D1784506

PSYCHOTHERAPY
IN CHILD GUIDANCE

Psychotherapy in Child Guidance

BY *Gordon Hamilton*

COLUMBIA UNIVERSITY PRESS
New York and London

A Study

of the Social Worker's Role in Psychotherapy

at the

Jewish Board of Guardians

COPYRIGHT 1947 COLUMBIA UNIVERSITY PRESS

First printing 1947
Seventh printing 1963

Manufactured in the United States of America

Foreword

In *Psychotherapy in Child Guidance* positive commitments are made in both the theory and the practice of child psychotherapy. The concepts presented here are offered by the author in a pioneering spirit, without dogma and with the hope of fostering progress in a highly important controversial field. The pattern of child guidance activities of the Jewish Board of Guardians is described ably, thoughtfully, and with the caution which characterizes true scientific exploration. It is inevitable that this book will be widely read and discussed. It will be welcomed by some and attacked by others. One thing is sure; it will not be ignored.

Why a book about psychotherapy written by a social worker? Is this an anomaly? I do not think so. Casework is an applied social science. The social sciences have a fundamental link with dynamic psychiatry, just as has medicine. In fact, modern psychiatry is the logical connecting bridge between medicine and the social sciences. Dynamic psychiatry no longer confines itself to mental disease per se, but more broadly concerns itself with the whole problem of human adaptation. The traditional interest of casework in the phenomena of social adaptation and in family problems brings it very close to dynamic psychiatry. Psychotherapy, therefore, is inevitably a matter of concern to the modern caseworker.

This book formulates the principles of psychotherapy which are the foundation of the Child Guidance functions of the Jewish Board of Guardians. The work is carried on by a clinical team—caseworker, psychologist, and psychiatrist. Diagnostic evaluation is a combined responsibility. The caseworker administers the therapy; the psychiatrist plays a systematic role in the conduct of cases through a plan of regular consultation. A basic pattern of close, continuous coordination of caseworker and psychiatrist underlies the entire clinical program.

The rationale for the program rests on the premise that the social and emotional problems of children and parents are the legitimate concern of a psychiatrically oriented social agency. In this frame, psychotherapy becomes a valid function for such an agency, assuming that the personnel possess or acquire the necessary technical training. It is recognized that the present curriculum of social work schools does not equip workers for this responsibility. In order to qualify personnel for therapeutic responsibility, caseworkers are given additional systematic training in the personality growth of children, in psychodynamics, and in psychotherapy. One point must be made clear: in receiving this specialized training, caseworkers are being prepared to function as psychotherapists, with the safeguard of continuous collaboration with staff psychiatrists. This should be the basic condition of the training of all workers in psychotherapy.

The theoretical orientation emphasizes the need for a comprehensive understanding of the scope, nature, and causation of the child's emotional difficulties and, secondarily, adapts treatment methods to such understanding. This point of view implies that the total range of the patient's problems must be clearly defined as to causation, unprejudiced by the conventional, time-bound limitations imposed on the respective roles of psychiatrist and caseworker. After the etiology is properly formulated, specific therapeutic responsibilities can be selectively delineated in accordance with the capacities and limitations of the particular therapist, whether psychiatrist or caseworker. In addition, of course, the therapeutic goal and method must be further modified by the capacities and limitations of the particular child guidance organization, the characteristics of the patient's environment and personality. A fixed technique of therapy is not espoused, but rather treatment concepts are constantly molded to an increasingly precise knowledge of socio-economic and psycho-dynamic causation.

Phenomenologically viewed, deviations in social adaptation are oriented, on the one hand, to environment and, on the other, to vicissitudes in emotional growth. Both the structure of the environment and the structure of the individual personality are part of the problem. It is self-evident that the social worker cannot treat social ills as abstractions, without adequate knowledge of people, since in the last analysis social ills are expressed through the behavior of people; nor can the psychiatrist treat individual persons without knowledge of social patterns. Neither the caseworker nor the psychiatrist, as at present trained, is equipped technically to deal with the whole range of the problem. The total task, by its very nature, requires a fusion of the highest order of efficiency of the special skills of both professions.

If one schematizes the components of the problem in terms of levels, progressing step by step from outer social realities to the inner functions of personality, certain broad correlations suggest themselves regarding the respective areas of responsibility for caseworker and psychiatrist.

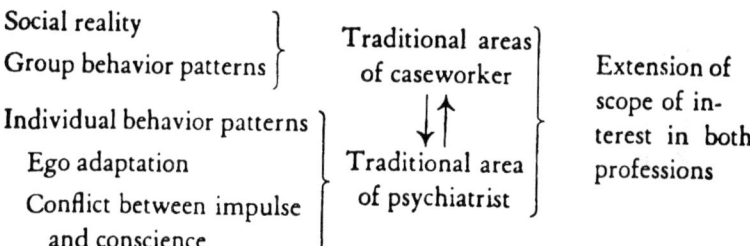

Social reality		
Group behavior patterns	Traditional areas of caseworker	Extension of scope of interest in both professions
Individual behavior patterns		
Ego adaptation	Traditional area of psychiatrist	
Conflict between impulse and conscience		

With an increasing appreciation of the complexities of the phenomena of social maladaptation, the caseworker has been impelled to extend his sphere of interest into the realm of individual behavior; the psychiatrist, similarly, into the realm of group behavior, social patterns, and social pathology. This does not mean, as has been alleged, that the caseworker surrenders, nor that the psychiatrist renounces, his professional identity. On the contrary, each preserves allegiance to his primary area of specialization. But the inevitable extension of interest, as above illustrated, makes it possible for both professional disciplines to operate more effectively in their respective areas of specialization and, what is most important, provides a favorable basis for the integration of the special skills of both disciplines.

The dynamic level at which the two professions meet is the so-called "ego level." "Ego" is a term which represents the organizing functions of the total personality. These functions, adaptively patterned, are oriented both toward the outer real world and toward the inner conflicts between impulse and conscience. The dynamic link between social reality and the unconscious is the ego. The link between individual motivation and group motivation is the ego. It is at this level that the areas of special interest of psychiatrist and caseworker meet. Close cooperation of psychiatry and casework in the field of child guidance may shed significant light on the problems of ego development in children.

Still there is the insistent question: Why does the caseworker assume the role of therapist, rather than the psychiatrist himself? This challenge is not simply met with the negative argument that there is a current scarcity of trained psychiatrists. There is a positive rationale for such a plan. From the social worker's point of view it is difficult sharply to separate social problems from psychological ones. The social worker is primarily concerned with the interaction of individual persons with social realities. Properly to understand this he must have precise knowledge of ego-adaptive functions and their relations, both to external social realities and to unconscious conflicts. Psychotherapy is a function derived from the dynamic nature of the patient's problem, not a technique arbitrarily patterned to suit the conventional training of any single profession. Good psychotherapy must be essentially the same process whether executed by one profession or another. Theoretically, psychotherapy could be administered by general practitioners of medicine, caseworkers, psychologists, as well as by psychiatrists, providing, of course, that it is supported by rigorous technical training, and that standards are maintained by adequate supervision. Caseworkers, already trained in understanding social problems, can receive additional technical training in the interaction of the individual personality with social situations, and thus become equipped to perform certain levels of psychotherapy.

It is common knowledge that some caseworkers prefer to deal exclusively with "social realities" and react with discomfort when confronted with unconscious mental mechanisms. Similarly, some psychoanalysts show discomfort when social realities are discussed. It is fair to say that these are examples of defensive reactions in both professions. Apparently such persons arbitrarily constrict the area of their professional concern in order to ward off feelings of discomfort and anxiety. In several instances, psychoanalysts have told me personally that if they functioned professionally in a social agency, they would be spoiled as analysts; it would injure their special talents for perceiving and interpreting unconscious motivation. This is the ivory-tower psychology of the psychoanalyst. It is outdated. I take the opposite stand. The psychoanalyst is likely to be a better psychotherapist and is likely more exactly to penetrate the meaning of unconscious motivation when he has the advantage of precise knowledge of the social realities which surround his patient. Armed with such knowledge, he is able to formulate correctly the relevant patterns of ego adaptation which, in the final analysis, are responsible for significant changes in the balance of unconscious forces.

It has been my experience in the past that caseworkers sometimes found it difficult to profit from consultations with psychiatrists because they could not easily bridge the gap between their formulations of the problem on the level of social disturbance with the psychoanalyst's formulations of the same problem in terms of certain configurations of unconscious distortion. The missing link between disorders of social adaptation and the correlated unconscious distortions is a definition of ego functioning. In order, therefore adequately to reconcile manifestations on the social level with manifestations of the individual's unconscious, it is indispensable that the caseworker and psychiatrist get together on a formulation of ego integrative patterns which would serve simultaneously as a foundation for understanding the social disturbance and the correlated disorders in the unconscious.

In recent years there has been emphasis on the application of the valid, time-tested concepts of psychoanalysis to modified forms of psychotherapy. Current developments in modified psychoanalytical technique—"brief psychotherapy," group psychotherapy, and certain changes in the concepts of child therapy—reflect this trend. The application of psychoanalytical concepts to the problems of child guidance is no new trend. In the field of child behavior there has been another significant emphasis in recent years. The error of basing our knowledge of the growth of child personality on the retrospective analysis of adult patients has become clear. Therefore, it has become necessary to accumulate precise knowledge of the growth of child personality through direct observation of young children. The psychiatric staff of the Jewish Board of Guardians is composed exclusively of psychoanalytically trained psychiatrists. The clinical program represents a

considered application of the concepts of unconscious conflict, transference, resistance, and the corresponding ego defense patterns to the
task of therapy. Faithful allegiance to a policy of continuous critical re-
evaluation of concepts and methods in psychotherapy provides a basis
for steady growth through gradual refinement of the social and
psychodynamic principles of diagnosis and treatment.

Nathan W. Ackerman, M.D.

New York
August, 1947

Preface

WHEN I was asked to make a study of child guidance at the Jewish Board of Guardians in New York, I had some reservations, having understood that the practice of this agency was so exceptional that I might not be able to reconcile it with accepted disciplines in social case-work. I asked, therefore, to be allowed to spend some time in preliminary exploration before giving an answer. What I found was so interesting to me, and I believed so significant for the field, that I agreed to make the study of which this report is the result.

The problem which presents itself for description and analysis is: In what way is psychotherapy related to social casework, and may it be appropriately practiced in a social work rather than a medical setting, and if so with what safeguards and controls? The problem was the more challenging to me, since in a book written some years ago I had made certain statements about the relationship between psychotherapy and social casework which I now saw were incomplete. I had said: "Case work differs from *psychotherapy* chiefly through the level on which it operates in regard to psychic conflict." [1] But here I had made the mistake common at the time to the field of equating the term "psychotherapy" with depth psychology, or psychoanalysis. The term "psychotherapy" is not coextensive with, nor should it be used as a synonym for, psychoanalysis, nor is it an art and science peculiar to the medically trained psychiatrist alone. The wise modern educator utilizes certain psychoanalytic concepts in the learning process, and the social worker who enters the field of family and child guidance must make a special adaptation of psychoanalytic principles and techniques appropriate for the objectives of his own practice. The dictionary definition of psychotherapy is any measure, physical or mental, which favorably influences the personality. But the personality is not only a psychosomatic but also a psychosocial unit, and in the field of parent-child relationships psychosocial interactions are especially significant.

[1] Gordon Hamilton, *Theory and Practice of Social Case Work*, New York, 1940.

Though treatment of the mentally ill person remains a medical specialization (though even here the lines cannot be too arbitrarily drawn), treatment of the emotionally disturbed or character distorted personality cannot be restricted to the practice of medicine. Social work is concerned with social adjustment, but often it cannot assist the emotionally disturbed client to a "social" adjustment without helping him to effect inner change. This calls for a direct treatment approach through psychologically oriented interviews. There must not only be greater harmony between body and mind, among internal mental processes, but also between the person and society, nor can the line between dynamic and symptomatic cure be too sharply drawn. Alexander suggests that the analyst must decide "whether a primarily supportive or uncovering type of treatment is indicated, or whether the therapeutic task is mainly a question of changing the external conditions of the patient's life." [2] For social work the latter has been generally considered to be the appropriate role, but, as we shall see, in child and family guidance the approaches of psychotherapy and social therapy are interdependent.

While the purpose of this study is to describe adaptations of therapy carried on by social workers at the Jewish Board of Guardians, the findings are, I believe, susceptible of general application by those social caseworkers who are willing to equip themselves as therapists. I should say at the outset that I believe the evolution of psychotherapy is a specialization, though a legitimate and appropriate specialization, within the larger field of social work. Although therapeutic, as well as educational and social science, principles must suffuse the whole range of practice, psychotherapy calls for greater knowledge of psychopathology and more skill in the transference relationship and other clinical disciplines than is necessary in all types of social casework.[3] It is not within the scope of this book to describe the role of the psychiatrist in the child guidance unit.

The method used in this study is descriptive rather than statistical and does not attempt to evaluate in terms of success and failure.

[2] See J. F. Brown and K. A. Menninger, *The Psychodynamics of Abnormal Behavior*, and Franz Alexander and T. M. French, *Psychoanalytic Therapy*, p. 5.

[3] See Chapter XII.

Blocks of cases were drawn at random, samples of the years between approximately 1930 and 1942, in order to gain perspective and to clarify trends. In addition, a large number of current cases were furnished by the staff, out of which the writer selected those which seemed best to illustrate practice. Cases showing very unusual problems were eliminated. This did not, however, permit the selection of either pleasant or easy cases. The child guidance case load is made up of families and children who are there because they are disturbed, have problems, and need help.

The usual safeguards of changing all names and identifying information have been taken.

After trying several arrangements for the presentation of not-too-easily-manageable material, since the cases were long and, for the most part recorded in full detail, the device was adopted of looking at the therapeutic process from two angles, namely, the clinical diagnostic and the social and ego patterns of functioning under age groupings. It must be understood that this is a somewhat arbitrary device, since children do not fall into absolute categories, and the whole picture must be considered in every case. Therapy can be addressed neither to a clinical type, as such, since there were few pure types, nor to an age range, as such, since developmental stages overlap, but must flexibly adapt itself to a person with mixed clinical facets and shifting emotional phases. Nevertheless, since there are certain treatment considerations growing out of clinical diagnosis and also differentiation according to age levels, this arrangement may prove useful. Finally, although a consistent theoretical (psychoanalytically oriented) structure has been assumed throughout, it is recognized that the application of principles should be extremely elastic. Moreover, the theoretical structure itself is under constant revision and, therefore, progressively changing.

I am indebted for most generous and understanding support throughout this study to: Mr. Herschel Alt, Executive Director, and Miss Frederika Neumann, Director of Casework Services, of the Jewish Board of Guardians; to the supervisors who gave unstintingly of their time, both in discussion and in reading various drafts of the material as it slowly evolved, and to the workers whose cases are used for illustration. Mr. S. R. Slavson kindly reviewed the material on group therapy. I am particularly appreciative of the help given by Mrs. Yonata Feldman in critical analysis and demonstration of the case material itself. My grateful acknowledgments go to Dr. J. H. W. van Ophuijsen and Dr. Nathan W. Ackerman, whose seminars and conferences were most stimulating and instructive. The same psychiatrists gave a patient and critical reading of the manuscript as a whole; Dr. Margaret Hitchman reviewed several chapters, and Dr. Peter Neubauer the chapter on adolescence. Dr. Hyman Spotnitz gave encouragement to a radical position for case-work adaptations in psychotherapy.

Gordon Hamilton

New York
August, 1947

Contents

Introduction

by HERSCHEL ALT

Two important considerations prompted the Jewish Board of Guardians to have this study of its child guidance program undertaken. The first was the conviction that a comprehensive description of the agency's program would serve as a basis for continued critical evaluation, as well as modification and refinement in its own practices. The second was the belief that the experience of the agency and the specific treatment methods which it has developed would prove of general value to the social work and mental hygiene fields.

More than two decades have elapsed since the Jewish Board of Guardians turned to psychiatry for help in dealing with problems of delinquency and behavior disturbances in children, and more than ten years since the agency recognized the value of direct psychological, as well as environmental, treatment and began a quest for methods which would be most effective in helping the particular types of children it undertook to treat.

Many of the essential qualities which now characterize its child guidance program grew out of the consistent effort which the agency devoted to the problem of developing a method for psychological treatment. This endeavor moved through various stages: first, diagnostic concepts were established and utilized in planning for all children who came to the agency; then, specific treatment methods were developed; finally, a program of training was undertaken to prepare the staff to carry the responsibility for this special treatment program. The in-service training program has been progressively elaborated as diagnostic and treatment concepts have changed and grown.

Another significant aspect of its growth can be seen in the way in which the structure of the agency has developed. In the beginning, a child guidance clinic was established, and for a time it constituted a separate functional unit. Later, as psychiatric principles were incorporated into all aspects of the agency's program, the clinic was absorbed into the agency itself and ceased to exist as a separate entity. The absorption of the clinic could have meant a denial of the value of the child guidance clinic methods in the agency program. On the contrary, it actually signified the recognition of the usefulness of a comprehensive clinical approach to all problems of child behavior and the integration of that approach in all the study and treatment procedures of the agency.

The dissolution of the clinic as a separate entity was only a step in establishing clinically oriented procedures in the total child guidance program. Application of diagnostic criteria to each case is one illustration of the clinical approach of the agency. Diagnostic categories which are clearly defined and consistently utilized provide a basic frame of reference for comparing the character of problems as well as the effectiveness of the treatment methods employed.

A basic premise in the program of the agency is that in work with children the most complete fusion of social casework and psychiatry, as a basis for both diagnosis and treatment, is essential. This is true because the child cannot, by himself, alter his environment and must look to adults for its amelioration and the removal of undue pressures and burdens. This difference in the needs which children and adults bring to the treatment situation should be fully recognized. Psychotherapy with adults, may, in the main, be focused on strengthening of the capacity of the adult to make choices and to deal with his own reality problems. This is not sufficient, however, in the case of the child, who is dependent upon his parents and other adults for many of his basic needs, and whose capacity to alter his environment is limited. Direct psychological treatment and environmental modification must therefore remain two aspects of a single effort in helping children.

The importance of this broad yet unified approach to the treatment of children was fully recognized by the early child guidance clinics and was reflected in their plan of staff organization, which included psychiatrist, psychologist, and psychiatric social worker and which assigned to each responsibility for different aspects of study and treatment. This emphasis on combining social and psychological understanding in the study and treatment of children may be said to have reached its logical development in the Jewish Board of Guardians, where responsibility for both aspects of treatment are vested in the worker. The psychiatrist continues to be an important member of the professional group. He functions as a teacher and consultant and—with the social worker and the psychologist—as a member of the diagnostic team. He is the person primarily responsible for establishing limits of the therapeutic program both as to types of problems to be treated and psychotherapeutic methods to be employed.

The unification of responsibility for treatment in the caseworker helps to assure not only the full assimilation of psychiatric knowledge into efforts to bring about changes in the environment of the child but also that the psychological treatment is carried on in the light of the total environmental situation. The value of this arrangement becomes even clearer when we recognize that perhaps nowhere outside the therapeutic situation does the child so fully reveal his feelings and his attitudes toward members of his family and others in his environment. The understanding thus gained by the worker not only serves as a focus for the treatment plan but also helps to make sure that all aspects of treatment are sensitively geared to the needs of the child and the methods that will best help him.

The historic responsibility of the agency for the treatment of delinquent children and the important part which environmental factors play in the etiology of delinquent behavior has further served to emphasize the importance of reality experience in the lives of children. The recognition of this fact has been responsible for the reliance of the agency on diverse treatment methods and its continued utilization of planned living situations or milieux as important therapeutic tools. Environmental treatment resources of the agency now comprehend its interview and activity group therapy programs, summer camps designed to provide a treatment experience, and a special school for seriously disturbed and delinquent children. Psychological therapy, alone or in combination with various forms of environmental therapy, may therefore be utilized. This more comprehensive treatment program provides a unique opportunity for observing the interrelationship of various treatment emphases. Furthermore, knowledge gained in the practice of one form of therapy may be useful in clarifying other methods. Thus, the understanding of child behavior gained in the clinical situation has been utilized as a starting point for the planning of a healthy and healing environment at the Hawthorne and Cedar Knolls schools.

Questions concerning the types of attitudes on the part of adults toward children that will restore confidence in youngsters who are hostile and suspicious of all authority have been studied through the experience gained in the clinical therapeutic relationship. On the other hand, the recognition of the need of certain types of children for limitations upon freedom and choice has helped to bring some of the clinical treatment methods into broader perspective and to clarify the extent to which individual psychotherapy alone meets the child's problem and how far it needs to be combined with other treatment measures.

Following the assumption of responsibility for public assistance by governmental agencies, family service agencies, for over a decade, have moved more and more towards "counseling" or treatment services for the family as a unit, or for its individual members. With the changes which have marked our social life during this period, particularly during the war and postwar years, child caring agencies, too, are finding themselves called upon more and more to serve children presenting behavior problems. As a result, some family and children's agencies have undertaken to provide psychotherapy as part of their service, and all find it necessary to define the relationship between their accepted functions and psychotherapy in more specific form.

Two differing points of view about the relationship between psychotherapy and the practice of social casework, as carried on in these agencies, can be identified. One moves from the assumption that the client retains many personal strengths which the caseworker can help him mobilize to meet his own problem, and that facing reality will call forth the client's own capacity to deal rationally with his situation. While granting the validity of this approach in many instances, the other viewpoint assumes that the client's responses to his situation reflect his total life experience, particularly his primary relationships with parents and other members of his family. The latter point of view recognizes the neurotic as well as the mature elements in the client's behavior. Treatment focuses not only on strengths but also on crippling conflicts in the life of the client, and seeks to bring about a greater degree of personality integration. Practice which is in accord with the latter assumption tends to utilize methods which are akin to formal psychotherapy. No attempt is here made to affirm or to deny the validity of any one approach. Different levels of treatment may be appropriate in relation to different types of social situations involving individuals with different personality strengths. However, all therapeutic programs for children and adults should be based on clearly defined diagnostic procedures which stem from a unified theoretical framework, no matter what particular level of treatment may be indicated.

The treatment methods which the book describes—particularly the way in which direct psychological treatment, modification of environment and reality situations are combined—should, we believe, prove useful to the family and children's field in clarifying various levels of treatment as well as methods to be employed. The publication of this book may introduce a new dimension in social work, which embraces a diagnostic framework as a tool in understanding and a method of treatment grounded in a well-defined theoretical base.

The literature on psychotherapy with children is still limited, and available authoritative texts are few in number. Furthermore, the psychotherapeutic methods and processes in work with children have not, up to the present, been clearly systematized and fully described. Moreover, a description of its treatment methods should be specially useful, because the Jewish Board of Guardians has for more than a decade been engaged in the practice of psychotherapy with children; this has been carried on in the same agency setting, with a number of the same practitioners participating in the program throughout the period. In addition, the agency has critically evaluated its methods and both modified them and elaborated them in the light of results and increased knowledge.

Our nation is now on the threshold of a broad expansion of mental hygiene services under the leadership of the Federal Government. This development, which is long overdue, has been accelerated by the increasing awareness of the extent of mental disorders and social maladjustment revealed by the war and also by a growing public understanding of the possibilities of successful treatment. A primary requisite for this expansion of services is the training of additional psychiatric personnel—psychiatrists, social workers, psychologists, and nurses. The psychotherapeutic methods described in this work should prove useful not only in the training, but also in the expanded treatment programs which we hope will be undertaken in the immediate years ahead.

These comments would be incomplete without an expression of appreciation of the agency to Professor Gordon Hamilton. She brought to her task a broad perspective and skill in identifying with the philosophy, objectives, and methods employed by the agency. Furthermore, she was able to make the study process one in which many in the agency participated and therefore a rich educational venture for the entire staff.

We are also greatly indebted to the trustees of the Nathan Hofheimer Foundation and the Marion R. Ascoli Fund, for their deep and sustaining interest in mental hygiene and for their contributions to the Publication Fund of the agency, which made this study possible.

PSYCHOTHERAPY
IN CHILD GUIDANCE

Chapter I

CLINICALLY ORIENTED SOCIAL CASEWORK

Although all Western cultures have created and promoted extensive programs for the education, health, and welfare of children, in the American commonwealth the concepts of child guidance have had a somewhat special development and hold a unique place. Even the word "guidance" carries unusual meaning, since in the democracies it is assumed that the individual contributes to and helps shape his social economy and culture quite as much as that society teaches him to conform to his culture. This has increasingly meant that education and all the more enlightened forms of therapy have been concerned not only wisely to restrain, as was done in the older types of pedagogy, but creatively to release the energies of the individual. More and more has this been applied to the rearing and teaching of children.

New Perspectives for Children

During the last twenty-five years, along with the phenomenal development in American psychiatry and in large part due to its discoveries, there developed a deeper understanding of the nature of children and of the growth process itself. This understanding has been felt in the schools, in hospitals and clinics, and in the whole field of family and children's services. Dr. Lowrey [1] has dated what he calls the "new era" in psychiatry as the second decade of the century, 1909–1919. These were great years, too, in education, and in

[1] See Lowrey, "Psychiatry for Children," *American Journal of Psychiatry*, CI (November, 1944), 375–388. "A new era started in psychiatry in 1909 when Healy began his work at the Juvenile Psychopathic Institute." He quotes Healy as saying that at that time, with a few exceptions, "there was not even the semblance of anything that could be called a well-rounded study of a young human individual. . . . Even physiological norms were not available; standardized mental tests had to be developed . . . and the importance of knowledge of family attitudes and conditionings was barely realized."

pediatrics, and they saw the beginnings of security and welfare programs for children.[2]

In any concept of therapy we must recognize how needs are gratified. Some needs must be gratified concretely, while other needs must be met through a process of education and reorganization of the functions of the personality; the latter are assumed to be the special area of psychotherapy.

The most basic "treatment" of the child lies in gratification of real needs—subsistence, family life, health, work, education, play, religion, and group associations. Subsistence needs must be met by the production of income; other needs by appropriate fulfillment. Affectional needs are met through real relationships. There is no substitute for income, housing, food, and shelter, and there is no therapeutic substitute for family relationships. Therapy can never adequately be substituted for life experience. The methods through which any society provides natural or planned methods of gratification are culturally determined. The area of social security, the public welfare and the common good, has been steadily widening through the collective action of the people. Social work has always played an important role in furthering goods and services—in the field of public assistance and other forms of economic maintenance and the preservation of health, supplementary family care (as in institutions, foster homes, and day nurseries), creative activities (such as group work and recreation), and so forth. It has always carried on counseling service, aimed to strengthen family life and develop the individual's capacity to make rewarding vocational, educational, and social choices for himself, but this has often been regarded as incidental to the function of enabling persons to use social resources. Its growing skill in psychotherapy, which is the concern of this book, has been least understood.

There can be no solution of human problems so long as want and crude hunger persist, and there can be no democratic solutions except on the basis of economic security, civil rights, and a tolerant and cooperative fellowship of human beings. Physical, mental, eco-

[2] In 1909 was held the first White House Conference on Children, resulting in the beginning of a charter, in principle at least, for economic security. The Federal Children's Bureau was founded in 1912 in response to one of the recommendations of this conference.

nomic, and emotional needs are interrelated, and even the most practical program for human welfare must be undertaken with regard for human personality. Social services should be geared to the purpose of social betterment and social development, quite as much as to the immediate gratification of a basic need. The first task is to make programs substantial in a material way, and the second—interrelated and no less important—to make them conducive to the growth and social contribution of the individual. There must be not only protection of rights but also adequate fulfillment of needs. For the latter, the role of the family is of primary importance. "Affect hunger" is as crippling as is starvation of the body. Social workers are familiar with the results of both economic and affectional deprivation. The worker in child guidance sees, perhaps, fewer extreme instances of physical neglect and abuse than of distortions because of rejection, rigidity, and lack of love in the home.

In social casework we may validly designate the two first decades of the twentieth century as the period before the assimilation of psychiatric concepts. *Social Diagnosis,* the significant book of the pre-psychiatric era, by Mary Richmond, clarified for social work a method of approach to the environment based on social evidence and social manipulation. The concepts of the inner and emotional life, along with those of education, and most of the social sciences of the time, were largely rational and intellectual. Bit by bit, with the increasing complexity of living, the development of all the sciences and particularly the extraordinary advances of psychiatry, it has become clear that we are "one world," not only in the interdependence of the sciences, of nations, and of persons but also with regard to individual personalities interacting within society and culture. Within any personality there must always be a balance between inner and outer, between instinctual drives and reality, if there is to be growth, adaptation, and achievement. While the individual adjustment varies with the immediate culture, culture itself, in our civilization, is transmitted most effectively through the home. Parental influence is most important, although other forces contribute, to a greater or lesser degree, to character formation. Social-work interest in this newer branch of medicine was intense and eager, because psychiatry seemed able, for the first time, to throw light on one of the most baffling aspects of the social-work problem. For a long time social scientists and social reformers alike had been aware of external or overt causes of distress, such as poverty, disease, unemployment, and also of inner and more personal causes of unhappiness and unadjustment. But the latter were often approached as if they were separate planetary systems, instead of two arcs of the same circle. The relation of one to the other was little understood. To be a practitioner in the field of emotional disturbances calls not only for intimate knowledge of the personality but also for knowledge of the interplay of social, economic, and cultural forces.

From Guidance to Therapy

The rise of the child guidance movement, which was largely a product of the newer psychiatry, is usually dated from about 1921, when the National Committee for Mental Hygiene, backed by the Commonwealth Fund, entered upon a program for the prevention of delinquency. The forerunners of this movement—in Chicago, Philadelphia, Baltimore, and elsewhere—are well known, and some of the most distinguished pioneers both here and abroad made their contributions early. These beginnings have been adequately recounted.[3] Dr. Lawson Lowrey,[4] who identifies 11 psychiatric clinics for children in 1919, finds 776 in the United States in 1939. These clinics for children were of many types, most of them closely following hospital models, others an educational pattern, and still others the "demonstration" type of clinic, described by Stevenson, Witmer, and others.

The practice of the Jewish Board of Guardians, founded in 1893 as an agency to give aid to prisoners, as it evolved from the care of the adult offender to the treatment of emotionally disturbed children, has paralleled in many respects the development of the child guidance movement throughout the country. It was somewhat atypical, however, because its clinic was from the beginning under the auspices of

---

[3] See Stevenson and Smith, *Child Guidance Clinics,* and Witmer, *Psychiatric Clinics for Children,* and other titles listed in bibliography.

[4] Lowrey, "Psychiatry for Children," *The American Journal of Psychiatry,* CI (November, 1944), 375-388.

a social agency. Like other social agencies, the Jewish Board of Guardians had its pre- and post-psychiatric periods, and like others it had moved from working *around* and *for* the child to working *with* the child. Just as the early child welfare workers placed children, but rarely *saw* children in the sense of understanding them, so treatment of the *problem*, delinquency, came at last in child guidance, to mean seeing and treating the "problem" *children*. When this occurred, certain traditional functions, such as parole, were clearly seen to be governmental and were therefore transferred to the appropriate state and municipal authorities. This perception of public responsibilities was not only correct, but it freed the agency for its central purposes of demonstration, education, and development of special skills in the treatment of behavior problems.[5]

In another respect the agency was atypical, since it had never subscribed to the once-accepted division of labor in which the psychiatrist treated the child and the social worker the parent, nor was a sharp distinction ever made between direct treatment and favorable reconstruction of the environment. It was interesting that whereas use of relationship in "attitude therapy"—a term invented by Dr. Levy [6]—was an experiment in which social workers had responsibility only for the direct treatment of parents, at the Jewish Board of Guardians the therapy was carried on with both the children and the adults. The fact that the consulting psychiatrists were regular staff members (on full or part time) [7] had led not only to the necessary clinical controls in the practice of therapy but also to an unusual amount of sharing of knowledge and skill between physicians and social workers. The evolution of the social worker into a therapist was from the beginning inevitable.

In the three decades since the founding of the first Children's Court in America, leaders in the field came to see that "delinquency" was the result of conflict between man and his environment and, even more significantly, that this conflict was between the *inner urges* of

---

[5] Alt and Stein, "After 50 Years: an Agency Looks Ahead," *The Jewish Social Service Quarterly*, XXI (December, 1944), 99–108.

[6] Levy, "Attitude Therapy," *American Journal of Orthopsychiatry*, VII (January, 1937), 103.

[7] By 1940, 68 instead of 48 psychiatric hours were given weekly. In 1941, with 56 caseworkers and 6 group workers, there were 6 psychiatrists and 2 psychologists.

man and the pressures exercised upon him by society. It was recognized that delinquents and criminals were emotionally disturbed or ill, not inherently wicked. It became clear that manipulation of the environment, which some of the social scientists were prescribing, would in many instances be insufficient. The individual himself must be treated. As Dr. John Slawson had pointed out—"education to which the maladjusted person has been subjected for many years will yield no results—it must be therapeutic, creative and concretely related to experience in living and answer the needs of the specific illness of the individual." [8]

Though before the establishment of the mental hygiene clinic it had been known that the delinquent person needed friendship, not punishment, the services given inevitably had the protective and somewhat disciplinary flavor of the times. While one can see clearly that by about 1930 the idea of punishment had yielded to the idea of treatment and that faith in progressive educational methods was growing, the educational approach of most workers was still highly active and intellectualized, and their approach was to manipulate the environment on behalf of the child rather than to stimulate the growth and self-directing activities of the child himself. Delinquency had been imperfectly understood in that it had been differentiated too sharply from other forms of personality disturbance. Even Aichhorn had not yet clarified his "state of latent delinquency" or what constituted "susceptibility" to antisocial behavior.[9] During the first twenty-five years of child guidance the etiology of symptomatic behavior had been pursued, and the startling discovery had been made that parental attitudes are significantly causal.[10] There had been at first a disposition to conclude that the nature and severity of the problem was wholly determined by the parental attitudes and that these, in turn, determined the prognosis, but soon it began to be recognized that less tangible factors in the total personality, rather than the prob-

[8] Slawson, "Social Work Basis for Prevention and Treatment of Delinquency and Crime; Individual Factors," pp. 590–599.

[9] Aichhorn, *Wayward Youth.*

[10] In 1936 Healy and Bronner, in a study for the Yale Institute of Human Relations, *New Light on Delinquency and Its Treatment,* reported that delinquents as a group proved to have the worst developmental histories—91% having been extremely disturbed because of "emotion provoking relationships."

lem alone or the kind of treatment selected, suggested the prognosis. What precise factors predisposed the personality, either constitutionally or environmentally or both, to antisocial behavior, were not known. It was seen, however, that indulgent, inconsistent, or repressive parental attitudes toward the child seemed equally thwarting to full personality growth. It was observed that repressive measures in treating delinquents clearly did not work well, and an explanation was sought.

Healy, followed by Alexander, Staub, and others, had made plain that the behavior tendencies which enabled people to live in the community are acquired during the individual's early developmental periods; that neither psychological insight nor social control alone is sufficient to solve the "disease called crime." The instability lies in the balance between social restrictions and social gratifications. In a broader sense the social milieu exercises a later and generally less potent influence than does early family environment. Acknowledging the futility of "treatment" by methods of reform and the difficulty of treating older offenders by any known methods, Alexander and Healy had thrown out the hope that cooperative efforts, based upon the psychoanalytic understanding of psychiatrists and social workers, would have something to offer. They also believed that insight and emotional change must be coupled with a "convalescent" reconstructive period to consolidate strengths [11] and that prolonged psychotherapy at an early age was the most hopeful possibility. It was not enough to see the child with new eyes; it was not enough to see the child genetically. To help effectively it was imperative to make as early a start as possible, since causes of delinquency are not only hidden but also very deep. The moment one began to study the whole child it became evident that the "delinquent" could not be set apart in an arbitrary way from other disturbed children, although some of the predisposing factors could be ascertained. What was very certain was that the roots of *all* behavior lie in the subsoil of the early years. Interest was then directed to all deviations in behavior which etiologically might be traced to early

[11] Alexander and Healy, *Roots of Crime*, pp. 294 *et sqq.* Also Alexander and Staub, *The Criminal, the Judge, and the Public.*

home factors, and this immediately involved the social work profession, whose concern so long had lain therein.

The shift in guidance technique, brought into practice through understanding the nature of the transference, was made complicated in an agency dealing with delinquency, since it had been observed, without full realization of the implications, that the delinquent child seemed to have great difficulty in using a "casework relationship." He and often his family did not easily accept this kind of relationship, and this very resistance pointed the way to further study of the nature of delinquent behavior as over against neurotic disturbance, which had been much more fully explored by psychiatry at this date—the important point being that to the study of causes of delinquency was now added the concept of the wish to use help (or, more typically, the resistance to help)—together with the beginnings of a more dynamic concept of personality. As relationship was better understood, interpretation became less abstract and pedagogic. There was for awhile, however, a mistaken notion that relationship alone was sufficient, and there was temporarily a dropping away of the familiar ancillary social services. Fortunately, it was soon recognized that casework could share psychiatry's concern for personality change without sacrificing its social purposes and techniques [12]—in fact, that social experience could itself contribute to personality change.

From about 1930 on the workers were faced not only with the need to understand the outward and obvious clashes of the antisocial or delinquent child with his environment, but also the internal conflicts of the psychoneurotic. Especially with the shifting picture of the growing child and the immediacy of his home and family problems was it impossible to distinguish one as wholly the province of the psychiatrist, and the other of the social worker.

Psychoanalytic Orientation

The child guidance movement had not only brought psychiatric theory into the practice of social work, but a psychoanalytically oriented type of psychiatry which threw immediate light on the oldest concern of social work, namely, family interrelationships and inter-

[12] Witmer, *Social Work*, p. 439.

actions. Classical psychiatry had been grounded in medical practice, having mental illness or psychosis as its chief preoccupation; psychoanalysis gave the first clue to an understanding of the cases with which social workers were traditionally involved—those persons with behavior problems and neuroses whose conflicts showed themselves in failures in family life and in social and economic functioning. All attempts to explain behavior, from original sin to defective brain structure, had been abortive until Freud's great concept of unconscious conflict, the emotional forces within the personality, and the irrational character of much behavior revolutionized the therapeutic approach. Man's struggle with himself, the central focus of philosophy and religion, became a clinically usable constellation of ideas. Treatment could for the first time be addressed to the inner conflict as well as to the outer circumstances.

In agencies or clinics using psychoanalytical concepts, social workers had first been made aware of the deeper instinctual drives, and only later, as knowledge of ego psychology [13] became incorporated in their training, could they comprehend the nature of the defenses, as well as such phenomena as transference, resistance, and sublimation. In the early phases of this development the nature of internal conflict was not well understood, and workers were haunted either by a not unwholesome, yet unrealistic, fear of "getting into" the unconscious or else believed they must follow as closely as possible the classical psychoanalytic techniques. Finally it was recognized that while the ventilation, interpretation, and reintegration of feeling are important in order to obtain a therapeutic result, in the adult as well as in the child, many combinations and variations in treatment are possible.

The main purposes of social casework are not primarily adapted for the treatment of deeply repressed material (the forces of the id), but are applicable in an approach to the defensive structures of the

[13] As Anna Freud has pointed out in her introduction to *The Ego and the Mechanisms of Defense*, p. 3. "Many analysts had conceived the idea that the value of the scientific and therapeutic work done was in direct proportion to the depth of the psychic strata upon which attention was focussed . . . but the investigation of the id and its mode of operation was always only a means to an end . . . the correction of these abnormalities and the restoration of the ego to its integrity."

ego once the purpose of these dynamisms in protecting the ego against instinctual demands is understood. The caseworker does not use dream material except incidentally, but "the ego," as Dr. Franz Wittels says, "is best studied in our waking hours." Social workers cannot "treat" the unconscious any more than they can "treat" the past, but neither can they dodge the unconscious or the existence of the past in the present. In all men feeling is partly conscious, and its motivation is partly unconscious, and the line cannot be too firmly drawn. In the present concept of therapy, the attempt is to gain access to thought and feeling, with the understanding that the patient must always involve himself in any real change. A person has both conscious and unconscious processes at work in him. Whatever goes to make up personality must be understood by any therapist. Psychiatric knowledge, intuition, relationship, experience, and social services are all part of the adaptation of therapy to casework hereinafter described.

While during recent periods one can see interest swing back and forth between more effective use of the environment and "relationship" as the chief medium of treatment, the community-centered aspects of conduct disorders and the established grouping of social services, including institutional facilities, helped to keep the social agency in the middle of the road between actual social experience and the therapeutic relationship. Moreover, the perception that a client must do his own changing, cope with his own environmental and inner difficulties, is balanced by the deepening understanding of the diagnostic process and of the part played by the unconscious in the way the total personality is able to function in a real world.

The social worker knew that the person could not be separated from his environment, and he was already trained to handle many elements in the environment. He also knew pragmatically that the ego had considerable plasticity and ability to adjust. He had seen many such adjustments and had had a hand in not a few. The question was soon to become: in what ways could psychosocial therapy affect the functioning of personality? Obviously, in any such consideration adequate understanding of personality structure is essential. Diagnosis of the whole clinical development of the illness is tied in with understanding the development of the total personality, both within itself and as a reaction to those familial and cultural influences which are the social worker's stock in trade. Psychoanalysis had explained the nature of genetic development; the social worker had seen familial influences operating. These angles of vision were more and more converging. As Dr. Ackerman points out: "the dynamic level at which the two professions meet is the so-called ego level." [14]

Perhaps because child guidance agencies were dealing with "delinquency," they continued to strike a balance between social and clinical considerations. Psychotherapy, as practiced at the Jewish Board of Guardians, aims at a fusion of psychiatric and social skills in a characteristic "design" of direct therapy and life experience (social-clinical rather than purely clinical),[15] with varied adaptations and a flexible combination of methods. Among recent developments the most striking note is the fresh consideration of and the renewal of energy devoted to an educational program of mental hygiene, not only as the first essential in the prevention of delinquency or even the basis on which effective therapy must operate, but also because the perspective is that of positive mental health and welfare for children.

The Clinical Unit of Practice [16]

In the Jewish Board of Guardians at first, psychiatric and social services coexisted. They were not really integrated. The workers at that time were insufficiently trained. There was little theoretical knowledge to aid them in using the consulting psychiatrist, still less in learning the necessary skills. The role of the psychiatrist was at first diagnostic and directive to the caseworker carrying on the treatment. Later, very disturbed children were occasionally treated by the psychiatrist, but as most of the children were disturbed, the line of demarkation was not easy to establish. At the Jewish Board of Guardians there was, therefore, a departure from any "therapy" which taught the manipulation of attitudes at a conscious level in the adult,

---

[14] See Foreword

[15] As a point of departure from what was later to be called "functional" casework see Dr. Jessie Taft in "The Relation of Function to Process in Social Case Work," *Journal of Social Work Process*, I (1937), 1–18, in which "therapy" is differentiated.

[16] See Chapter XII.

or from any psychology [17] which tends to separate out a few processes for general use, but without diagnostic study. Rather, it was assumed that there should be continuous free interplay between the developing social and psychiatric sciences in a genuinely integrated endeavor, with a common conceptual scheme and a common method of communication. It was the more imperative since it had been found that real fusion could not take place across the barrier of different languages. Clinical assumptions and a precisely understood terminology had to be shared if the concepts were to be effectively translated into practice.

Underneath everything was the conviction that social casework and psychoanalytically oriented psychiatry should be fused—not merely in purpose, for a common purpose in child guidance was already accepted, but basic knowledge about personality and social forces must be fused if new roads were to be built in what was still a wilderness. The fact that social work more than any profession, except perhaps education, has the chance to look at families and children before emotional illness and disturbance become chronic gave that conviction the utmost significance. In short, the idea of a unified approach, accepted on both sides, makes for a peculiarly stimulating and rewarding partnership. Therapy cannot be completely set apart from casework, but neither do psychiatry, rooted in medical practice, and social work, in social practice, have the same jurisdiction. If psychotherapy is not the whole of medicine, neither is it the whole of social work, but whereas psychiatry draws on medical techniques, sedation, drugs, physiotherapy, psychoanalysis, and so forth, social work draws on social services. Social treatment continues to modify, as well as to be modified by, psychiatric treatment—but though psychotherapy is shared by physician and social worker, the special equipment and contributions of each need not be confused.

The importance of regular consultation with the medically trained psychiatrist is inescapable, since both behavior disorders and psychoneuroses represent complicated maladjustments which may be rooted in organic disease or psychosis. The fact is that psychiatrists must be

[17] See Rogers, *Counseling and Psychotherapy,* and similar approaches in social work and psychiatry.

readily available to and, whenever possible, part of any social agency staff, whenever the social agency is doing psychotherapy, just as it seems obvious that social workers should be part of the unit in medical institutions. The psychiatrist is especially responsible for guidance in the diagnosis and treatment of intrapsychic matters, and the social worker in social aspects of familial problems.

Definitions of Psychotherapy

The term psychotherapy is an old one and has often been misused. While it includes all forms of treatment by "psychological" means, this in itself is somewhat vague. From the various psychiatric descriptions and definitions we may say that psychotherapy is regarded as rooted in a two-person relationship in which one is therapist, or helper, and one the "patient," or client. It is assumed that the patient consciously involves himself to some degree in a therapeutic process and that the transference is used as the chief medium of treatment. The psychodynamics of personality must be understood, and the treatment is based on diagnosis. In the specific adaptation of psychotherapy, hereinafter described, though subscribing to the above definitions, we go farther in emphasizing the importance of a comprehensive approach to the child's life experience.[18] Psychotherapy thus conduces to a reorganization of the social milieu, as well as of the forces of the personality itself in a healthy growth process. Certain other emphases and modifications arise, since the psychotherapy is addressed to the total functioning of the person, not solely to the unconscious conflict as such.

The term psychosocial therapy, were it not so clumsy, would more precisely describe the purposes of child guidance. Psychoanalysis as a self-contained method is believed not to gain, especially for the adult patient, by having social services added: psychotherapy for children to a large extent derives its strength from a combination of psychological and social therapies. There must continually be alertness, particularly in treating children, to the child's own reality. The chief argument in favor of restricting psychotherapy to a medical endeavor rests on the belief that otherwise disease may be overlooked. The chief

---

[18] See Chapter VII and the following chapters.

argument against its being solely a medical endeavor is that the life experience of the child may be minimized. Much of the difficulty can, we believe, be dissipated if psychotherapy is practiced in relation to a clinical team and within agency controls.

The purpose of psychotherapy is to assist the client toward fuller and less distorted satisfactions; toward better integration of himself; toward self-direction and more creative or more comfortable social functioning. This should mean less anxiety, more healthy and normal enjoyment, better adaptation to the demands of society in work and play and other associations. Therapy does not aim to make a person conform to harsh and depriving conditions or to become as normal or mature, as a theoretically "average" person may be, but within his own capacities to achieve a more adequate use of all his faculties. Therapy is especially important with children, since whenever pressure from without can be modified, or inhibitions removed, the forces of growth are on the side of the therapist. In adults, even though some personalities are far more rigid than others, some changes can and do take place under favorable therapeutic and educational influences. Therapy uses various combinations of expressive or release techniques, reeducation, insight and support—the whole attuned to self-restorative forces in the personality and assisted by whatever social resources are available. There is a mistaken notion that the therapeutic intent is to control the client, whereas just the contrary is the case. Therapy is a controlled, not a controlling process. To an unusual degree the therapist must be a self-aware and self-controlled person, but the aim of the therapy is to make the client more self-aware and self-directing. The phrase "nondirective [19] therapy" or "counseling" suggests that other forms of therapy are regarded as authoritarian. Psychotherapy, since it is based on diagnosis, is a *directed* technique, but in child guidance methods of persuasion suggestion and authoritative advice are little used. Rather, an attempt is made to understand the person so as to assist him in self-understanding; to support, so that the strengthened ego may be more able to bear up under strain; to interpret, so that new insights may be synthesized and new habits of feeling and thought may emerge.

[19] Rogers, *op. cit.*

Recapitulation

From about 1921, child guidance was increasingly psychiatrically (in part psychoanalytically) oriented. The nature of the genetic aspects of behavior was studied; recognition that behavior was, in part, unconsciously motivated affected the approach; release of feelings came to have more therapeutic significance than did a rational pedagogy of imposed "guidance." There were important attempts to distinguish between the antisocial child, whose problem is learning how to live with or relate himself to anyone, and the child whose intrapsychic conflict makes a permissive relationship inadequate, when it becomes necessary to gain access to the conflict which is causing the behavior. The concepts which explained personality structure were found equally significant for all work in interpersonal relationships: on the one hand, diagnosis was becoming more adequate in terms of the total personality picture, and therefore treatment objectives were clearer; on the other hand, there was growing recognition that a person learns from those he trusts and that the transference relationship may be in itself the dynamic for change, growth, and integration of the self.

The grouping of professional services in a working team or unit with adequate psychiatric consultation and social work supervisory controls has obviated the misconception that plagues so many persons—that only psychiatrists can effect personality change, or that personality change can only be induced through deep therapy. Change is a relative thing. A person may change as a reaction to a change in his situation; children change more than adults, but experience has shown that under various influences a person may be helped to change his attitudes, adapt his behavior or outlook, and release new energies which have the effect of changing the direction of his life.

In a unified approach at the Jewish Board of Guardians it is no longer assumed that a "therapist" must do one kind of treatment and a "caseworker" another, but it is recognized that psychosocial therapy [20]

[20] For a full discussion of the principles of therapy see Chapter VI. In certain clinics a sharp demarkation is made between the roles of "therapist," usually, but not always,

should be adapted to the problem—all direct therapy being oriented fully to the social situation, and the whole social treatment being clinically oriented. Psychotherapy, as carried on through casework and group work, in the two-person and multi-person situation, is always strongly supportive of the living experience itself. Thus, psychotherapy brings in concepts of progressive education which, in turn, owes much of its own theory to mental hygiene; it includes the growing science of interpersonal relationships. Its aim is to help the person to use or conserve or release or build or rebuild his own strengths. Inasmuch as children are the direct beneficiaries of the program, therapy, allying itself with both the natural processes of growth and the social forces in the environment, may often offer a hopeful outlook.

a psychiatrist, and of social worker. In some clinics there may be graduated shifting of roles. This book emphasizes child guidance *therapy* rather than the therapist.

Chapter II

THE DIAGNOSTIC PROCESS

IN CHILD GUIDANCE

In therapy, when change in the person is the chief aim, adequate diagnosis must be kept at the center of the process, and both practical aid and the provision of an educationally or therapeutically conditioned environment will subserve the therapeutic intent. The psychiatric concept of wholeness, or integration of the self, both among its own constituent factors and in the running stream of life experience, does not mean that casework treatment is necessarily directed toward a total change in personality, but that understanding the person-social configuration is everywhere necessary. At one time the symptom of stuttering, let us say, might have been attacked as an isolated phenomenon, whereas now understanding this particular symptom would lead to consideration of the significant interactions, and treatment would attempt to involve the whole self or personality of the child on his own behalf. The caseworker may "partialize" in treatment, in the sense that the client and he will work along one step at a time, or on a bit of this surface or that, or from this angle or that, but the diagnostic process in child guidance insists on a comprehensive picture of the situation, the person, and the person reacting to his situation, including those earlier experiences which have contributed so much to shaping his character.

In the relationship life of the growing child it is not easy to draw a sharp line between the pathological and the normal. The "personal equation," as important for social work as Einstein's relativity is for physics, is the balance between internal strains and external cultural, social, personal, and economic pressures. The social worker must be able to distinguish between cases in which there is deficiency in parental affection, causing genuine affect hunger, and cases which show marked social pathology of an objective sort, as in defective, diseased and deteriorated families. He must be able to distinguish rejection, whether covert or overt, from gross neglect; the essentially healthy but egocentric person, who may show minor disturbances or habit disorders, from the real deviations; the essentially normal child with mild situational problems from the dwarfed, warped, or sick child; he must distinguish completely disrupted and disrupting homes from those that have possibilities of modification and reconstruction, and finally he must understand the fluid and shifting picture of child development. In this last he must discern what part of behavior is reactive to a current situation and what already has become a character trend.

The Official Classification and the Clinical Picture

The standard psychiatric classifications [1] have not been found entirely adequate in child guidance work, and they certainly do not suffice for the familial concerns of the caseworker. There is always a question raised about the propriety of the making of psychiatric diagnoses by social workers but no one would deny that a social worker treating children and their families, removing children from the home, dealing with truants and school problems and all the rest, should *understand* the significance of such terms as "primary behavior disorder" [2] along with broad classifications of psychoses, psychoneuroses, mental defectiveness, convulsive disorders, and so forth. The terms "psychoneurosis *with behavior disorder*" and "behavior disorder *with neurotic symptoms or traits*" came into usage because the old categories were too broad and not sufficiently clarifying.[3]

---

[1] The Jewish Board of Guardians has, in the main, followed the Lewis Classification— *Outlines for Psychiatric Examinations*—but with certain refinements which will appear in later discussions. It is unnecessary to recapitulate here the standard classifications of mental illness with their characteristic syndromes.

[2] In this book the author uses the term "primary behavior disorder" to describe a person whose life shows the pattern of behavior designed to relieve unconscious tension through "acting out" in ways not well adapted to reality. Diagnostic terms in behavior problems are not so well standardized as are the other clinical categories. Under the Lewis Classification "Special Behavior Disorders" are given the subgroups: habit disorders, conduct disorders, sex perversions, and disabilities in reading, writing, and speech.

[3] Although at the outset of this study the writer was assured that there would be a large incidence of "pure" primary behavior disorders, this was less common than mixed types. Several years ago a study at the JBG showed that about 80 percent of the cases

These failed to show that a disturbed child might be capable of functioning both on the neurotic and on the primary behavior disorder (narcissistic-preoedipal) level. With every neurosis there must be some behavior disorder; there may be behavior disorders with neurotic traits or with incipient psychoneurosis (or psychosis). The classification is usually given according to the dominant grouping of symptoms, e.g., psychoneurosis with behavior disorder, or primary behavior disorder with neurotic traits. For a full clinical diagnosis one must always have the syndrome of symptoms leading to the official description. As Miss Frederika Neumann has pointed out: [4] "One of the soundest disciplines to which caseworkers can be subjected is that of learning to think clinically . . . to subject symptoms to scrutiny in their context; to absorb the idea that a diagnosis is a vertical as well as horizontal concept." It can certainly be said that the trend to the treatment of younger children makes adequate differential diagnosis imperative, since the prevention of neurosis as well as of delinquency is in the fullest sense the opportunity of family and child guidance work. The problem is particularly important, since in family guidance not only must a clinical descriptive diagnosis be made of each person under individual treatment, but a diagnosis and evaluation of the family constellation, its balance and potentiality for improved functioning, must be dynamically formulated.

In order to have a diagnostic picture adequate for the practice of psychotherapy, one must ascertain the type of abnormality acquired at certain periods of life by a certain type of personality under certain conditions. One must consider not only the clinical development of the illness (including behavior disorder as "illness"), but its place within the functioning of the total personality. The diagnostic term, to be of value, should be an accurate, recognized, and precisely used symbol for the constellation. To understand the phenomena of re-

---

were diagnosed as primary behavior disorder, 7 percent as psychotic, and 7 percent as psychoneurotic, and the rest miscellaneous. According to a statistical analysis covering the period July, 1944, to June, 1945, 40 percent were diagnosed as primary behavior disorder, 42 percent as psychoneurotic, 3 percent as psychotic or prepsychotic, and the rest miscellaneous. A further analysis of the 40 percent diagnosed as primary behavior disorders revealed that 17 percent, or close to one half, included neurotic traits.

[4] Frederika Neumann, "The Use of Psychiatric Consultation by a Case Work Agency," *The Family*, XXVI (October, 1945), 216.

gression, transference, ambivalence, and so forth, which inevitably
take place during intensive psychotherapy, one must also understand
the dynamics of the emotional age level. Although there have been
recent swings in certain schools, both in psychiatry and in social
work, away from consideration of the so-called "psychosexual" development, we believe that any worker who hopes to treat behavior
disorders and psychoneuroses in a responsible fashion must know
fully the underlying theoretical assumptions, as well as the major
criticisms of these assumptions.

There is something of a dilemma here, however, since in psychiatry
itself there are emphases, indisputably two aspects of the same knowledge, which are as yet imperfectly reconciled. One is the traditional
clinical concept that emotional disturbance is an "illness" with known
symptomatology, the other the concept of the disturbed person and
his difficulties in functioning in or adapting to the world around him.
As soon as symptoms are isolated it is suggested that attention should
be given to that particular configuration and its etiology. Yet the
"illness" must be understood *within the context of the whole person,*
of the family, and of the social milieu. Thus, the functioning of the
total personality, its strengths, its social and ego patterns, the defenses and other adaptations to reality, becomes dominant in the
evaluation of the case as a whole. The normal person can best har-
monize his instinctual tendencies with outer pressures, the neurotic
is more fixated to the nonsocial infantile tendencies within him, so
that part of him is less adjusted to the rest of him, and the conflict
comes out in disguised ways as symptoms. In primary behavior disorder the personality has come even less into adjustment with reality,
and in the psychopath still less. Diagnosis represents the contribution
of science to art, the core of knowledge at any given time in the life
of a profession. Any social worker practicing therapy must have
enough clinical understanding not only to treat but even to make
effective use of the psychiatrist's contribution.

Dynamic Aspects and the Emotional Age Level

The level of development and of arrest is of the greatest importance
in understanding the nature of the end result. Therefore, a proper

classification does not arise from a grouping of the behavior symptoms alone, but in the light of the developmental factors or emotional age when the disturbance arose. Character structure in the growing child has in it elements of constancy and of fluidity. It is no longer thought to be true that the constitution with which the child is born is permanently and immutably formed; that the limits of growth or of intellectual capacity are fixed, even though the color of the eyes and hair and the gross physical and mental characteristics do not seem subject to change. The child takes along with him in his growth process something from every level of his experience. In the adolescent and in the adult we shall find, if our observations are sufficiently complete, something of all that he has lived through—both in his present character and in whatever may be his present problems. No diagnosis using the categorical or classification form alone can fully define, though it may imply, this flowing stream of the personality. "Anxiety hysteria" tells very little about a child. One cannot split off current functioning from the history itself. The clinical findings must coincide with the psychological development, and vice versa. It is very hard to determine just when the ego may be said to develop, as it is a continuous process, and while we can roughly distinguish how and when the child passes through identification to object relationship and the critical period for the formation of the super-ego, these phases, too, have a certain fluidity and range. Skilled workers would make at least as much differentiation in treatment among *age* groups—young children, latency, and adolescence—as among *clinical* classifications—psychoneurosis, primary behavior disorder, psychosis, and psychopathic personality. Diagnostically, the habit of looking at these disturbances retrospectively through the developmental history not only tells what the problem is, clinically speaking, but what in an over-all way one should attempt, and in a limited way can predict, in treatment. With changes in personality in the older child or adult, one must always ask what sort of changes. When did they take place? For instance, with schizophrenics the changes typically occur at the onset of puberty; if extreme loss of interest, neglect of possessions, and so forth, occur in the young child, one must think of the possibility of organic disease.

The importance of these and all other diagnostic distinctions lies in the therapeutic objective. One must determine motivation within the context of the whole problem in order to understand the symptom used. The therapeutic aim is to gain access to the child's ego; to strengthen it if possible, in order to help the child deal with his own drives. The diagnostic process inherently reaches for causality. There are four main sources of understanding utilized in the social work approach, namely: (1) psychogenetic history; (2) direct observation of the child or other person during the interview, including his way of relating himself; (3) the use of examinations, consultation and tests from other disciplines, and (4) the environmental study. While all these methods are used in any field of casework, there are certain emphases especially appropriate for child guidance diagnosis, to which we shall give consideration here.

The Primary Self and the Habit Disorder [5]

In order to understand the nature of the habit disorder, which is the earliest deviation, the worker reexamines the dynamics of infancy. Constitutional factors may have started the child with a strong or a weak structure, predispositions to this or that character formation, or certain sensitivities not now fully understood. Some children seem to be born with a great deal of aggression, others seem to have special susceptibilities for feeling rejected, even when there is not much rejection discernible. May there not be an "allergy" for rejection which makes some children especially vulnerable? Then, there are prenatal influences to be considered, and the question of the relation of birth to anxiety.[6] The experience of birth was considered by Freud to be a prototype of the anxiety reaction developed later. A disturbed pregnancy does not necessarily mean an unwanted child, but in some instances it may point to a neurotic conflict. The question of easy or traumatic birth experience is noted, even though the social worker's task begins with the parent-child relation in its *social* aspects. A record of the mother's previous abortions should make one wonder

---

[5] The developmental stages are reconsidered from the point of view of therapy in Chapters VIII, IX, and X.

[6] Greenacre, "The Biological Economy of Birth," in *Psychoanalytic Study of the Child*, pp. 31–52.

what might be the deeper significances underneath the conventional rationalizations. Some parents frankly say that the child was an accident, and others that they would have much preferred a child of the opposite sex. While such preferences are normal the intensity or duration of feeling may be suggestive. Many parents do not say these things openly, but express their anger and disappointment indirectly through complaints or emotionally charged accounts of childbirth and early sufferings.

The succeeding dynamics are found in the nursing experience, the nursing baby being generally conceded to start with an advantage. The fact of nursing is important not only because the act which, aside from developing the child physically, directs the baby's interests (along with his pleasures) to the outside world, but also because under favorable circumstances it insures adequate "mothering." This is important not only in its more familiar aspect of loving, but because it is in this "climate" that the ego functions best develop. The baby must be loved to proceed with the business of growing, but he also needs an admiring audience. True, the baby will sit up and walk whether loved or not, but feeding and habits of speech seem to be particularly sensitive to the quality of the mothering. A progressive emotional development between parent and child enables the child not only to have feeding satisfactions but also to learn to perceive, to touch, to play, to laugh back, to feel secure when being moved about. He is encouraged to crawl and to walk by the outstretched arms and the voice of mother and father, their love leading to his independent functioning. Here one can see how intertwined from the earliest months of life are the ego and the instinctual satisfactions which make for growth, and later for full adjustment. At all ages the child must be helped and encouraged to grow up.

The child first distinguishes whether the mother is there or not there, and later he recognizes the mother. This is not true object relationship, since babies are normally autistic or narcissistic. The infant uses the persons about him for his own ends; in the deviations such as primary behavior disorders this mode of relating oneself persists into later life. Not only is identification, after self-love, the most primitive form of love, but it also continues all through life as one aspect of love. Primary identification takes place before the child can distinguish the difference between himself and his parents. The mature person achieves the ability to distinguish others as different from himself (object love), but he also carries a layer of this earliest ability to identify with other persons in sympathy, or "empathy." Indeed, the therapist must have a large portion of this form of intuitive understanding guiding his perceptions if he is to enter into a living, feeling relationship with his patient.[7] The baby knows how the mother feels when she is nursing or handling him, and he reacts to tenseness or anxiety or disgust. Because the mother offers the baby satisfaction and comfort when feeding him, changing diapers, and so forth, for the child it is an easy step from loving the *satisfactions* to loving the *giver* or image of these satisfactions. A young child makes identifications with little regard to the sex of the adult. If the giver of satisfaction should fail to give fully and warmly, it is easy to see how the primary identification process would break down and a condition of secondary narcissism take its place. A child will, however, in therapy, start all over again to relate through identification, as we shall show later.[8]

For approximately the first year of life it is normal for a baby to use every outside stimulus to gratify his wishes; to be as much of a baby as possible is good for him. Gratification is necessary and appropriate; if gratifications and stimuli are lacking, there is retardation; if gratifications are excessive and prolonged beyond early infancy, without the balance of necessary restriction and encouragement toward learning to do for oneself one may see the beginnings of infantilization. The mother who keeps her little boy or girl overly dependent at four or five years of age is not forming a new habit, but is using methods formed in the child's infancy. In babies who have been totally deprived of mothering, such as foundlings in a large institution, personality growth may be completely arrested in the narcissistic stage. The child develops self-dependence through increasing mastery of physical and social experience in a warmly supportive atmosphere.

Deviations in the earliest stage of the selfhood express themselves

7 See p. 126.   8 See "Dynamics of Change," p. 131.

as habit disorders. If the baby does not get adequate mothering, he is forced back to his own body for pleasure and attention, and the ordinary thumb-sucking, masturbation, and other body play may be prolonged or intensified as "autoerotism"—extreme physical indulgence having somewhat similar effects. The child thus forced to love himself prolongs his infancy, does not outgrow his infantile habits, which, if not treated, continue as part of the permanent personality structure. The rejected child only partially grows beyond this stage or regresses to secondary narcissism, which shows itself in habit disorders. One must be careful to distinguish between the perfectly normal autism of the little child who has not much "social" sense, from excessive body pleasure aberrations of this period occurring because the child has been thrown back on itself for gratification. Frustrations normally occur in weaning. Regular feeding periods, supplementary foods such as cod liver oil, which the baby may not like, toilet training, and so forth, if constructively handled by the mother should permit the ego to get off to a good start; if destructively handled, the baby may be overwhelmed, antagonized, or otherwise handicapped.

Interest in the body and bed-wetting and soiling are normal for all infants. Obstinacy and rebellion are useful in toughening the ego. When the child conforms because of fear of punishment, there may result neurotic traits, or else the child, casting aside dependency altogether, may act out his impulses in overt misdeeds. If the child conforms because of receiving a reasonable amount of love and approval, sublimation and social development result. Both habit and conduct disorders stem from the earliest years as reactions to an inadequate mother or mother substitute, and excessive residual traces shown later warn us of a degree of obduracy in the prognosis. One must think of the retention of childish habits as disorders only if they are inappropriately prolonged or unusual in quality or quantity. The child with marked habit disorders is usually a passive child, self-preoccupied, whereas children with conduct disorders (discussed below) are obviously and aggressively in conflict with their environment. It is easy to see why each type described would have great difficulty in developing a capacity for relationships. In practically all disturbed children some persisting habit disorders are likely to be found.

Reaction to the "Parent as an Individual"[9] and Conduct Disorders

The next chronological deviation in the development of self has to do with conduct or reaction against someone outside the self. Secondary identification takes place when the child learns that there is a difference between himself and his parents. As not all of his wishes are immediately gratified, he loses his feeling of omnipotence and realizes that the parents are something he cannot control. He becomes aware of his helplessness, and his parents begin to seem to him omnipotent. He loses his feeling of narcissistic perfection, yet wishes to regain it, and he strives to do so by identification with his parents, by trying to be like them. The super-ego development originates because of parental prohibitions, which arise in many little ways, but especially in relation to body habits already described, including thumb-sucking and masturbation. The mother normally does not accept the "crude and passionate elements" in the child's instinctual strivings, but acts intuitively to replace these with sublimated forms of tenderness and affection. Since the child loves through identification, he also tends to reject and repress these crude impulses and follow the example set, gradually internalizing parental prohibitions. But this expected development from the pleasure principle to the acceptance of reality is made hard, if not impossible, if there is undue harshness or inconsistency in the parental attitude.

Little children who normally enjoy seeing or playing with excreta also enjoy, a step farther along in their growth, smearing food about. The associations, through the mother, of feeding and toilet training are very close and easily confused; table manners and toilet manners have interchangeable values for the young child, and parental prohibitions in one area are carried over into the other. Quite routinely the average child may take the parental attitude in toilet training over

---

[9] This and the concept of the "parents as a couple" are attributed to Dr. J. H. W. van Ophuijsen, "New Fields for Psychiatric Case Work," in *The Case Worker in Psychotherapy*, pp. 10–15.

into inhibitions about eating, going through a phase of disgust over certain foods which seem to him "dirty." Normally, children outgrow these fancies if the parental attitudes are natural and serene, but if this situation is badly handled the desires are not given up, but are continued underground. Temper tantrums, which are a sort of generalized outburst of rage, not directed at a specific object, as quarreling is, stem from the level of infancy. The student of child guidance cases is at once struck with twin facts in the history of delinquent children: the amount of harshness, inconsistency, and actual hostility in the parental background either directed at the child itself or shown in marital quarreling, or more likely both; and the monotonous recurrence of a history of feeding difficulties and unwise toilet training.

Before three, the child reacts to each parent as an individual; that is, in a conduct or habit disorder the child is reacting to a *single* person, typically the mother, although sometimes the father or other parent substitute. The child is not yet conscious of the parents as a couple, although even before three he will have received some impressions and developed some fantasies about the physical relationship. Conduct disorders [10] may be transitory and will persist only when there are severe parental frustrations, harshness, or lack of love for the child. The child does not think it worth while to please his parents, since he cannot seem to get love on any terms. The child then tends to renounce parental love, and to retain aggression as a characteristic pattern. Only by experiencing love can a child love back. When the child has little love, he must continue in or fall back upon his narcissism. Such a child now cannot form normal love relationships. He uses the parent for his own ends, but he does not deeply love the parent, because his love is frozen or fixated within himself; he continually wants the parent or other person to love him. The child does not get enough from either parent to incorporate a super-ego (of which conscience is the conscious part), so there are defective controls. Conflict then remains outside, between the individual and the restraining environment. If the disorder persists, there will be more and more frustrations, and often the child will

[10] See Chapter III.

say that he does not want anything to do with his parents. Profound disgust as well as aggression is characteristic of the primary behavior disorder. Early rejection or inconsistent handling leads to inconsistent impulsive behavior, weak ego formation, and a poorly integrated character.

Our concept of neglect should include not only those babies who never have been mothered but also those who have never been limited in any way. Wise mothering includes wise protection and necessary prohibition. The truly "neglected" child has been neither loved nor restrained. Intimidation or severe deprivation seems to lead most to the frustration-aggression forms of behavior; over-protection or indulgence, solicitude and inseparable contact, most to infantilization.[11] Good mothers and fathers, however, prepare the young child for the mastery of his next problem in social growth.

"The Parents as a Couple" and the Oedipal Conflict [12]

From approximately three to seven, the so-called "oedipal" period, the child begins to recognize the relation of his parents to each other, or as a couple. Normally, at this period the boy child wants his mother for himself, and the girl child, the father, and the essence of the growth experience is that the child must give up his wish to possess either separately. In a wholesome situation the parents together help the child to repress these drives, the boy to identify with the father, and the girl with the mother, and at the same time to renounce jealousy. Thus the child emerges with a constructive identification with his own sex and affection and admiration for the other, rather than any undue possessiveness. The child becomes aware of the inter-relatedness between his parents, learns to accept this as reality and to repress his impulses, hence the development of the mature super-ego. In neurosis, these problems are not solved; there is insufficient or incomplete repression. The fact that the child has not given up the parent of the opposite sex as a love object remains the weak spot throughout his life. This child grown up is familiar to social workers as the person who brings into marriage every version of unresolved

---

[11] Levy, in *Maternal Overprotection*.   [12] See footnote p. 28.

parental attachment and ambivalence. They are the parents of large numbers of the "guidance" population.[13]

The normal child, helped by secure parents, learns to accept himself and the reality of other persons, builds up constructive defense mechanisms against the crude expression of the drives, and also sublimates these through the ordinary achievements and satisfactions of growing up. In normal super-ego development the child's aggression is turned against his own censored impulses and acts. Under favorable circumstances, the child makes his adjustment to the fact that the parents belong to each other as well as to him and passes comfortably to another stage of development. In the deviations the child who has had an unsatisfactory parental experience does not resolve his problem, and he does not enjoy a secure latency for ego building.[14] To avoid anxiety, he regresses—clinging to the old dependencies and resistances, unable to move toward a more mature object love—or he partially resolves his problem by throwing up a defensive structure bound with anxiety. Thus he is enabled to function as long as the defenses hold. The instinctual drives of the child are not bad; they are essential to growth itself. The mischief comes when in the necessary social and ethical maturation of the total personality the impulses run amuck, as in the delinquent, or are perceived as bad and dangerous, as in the psychoneurotic.

The mild phobic disorders, characteristic of the ages from three to five (generalized anxiety being not much seen before the age of four), such as fear of animals or the dark, may become invested with much deeper anxiety, involving fear of punishment by the parents. The psychoneurotic symptoms, which represent the internal conflict between the repressed wishes and the forces of the ego, are usually greater during the later half of the oedipal period. The psychoneurotic deviation represents a disturbance in the "sexual" area, stemming from the incomplete resolution of the oedipal conflict and infantile anxiety. "Sexual" is used throughout this study by the writer in the broad sense of life energy which normally flows into ego strength, security, and capacity for object love. Any disturbance in

[13] See Chapter XI.   [14] See Chapter IX.

the "sexual" area always involves disturbance in ego functions as well.

The child with a primary behavior problem brings to the solution of the oedipal situation little experience in loving to help him. In a sense he must by-pass the whole business, as he did not get enough help from the parent to solve it. He has little but failure and aggression to bring to bear. As he has never adequately possessed his parents, he cannot be said to relinquish them. He has not experienced enough love to be able to sacrifice for it—"I should worry about my parents, they never did anything for me." For him the conflict can remain unsolved—"go hang," as it were. On the other hand, the child who has experienced love, but not enough for security, has already paid too high a price for it and is still willing to pay too high a price. His feelings are ambivalent, showing both love and hate, so his efforts are confused and ineffective. He has conflict about his instinctual drives, which he dimly feels he should solve. He is the anxious child, the psychoneurotic.

An important aspect of differential diagnosis in behavior disorders appears in our use of the concepts *preoedipal* and *oedipal* type or group,[15] because the time of onset helps to clarify the nature and severity of the disturbance. It is true that these syndromes are not to be found in pure form in the very young child, because the primary behavior disorder may, in going through the oedipal period, take on some characteristics similar to those of the psychoneurotic, although the total clinical picture, seen in latency or adolescence, differs from that of the psychoneurotic in that the person has a warped character and acts out his unconscious tensions, whereas the neurotic has crippling inhibitions. Primary behavior disorders are always reactions to environmental influences. Both habit and conduct disorders arising in the preoedipal stages of development may persist in later life with or without marked oedipal involvement. Anxiety culminating during the oedipal period may be either acted out in conflict with society or internalized in psychoneurosis. If the acted out behavior has oedipal content one would place the child diagnostically in the neurotic group of behavior or character disorders. Thus, dissocial character formation (primitive hostile aggression)

[15] This differentiation is carefully made at the Jewish Board of Guardians.

does not preclude the development of neurotic conflicts which may be superimposed to a greater or less degree, leading to a delinquent "symptom." All the personality is expressed through the ego functions. One cannot consider the impulsive life *or* the ego structure, but their interaction, which in favorable situations works into as strong and adequate a functioning unit as does the heart in the human body. In child guidance one sees the cases in which damage has been done. Whether all children and all cultures have some version of the oedipal struggle is for research to determine but certainly oedipal material is prominent in child guidance problems.

From Latency to Adolescence

During the ages approximately from six or eight to twelve, inclusive, the child has a relatively quiet emotional development, actively identifying with the parent of the corresponding sex, repressing forbidden drives in a healthy way, forming new contacts, and sublimating his drives through activities, interests, school, and so forth.[16] The early part of this period is when obsessional symptoms may develop—or even earlier. If the oedipal situation has not been constructively solved, torturing thoughts, disguises for the unconscious preoccupation with the parents, arise, accompanied by anxiety. If obsessional symptoms do not serve the purpose of keeping repressed the unconscious thoughts, compulsive symptoms may develop. The compulsive neurotic has never overcome his earliest infantile attachment to the parents as love objects—ambivalence is very strong in his relationships. After the latency period (although in disturbed children there is characteristically no latency), which is generally favorable for casework treatment because of the consolidation of emotional gains with good ego defenses, the balance is again upset by the onset of adolescence. With adolescence the urge of psychic energies, because of the biological development, again becomes insistent. The ego and the super-ego, which structurally were strong enough for the quiet period of latency, are threatened by the increased tensions. At adolescence the oedipal situation is reactivated. If the child has had a secure development, he rides the storm successfully, turning his energies

---

[16] See pp. 247 and 265 for the "inadequacy constellation."

in the direction of appropriate heterosexual objects. Diagnostically, it is very important to remember that a good deal of instability is to be expected. The boy may show love attitudes toward the worker, as toward any older mother figure toward whom his affections are directed. A certain amount of homosexuality is normal in pre-puberty and adolescence, but the worker has to be on the lookout for excessively feminine behavior in boys or masculine drives in girls. If there are signs of confused identification, the young person may have a great deal of anxiety about these feelings unless he is helped to resolve them.

History Taking and Observation of Behavior

As based on the foregoing, history taking becomes a precise instrument in regard to both the clinical picture and the emotional age level, in the normative sense, against which deviations can be properly discriminated. History giving and taking with regard to an adult or an adolescent involves spontaneous, if not wholly "free," association, with therapeutic elements of catharsis and potential insight. In child guidance the process is modified by the fact that in most instances the parent who gives the history about the child gives it, indirectly, about himself. There will often be blocking, or withdrawal in panic, as an already anxious or guilty parent partially glimpses his own role in the problem. Because it is necessary to determine with reasonable immediacy whether a case should be treated by this agency or elsewhere, a certain amount of history must be secured for tentative diagnosis. In many cases the process of history taking leads into a transference relationship with the parent who is to be a partner in the treatment. It is a mistake to assume that *first* one establishes a "relationship" and *then* one obtains the history, since the former is an aspect of the latter. At any rate, with the double patient focus there is no substitute for securing a knowledge of the predisposing factors in the child's early, especially his familial, environment in order to ascertain the dynamic factors in the total clinical picture. The worker needs also to know what the problem is now thought to be by parent or teacher or others—with regard to sensitivity, withdrawal, rebellion, and failure to get along with other children.

The problem is further complicated, since the parent who gives the history about the child tends to feel that now the matter is completed. If, however, she is helped to take responsibility, she will bit by bit disclose, with or without questions (though one should not be afraid to ask appropriate questions either in regard to the child or herself) significant facts in her own life experience. For instance, it may be evident at once that she did not want this little boy, but why she did not want him must wait to be divulged after greater security in the relationship has been established. One is careful not to delve for childhood memories prematurely, as this only arouses defenses. In all history taking it is important to find out the positive aspects—to help the client discover in himself those talents and capacities which when psychic energy is freed he can use for a fuller and more satisfying life.

It has been the fashion recently to underestimate the historical method of enquiry, but this is shortsighted and, in child guidance, inadmissible. There is no substitute for the historical method of establishing the diagnosis, since the development of the problem points to different types of illness. History is important because it tells us when some deviation started, and knowing when it started and under what circumstances, we are in a better position to know what it is today. One does not seek to know the past because one is going to treat the past. One seeks knowledge of it because it is part of the present structure. One can only treat the "current" personality in its present circumstances, but one can understand the person best by knowing when the deviations and fixations occurred and what were the traumatic incidents which are now scars and to which he is still reacting. It is the inappropriate persistence of the past into the present which largely occasions treatment.

True diagnosis is derived not only from the history but also from direct observation of the functioning of the person during the interview. In the early days of child guidance the social worker was assigned the role of getting the familial history from the adults about the child, while the psychiatrist observed the child in a psychiatric examination, which provided a cross-section picture of the child's behavior. In child guidance today, the worker also must acquire the skill to see and understand the child through his behavior—the way he relates himself in the interview or play situation. As the history prepares one to know what to watch for, conversely, what one can observe tells something of the child's psychological development. What information can be gained by observing the ways in which the person functions in such a relationship which can be used in addition to the data of the life chart? What is recurrent? The psychosocial influences result in varying symptomatology according to the developmental level reached when the unfavorable stimulus hit the personality. But processes leading to symptomatology have been more clearly charted than the processes leading to character formation. Not all childish peculiarities develop into neurotic formations, some being absorbed within the range called "normal," some leading to antisocial or other deviations.

Character diagnosis, patterns of social and ego functioning, are perhaps especially the concern of the caseworker. As we know, the ego "has two perceptive surfaces, one directed toward the instinctual life (inner perception), the second directed toward external reality (sense perception)." [17] The chief function of the ego is to bring subjective needs and wishes into harmony with external circumstances or "reality." The "character" of a person is his typical behavior in all sorts of circumstances. This character is not wholly inherent (biological and constitutional) or imposed from without (social environmental); it is also self-formed through interaction with the environment. Whenever there is a breakdown in adaptation one must ask oneself, is this superficial or involved? Is this behavior reactive, or does it represent a deviation in personality? In adults behavior is not often merely a reaction to a situation, but the more disturbed the person and the greater the irrationality, the more rigid and total are the responses and the less is the behavior likely to be a true reaction. The therapist comes to understand the difficulty, not only from the historical approach, but through the request itself and discussing the client's attempts to deal with his problems. The parents' request for guidance is always accompanied by defenses against it, out of which the treatment situation is gradually opened up.

[17] Alexander, "Development of the Ego-Psychology," in *Psychoanalysis Today*.

In child analysis it was discovered that current observation of the child added something new and significant to the methods already evolved, and in fact these observations have served as correctives to earlier assumptions based only on the recall of repressed material in the adult. The child is actually still in successive and shifting phases of adjustment and nonadjustment to his environment. Though the conflict may be already partially, or even wholly, internalized, the conscious ego, which is the most plastic part of the personality—more plastic in children than in older persons—is accessible to the case-worker, who must be taught to notice and to comprehend the meaning of what he sees in the child's current functioning. The child expresses himself more fully in action and movement (play) than does the adult, the transference relationship being the "culture" in which these meanings emerge.

The worker must be acquainted with fantasy, must know at what ages and to what degree it is entirely normal and when it is in border-line areas. He should be able to follow the child's projections in play, the special choices and repetitions in play material, day dreams, series of anxiety dreams, and so forth. He notices the various types of personality picture—the unreasonable, illogical, amoral, demanding, infantile person and the stubborn, dependent, passive, withdrawn, fearful, suspicious, or irritable moods—since these observations will direct him back to the etiological basis in the psychological development, discussed above. The eye cannot truly see what the mind has not been taught to understand.

One must clear away the underbrush and see whether one is dealing with a child having a severe conscience or too little conscience; the "behavior disorder," who acts out his impulses under tension, or the inhibited child. One must notice all fears and be able to grasp what a person is expressing in his play or words, or both, since in young children play is substituted for verbalization.[18] Motor behavior, especially in young children, its goals, quantity, and quality, is important as part of the diagnostic picture. What is normal for the age range must be a constant corrective. The child will tend to show toward the worker some of the same behavior which he shows toward the parent.

[18] See Chapter VII.

This charges the interview, whether play or verbal or both, with meaning. As the transference develops, the interview is even more charged, and dominant characteristics can be observed. Because the classical behavior problem child is aggressive and cannot relate easily, whenever one sees wariness, hostility, suspicion, and inability to relate, with marked projection, an important diagnostic window has been opened. When there is a quick positive transference, perhaps changing to alternations with the negative or covered up by negative, one may legitimately look for hitherto unrevealed symptoms of neurosis, always allowing, however, for the shifting picture the child presents of his whole personality, now of one facet, now of another. Workers should be as familiar with ego and social function patterns as with syndromes which pertain to illness. Norms should be more fully worked out and made available—including general appearance, adaptation to reality, the image of the self, degree and type of self-control, affective tone, and ways of relating oneself.[19]

Looking at the child from the angle of *reality acceptance,* one can see great differences in a child's grasp on reality, his skills, for example, the degree and kind of fantasy he indulges in, and the mobility pattern. The *image of the self* may be one of self-esteem, self-confidence, or the reverse. He may have a good sense of goal and achievement, or he may be insecure and self-depreciating. With regard to *ego integration,* he may have self-control or be scattered or impulsive or egocentric; he may be able to complete tasks, or he may be easily frustrated and "fall apart" before one's eyes in aimless or destructive behavior. Can he accept limitation—too readily or not at all? One must notice the *affective tone*—spontaneity or repression; depth or brittleness or shallowness; rigidity or flexibility; and appropriateness of response. Finally, the *relationship pattern:* primary narcissism or little relationship (normal for infants and toddlers); poorly developed or limited relationship; passive dependency and defense, or active offense and aggression, or detachment; the quality of object, but immature, relationship; excessive submission, or guilt and fear

[19] At the Jewish Board of Guardians Dr. Nathan W. Ackerman has proposed a detailed chart for observation along these lines.

of punishment; ambivalence, with other mixed types of relationship, such as disturbed identifications. The psychoneurotic gives himself more fully in relationship than does the behavior disorder, but with anxiety.[20] The psychopathic personality has shallow and unsubstantial ways of relating himself; the psychotic is autistic, and so forth. Partial and limited, rather than full, capacity to relate roughly corresponds to the preoedipal and oedipal stages (correction being always made for deterioration). In a play interview everything a child does has some significance, and what he does first may have special importance. Is the shooting of a gun random behavior? Or is he expressing some of the aggression already complained of by his parents? When he will not use the finger paints because they get him dirty, why does he fear being dirty? One may see here what one may also confirm from his history, that the mother does not like to have him get dirty, and one would find data, no doubt, in the story of his toilet training. When he says to the worker "You do it," supposing that the worker reads this literally and says, "See, I can do it (finger paint), and it all washes off easily," what has happened? This may be false reassurance, but it comes about because the worker does not understand what the child is trying to say. He may be expressing fear, and one does not wash away fear so easily.

Suppose at an interview a child is afraid to leave the mother and approach the worker. The layman readily assumes that he is afraid of the worker, yet it may be more correct to see that he is afraid to turn his back on his mother; afraid she will run out on him or otherwise let him down. A little girl may come straight up to the worker and say as her first remark: "Have you a daughter?" Why does she ask this, instead of saying, "Can I play here?" or "Have you a son?" or anything else. Perhaps this child is saying, "Will you be my mother?" When the worker, translating literally, says "No, I haven't a daughter," she may have missed the cue altogether. The clinical caseworker has to learn to read the language of behavior, just as the scholar must know his classics. Whether by taking history or by observing the immediate scene, the caseworker must be able to draw

[20] See pp. 74 and 151.

cautious inferences as to the nature of the repressed material, even though he may not actively stimulate its uncovering or interpret it as it emerges in the interview or through play. Finally one must know what the person wants of the worker and what effort he is to make or can make to get what he wants. The gaining of understanding is *always* focused to the need or problem as presented by the client.

Psychological, Medical, and Other Data

It is not practicable to discuss here the use of special examinations and studies familiar to social workers other than to reemphasize the interrelatedness of all the findings of science with regard to behavior. Physical, psychosomatic and psychological as well as psychiatric findings must be considered. In order to determine the state of health and the level and quality of psychological development, examinations are made as indicated.[21] In addition to the standard intelligence, educational, aptitude, and achievement tests, thematic apperception and projective techniques are much used. Not only are they significant educationally and vocationally, to determine mental capacities, but also the discovery of skills is important therapeutically to suggest lines for sublimation and strengthening the ego. The Rorschach test is not only an aid in psychiatric diagnosis, for example, between behavior disorder and psychoneurosis, between psychopathic personality and behavior disorder, between puberty crises and psychotic manifestations, between conversion hysteria and organic disease, between intellectual and emotional retardation, but it also throws light on personality dynamics. It is revealing as to patterns of social response, or ego functioning, flexibility or rigidity, quality of the affective reactions, and capacity for relationship. The Rorschach describes the quality of intelligence more than the actual level, and whether the child functions with or without anxiety. Intellectually aggressive children show up clearly here. Given the preparation of the child, there is value in having this diagnostic aid, if indicated, fairly early in the

---

[21] It is not possible to trace the contribution of psychology to the child guidance movement. The earliest use of the psychologist at the Jewish Board of Guardians, as in other agencies, was largely to take the I.Q. as a measure of intellectual proficiency. Gradually the use of psychological material has become dynamic, an integrated diagnostic tool.

contact. The findings should be reviewed by the psychiatrist and integrated with the whole diagnostic picture.

The fact that the consulting psychiatrist is a physician makes regular medical examination in behavior disorders less imperative,[22] but all records are routinely reviewed and the child may be referred for medical consultation. This should not be taken to mean that medical examinations are unnecessary, but it is often sounder to associate them with other routines—such as the health examination and follow-up in the school—rather than to subject the often frightened and resistive child to examinations which must, in the problem context, carry all sorts of implications. The psychiatrist also helps to screen out cases of psychopathology—psychosis, or severe psychoneurosis. The practice of accepting cases of psychoneurosis as well as of behavior disorder in a social agency makes such screening particularly necessary, since child guidance workers usually treat by direct therapy only such cases as are psychological in origin (with no serious active disease process). Workers must be alert to signs of either physical or mental illness, taking pains to get a precise symptom picture—the onset, the duration, and the recurrence, if any. Stomach upsets and vomiting, chronic colds, asthma, convulsive disorders, and so forth, may all be present in a child guidance case load, and particularly for children, it is important to understand the interaction of bodily symptoms and home environment, because therapy may arrest in children a psychosomatic process before it becomes irreversible and the whole body adapted to the deviant function. The decision as to whether or not a medically trained therapist is needed is an important one.

A puzzling type of medical consultation sometimes arises because the parent not infrequently erroneously attributes the child's behavior to a physical cause. Even though the worker may quite correctly infer that this is a form of resistance to treatment and that no disease process is likely to be found, obviously he must consent to the examination, although he may, and probably will, warn the parent that the examination may prove to be negative. Determined demands for a

---

[22] The role and function of the psychiatrist in diagnostic procedure, though constantly assumed, is not described in this study. He examines patients whenever indicated.

physician are likely to arise when the trouble inescapably seems to point to the parental relationship and the parent frantically tries one projection after another to establish the point that the difficulty must have another cause. In self-justification rejecting parents often insist upon a psychological examination to prove that the child is dull and hopeless and that the fault is in his defects rather than in the home.

Social environmental study, except for the great attention paid to psychogenetic history and parental emotional environment, does not differ in child guidance from similar disciplines long familiar in social casework, and so will not be discussed. The school environment is properly given weight not only as to program but also as to the reactions of teacher, principal, classroom, and schoolmates.[23] Educational retardation, such as slowness in reading and writing and arithmetic and speech disabilities, may point to personality disturbance. Psychosomatic manifestations in school, absences because of headaches, digestive upsets, and so forth, as well as the more familiar conduct disturbance should receive thorough diagnostic consideration. The anxious, shy, and withdrawn child, the overconscientious learner, the perfectionist—all should come to attention as early as possible. In the institutional setting, the whole life experience of the child is under constant observation—cottage parent, shop, school, and recreation. Camps and group experiences are increasingly used in modern child guidance as a laboratory as well as for their contribution to social adjustment. Methods of studying cultural factors are slowly evolving.

The worker trained in diagnostic procedure makes an orderly topical summary of the selected and weighted information derived from: the psychogenetic history; the observation of the child's functioning; the family constellation; the data from tests and examinations, and relevant environmental considerations. From these materials the diagnostic statement, including a clinical classification, at least for the child,[24] is precipitated. The therapeutic plan is also outlined. This diagnostic picture becomes the basis of conference with the consulting psychiatrist. The diagnostic area for child guidance is *always* inter-

[23] See Chapters VII and VIII.

[24] At the Jewish Board of Guardians workers are encouraged to place the child's problem, if possible, within one of the broad clinical categories.

personal, but subsequent or supplementary diagnostic statements about other individuals in the family group may be also formulated then or later.

Recapitulation

All psychotherapy rests on psychological understanding. Psychotherapy must be based on an adequate diagnostic procedure which includes clinical orientation. The symptom picture and its etiology necessitate understanding not only the genetic development of the personality but also the social and ego patterns of current functioning. Although stages of growth must be understood in order to determine the onset of the difficulty which in part defines the clinical picture, the total growth process of the individual must be kept in mind in order to estimate retardation, arrest, regression, and other deviations from the normal. Observations of current deviation alone are not sufficiently exact. All potentialities for independence and full object relationship are present and develop from birth onward; the growth stages are overlapping, and residual traces exist at all age levels. In therapy one must understand the outer circumstances of the client's life, social reality, and the unconscious drives as they appear through attitudes and behavior. Adaptive and defense patterns are clues to the formulation of the therapeutic problem. One must appraise the degree of tolerance for frustration and anxiety and the adequacy of function at the ego level.

The psychiatric diagnosis should be routinely reviewed by the psychiatrist, but the worker who does not have matured ability to understand the nature of personality is not equipped for child guidance work. The psychiatrist, psychologist, and caseworker must speak a common language, both as to the clinical picture and the social and ego patterns of character formation and function. The terminology, not only for children's disorders but also for social, economic, and cultural problems, should be much more precise if practice is to move into disciplined treatment and scientific research. The main object in all diagnostic procedure is that it shall be thorough without being rigid and that there shall be selection and control in the use of appropriate methods. A complete diagnosis, adequate for the therapeutic objective, is not static and should be the product of the integrated working unit or team.

Diagnosis of physical and mental illness is ultimately a medical specialization, but to diagnose, in a modern sense, does not mean that one must proceed alone. The resources of psychometric, apperceptive and other tests by the psychologist, as well as those of the psychiatrist and the social worker, are indispensable. Although cultural influences have not as yet become fully clinical knowledge, as have other data, the social worker who has a special obligation to understand the culture within which he and his clients exist must assist in the formulation of this essential subject matter as rapidly as possible. External and intrapsychic conflicts are dynamically inter-related.

Chapter III

THE CHILD WHO ACTS OUT HIS IMPULSES

THE CHILD who acts out his impulses (the primary behavior disorder) is apt to be regarded by parents and society as a "bad," rather than a "sick," child. To the caseworker he is a child who, like other children, needs to be understood in order to be effectively helped. According to a catch phrase, the only way to stand the "behavior disorder" is to understand him. Examination of the history of child placing shows that at one time only "good" children were placed in foster homes, while "bad" children were sent to institutions. Later it was found that the "bad" children were most in need of warmth and attention. The lesson was learned over again in child guidance. The child whose conflict is largely with the environment, that is, the primary or reactive behavior disorder, needs a special kind of interest and acceptance from the persons around him.

The Clinical Picture

The classical picture of the primary behavior disorder [1] is an extremely aggressive child who acts out his impulses. However he feels, so he acts. This is because he has a deficient super-ego, or internal moral authority; he is neither restrained from within nor, since he has a poor perception of and adaptation to reality, held back by social controls. The aggression may always be interpreted as reaction to the restrictions and frustrations of the early (usually parental) environment, which is why some would prefer to use the diagnostic terminology "reactive behavior disorder." It is also primary, since it starts in the first years of life. With monotonous regularity one finds that these children were rejected and have had inadequate experience of love. Many troublesome children who have well-meaning and affectionate, but unwise, parents behave badly in one situation or an-

[1] See the formation of habit and conduct disorders in Chapter II.

other. Such children may behave well when they are visiting or when at school. They do not warrant being classified as true behavior disorders but show situational disturbances. But in the case of the true behavior disorder "the iron has entered into his soul"; he has the established pattern of hurting and being hurt under most circumstances.

The normal child has a certain amount of conflict with the educational environment of the home. Neither home nor child is perfect, and misbehavior is to be expected. As he is taught day by day to modify the expression of his needs and urges, he relinquishes some of his aggression for love. We have shown in the preceding chapter how in the earliest disturbance of the personality, namely, the habit disorder, the aggression is used to cling to auto-erotic pleasures, since other satisfactions are denied.[2] Traces of these habits are usually found in the older disturbed child—nail-biting succeeding thumb-sucking, and so forth. In conduct disorders—temper tantrums, feeding difficulties, and other manifestations, the aggression is always directed outward toward someone else. It has the purpose of destroying or removing the object. With adequate love at an early age severe conduct disorders do not seem to arise or to continue. In normal development the child who goes through phases of "destructiveness"— cutting and tearing or breaking and punching holes in the wall— soon begins to consider his parents' wishes in these matters. As he identifies with the parents his ego develops negative and prohibiting attitudes toward such wayward impulses. The child is aware of the possibility of punishment or of withdrawal of parental love if he misbehaves. "There is, therefore, a period of struggle between the aggressiveness . . . and the love for the parents."[3] The aggression then is used, on the one hand, to repress the urges over which the conflict developed and, on the other hand, to inhibit the ego in ways which permit gradual adaptation to reality. Aggression is healthy and necessary for survival. It exists in the normal, the neurotic, and the

[2] See p. 26.
[3] See Jewish Board of Guardians, Primary Behavior Disorder in Children . . . Two Case Studies, p. 17.

behavior disorder alike. It is the kind, cause, degree, and method of discharge which suggest the diagnostic classification.

The process of displacement of aggression occurs in relation to each demand made by the parents on the child. The loved child experiences a world of reality which is not too painful and internalizes a conscience which is not too severe. The rejected or badly handled child, who has known only a severe and painful reality, cannot succeed in the same way. His frustrations disappoint and anger him. Displacements and internalizations then take place only partially, if at all, and so he continues to act out his impulses without inner restraints. There are two kinds of aggression to be expected: [4] hostile or infantile (preoedipal) and erotic (oedipal) aggression. The terms "oedipal" and "preoedipal" accent the point of onset and therefore the content and quality of the conflict. Actually, in all erotic aggression there is a layer of earlier hostile aggression. In experiments with group therapy and in camps run by group therapists for troublesome children, the observer is almost overwhelmed by the amount of overt aggression, destructiveness, sex behavior, obscenity, and so forth, which is released when the environment is permissive. It is not easy and perhaps not important too sharply to distinguish erotic from hostile aggression, except as it is another clue to the level of the child's total functioning. In primitive destructive hostility the child's hand is against every man, and every man's hand is against him; in erotic aggression the conflict is related to the marital disharmony in which the child became involved during the oedipal period.

In normal growth the child, through identification, incorporates the parental "no." Later other constructive identifications enrich the super-ego, and he is further socialized through identification with teachers and other persons, including playmates. To the behavior disorder, the child who has not internalized educational demand through identification, to be good means being imposed upon, put upon, or giving in. All primary behavior disorders have the pattern of trying to provoke. Such children expect punishment, which they

[4] Another theory speaks of "eroticized aggression."

will, however, dodge if they can. They enjoy their "badness"—the expression of their impulses—but they do not enjoy the consequences unless these happen to fall in with an instinctual gratification. Narcissistic, preoedipal, hostile behavior (the hoodlum and gangster types) is sometimes thought of as "genuine" delinquency; the oedipal types, as neurotic delinquency or neurotic character formation. The latter persons relieve unconscious tensions by acting out the neurosis which has been built into the character structure.[5] They usually act out so as to ensure their own punishment.

Neurotic traits may be superimposed upon an earlier structure of habit and conduct disorders. Prior to the oedipal situation, that is, before about three years of age, the conflict is between the child's body and motor urges and parental restrictions. The neurotic trait, according to Dr. van Ophuijsen, is the manifestation of an internalization of aggressiveness and its resulting unconscious conflict. "The conflict, in this case, belongs to an earlier stage of development than the conflict which causes the psychoneurotic symptom [6] or, the psychoneurosis." The grown up "neurotic character," like the primary behavior disorder, acts out his conflicts. The distortion also shows itself in antisocial behavior. To quote Glover, "the pathological character formation has somehow dealt with instinctual drives, in part at least, without the aid of repression." [7] Such a person does not make the conventional social or reality adjustments. In other cultures, with different family mores and constellations, what is repressed has a different content, and what is acted out is social or antisocial with respect to that particular culture.

The person, who through sexual or other deviation, exploits society in some fashion, shows that from an early age there has been an abnormality in the development of his super-ego. Antisocial characters may, however, also show neurotic conflicts.[8] There is some super-ego formation in almost everyone which permits the person to shift back and forth between symptoms and antisocial acts. Guilt

[5] See pp. 114 et seq. for further discussion of neurotic characters.

[6] van Ophuijsen, "Primary Conduct Disturbances; Their Diagnosis and Treatment," in *Modern Trends in Child Psychiatry*, p. 37.

[7] Glover, "Pathological Character Formation," in *Psychoanalysis Today*, p. 218.

[8] See pp. 119-120.

is a tension between ego and super-ego, when impulses are felt to be dangerous. The primary behavior disorder, preoedipal type, is one who discharges all his offensive impulses into the environment. He has little capacity for standing any tension whatever. It is, perhaps, not quite true to say that he has no guilt, as without any super-ego he would be a monstrosity, but the guilt is likely to be a "social guilt" in that he knows that what he does is disapproved of, but he himself does not disapprove of it. He knows he isn't supposed to do these things, but he lacks the inner inhibition, repression, and reproof which occur in normal super-ego formation.

The child with a primary behavior disorder is selfish and self-centered. Continuing to want infantile gratifications, he becomes angry if others receive more than he does. For the same reason he finds it hard to accept routines and disciplines of any kind, and tends to project blame for his misdeeds on others. Such a child is forever demanding, wheedling, wangling, and dodging the expected blow. The catch line "there are no problem children only problem parents" should be carried a step further. The child who has "problem parents," unless successfully treated will continue all his life to have a "parental" problem. For the preoedipal type of behavior disorder the adult world remains perennially the enemy. He must continue to attack, outwit, exploit, since he knows no other way to succeed. In the interview he will try to provoke the worker into being as rejecting as is the actual parent.

Examples of Children Who Act Out Their Impulses

A primary behavior disorder, preoedipal onset with habit disorder, is Karl, aged seven, who fights repeatedly with the children at school and with his younger brother.

Mrs. P. was very disturbed during her pregnancy with Karl because of the death of a close relative in the family, and she had a great deal of difficulty with vomiting and feelings of unhappiness and worry, and a period of false labor. Immediately after the birth Mrs. P. became ill with a streptococcus infection, complicated by double pneumonia, and she remained in the hospital for eight months, during which period there was some question as to whether she would live. Karl was placed at the age of one month in a home for infants, where he remained for eight months. He was bottle fed until he was two, and ate solid food after the age of one year. When he was ten or eleven months old he spent a period of time in the hospital with ear trouble and a high temperature. Mrs. P. noticed his overactivity at seventeen months. At the age of two it was necessary for him to return to the hospital for a minor operation. There was a tonsillectomy when Karl was almost three, measles and whooping cough at the age of four. The mother's difficulties in managing him became much worse after his brother's birth. There was a stealing episode when Karl was four, when Mrs. P. took him to the police station to frighten him, and there has been no repetition of this difficulty. He continues to have enuresis.

The mother is infantile and quick to anger against the children (she says Karl nearly killed her at birth); the father is away from home a good deal and inclined to punish the children, although he sometimes takes them for outings. Despite the poor parental attitudes, both parents have some concern for the children; the boy has good intelligence, is handsome and appealing, and a good deal of his difficulty can be ascribed to very early traumas, as well as loss of the mother as an infant. The deprivations and frustrations account for the aggressive behavior. The rejection seems, in part at least, also attributable to severe reality factors.

A primary behavior disorder, oedipal type, with earlier habit and conduct disorders and neurotic traits, would be found in the following:

Sylvia was a seven-and-a-half-year-old girl, with a brother nine and a sister five and a half, referred by the school as perverse, extremely destructive, her behavior being such as to upset the whole classroom. Although she could get good grades, she truanted. At home she was stubborn, negativistic, aggressive, hyperactive, stole money from the mother and art materials and pictures from the father, a painter. She has always masturbated.

Sylvia's brother was one and a half years old when she was born. She was unwanted, and the mother considered an abortion, but did not go through with it. It was a difficult pregnancy, and the mother fainted a number of times and had continual nausea. The mother suffered shock during the delivery. Sylvia was never breast fed, as the mother's milk had dried up. She refused the bottle, and the mother made a play of two or three hours with the child at each meal.

The child, who had been urged to eat to "please the mother," easily learned how to provoke the mother, and with the provocative circle once well established, she tends to continue this form of behavior to get what she wants.

At nine and one half months the child fell out of her crib and fractured her skull. She was immobilized for six weeks (a major frustration). After that she was "spastic" for some time in that there were jerky movements on her right side. Recovery was thought to be complete. She walked at ten months. There was no pressure on toilet training. The mother was pregnant when Sylvia was fifteen months old, and her sister was born when the child was two. The mother felt that the first unusual behavior she noticed in Sylvia was at this time. She was very jealous, wished to crush the baby's head, and destroyed possessions belonging to her. Many of the other symptoms appeared to develop when Sylvia was three; at this time the family was living with the father's parents, who were depriving and repressive in relation to Sylvia. Her aggressiveness, negativism, stubbornness, and destructiveness were evident then, but have increased in intensity in the past year.

Sylvia entered school at the age of five and had difficulties there from the beginning. She had many friends and used the money she stole to treat them. She wanted to spend a great deal of time at her friends' homes, but her mother limited this because the child was constantly quarreling with them. Also she was fearful that Sylvia would steal articles from them.

The father, a commercial artist, worked long hours and did not take much responsibility for the children. However, there was a long period several years earlier when he was unemployed or was doing art work at home, and then he was active in disciplining and training Sylvia. He was inconsistent in handling her, alternating between severity and frequent beatings and periods of acceptance and leniency. According to the mother, her husband was irresponsible and undependable and she had to keep after him continually to get him to work on time, etc. After the birth of the youngest child five and a half years earlier, the family was in dire straits; Mr. J. was depressed and told his wife that he had considered turning on the gas and killing himself and the rest of the family.

When aggression is freely expressed throughout a family circle, this probably accentuates the child's tendencies to aggressive acting out. When the parents quarrel, this child gets the feeling that she can have her father's love if she fights for it.

The mother, herself neurotic, was depressed and suffered from various pains, headaches, and numbness in her hands and feet, for which her physician could find no organic basis. The mother felt that she "takes it" from everyone—her in-laws, her parents, her husband, and her children—and that no one helped her or saw her viewpoint. She was overwhelmed by her household duties, her financial situation, and what she felt was her constant struggle with the children. Although she considered all three of her children problems, Sylvia seemed to be the most disturbed one, and the mother indicated that she and her husband had somehow handled her more severely.

Although physical and neurological examinations showed a healthy child, an additional deprivation was shortsightedness, for which the child wore thick lenses. She had a slight eye tic after masturbation diminished. Sylvia liked to paint and draw, and created unusually colorful and interesting designs. She read excessively, but her mother attempted to limit this, as her physician had advised that it was harmful for the child's eyesight.

In this case the frustration-aggression pattern would seem to be quite fully established. In her approach to the worker Sylvia was cautious and politic. For a number of weeks she brought the worker a present each time to ward off the expected attack or punishment. It took her a long time in a permissive atmosphere to express the hostility which when released was, as one would expect, violent. The oedipal material can be seen: in the identification with the artist father; the eye defect through which her mother punishes her; the interesting development of a neurotic trait (or symptom?)—an eye tic after masturbation was relinquished; and the aggression toward the prohibiting mother, which Sylvia now releases on the worker. Although an alternative classification of psychoneurosis with behavior disorder might be made, the dominant pattern throughout the case was that of abnormal use of active aggression.

The following case (a foster child) shows some of the characteristic reactions of the primary behavior disorder, oedipal type, with conduct and habit disorders and neurotic traits.

This little boy, aged seven, was referred by the settlement because of very aggressive behavior toward other children, with marked stubbornness, disobedience, and temper outbursts. In addition, he was dirty, untidy, a poor eater, and a nail biter. This behavior was shown at school and at home. He was afraid of the dark.

Omitting the history, which has many complicated social factors, we may show some of the behavior in the play interviews.

When Harry was first seen, he was maturely dressed, and there was a striking mixture of independence and timidity in his manner. He had been told that he was to see someone at the agency because he was "bad." Worker now told him that she understood he was having some difficulty in getting along and that she was going to help him. Harry was uninterested; he would rather stay with his friends or the superintendent, who gave him ice cream every day. He was not interested in the usual play things and demanded guns. In his next interview he became fascinated with darts and played without including the worker unless a dart got stuck and he, annoyed, asked worker impatiently to fix it. He tried to bargain for more time to play his game, but ignored the worker otherwise. At the third interview he became restless, explored the whole room, looked through the worker's desk drawers, and became more curious about the toys. The worker allowed him freedom and made little comment on his activities other than friendly attention. He left early, but indicated that he would come back.

At his next interview he complained of the materials and, finally, with a little help from the worker, settled down to tracing soldiers with a carbon, asking to take the pictures home. He was allowed to do this. At the next interview he was more demanding, wanted the tracing paper and all the pictures from the book. He was allowed to take his favorites only. He bargained a great deal about time. The worker conceded some minor points, but held firmly to the appointments and the general schedule. In the seventh interview he, for the first time, permitted participation by the worker in his drawings (illustrating the typically slow way in which the behavior disorder permits a relationship to be created). In the eighth interview he included the worker actively in his games of aggression. He fought from behind a chair, but the worker, who is to him a "Jap" or a

Nazi, could have no protection, and was always killed or wounded. Nevertheless, including her even in a hostile way showed the beginning of relationship. In checkers he cheated to win. The worker helped him occasionally on moves and sometimes gently reminded him of the rules.

It was during his eighth interview that a more positive relationship began to develop. He was anxious to come, impatient at waiting, resented having to leave. He wanted to control and possess the mother person, and his aggressive play had an erotic quality. In the ninth interview he expressed some jealousy of the other children in the office, involved the worker deeply in his drawing, becoming very dependent on her.

In the next interview he was defiant and demanding. He climbed onto the window sill and fantasied that he fell off and was killed by the worker—"And what then?" "Someone would kill *you*." (Release of his hostility occurred here, breaking through the play defense.) After this, Harry again was babyish, demanding, and whining. He played a little with dolls, with obvious sexual symbolism, but was furtive about discussing his play. After this he was upset, hurt himself, wanted sympathy, was restless, wanted to go home. The worker comments that he was upset and made no attempt to keep him. He was disappointed; reiterated goodbyes.

This boy goes through a cycle of suspicion, wariness, protestations of concern for his father, extreme aggressiveness, alternating with dependency and possessiveness, including a considerable erotic component. His continuing to draw rather than talk indicates resistance. By being silent, not expressing the forbidden feelings, he remains in a state of infantile security. As an infant, he can safely gratify his wish to be near the mother.

In a presentation by staff members of the Jewish Board of Guardians of two cases of primary behavior disorder,[9] "aggressive behavior disorders present since childhood" which "do not seem to be explainable on the basis of pathological processes, but do seem to be patterned reactions to unfavorable environmental influences," similar phases are described. Sometimes at the start the child is preternaturally good instead of unpleasant. Initial sweetness and light are evidenced because the child is expecting punishment. When this is

[9] Jewish Board of Guardians, Primary Behavior Disorder in Children . . . Two Case Studies.

not forthcoming and he does not yet know how to respond to the unaccustomed positive relationship, he must fall back on his usual provocative pattern of aggression.

In his next interview he was reserved, shy, and well-behaved; was very anxious to win at checkers, cheated less, but begged for a prize. He showed some feeling of guilt because of his demands. As the relationship deepened he insisted that the worker must read to him. (His mother always read to him before he went to sleep.) He began to be aggressively affectionate. As he continued to press for a prize, the worker suggested as a prize a story book, which he could share with her. (This was a constructive move, tending to divert an erotic aggressive interest in the worker into other shared channels.) He leaned against her as she read, was relaxed, friendly, and comfortable. His anxiety was relieved through this sublimation. After this there was a return of violent hostile aggression, with Nazis and Japs hiding in the worker's house, and in the play it was clear that he still wanted to separate mother and father. Great hostility was now expressed through play toward the father image. He no longer killed the worker, but overpowered and wounded her, making her repeatedly his prisoner (trying to possess her utterly). This he repeated over and over again with mounting excitement, then protested that he would not come next week; he did stay away. During his absence his mother reported that he went around with his fingers crossed that nothing might happen to him (use of magic).[10] He was also afraid to go to a barber shop and have his hair cut (castration fears). When he came back he insisted on wearing his overcoat all buttoned up, and he very coyly and shyly went through a play which ended in the worker's having to purchase two tickets for a raffle book. He was very seductive, the worker remaining friendly and matter of fact. He entered into constructive activities of building an airplane, for the first time, although protesting into the dictaphone that he only liked to play war. He seemed friendly and positive again, and was now able to bear some frustration in his play with the worker (he can sacrifice for love).

His violent acting out of aggressive wishes against the father, possession of the mother, fear, guilt, and invocation of magic to ward off retaliation are all characteristic patterns. The beginning (under treatment) of super-ego formation—sacrifice for love—can be seen.

[10] See p. 59.

An eleven-year-old boy, Alan, referred by the mother; was annoying, demanding, never satisfied with anything; a bright boy and a good student at school until recently, when he had been truanting. He was aggressive to his mother; hit and kicked her. He had always been a problem. Alan was an unwanted child, and pregnancy was accidental. His mother decided to make the best of it, but was ill a great deal. She would have preferred a daughter. Instruments were used at his birth, and he was given rather severe toilet training. He slept in the parental bedroom until he was five. During the first eight years of Alan's life, when he was an only child, his mother overprotected and overindulged him. She had many fears that injury might befall the boy. She never let him cross the street alone. She took him with her wherever she went. Alan had been very jealous and was repeatedly punished by his mother for his hostility to a younger child. A report from the previous summer, when Alan had been in camp in care of another agency, showed that he had been much teased by the boys because he was babyish; he fought a good deal, biting and scratching. He had a scarcely noticeable lisp, which he regarded as "an incurable ailment." He had occasional choking fits when he was upset. No medical basis was found for this.

The diagnosis was primary behavior disorder, oedipal type, but there were enough neurotic symptoms to suggest psychoneurosis with behavior disorder. Alan is bold, demanding, but also infantile and dependent; intensely jealous of the baby; resentful of his mother's interfering with any of his pleasures, especially since she used to indulge him greatly. Sibling rivalry is very intense for a boy so much older than his brother. The marital adjustment of the parents is very poor. The mother, whose history is omitted, is neurotic, and the father, for occupational reasons, absent much from the home. The mother, who had not wanted the child, compensates for her guilt by tying him to her.

Alan was a big, stockily built boy, very aggressive, bold, and demanding. When he first came into the office he was sarcastic; said he didn't like to come; that he didn't need to come; that he didn't have any problems, and whatever he had were his own business. The worker said lightly that would be swell if he really could keep everything as his own business, but that it seemed that when he hit his mother or brother he made it their business, too. He laughed. "OK, but what are the consequences?"

The worker asked if Alan would like to be helped against the consequences. He responded by talking about magic and radio, saying that his
mother felt that he really liked to fool people. He does like to fool people.
Worker agreed that it is a lot of fun. When the worker showed an interest
in his exploits, he promised to bring his magic set to show her.

Several elements here are characteristic of the primary behavior
disorder—a warm response is elicited when worker feeds his narcissism by taking an interest in his exploits. The worker's offer to help
him to avoid the *consequences* of his behavior pleases the boy. The
behavior problem child enjoys *provoking,* but fears the retaliation or
the consequences. He uses magic because he feels too weak to overpower the enemy single-handed.

The little child finds the outer world of reality very big and often
menacing. If parents have been kind and wise and have helped the
child to manage his aggressiveness and fears in relaxed and friendly
ways, the terrors without are not too overwhelming. Every child has
some episodes of primitive fears and dreams of devouring wolves,
giants, dragons, and other monsters. These myths and fairy tales of all
literatures which appear so bloodthirsty are in every child's unconscious. Because of the protecting parent, these do not bother him too
much or too long. As he progressively gets stronger and older and as
the parents continue to love and not unduly punish, he takes care of
these fantasies in play, in stories, and in other appropriate ways. But
it is also normal for the little child to find a magic talisman—a
favorite toy, a special blanket, or other comforter—that will protect
him from the dangers lurking without. Thus, he aids his weaknesses
by a device that will ward off or control the dangers and assure him
love and security. It is assumed that it is his own aggressive wishes
that are projected onto the big black dog or wolf or man who will
bite him or eat him up. Normally he resolves these dangers (parental
equivalents), as he passes through the oedipal phase, uneventfully
and with little discomfort. The primary behavior disorder, however,
who has experienced in reality harshness and deprivation, has less
bound his aggressive impulses, so, fearing retaliation, he resorts frequently to a magic device to help him or continues to use it in fantasy and at later ages than does the secure unfearful child. Many chil-

dren continue in fantasy the illusion of "superman," the more so if in fact they are defeated, weak, angry, and overwhelmed.

For behavior disorders, as for this boy, a magic device may be invested with intense feeling. He continues to use a magical method to control or to dominate the situation, since he cannot find a solution in the too-frustrating reality. Whether the magic is to bind his aggression toward his mother (he "always wants to hit her") or to possess her completely and make her love him, we cannot discuss here. In any event, it serves the purpose of increasing his sense of invulnerability, which makes the delinquent think he won't be caught—at any rate, not this time.

In the next interview he brought his magic set and showed his tricks to the worker. They got along well. He tried to teach the worker to fool people. The worker, unfortunately, had to break an appointment with him, and Alan immediately retaliated by staying away himself. When he was brought back by his parents he was very resistive. (His magic hadn't worked; the test had failed.) He stood rigidly, wouldn't sit down, said he had come only for one reason, wanted to get it over with and get away. Worker must stop writing him letters; he didn't want to come in any more. Why had he decided this? He isn't here to discuss it, but to tell the worker. He ran out of the office. The worker had disappointed him as his mother had—he wanted her, and she wasn't there.

Sent back again, he rushed into the room saying he would "fix" the worker. "I'll bring my gang to do it." He was prepared to rush out, but the worker suggested that if he wanted to "fix" him it was only fair to tell why. He said because the worker had told other children he was crazy. Why should worker think he was crazy? He was so angry that he couldn't talk about it. The worker continued to express a calm interest in him. "That's enough—you are bothering me again. You'd better watch out." The worker said she was concerned about him; that he seemed more unhappy than angry. "I want to help you"; but he was still mistrustful. He rushed out to "call his gang." The worker told him mildly that she hoped he would come back. He came back by himself, but was very disturbing, making silly noises. The worker was relaxed, accepting, friendly and interested in all his exploits with the gang, with magic, etc., of which he constantly boasted.

This "interest" is not a form of manners, but stems from the worker's understanding that the boy needs to be built up. He appears tough, but actually he is weak. His pattern is a thorough-going one and he hits out in every direction. He is destructive and noisy, like a four-year-old. He is fighting for his "rights." Because of extremely pathological home conditions and his beginning delinquency, it seemed best to continue the treatment of this boy in the school maintained by the agency.[11]

While a court commitment often has merit because of its authoritative finality in helping a child to settle down, the accompanying punitive elements would have no therapeutic value. It is unfortunate that the value of the restraining limiting environment, which is often necessary and actually helpful, is likely to be impaired by its associations with humiliation and punishment in many institutions.

He continued to be difficult at the institution; showed a tremendous amount of aggression toward other boys at his cottage; was lazy and uncooperative. His only interest was his magic. He and his mother fight about the magic—"and what battles!" The worker encouraged him to put on a magic show for the boys. He enjoyed doing this. He began to relate to the worker only on the basis of an audience for his magic, his boasting, asking her to do special favors.

The second worker, understanding his need for magical power, helps him by making use of his talent for showmanship to sublimate his interest in magic and avoid letting it become another battleground between him and his mother. He begins to reach out for relationship by talking of his troubles, his feeling that he is "crazy"—anyone who doesn't love one's mother must be crazy. This is probably a different feeling from that of "going crazy" in the obsessional.[12]

He felt that if he ran away from the institution, i.e., from the worker (who was acting as his super-ego), he would get into trouble. When he was at home on leave, he brought back pictures of himself (narcissistic satisfaction). The worker admired them, and he began to speak more freely. He admitted jealousy of his little brother, how he fought with his

[11] See pp. 161–162 on therapeutically conditioned environment.
[12] See p. 111.

mother, how he attempted to get back at her for lying to him. He continued to be very demanding; asked for sneakers, for leaves, and for
presents. He again went home with expectations and returned full of
disappointment, as his mother constantly thwarted him. . . . He ran
away. When he came back he discussed the home situation, accused his
mother of unfairness; maintained that he had gone home to get things
straightened out; tried to force worker into the role of arbitrator between him and his mother, was very angry at her refusal to "judge him."

He still demands for his battered, but narcissistic, ego that the
worker shall be the mirror of his accomplishments. This boy endlessly
recreates the needs of the young child for admiration and support for
his efforts to grow up. The worker, like the mother, is unfair. To
"judge him fairly" means to him that the worker must be wholly
on his side. He is disappointed also because the worker does not help
him against his bad impulses. Such a boy is afraid to love the worker
because one day she will fail him. He is not yet ready to please her,
yet he is even now uneasy. The crisis in the transference approaches
when he can no longer get pleasure by suiting himself.

He was able finally to bring out a feeling of resentment that the worker
had not reprimanded him for running away. He felt worker was insincere in saying she would like him no matter what he did. It might
work with some children; it wasn't going to work with him. She should
have disliked him and become angry. Asked what this reminded him
of, he said his mother would have reacted this way. He was surprised
at making this connection. In the next interview he said he was a pretty
rotten sort of person, and worker connects his suspiciousness and resentment of his mother with his feeling about the worker. He was able
to recognize for the first time that the worker's liking for him was based
on her understanding of his need for help. He asked the worker to go
with him to the dentist and to do other practical things for him instead
of merely demanding gifts and attention.

After this there is a marked change in the use of transference. Alan
begins to confess his sins, feeling a great deal of guilt. This is a step
ahead. Police officers often try to force a delinquent to an early "confession." This not only is unreliable but also does the child little good.
Therapeutic confession arises within the transference. He has stopped

accusing others. He admits his angry feelings about his younger brother; that he has always wanted to hurt him, and then his stealing. He has begun to assume blame. He can trust, and therefore he can confess. He gives himself to the worker in the full-blown "neurotic" transference. He is developing a new portion of super-ego, which grows in layers. There is a guilt tension now which he cannot bear. The confession is an outlet for this tension, which is more constructive than running away or fighting. He recognizes his dependence on someone else. This helps to socialize him. To have even one other person know and accept you for what you are builds a bridge into society. The child may give up infantile desires if someone loves him enough. Without guilt feeling or awareness of guilt, growth is impossible.

We see how a boy with behavior disorders is changing into a boy with neurotic formations. This is growth. The boy's capacity to form a relationship has expanded, but with his acceptance of another person's influence he must feel anxiety. He began with negative transference; now it is changing to positive. He is no longer able to make a decision without communicating with the worker as an external moral authority (parent). Later, if growth proceeds, he will internalize the moral authority, but for the behavior disorder the conscience is a tenuous affair and easily shaken. The relationship which started because of the boy's need to be cared for as if by a good and always giving mother is now both stronger and at the same time more ambivalent.[13]

A six-and-a-half-year-old boy was brought to the agency by his mother because he fights in school and at home, is stubborn, restless, jumpy, and hyperactive. He bites his nails and blinks his eyes. He calls his mother vile names, hopes she will drop dead, defies and dominates her. The other children won't play with him because of his wild behavior, threats, and destructiveness.

The child was interviewed by the psychiatrist, and the diagnosis was established as a primary behavior disorder, with conduct and habit disturbances and neurotic traits. The extreme reaction to the mother, with hostility, nervousness, physical and verbal attacks, indicates the oedipal

[13] For further discussion of treatment principles see pp. 148–153.

disturbance, i.e., the youngster was having a hard time relinquishing his mother as a possession.

The significant facts of his history, which account for the boy's difficulty, were that the first child, a boy, died during childbirth, as the physician decided to save the mother's life instead of his. The second child was a much wanted boy, especially as the mother grieved over the earlier loss, and Harold, the third, was not planned for, and the mother was much disappointed because he wasn't a girl. He was weaned abruptly at two and a half months, because of the mother's lack of milk, and kept on a bottle until he was five and a half years old, because he would not give it up. Toilet training from three months was severe, and he was whipped for soiling. From the time he was thirteen months old Harold was an active and aggressive infant. He had a tonsillectomy at three and a half, and was in the hospital; he had measles at six followed by ear abscesses and rheumatic fever, which cleared up without organic damage. Because of his hyperactivity and his mother's fear of his hurting himself, he has rarely been out of her sight, which meant thwarting and restraint.

In this picture of rejection, with severe early discipline and a neurotically fearful overprotection instead of sustaining affection, the mother's own history of a very traumatic childhood accounts for her anxiety, rigidity, and unconscious hostility. She is now defensive and self-righteous, her hostility veiled in self-sacrifice. The father is an easygoing, indulgent, rather uninterested person. The marriage is reasonably happy. The oldest boy is reasonably well adjusted. The problem is centered in Harold, who reacts to the rejection and frustration with extreme aggression and resents the controlling but unloving overprotection.

After an illness and convalescence, when the boy was worse than ever, the aggression markedly increased. He would show her, he said, that he was a really bad boy. He said obscene things to strangers, lit matches, ran around incessantly, wished both mother and father dead, was physically and verbally provocative. The boy's exaggerated behavior was largely reaction to his feeling that hospitalization was punishment and a further rejection.

Rejected children usually interpret any form of placement, including hospitalization, as punishment.

Omitting the treatment of the mother [14] and turning to the boy, we shall see in the play interviews a mixed-type behavior disorder.

The mother brought Harold promptly and regularly for treatments. He did not want to come. She persuaded him by bribing or fooling him— making him think that it was a club where he could play or that she would give him a treat afterwards.

The boy was a strained, thin, solemn-looking child, frequently showing apprehension and other defiances. He clung to his mother for fifteen or twenty minutes at the beginning of each interview, then relaxed a little and began to play quietly with the material, but the mother must also stay. She often commented sarcastically on his "good" behavior at the office and his unrest at home. He played with blocks or clay, paying no attention to his mother or the worker. After the first interview, he permitted the mother to sit in the adjoining room, making frequent trips to see if she was there. (Most children Harold's age will relinquish the parent much more quickly at the office.) He was constantly on his guard, showed no interest in the worker except when he was intrigued enough to be willing to write his name on the calendar for a subsequent appointment. His play always had the component of death or destructiveness of some sort. With frank resentment, he kicked the wall and started to throw things out of the window, which had to be stopped. He stopped his good behavior and reacted with violence, applying to the worker obscene adjectives.

This is a characteristic opening gambit for the behavior disorder— a period of unnatural goodness which is only disguised wariness, suspicion and fear, and exclusion of worker from his talk or play. In the quiet, accepting, and permissive relationship tension mounts, breaking out at last into overt aggressive acts and with violent reaction to the slightest limitation (or frustration). Such children have a low threshold of control for tension and must "act out." The worker "intrigues" him by playing into his narcissism.

The worker was quiet, firm, completely good-natured, tidied up the strewn toys without criticism and was rewarded in the fifth interview by one or two gestures of help and a smile, although he always left without saying good-bye. In the sixth interview he began to play with a gun, including the worker for the first time in his play by shooting her dead,

---

[14] See Chapter X. Parents are always involved in the treatment.

which gave him great pleasure. He said the office was a hospital. "No, it is not a hospital. Do you think I'm going to hurt you?" "Yes, it is." (Fear of hospitals because at three he had a tonsillectomy.) "It's not a hospital and I'm not going to hurt you." He replied by even more vigorous shooting at the worker. He said to his mother, "I hate you; shut up." He tried to hit the worker. He was gently restrained. "You are good and mad at me, Harold, I guess." He wasn't allowed to throw clay at worker. He then violently made a phallic symbol out of clay, which he insists is the worker's. Worker, who was a woman, commented in a matter-of-fact way on the difference between boys and girls, and his interest in this explanation was marked. He became more agreeable. They played school at his request. He introduced himself as if he were a new pupil, but he was the teacher, and everything the worker did must be wrong and punished and marked zero. In successive interviews the worker was permitted to rise from zeros to occasional B's. He responded affirmatively to worker's good-bye.

A positive relationship is now growing, but only, as we see, after a half dozen interviews in which the worker is permissive and attentive to all his interests and legitimate wishes.

In the next interviews he made a picture for the worker, built blocks more constructively, and admitted that he was made to come by his mother because he was "bad." The worker accredited and praised whatever he did constructively, and any little bit of verbal admission was carried forward with him. He vacillated: "I'm not coming at all—maybe I'll come in two weeks." (From pure resistance to ambivalence.) He was assured that the worker wanted him to come and expected him—could help him overcome his "badness." All children are bad sometimes. They aren't bad all the time or bad all the way through. He did not believe this.

With each interview he displays more overt aggression. No restrictions except a time limit or restraint from physical attack are put on him.

When he splashed water or paint on the worker she commented mildly that she knew he wanted to hurt her, but he must not do so. He turned to verbal aggression. He used vile language. He was frightened; he expressed fear of retaliation for what he had done to worker in a fantasy—saying that he had been bitten by rats. He had to reassure himself by

taking worker down into the cellar, clinging to her hand. Worker participated and reassured him that she was not angry with him, using his
language of the rat story fantasy. He was relieved, but insisted that he
would never come again. He alternated between play with modeling and
drawing pictures full of sexual symbolism and his own frank sex comments. Occasionally he carried on mild episodes of school play with the
worker. They chewed gum amicably together for awhile. Then, angrily,
"You are so bad." "Why am I, Harold?" "You made your mother sick;
you made her die; you killed her; you shot her." This is the first time
worker was definitely associated with the mother figure. The bad one
ought now to be put to bed in play. He wished to lie down with her, but
became anxious. He wished to telephone his real mother, telling her that
he had been playing very quietly and had drawn her some nice pictures.

He was afraid to leave after this episode, the erotic aggression
and the fear of retaliation (castration) all having been brought to
the surface. Because the worker does not condemn the sexually aggressive wishes, he becomes anxious. He tells himself on the telephone
that he should be a good boy for mother. When he says or does "bad"
sex things, he is beginning to feel that they are bad. In the early super-
ego strivings he projects, saying that the worker is bad.

The worker recognized that he feared that his mother (or the worker)
would be angry and reassured him that the worker is not angry with him.
In later school play he permitted the worker to be right occasionally and
gave her some commendation. Whenever he threatened to leave and not
come back, worker was matter of fact and friendly about saving the time
for him. She wisely never tried to placate. He smoked a cigarette—"I'll
puff it and puff it until my mother suffers." He is surprised that worker
doesn't interfere. He comes close to the worker and leans against her,
and his sex talk at intervals is of the gutter variety. He had a little song
which he often sang: "I am a child who loves no one." Whenever he
showed any positive feeling for the worker, he always followed it by an
outburst of hostility. After a repetition in play of putting worker to bed
because she is bad, he tried to lift her dress. "Is this something he wanted
to know about?" (worker's body) "No, I want you to die. I want to see
you lying down and sleeping. I want the pole to fall on your head and kill
you." "You feel there is something bad and wrong with what you want
to do, Harold?" For answer he made angry sexual comments of an ag-

gressive kind. The worker here got him to paint and model boys' and girls' bodies, and they discussed sex differences in his models. The worker answered questions. He was absorbed, relaxed, and attentive.

This is a good example of sublimation of the direct erotic aggression into an intellectual dramatization and discussion of his problem, the worker handling only the obvious foreground material—not relating what is going on to the deeper mother conflict. She permits him to have sex curiosity and to satisfy it in safe ways. She does not frustrate. By modeling and discussion the tension is drained off and sublimated. At his age crude and direct expressions of sex interest are not unusual. The conflict between the instinctual drives and the restraining environment is now fully out in the open. When he is in the first phase of aggression he fears to put the hostility where it belongs—mother-worker; now he can attack but he believes the worker must hurt him in retaliation. The overtness of the erotic (oedipal) aggression is a desperate denial of his submission to the mother's castration. The child wants to possess, but feels in danger. After this the aggressive behavior lessens and he is more childish— demands more love and attention.

He used pet names; he called for help in play situations. He repeated "Hurray, I'm saved." He called her "Mom." Sometimes he played with brown paint, smeared it over everything, was soon anxious—was reassured that it was all right, enjoyed himself thoroughly (this is, of course, referable to the severe toilet training mentioned in his history). He washed himself and made everything tidy again, and eventually seemed much relieved that he was allowed to do this. "Now I have a new pair of hands," he said at length. Was very pleased with himself. (Direct gratification was permitted with subsequent washing away of guilt.) Phases ensued in which he attacked the worker, alternating with infantile demands. He took the worker's things out of her desk. "Why do you want so many things?" Fiercely, "Because I want you." He was afraid after this admission. Although often destructive he began to ask for things instead of grabbing. He was occasionally affectionate. He wondered if worker was married. His mother must have been married twice to have two sons, he said. He asks where babies come from. They talked quietly and seriously about it. He moved from anxiety about sex differences to anxieties about birth (see earlier history). He became jealous of another little boy client. When he was less outwardly aggressive he began to develop tic-like movements of the head, which the psychiatrist thought was not serious.

These may have been, in part, a substitution for his hyperactivity. Perhaps, too, the acting out and fantasies had been inhibited too often because of the limitation against personal attack.[15] Waves of acting out and inhibition may be expected when the danger gets too great. The violence of this little boy's behavior makes it difficult to be as permissive as might be theoretically desirable. Also, if too extreme violence is permitted the anxiety may prove overwhelming. Phases of doubt and ambivalence would ensue.

In his play there was still much aggression, but his bombs and darts did not always kill. Sometimes his victim was saved. He made storms—"God makes storms and punishes bad people with them." They discussed his fear of storms and of death. He teased: "What if I don't come back?" "I'll miss you." He flirts: "So you'll only have to miss me for a week. My mother says I come here because I am bad." "Yes, I'm helping you with that. Do you think I mind your being bad?" "No, I know you like me." Once when he soiled the worker's new dress with paint she became genuinely annoyed (he was certainly a handful for any worker) and he was extremely frightened. They worked his frightened reactions through in the next interview by recognizing the fears which underlay the aggressive behavior. He dictated spelling words in his play—"man," "father," "little baby," "hits," "wants," "yes," "no," "strict," "not," showing his area of conflict again. He rarely brought his father into his discussion or play, but after his spelling play he wrote him a loving letter. He began to play out some fantasies of childbirth with his dolls.

During this period there was marked improvement in his behavior at home and at school, but just at this point he, unfortunately, developed rheumatic fever followed by regression, since he had been sent away from home and indulged as a patient.

He came to see the worker. "I've had a birthday, but I got badder," he announced. He didn't know in what way he was bad—he had forgotten everything. (Of course he remembered very well—the hospital experi-

---

[15] Frank interpretation in this case might have been wiser.

ence and his mother's sending him away, as well as the nature of the treatment.) "If I remembered, I wouldn't tell you anyway." "I can help you better if you tell me." He started with mild aggression, but gave the worker good marks and ended sweetly enough. Worker gets him to express some of his fears about the hospital.

It was unfortunate that when he was just beginning to play out some of his fantasies about childbirth the hospital intervened as a terrifying reality. He denied most of it, especially that he feared being sent away. Rejected children, especially, may deny what they most fear.

He had a tooth extracted and again regressed, smearing with the finger paints and acting like a baby. (Any traumatic incident is apt to be reflected in regression.) This didn't last long. Affectionate relationship began again and gentle school play. In school he was fortunate in having an understanding teacher who didn't think he was especially bad. The worker encouraged the teacher to a neutral but warm handling of the boy, without overindulgence or much discipline. He discussed his teacher. He liked her, and he believed she liked him. He was good and bad, he guessed. This was the first time he had seen anything good in himself. Sex aggression was now wholly verbal, slangy, less intense. He felt able to like worker without being afraid of being hurt. He was able, however, to express quite directly, or in transparent play, the ideas about sex which bothered him: fears about the loss of his penis. The worker helped him by making specific his fears of retaliation, being hurt, and loss of the penis.

He can now like the worker without fear of punishment. Earlier, if he liked the worker, because of his distorted perceptions, he thought it would mean injury to himself. As in many other instances, it may be necessary for a worker to use simple educational techniques, as here, by explaining that the boy will not lose his penis because of his "bad" thoughts, nor even because of his behavior. The severity or violence of the boy's behavior is not an indication of poor prognosis. The fact that he is able to act out and express so much erotic and hostile aggression in play and in words is essential to his progress. Gradually he is being helped to internalize his aggression so that he can achieve normal object relationships.

Recapitulation

The dominant characteristics of the primary behavior disorder are extreme aggressiveness, a deficient super-ego, or little feeling of guilt, and a high degree of self-love, or narcissism. The behavior disorder child elaborates his aggression into a character defect as the psychoneurotic elaborates his anxiety.[16] He may elaborate all the aggression outwardly into dissocial behavior, or part of it, internalized, may appear as a neurotic trait. The aggression may be hostile, nonerotic (preoedipal), or erotic (oedipal), or it may show both phases. It may be active, as in temper tantrums, rebellion, fighting, or running away, or passive, as in stubbornness, obstinacy, disobedience, unwillingness to change unapproved habits. Outwardly these children are supposed by their parents, school teachers, and neighbors to be antisocial; actually, they feel put upon and mistreated. In their opinion they are more sinned against than sinning. Having had few or no rewarding relationships at home, they expect none elsewhere. Having had no strong or loving adult with whom to identify as little children, they do not identify with a stranger. Disillusioned from the start, they carry a chip on the shoulder, expecting the world to knock it off, thus giving them leave to fight back. Because they are weak, they boast and use "magical" means to overpower the enemy. They do not know that they provoke. To them their aggression is always a retaliation— "retaliation" in advance. They are demanding, not giving. They must possess all and return nothing. They have had no reason to believe that people will love them if they are good—still less if they are bad. They are constantly prepared to defend themselves. They cannot sacrifice their will or their aggression for love, because they have had no experience which makes this worth while. "My parents never did anything for me, so I must look after number one," they say. They are wary of all relationships, because their own relationships have failed them. They have learned to be hurt and to hurt—to make other people suffer. In the oedipal situation, although the neurotic composition shows much variation, they are often more angry than jealous, because they have possessed so little. The amount of guilt and need for

[16] See Chapter IV.

punishment for bad behavior also varies. Initially, in the primary behavior disorder, the child has little tolerance for "therapy," wanting real gratifications in the life experience. The oedipal types may come into relationship more easily than the preoedipal types.

For any primary behavior disorder, treatment is likely to be protracted because of the deep level of fixation and because the growth of the super-ego is bound to be slow, with much vacillation and regression. One cannot say to these children, "Now let me see you be good for a change." They have to change to be good. It is quite striking that the "worst" behaved and most violent children, if not psychotic or psychopathic, improve, if treatable at all, both absolutely and relatively, as much as the milder types. Psychopathic personalities and those with full-blown neurotic characters do not respond well either to direct psychotherapy or to conditioned environment, but often younger delinquents with very disturbed behavior are responsive to an atmosphere of acceptance without punishment for nonconformity. In other words, the form which the behavior takes seems less important in prognosis than are the dynamics of the diagnosis, coupled with evaluation of potential strengths in the ego—the existence of previous love relations, intelligence, talents, and so forth, coupled with favorable environmental opportunities. The dissocial character development does not preclude the possibility of neurotic traits or of neurosis itself. If the worker is patient and sincere, the aggressive personality may come to identify, begin to discriminate, and thus be freer from impulsive action.

Chapter IV

THE ANXIOUS CHILD

WE HAVE seen that traditionally the children brought to the attention of court or protective agency and in large numbers to any child guidance clinic, are the extremely aggressive children who act out their impulses—the "primary behavior disorders." Such children, in overt conflict with the home or the school environment are readily identified, and since the aggression makes others uncomfortable they are likely to be referred for placement, discipline, or treatment. Whereas the primary behavior disorder is a direct reactive disturbance to environment, the psychoneurotic child is no longer purely reactive, but already has, to some extent, an intrapsychic conflict of greater or less intensity, depth, and complexity. Anxiety comes with this repression of the impulses leading to symptom formation.

It is this concept of internalized conflict which has revolutionized the approach in social casework, as it has that of classical psychiatry. As long as social workers thought they were dealing with children frankly in conflict with their environment and as long as personality could be regarded as independent of the environment, so long could each case be artificially bisected, using one approach for the "person," and another for the "environment." If the environment was unfavorable, then the solution might be to remove the child to a more favorable situation. But if the conflict lies within the child's personality, then the approach can no longer be dualistic, and purely environmental shifts are of little avail. The child placing field for a long time continued to move children from one foster home to another, with ensuing failure after failure, not realizing that the child who had internalized his parental conflict must react to the new environment as to the old and that treatment, therefore, should be addressed to these inner conflicts. Aggression is not always discharged outwardly, but may be turned inwards against the life energies themselves. True, the anxious child may be aggressive and destructive—the expressed behavior being an overcompensation for feelings of weakness, of inferiority, of being overwhelmed. The outward behavior may appear like that of the behavior disorder, but the composition and quality of the behavior is different, because genetically the onset was different. The anxious child has a higher, more discriminating level of organization, and he functions in a more complicated way. This does not mean necessarily that he is harder to treat, but it does mean that anxiety must be understood in considering his total adaptation. The degree to which neurotic symptoms impair functioning differs greatly.

The anxious child who obtains gratification by being sick or can replace his neurotic suffering by an organic disability is likely to be taken to a medical institution. The children, however, to be found in the social agency case load are likely to show a mixture of conduct disorders, bodily symptoms such as dizziness, vomiting, or stuttering, residual habit disorders, and many fears. Just as a behavior problem, breaking out at eight or nine, is almost always preceded by a history of early conduct and even earlier habit disorders, and possibly neurotic traits, so the psychoneurosis may show behavior deviations as part of the "symptom" picture. Unless withdrawal, shyness, or anxiety states are unusually severe, parents are likely to refer those neurotic children who have some disturbances in conduct uppermost. They do not know that the child suffers, but he is causing them inconvenience.

As usual, then, as far as the child guidance agency is concerned conduct deviations are the aspects which are visible, like the tip of an iceberg, but it is the submerged part that makes for shipwreck. It is the diagnostic rule, however, that whenever there is a history of fears or current expressions of anxiety, psychoneurosis should be suspected. At any given stage of development the child may show some aspects of the behavior disorder and again some of neurosis, or a shifting pattern may be observed even in one interview. Treatment must be sensitively attuned to what is actually dominant at the moment. In an adult or an older child the picture is almost always mixed, and problems arising from the deeper and older layers of the personality structure must be apperceived. As Anna Freud puts it:

It never happens that the libido expresses itself wholly in manifestations of the latest phase of development; some part of it invariably remains attached to earlier modes of expression. To ensure normality it is sufficient if the major proportion of the libido reaches the organization appropriate to the needs of the child. . . . It is essential for the development of a rich and vivid personality that this part of character formation (the establishment of a definite proportion between id strength and ego strength) should not be terminated too early.[1]

The opportunity for the therapist comes precisely because he can, in favorable cases, help to reduce the crippling guilt and through ego building—gains in achievement—to alter the balance between ego and impulses and in this way help the child, as the parent has not done, to manage these impulses more rationally and successfully.

The Clinical Picture

The child with neurotic conflict is the child whose life energies are blocked and distorted because they are partially fixated in infantile wishes and impulses which the child's ego rejects. In the struggle between the urges and the frustrating reality the "bad" desires have been "turned backwards," rather than successfully repressed. If the unresolved conflicts persist and the tension mounts, one may see either a situational kind of anxiety, that is, the child is anxious under particular circumstances ("anxiety state"), or the child is anxious under most circumstances. Anxiety and inhibition are sometimes diffuse, sometimes bound up in symptoms. Whenever there are physical symptoms, they are regarded as anxiety equivalents, and it must be determined whether these are part of a disease process, or psychosomatic, or psychogenic. In regression the ego refuses to acknowledge that the dangerous desires belong to him at all. The child becomes the helpless, innocent baby. This picture of temporary regression after illness or shock or other disturbance, or the birth of

[1] See Anna Freud, "Indications for Child Analysis," in *The Psychoanalytic Study of the Child*, pp. 137 and 142.

a younger sibling, is familiar. The neurotic child may either be overtly anxious or have deeply disguised anxiety, but in the latter event evidence of fears (under close observation) will always be found. Sometimes symptoms are also present or in formation, as well as timidity, withdrawal, and poor capacity for relationships. The child is actively distressed and usually appears to be distressed. Most children suffer at one time or another from certain fears—of being hurt, of animals, of the dark, of withdrawal of love when they are naughty, but these fears are neither persistent nor disabling. These occasional fears are as normal as is a reasonable degree of naughtiness in the growing child. In fact, it is assumed that the birth experience itself [2] starts most infants off with the sensation of being hurt and, perhaps, frightened, which may make for chronic tensions, especially when labor and birth are difficult. Whether constitutional factors or traumatic birth experiences or both predispose some children to greater anxiety than others is not known. But certainly not all children outgrow childish fears as parents like to think they will, and some children seem to suffer excessively from anxiety tendencies.

If the parental environment has been too strict or threatening or inconsistent toward the child, if the child has had frightening physical or social experiences, or if he has been drawn into and made a party to the parents' own neuroses, he does not have enough help from the parent in gradually mastering his primitive impulses. Love and hate struggle within him. Menaced by his own desires and mixed feelings of resentment, he tries to bind these impulses by repression and other defenses—but always with rising tension or anxiety, for fear the bonds will break. It is a mistake to imagine that such anxiety is unconscious; the child is aware of his fears. The part that is unconscious is the repressed conflict (and hostility) which may express itself through worry, bodily symptoms, or in some other way. The anxious child accepts discipline and fears to offend, although he may behave very badly. We should not, however, assume that the submissive, compliant child is always neurotic (anxious). This may be merely the way his character has developed. The psychoneurotic is

---

[2] See Greenacre, "The Biological Economy of Birth," in *The Psychoanalytic Study of the Child*, p. 31.

all his life a struggler. He strives to please, to get more of that dearly prized commodity affection or "acceptance" about which he always feels uncertain. He fears failure; he fears that he will be laughed at, or scorned, or teased. He is a perfectionist, but in reality he has often been put at tasks beyond his capacity or suffered from overexacting demands. His whole being is filled with guilt feelings and self-criticism, leading to withdrawal, undoing, and self-punishment. Excessive fantasy easily substitutes for the painful reality. The child may outwardly become "painfully good"—the popular phrase being very descriptive.

To compare characteristic patterns: [3] the child who has the primary behavior disorder fears attack from without; the anxious psychoneurotic child feels that his danger comes from within, that is, from his own primitive desires. The former has a deficient super-ego; the latter, a too severe super-ego. The former will say to the worker, "You are bad," or possibly, "My mother is bad," or possibly, "My mother says I am bad (but I don't believe it)." The anxious child is sure that *he* himself is bad. The anxious child suffers unless or until he has set up adequate defenses against his wayward impulses; the child who has the behavior disorder gives rein to his wayward impulses. The child who acts out has experienced so little love, that he has never learned that it is worth while to sacrifice for it. The anxious child has always experienced some love, but never enough and never good enough, not consistent, but rigid, or dutiful, or intermittent. He has learned to value it too much and to pay too high a price for it. It seems to him that he has only been loved when he was good and lived up to exacting parental expectations. He has never had the healing and nurturing assurance that he is loved in good weather and foul, that he is loved even when he is bad, that he is loved with all his badness and his goodness. Thus, he cannot accept the "badness" in himself. He fears and represses it. He protects himself against the lurking "badness" with the aid of various defenses [4]—denial, a common defense for a little child ("It isn't there," "I didn't do it"), reaction formation, as in being excessively good or kind instead of cruel and

[3] For treatment considerations see pp. 148–153.
[4] See Anna Freud in *The Ego and the Mechanisms of Defense.*

mean, isolation, and so forth. But if the defenses do not succeed in holding back or damming up or diverting the wishes, the anxiety breaks through or the neurotic symptom permits the gratification of the wish in disguised form.

The behavior problem, classically, is more deprived than is the neurotic child. Wary of love, because he has had so little of it, he fears relationship with anyone because it limits his aggressiveness. Commonly his defenses are guile, suspicion, keeping out of reach, hitting out first, deceptive conformity, projection and identification with the aggressor. The characteristic play of the primary behavior disorder is in the form of an actively expressed aggression, such as shooting and competitive, dispersed, and relatively impersonal games. When such a child does include the worker in his game, usually as victim or in a subordinate role, it is the beginning of positive feelings. The play of the neurotic child is more patterned and more personal, almost always with relation to persons in the family and soon including the worker.

The behavior problem boasts, "I don't care if my mother does not love me," and whistles to keep his courage up; in his heart he knows she doesn't. The psychoneurotic says, "I know my mother loves me, at least, I am sure she does, at least I *hope* so" (showing his ambivalence and uncertainty). Subjected to shock, separation, painful operation, or illness, the behavior problem resents separation as a personal threat or insult. The anxious child fears loss of the always precarious love. The behavior problem says "no" to other people; the anxious child is forever saying "no" or "don't" to himself. Out of the conflict between his desires and the prohibiting realities he has achieved a very strict internal censorship. When others hurt him, he doesn't allow himself to hurt them directly. If he must hurt them, he does so in devious and usually unconscious ways. For the most part he arranges matters so that he himself shall be hurt.

While the neurotic child has a stronger grip on reality, a more highly organized ego in the sense of values, than has the primary behavior disorder and is therefore able to make better social adaptations, he does frequently show severe distortions and disturbances.

While his need to be closely attached to his family, particularly to his mother, is very great, and his partial gratifications have given him more capacity to relate himself to people than has the child with a primary behavior disorder, he does have some trouble with his relationships. The child who has a behavior disorder has poor and limited capacity to relate; the psychoneurotic, who potentially has full capacity to relate, is inhibited by anxiety; the normal child has full capacity to relate, but without anxiety. In the psychoneurotic the dependency needs are urgent and the mixed feelings of love and hate are strong. In the psychoneurotic one must expect readiness to form a positive (later ambivalent) transference, even though it is a very passive, dependent sort. Because he suffers he is already receptive to the therapist who wishes to help him. The psychoneurotic not only is liable to fears of all kinds, including nightmares and night terrors, but may show food fads, sleep-walking and diffused body aches, pains and complaints. He is always a sensitive child, with marked feelings of inadequacy.

The child who is charming, seductive, insincere, provocative, ingratiating, overconfident, boastful, and aggressive in various ways suggests that the worker consider the possibility of behavior disorder; the child who is overconcerned, negative about himself and his achievements, timid, shy, having a worried expression, preoccupied with stories or games of violence suggests psychoneurosis. The child who likes to figure things out, with disguised curiosity, without spontaneity, perfectionist in his play, critical, indecisive, persistent, suggests the obsessional, or compulsive neurotic, and so forth.[5] The anxious child feels weak, but whereas the behavior disorder in his feeling of weakness attacks, partly because of his established habit of retaliation and partly because of his feeling of magical invulnerability, the anxious childs needs to be hurt and feels extremely vulnerable. The delinquent feels that punishment is *retaliation*—and considers it unfair or unjust; the neurotic regards his as *retribution*, that is, as just punishment for his sins, and he derives some satisfaction from his suffering.

[5] See p. 111.

Illustrations of Anxious Children

A case which shows a mixture of neurotic fears and disturbed behavior will be shown first.

This was an eight-and-a-half-year-old boy, referred by the principal of the school because he was stubborn, willful, and did poor school work. He resorted to temper tantrums and other infantile behavior—sometimes wanting to be dressed and fed. He cried easily, was disobedient and abusive, hit the mother and used sex words to her. He had many fears—of darkness, of flies in the house; he feared that other children would come to kill him and hid behind the piano. He feared sounds, such as that of a window being opened, when there might be a man with a finger pointed at him. He was afraid to sleep by himself because of fantasies, which took the form of horses, of men losing hair and limbs, all floating towards him. They terrified him because they seemed to come in response to his wish. He vomited when he was excited, and had food fads. He was hyperactive, unable to concentrate, hostile to everyone, and considered himself bad and nervous. He had difficulty in getting along with other children. There was also a minor speech defect.

Jerry was born a year after his mother had had an abortion, and ten years later than an older brother. He was not wanted, the mother felt too old to have another baby and wanted to spend what money they had to further the education of the two older brothers. The parents would have preferred a girl. Pregnancy and delivery were normal. Jerry was breast fed for three months, but with supplementary feedings and many changes. Toilet training was begun at six months and completed at a little over a year; the mother was not lenient about this.

When Jerry entered school, at four years of age, he kicked and screamed, and also developed choreic movements (which were possibly masturbatory equivalents). He attended school only one month. He was reentered at five and a half years of age, and has had difficulties since that time. The disobedience, temper tantrums, and abuse of the mother occurred after his mother left him for the shop. His difficulties with other children began at this time. After his return from camp last summer, Jerry developed many of his fears, which have been steadily getting worse.

He told his mother that there was no use in his trying to be good, as she only loved her "soldier son." He has shown a certain amount of sex behavior towards the little girls in school.

The feeding difficulties began when Jerry was about two weeks old, and until last summer the mother found it necessary to prepare two meals, one for him to vomit and one for him to eat. At the time of referral this occurred only when he was excited, but there was much difficulty about food, particularly when he was with the mother. He had had an unusual amount of dental treatment, due to a fractured jawbone. Choreic symptoms appeared after a tonsillectomy, at four. A subsequent neurological examination showed no evidence of organic disease of the nervous system or chorea.

During the first three years of his life, the mother kept Jerry exclusively with her, caring for him "like an angel," changing his clothing many times. She felt that she had always kept him away from other children. Then, when he was three, she left him in the care of an older girl so that she could help her husband in their butcher shop, "to be away from Jerry." She had continued to work since that time, and for three summers had sent him to camp, although he fought against it. Her attitude varied from extreme overprotection to neglect.[6] At times she felt that the boy was nervous and she shouldn't scold or hit him; then she felt he was bad and she should send him to a boarding school. Having the other two children, she was able to leave one in the care of the other. Then she had to hire someone to care for Jerry if she wanted to go out in the evening. She was ambitious and felt that she had been cheated by her father, who believed in education for boys, but not for girls.

Until he was five, Jerry slept in the parents' bedroom. Since then he had been sleeping in the same room with an older brother. However, he slept with the mother and father whenever the older brother was home on furlough.

The parents were never harmonious. The mother, neurotically tied to her own mother, felt that her husband gave her no companionship or help with the children. She was anxious and aggressive in turn. The father worked long hours as a butcher, and his relations to the children were often irritable and disciplinary. The oldest boy was the favorite, the second boy showed marked disturbance of personality, with speech defects and shut-in behavior. Both brothers wanted Jerry placed, for the "peace of the family." They had never accepted him.

[6] Compare the picture of this mother in the discussion of stuttering, p. 104.

Jerry played with a group of boys about six and seven years of age. He called them his slaves and ordered them about. He had many fears—that they might rebel against his domination or grow older and not want to be "suckers," and then he would "lose his power." According to the principal and his teacher, Jerry was constantly fighting for attention in school. He threw articles on top of the closet, and when sent to the office as a disciplinary measure, he sat with his finger in his mouth. He reacted well to praise. If anyone got ahead of him, he gave up entirely. He sat in the classroom with his fists doubled up tight. He never entered into any kind of contest. Jerry ridiculed both his principal and his teacher, but did not disobey them.

Jerry was a thin, timid-appearing boy of normal intelligence, with heavy dental braces and one ear out of shape because of his constant pulling at it when an infant. Although at first afraid to leave his mother, he made an immediate transference to the worker and started to talk about his fears, his badness, and his feelings of inferiority concerning his appearance. He started "outlaw" games, with marked aggression towards powerful men, but desisted quickly, as this play aroused too much feeling of guilt and anxiety, and he turned to less threatening games, in which he lost very cheerfully.

The diagnosis indicated a beginning psychoneurosis, anxiety type, with behavior disorders. Although there were conduct and habit disorders the anxiety symptoms predominated and therefore the main classification would be given first. The therapeutic aim would be to prevent Jerry from developing further in his neurotic pattern, to strengthen his ego so that he could cope with his anxieties in more constructive ways. He should be helped to express his "badness" and his fears and to discuss them in such a way as to reduce his feeling of guilt. Quick transference is to be expected.

Nat, a ten-year-old boy, was referred because of immaturity, irresponsibility, school retardation, periodic enuresis, dislike of physical activity, dawdling, day-dreaming, not mixing well with other children, and compulsive behavior expressed in repetitive drawing. He had nightmares and exhibited fearfulness about locks on doors, sudden noises, etc.

The early developmental history, except for strict toilet training, did not appear significant. From three and a half, when the father deserted the mother (he subsequently divorced her), he exhibited excessive and often peculiar interests, consecutively, in flowers, music, fire hydrants, collecting band-aids, and ads. He needed to do things over and over again. Following separation from his father, he threw rocks or snow into baby carriages. He would not let people he had previously liked come near him. He developed asthma and enuresis. The boy had had a reading difficulty ever since he was able to read, which the mother attributed to a muscular eye defect, operated on when the child was seven. He was unable to progress beyond the early academic level and had developed no work habits. His I.Q. was 130.

Before the parents separated the child had a good relationship with both his father and his mother. Father's attitude towards the child was affectionate, gentle, warm, but irresponsible. The mother had had a deprived childhood, having lived with various relatives and having had no home of her own. She was now an intense, intellectual, driving, anxious, and unhappy person, aware of her own tension. Nat was very much afraid she would remarry and forbade her to do so. The mother described Nathaniel as being physically dependent on her and taking up all her time. She bathed him, took him to school, and helped him dress if he dawdled. She was all-absorbed in the boy, overindulgent and overprotective, and felt very much disappointed that although he was a remarkable child, he did not measure up to normal children.

Nat was attractive, but in speech and behavior appeared younger than his age. He was intelligent, sensitive, and artistic, having both musical and drawing ability. While he had related warmly to the worker, expressing his enjoyment of coming to see her, wanting her to visit him in his home, saying that he liked to talk to her, he also expressed a basic hostility against all women because of their depriving ways. Nat got excited easily. During these periods of excitement, which did not last long, he frequently touched his genitals. Nat was very insistent; he wanted to draw on the worker's arm, paste drawing on the walls, etc. He consistently found it difficult to leave at the close of the interview.

The clinging, dependent, ambivalent way in which the neurotic child relates himself may be clearly seen. In this case the psychoneurosis with compulsive features was not thought to be sufficiently advanced to contra-indicate casework therapy. His talents would be an asset in sublimation of the primitive impulses, and social therapy in ego building and self-direction, to supply masculine leadership, could be instituted to supplement the insight therapy.

Innumerable cases could be described to illustrate how the removal of a key figure from the family, as below, especially one of the parents, may precipitate or intensify an anxiety state. How long or to what extent the behavior remains reactive, how soon it is internalized, and how completely it is structuralized as an intrapsychic conflict must be diagnostically determined.

Tommy, eleven and a half, was referred because of difficulties in school, feeding problems, and many fears. He was restless, disobedient, had temper outbursts, ordered his mother about, and liked to play with fire. He lied, telling stories glorifying the father as a general or a doctor, and about the mother, saying that she had married a rich man. There was nail-biting and some history of stealing. He had many fears—of the dark, of being alone, and that his mother might get killed, so he would not let her go anywhere without him. He had difficulty in falling asleep, unless the mother also went to bed. He frequently had bad dreams, nightmares, headaches, and stomach-aches, and he vomited frequently. On the subway he was uncomfortable, fearing that the automatic closing doors might separate him from his mother. He was afraid someone would come out of the bedroom closet and hurt him. He was worried about nose-bleeds and possible illnesses. He felt that people on the subway were staring at him and sat in a certain place to avoid this. He showed much guilt about his behavior and his use of sex words. He had fears about his masculinity; that his voice was like a girl's; that the food he ate just remained in his stomach.

Tommy, an only child, was born a year after his mother's marriage. Pregnancy and birth were normal. After his birth, his mother became sick, nervous, and tired. Weaning was difficult, the child cried a good deal and did not want to eat. At this time Mrs. B. had left her husband, taking Tommy with her. When Mrs. B. returned to her husband, they moved into their own apartment. The home was again broken up for a few weeks when Tommy was fourteen months old; at that time the mother was operated on, and the boy was cared for by the maternal grandmother. The parents were also separated. Feeding difficulties continued until he was five years old. Since then he had loved to eat, and the problem had been to provide sufficient food (as a displaced demand for affection). He had whooping cough at twenty months, scarlet fever at three years, chicken pox at four years, measles and mumps at five. He had a tonsillectomy at two years, nine months, was very unhappy and cried a great deal afterwards.

The conduct disorders and fears began when he was five years old. Before the divorce of his parents there were frequent arguments between them. The father had many love affairs. Since the divorce the mother had been working out of the home at comptometry. Until he was seven and a half Tommy slept in his mother's room whenever the father was away from home. Since the father had left home permanently Tommy had continued to sleep in his mother's room.

Tommy could not sustain interest in his school work and showed marked variability in grades. He used bad language, bothered other children, and was not friendly. Tommy felt that his difficulty in school was due to his not liking to be ordered around. He would have preferred to be a business man telling others what to do (compensating for his feelings of inadequacy).

Tests indicated a minimal I.Q. of 114. Goodenough drawing test showed superior ability. Rorschach findings gave evidence of marked emotional and sexual disturbance. Medical examination showed him to be thirty-eight pounds overweight, with chronic sinusitis.

This is a neurotic child with some phobic avoidance of danger by either physical or mental activities, who is already using compulsive devices to neutralize or bind the fears. Psychosomatic processes apparently are starting.

This is a clear picture of anxiety engendered by partially repressed, hostile wishes against the father, which seem to the child to have caused the father's leaving. Loss, in itself, would not create a neurosis in an otherwise normal child; early traumata were involved.

The mother was an anxious person, who vomited frequently, complained of headaches, constipation, and hemorrhoids, and had bad dreams. There was a close relationship between her and Tommy. He called her "my little Pussy" and made love declarations. The mother seemed to permit Tommy's advances, and then when he seemed beyond her control started to beat and scratch him. She felt that Tommy could not change, because he had his father's character, and that she could control him only by saying he was killing her. She obviously enjoyed her seduction and his response.[7]

[7] Obviously in cases in which children are being given unwise direct gratification the outlook for therapy is dubious unless the parent is accessible to treatment; see Chapter X.

In a group of cases one cannot, of course, say that disturbances during pregnancy, or a series of illnesses, or a frightening operation, or
rigidly imposed standards, or even the loss of one or another loved
parent, or any other single factor predisposes the child to anxiety.
Study of these and similar cases, however, underlines *the constant
element* of some withdrawal of love or threat of such loss or inconsistency of discipline, often combined with immoderate or seductive
affection. The fact that the figures which menace are those closest
to the child and that he has usually little experience or achievement
to balance and sustain him augments his sense of helplessness. In these
circumstances, traumatic experiences, such as severe illness, removal
of the parent, or accidents of childhood, are felt to be punishment and
further threaten the depleted or shaky personality structure. Anxiety
in these children runs all the way from simple concentrated phobias,
anxiety in specific areas or situations to a generalized state of anxiety
in which many ego functions may be weakened, if not paralyzed, so
that the energies are not available for growth. The picture of a free-
floating anxiety which attaches itself to any symptom (anxiety neurosis) is really a matured, or adult, condition. In children, the anxiety
is almost always found imbedded in a situation presently active.

An example of the anxiety state—a type found frequently in children during the World War, with good prognosis, is the following.

An eight-year-old boy was referred by his mother because he had night
fears, could not fall asleep before eleven, and then only if his mother lay in
bed with him. He was terrified that robbers would come through the window and hurt him. He wakened early, and again he must run to his mother's bed for protection. Two and a half years earlier his father was drafted
into the army. The mother herself was an anxious, neurotic person, with
a very unhappy childhood, always conforming, very dependent on her
husband, and suffering a great deal from fears for his safety, although
he was in a relatively safe post. Before he was in the army, she always
feared an accident for him and was afraid to be alone.

The boy was planned for, but the mother was miserable during pregnancy. The baby was born feet first in a very difficult delivery. The mother
was sure he would not live. Developmental history, which was not very
complete, showed little of significance except extreme fear of dogs at four

and five years. After the father, who was close to the boy, left, fears became intense and general—of exciting movies or radio programs; of answering the doorbell; and the night terrors already mentioned.

Even with a neurotic mother there was probably enough love and security and support to have helped this boy solve his problem if things had continued normally. As it was, he became the recipient of all his mother's clinging love and anxiety, which drew him close to her in the father's place and thus aroused great anxiety and fear of retaliation.

He wrote rhymes about soldiers being killed—"there was a bomber up in the sky, and all the time the man knew he might die." At school the boy did well; he was logical, good, conscientious, and cautious. He worked hard for high marks. Lately he had become naughty in school and resentful of his mother. He talked a great deal about stupid little children who stood around waiting to be punished. (He, of course, felt that he should be punished for his bad thoughts.)

When he came for his interview, he was polite, friendly, and related immediately. Asked why he was coming, he said, in a very grown-up fashion, that he came because he could not sleep and was afraid of robbers and that he would be happy if worker could free him from this habit. He was afraid that the robbers would steal things from his mother and hurt him. His mother was nice, but sometimes she hit him and then he hit her—"This is my special cure for mothers." He expressed much fear that something would happen to his father (death wishes with ambivalence and anxiety). He started to draw impersonal war pictures, but moved rapidly to pictures of Nazi generals, all the drawings having strong sexual symbolism. He included worker readily in discussing his drawings. He was very much in earnest about coming back and verbalized that worker was helping him. (The neurotic child acts on the expectation of some help, based on satisfactions in the past.) He told his dreams. He and his mother were in a room with Nazi guards. He asked his mother whether the guards would be too strict and hurt him. His mother replied that he should tell them not to be too strict. They did not want to do anything to his mother, only to kill him. "A very scary dream," he commented. The worker agreed that it was a scary dream.

Like most neurotic children, he presented material so as to show that he understood not only that he had a problem, but that he was part of the problem. He "caught on" very quickly to his own self-involvement. Anxiety dreams which are often readily produced by the child who is in emotional conflict are accepted with friendly interest, but not usually stimulated or interpreted.[8]

A five-year-old girl, very nervous, insisting on sleeping with the light on, was very fearful of the dark, of wolves, and of ghosts; had frequent nightmares, cried easily, refused to leave the mother, was timid, did not make friends with other children, sucked her thumb, and bit her nails. On contact, this child was expressionless, unresponsive, and too frightened to move. She was actually immobilized by fear. She did not want to be separated from the mother. When she finally used play material, it was impersonal. She made a geometric design for a ring over and over again. She rejected the worker's attempt to model a baby doll, and her other suggestions.

The underlying anxiety can be seen under the defensive structure of making rings. Here there was passive resistance to contact. It is because the child was paralyzed with fear that she kept her distance. Even so, she was intensely aware of the worker through subterranean channels.

Allowed to reveal herself in her own way and at her own pace, this little girl drew a chair, but the worker must draw the person. (Often psychoneurotics include the worker in some way in the drawings as a way of relating themselves to the therapist.) The worker must draw a wolf for her, but then she was overcome with fear and retreated. The worker said: "See, I will draw a wolf and you can put on a piece of him—" but it took several visits before the child was able to do this. She had given all responsibility over to the worker and did not want to take it back; she was repressing her aggression and isolating herself defensively.

At this age, the emotion is largely released through a series of actions. Verbalization for so frightened a child may be very difficult. The worker has to speak the child's play language.

In the psychoneurotic there is always a weakness carried over from the preoedipal period; neurotic traits or symptoms precede the full-blown condition. We can see definite anxiety patterns forming in the following case of a six-year-old boy.

[8] See pp. 143–144.

Miles was referred because he was restless, fidgety, aggressive, ready to fight with all the boys at school, but insecure and easily frightened— of the dark, of being left alone, of being hurt. If he had to be still for a moment, he became jittery, making faces and grimaces. He acted like a "tough guy" at play school, but got very frightened if disciplined. He was diagnosed as a neurotic child with conduct disorders, his aggression being regarded as a defense to cover his fear of being hurt. He was alter- nately timid and withdrawn, and then subject to explosions of rage to relieve his tensions.

He was an unwanted child, born in very difficult labor. There were feeding difficulties from the start, with persistent vomiting. The gums had to be cut for his teeth to come through. He had a tonsillectomy at 3 and was held down when he struggled so that one of his ribs was broken. There was parental friction; the mother placed the child in a nursery at two in order to go to work. When his father was hospitalized for an incurable condition, the boy was four. His father left the house while Miles was asleep. When Miles awoke, both his father and his mother were gone, and a relative was there with him. He cried and was threat- ened with becoming ill like his father if he didn't behave. He was very anxious whenever his mother was out of his sight. He had so many fears that his mother would take him to bed with her, and he continued to sleep with her. Miles did not see his father except on very rare visits for short periods of time. He didn't know him very well, but seemed to have a good deal of anxiety about him. He didn't understand why he had no father and had asked his mother many times to get him and his brother a father.

This child had been beset by "normal" fears growing out of a real sense of danger and loss. The damaging birth experience and opera- tions, the partial loss of his mother at a crucial age and his father at a later crucial age, and the whole out-of-balance parental relationship made for anxiety states moving in the direction of anxiety neurosis.

Miles was extremely fond of his brother, who was two years his junior, and would do anything to keep the child's good favor. The little boy knew this and exploited it by threatening not to love Miles or kiss him goodbye if he didn't get what he wanted. This upset him very much.

When Miles first came to the worker he wouldn't take off his coat (that is, he wouldn't "open himself up" to another person). He said he couldn't come alone; wanted to bring his own gun; was wary and patronizing. He lectured the worker. (He met his fear of domination by trying to dominate her, discounted in advance.) He told worker he was there because his mother had told him that the agency would find out who was right. He wanted to show that he was right. He couldn't stick to anything in the interview. He fooled around, dawdled, and disparaged everything he touched. He was boastful and challenging, attempting to control the situation by a great show of logic and reason, using both verbal and motor aggression to hide his insecurity. In his second interview Miles came with a torn shirt, complaining that he had been beaten up. He displayed a wounded finger, which the worker bandaged in a matter-of-fact way.

He asked sympathy of the worker as one who was handicapped ("If I take punishment will you accept me as a baby?"), that is, he must take punishment in advance before he could reveal his repressed wishes. There had always been the threat of bodily injury if he did not behave himself; he had in his short life already been much hurt.

He elaborated a dream in which fish eggs grew to tremendous size and then ate the camp counsellor and the bed in one mouthful. He cut the fish's belly open and took out the bed. Thirty or forty snails came out. He insisted that this was true. He was an inventor of a pill that made people invisible; he had a secret workshop. He had silver boots to make him invisible and a magic belt to make him invulnerable, etc.

This boy had many oral fantasies and fears of being blown up or poisoned. Birth fantasies usually come earliest in a child's development, and oral anxieties earlier than fears of being hurt. It was, perhaps, less important for the worker to react to the oral and castration symbols than to understand how this boy had been hurt and threatened by adults. It was difficult to handle the fantasies, since he assured the therapist that all the stories were exactly true. But the worker can show that she understands the fears and wishes by using the child's images, thus giving partial gratification and lessening his guilt feeling. Invention is normal for young children and serves older persons in many harmless ways. It is the amount, quality, and purpose of fantasy that concerns the therapist. What is real for one person is not real for another. This boy had a poor perception of reality. He wanted to find out how much power he had to control the forces which threatened him. The worker personifies reality and gradually, by play experience and by bringing out his fears and wishes about his home situation, helps him measure his real self more accurately.

He had phobias about visiting certain places and touching certain things (phobias always having incest content). He had spurts of aggressiveness, played with darts, and became anxious if he thought he was not winning. When his mother came with him, he insisted on not being left in the room alone, and he hid a toy gun under his shirt "for protection."

To the third interview he brought from home a wrecked airplane to be patched up, which he wanted the worker to believe he had bought in a damaged condition. He wanted the worker to "fix everything." He was whining and dependent.

This is a very fearful boy who lacks self-confidence, a fact which he covered by the very weak defenses of being tough and powerful. There was a great deal of fantasy to bolster him against avenging fate. The therapy would have to include progressive exposure and disruption of the pathological patterns of the defenses in order to release the anxiety. The worker must be careful not to respond literally or in concrete terms, which would soothe the boy, but leave the anxiety intact.

In the next case the patterns are clearly shown in the play interviews.

Stanley, age five and a half, was referred by the mother through the school because he stuttered and had a nose twitch when emotionally upset.[9] Child was hyper-active and had temper outbursts when thwarted. Did not get along too well with other children (though they liked him, and he shared with them), because he fought a good deal, especially with girls. He had nightmares from which he awakened screaming. Expressed fear of wolves. There was marked jealousy of a little brother, against whom he openly expressed aggression. Worker noticed overconcern about cleanliness, fear of getting dirty, and marked curiosity and persistent questioning.

Stanley, born six years after his parents' marriage, was planned for.

[9] For a discussion of stuttering see p. 103.

Pregnancy was easy. Birth was difficult and protracted, and there was a breach delivery. The father wanted a boy, but the mother wanted a girl, and she was very much disappointed in Stanley and suffered from post-partum depression for two months. Mother had worked before her marriage and until she was in her sixth month of pregnancy. She resumed work when the child was nine months old, continuing until pregnancy with the second child.

Because of her illness and then her return to work a few months later, Stanley was reared by nurses. He was an easy infant to handle, never cried, at times seemed almost phlegmatic. He was not breast fed, was weaned to a glass at ten months by the nurse with great difficulty. He had one nurse until he was about nine months old, a twenty-eight-year-old girl, who was described by Mrs. B. as being very strict. She would not admit anyone to the room when Stanley cried, but was not rigid as far as habits and routines were concerned. At one year he was given to violent temper tantrums, which still occur when he is thwarted. Toilet training was begun at eight months, and good habits were established in one year. He sucked two fingers until fifteen months, and occasionally still sucked his thumb when he saw his brother doing so. The boy was constipated. He was a small eater, finicky about food. His mother felt that this might be due to the fact that the nurse forced the child to eat.

The second nurse was even more strict, put gloves on the child when he sucked his thumb, and tried to force him to use his right hand until his mother stopped this. Child still used his left hand. The nurse was described, however, as a warm person, and the boy was extremely attached to her, as she was to him, still visiting him occasionally.

The mother noticed masturbation at about two and was at first shocked, because she didn't realize that this is a universal habit. When the doctor informed her, she tried to handle the situation by ignoring or distracting the boy. Masturbation was for a time excessive, and later a nose tic ensued, but this habit, too, had subsided.

Mother first noticed stuttering when Stanley was three. It was during the summer that she was pregnant, and Stanley and his nurse stayed with the paternal grandparents. Stanley was playing with his little cousin while the nurse was occupied and was told by the cousin that nurse was going to leave and never come back. The boy screamed and cried and began to stutter the following day. That winter he was sent to nursery school, as his mother felt it was the only way to wean him away from the nurse. After a month he adjusted fairly well and stuttering subsided, but it became more marked while mother was in her last few months of pregnancy with John.

At the age of three and a half, several months after the nurse had left, Stanley had a bad case of tonsillitis. The boy called for the nurse and the father, but not for the mother, and she felt resentful at the time. He was subject to frequent colds, and at the age of four, shortly after John's birth, his tonsils were removed. He seemed to associate the birth of the child with his operation, and would ask his mother if she had pain like his pain. He had whooping cough following the tonsillectomy. Since then he had had a mild chronic cough, a "bronchial asthmatic" condition. He had a weak muscle in his left eye, and when he was tired his eyes appeared crossed.

Until the birth of the second child Stanley had his own room, but when John came, the room was turned over to him and his nurse and Stanley was moved into the parental bedroom. Later both children had their own rooms. The mother was afraid to let Stanley sleep with John for fear he might injure him.

Stanley was very curious about the birth of the second child, and it was difficult for him to believe that the baby would not come out of a belly-button. He continued to ask questions after John's birth and to express curiosity as to how the baby ate in the mother's stomach. Occasionally, when his mother combed his hair he would ask her to comb it so that he would look like a girl and wondered why he couldn't be like a girl.

The mother reported that Stanley had had two falls, which raised some question as to the possibility that this had been a self-punishment mechanism. When he was hurt in this way or was ill, he reverted to infantile behavior, demanding a lot of attention and making a fuss about himself.

He was found to be, by test, a boy of slightly superior general intelligence, with an I.Q. of 113. He showed fair achievement, good motor coordination, but was left-handed, with some confusion in writing letters and numbers, stuttering, and other evidences of insecurity.

In regard to cleanliness, the mother believed he was less fussy about this than he was before the age of three or four, when he would refuse to play in dirt or sand. However, he still asked that dirty hands be washed immediately. His fear of wolves seemed to date back to the time when he heard the Red Riding Hood story. He had always thought of his grandmother as a wolf, refused to sleep in the same room with her, and called her Hitler. Since September he had expressed a fear that someone might put dynamite under his bed.

The boy was not fearful with adults, liked to go places, and talked to everyone. He preferred men to women, and this was noticeable even at six months, when he seemed content to be held in a man's lap, but not in a woman's. He was inclined to be stubborn and want his own way.

The paternal relatives had overindulged Stanley. He had often spent week-ends or summers with them, and his grandfather and his father tried to make a "sport" out of him, in view of their extreme interest in sports. When he was two they bought him a baseball suit, which was much too big. Partly as a result of this, as well as of her own rejection of the boy, mother had felt that Stanley belonged to the father and his family, rather than to herself. As she worked after his birth and he was left in the care of nurses, she had limited contact with the boy. Mrs. B. felt extreme guilt in relation to Stanley; felt that he sensed her rejection of him and her preference for John and that this had aggravated the problem. She felt, too, that she had caused his stuttering (because she herself stuttered). The in-laws, as well as her husband, seemed to have aggravated this sense of guilt, as they were constantly pointing out the fact that she was too strict with him, did not show him enough affection, etc.

Mrs. B. has fairly good insight, as well as understanding of the children's needs. She is in conflict in handling Stanley as a result of her feeling of guilt. She tends to exaggerate the boy's difficulties and to see problems in what seems to be relatively normal behavior. Probably this is partly due to anxiety, and partly to too high expectations. She is a woman with a masculine drive, who had had satisfaction in her outside work and who finds it difficult to stay at home and care for the house and the children exclusively. She seems to be a frail person, not too strong physically, insecure, and markedly repressed. Neurotic parents many times do seem to produce neurotic children.

Mrs. B. had mentioned that Stanley had referred to having two fathers, one who is nice, and one whom he'll shoot full of holes.

It would seem, therefore, that while Stanley was more definitely attached to the father and, no doubt, got real affection from him, at the same time there is ambivalence in this case, and fear as well.

Stanley was in the kindergarten (second term). Mother reported his periodic difficulties there with other children, and general restlessness. She stated, however, that the teachers were very unprogressive and rigid. She asked for a psychological test; wondered whether perhaps Stanley was brighter than the others, and consequently whether his interest was not being held. Actually, perhaps, this reflected her anxiety, since she wanted to know if she had a superior child.

Stanley was a nice-looking youngster, chubby, with a rather serious, sober expression. At times he seemed to be slightly crosseyed. He stuttered only occasionally. He was always neat and clean, and evidenced fear and anxiety about getting himself dirty—for instance, when playing with the finger paints. He was bright, alert, and extremely curious, asking innumerable and persistent questions with a kind of obsession. He was outwardly friendly and well poised, but there was underlying tension, often restlessness and inability to decide what to do and what to play. There was need to maintain independence, to do things his own way, and to prove his adequacy. He had an unusual interest in mechanical objects, such as locks and clocks, which he liked to take apart. He loved to play with guns and knives. He had been testing the worker, expressing aggression indirectly toward her, as well as, to some extent, directly. He was extremely sensitive to any kind of suggestion, in that he seemed to fear that things might not be done the way he wanted, and one could see that unless given his own way he would probably become very stubborn and defiant. While he was able to release a lot of aggression in the interview, as well as to get satisfaction from playing with water and, to a lesser extent, finger paint, in general one sensed a pretty inhibited youngster, fearful and insecure, with a good deal of underlying hostility.

This boy has a neurosis of a mixed type with anxiety expressed in fears, night terrors, and hyper-activity. He has some obsessional traits. He was originally rejected by his mother—an insecure, repressed person with extreme guilt—left in the care of nurses, one of whom was rigid in her training, and deserted at the age of three and a half by a nurse to whom he was extremely attached at a time when his mother was again pregnant. The mother's own rejection of the boy (based largely on deep disappointment that he was not a girl) is aggravated by the attitude of the father and paternal uncles, who "possess" the boy, so that when the second child came the mother seems to have given up her struggle to attach herself to Stanley, and got all her satisfaction from the younger child. Stanley, already insecure, anxious and hostile, now has the added disadvantage of a loved brother to battle against. He shows ambivalence towards both parents; the aggressive impulses are repressed and reappear in night terrors, fear of wolves, fear of explosions, etc. These reflect projected anxiety with regard to his own aggressive impulses, which he fears will get out of hand. There are indications of conflict about being a boy and a drive to appease his mother by trying to be a girl.

In the history we see a child who has had a good deal of love from adults, especially men, but his experience with the mother figure and powerful persons close to him (two nurses in infancy), coupled with rejection by his mother, has resulted in deprivation and pushed the boy in the direction of inverted object choice. His own mother is tense, emotionally immature, swinging between rigidity and compliance. She has always been inconsistent in her handling of the boy. In this case the mother and the grandmother, rather than the father, have been experienced as the frustrating persons.

Play with water, paints, and clay had the purpose of releasing the boy from his fear of dirt. He related at once and included worker in his play, although he had a great need to maintain independence and do things his own way. He showed marked aggression toward the worker; shot the baby doll (a boy) and was uneasy about it. The lady doll he also shot, and sometimes the worker "for real." He showed apprehension about getting wet—only gingerly tried finger painting. He participated in the worker's drawings and made her participate in his. In the fifth interview he became more aggressive and was somewhat less anxious about getting wet with the bubble pipe. "I am having fun." "That's fine—it is nice to play like this, isn't it?" His play with dolls always reenacted closely the family scenes, and his desires and fears were very near the surface. Stanley's hostility toward his mother came out clearly, as he directed aggression at the women dolls as well as at the worker. This was also expressed overtly against the grandmother at home.

This sort of play is characteristic of the anxious child, who recreates immediately the familial persons who are the source of his conflict.

Soon the doll and the worker were used interchangeably. (The play behavior characteristically goes immediately into transference.) Both were now Miss J. "Why are you shooting at Miss J?" "Because she is bad—she did something to me." (Marked anxiety.) He was afraid at first to smear the brown finger paint. He complained that it smelled bad. Following the worker's example, he did the smearing and was delighted; he then became anxious. His hands must be wiped off at once. He then made a play in which the policeman would shoot him for his badness. His own fears overtook him after his regression.

This child's second nurse had instituted severe toilet training. The boy was never permitted until these play interviews to work through normally his satisfaction in excretion, and he still feels defecation is dirty. Children in a permissive environment quickly bring up those earlier unresolved instinctual tendencies, equating food with feces sometimes in a very flippant manner and with obvious satisfaction, sometimes with fear and disgust. This little boy, having learned that he should react with disgust, has turned against all "dirtiness." Stanley consciously has taken over the wish to be clean, with extreme reaction formation, but the struggle with the instinctual desires is still to be resolved. The worker's approval of his pleasure in the finger paints is helpful in diminishing his self-condemnation.

In the eighth interview he played very aggressive Nazi games. He is the Nazi. He is very bad. He is anxious. He was reassured that it is all right to play this way. He began to experience jealousy of other children who come to see the worker. He killed off, with violence, two lady dolls, one the maid and another who now doubled for both the worker and the mother. "You are mad at this family." "Sure, I feel mad. Shall I shoot the baby?" He roughly damaged the baby doll and became unhappy. Seeing his rising anxiety, the worker suggested that maybe shooting darts was too strong for this family and that he could use a pop-gun if he liked. He was relieved and shot them less viciously.

He now shot all the family except the maid. When he shot the mother doll, he said anxiously, "I am a good aimer." The worker said cheerfully, "Yes, you certainly are." He was reassured. He spent much time in sucking from the baby bottle, and there was much toilet play with the dolls. A little less anxiety—"Where is that rotten baby?" The baby was found for him, and he abused it thoroughly. He wished for handcuffs. "For whom?" "For my *brother*, of course." This frightened him and he ran to the toilet. After a series of interviews his behavior at home was worse and he stuttered more. He would not play with the baby doll. "I hate him." He showed his resistance in great distractibility. He left the interview early. After often shooting the worker dead, he would bring her alive again. He did this over and over. The worker said that it was all right for him to like her and to dislike her and that she understood—thus recognizing the ambivalence.

The way out of conflict about sex is to regress to infancy, but like all neurotics, he still feels that he is bad.

He began to tell stories, using many dirty words about a bad boy named Stanley. His mother gave him a licking. He was now verbalizing more. He discussed sex differences in the dolls; asked questions and was told matter of factly whatever he wanted to know. At intervals he seemed to need to play being a baby. He played out the parental bedroom, placing the doll children there. "I guess you are dreaming, Stanley." "Yes, this boy is dreaming that the wolf eats him up." After this he was anxious. "I won't be back again for some time," he told the worker. "I will save your appointment as usual for you," she said.

There are times when he showed affection, followed by great resistance. He talked a little more about his brother and blocks. "You don't like to talk about him, Stanley." "No." "I know you have trouble with him and I think I can help you." He smiled, "Maybe you can—maybe you can't."

The neurotic knows that it is hard to do anything, especially to get well. In every neurosis the total personality is affected; there is some damage to self-esteem, some sense of failure. The more mature the person, the less need he has for exaggerated dependence. As the child grows he learns that he can like someone else in and for himself, and in his social behavior he will be able to show greater elasticity in adaptation.

Recapitulation

The child guidance worker sees not only primary behavior disorders of mixed types but also neurotic children, particularly those who are manifesting conduct disorders and other disturbances. If the child shows any form of anxiety, overt or disguised, this is regarded as neurotic suffering or psychoneurosis. The child feels that he is bad and deserves punishment. The symptom (including certain neurotically determined behavior as "symptom") is always the result of an unsuccessfully repressed wish. In its disguised form the wish can be more easily tolerated by the ego. The final neurotic symptom is a fusion of repressed drives, super-ego restrictions, ego factors, and secondary gains. A neurosis means to have a special unit of the personality "encapsulated," or walled off, or arrested, although the rest of the person may function efficiently. There is always some pathological behavior, since the denial of inner reality disturbs in some way the outer reality. Too much of the child's energy is used in repressing the infantile wishes. "Infantile neurosis" is not an absolute classification, but it covers not only mixed types but also varying degrees of insecurity. Psychotherapy thus may be used for children with less severe conditions who do not yet have a fully structuralized neurosis —are not fixated in such a way as to resist development. A neurosis, however, always involves some degree of self-limitation. The goal is to move from generalized anxiety to uncover specific fears; to release emotions without the accompanying guilt; to reinforce energies for insight and ego-building. With resolution of conflicts, anxiety is diminished. The fact that the anxious child suffers and wants to be helped is on the side of the therapist.

Ventilation and release of the repressed fears and aggression may have far-reaching therapeutic benefits. For repression tends to spread, just as anxiety does, and if the child represses more and more into a rigid structure of negation, the ego cannot mature. The awareness of inner reality and the reduction of crippling anxiety free the ego so that it can use more energy in growing up, form more constructive defenses, and adapt better to the ordinary demands of living.

Chapter V

THE SEVERELY DISTURBED CHILD

ALL EMOTIONALLY disturbed children may be regarded as sick children, and it is only in an arbitrary way that we may differentiate the aberrations: the normal child reacting to an acutely abnormal situation, the child with a mild behavior disorder, and the anxious child from the deeply disturbed child. The fluid growth of childhood, the fact that pathological *processes* (diseases) are not always easy to distinguish from pathological *reactions,* makes diagnosis difficult. Both arrest and regression may be temporary, as when accompanying illness, or following the death of some member of the family, or in placement, or after the birth of a baby brother or sister. Or arrest may be generalized and permanent as in the infantile, or partially fixated as in the neurotic, personality. Or a neurosis may be superimposed upon or may utilize an organic condition. Or the personality may be biased or conditioned by constitutional factors not now fully understood. Science has not yet satisfactorily explained why the psychosomatic organism "chooses" or elects a special disease, even though some of the causes are separately identifiable. Not everyone exposed to the tubercle bacillus acquires the disease, nor does every child exposed to traumatic events develop a warped character.

Study of case records shows that a diagnosis is often changed by another psychiatrist or even by the same psychiatrist. A child may be classified as a primary behavior disorder, later as a psychoneurotic or a schizoid personality or as having a schizophrenic episode. The prevalence of mixed types and the lack of stability in the ego structure makes clinical entities not always easily distinguishable. The nature of the deviation must be observed and diagnosis made from appropriate sources, whether the deviation is in the intelligence, motility, speech development, achievement, relationship to parents or siblings, organic condition, or in several interacting areas. In normal growth there may be a temporary inhibition in any one of these areas; in disturbed growth the limitations are likely to be reflected in several areas. If the child has fixation or conflict in only one area and is otherwise normal, the prognosis naturally is more favorable. Just as there is overlapping among diagnostic classifications, so levels of growth are not absolutely fixed. There may be slow, rapid, strong, weak, uneven development, all within the range of the so-called normal. Yet we cannot be sure that fixation in one area will be self-healing; the traumatization may or may not be outgrown. The aim of child guidance is through early diagnosis and therapy to assist the self-healing process. Evaluation must determine what Dr. Margaret Mahler calls the "potential for reversibility." [1] In all diagnostic classifications there are milder and more severe types, variations as to flexibility and the basic capacity of the ego to function.

There are severe behavior disorders which are as unresponsive to psychotherapy as are the severe psychoneuroses and psychoses. Character disorders which are overtly antisocial or criminal are unsuitable for any sort of out-patient treatment. But the line between normal and defective "character" structure, especially in the young, is even harder to draw than between normal and abnormal body or mental functioning.

When a child is thought to be "nervous," he is usually taken by his parents to a medical institution or a private physician. Children thus referred are likely to show a high incidence of physical disturbances, —tics, vomiting and gastric disorders, enuresis, choreic movements, convulsive attacks, schizoid behavior, and so forth. Children found at a court clinic usually manifest extremely overt conduct problems— stealing, fighting, lying, sex deviations, waywardness, truanting, incorrigibility. The case load of a clinic in an educational setting is weighted by school retardation, reading disabilities, speech defects, as well as truancy. The grouping of symptoms for any type of agency is somewhat fortuitous, depending on professional resources, cultural attitudes, and other factors. When social agencies work with families in which there are sick, deteriorated, and delinquent person-

[1] Mahler, "Child Analysis," in *Modern Trends in Child Psychiatry*, ed. by Nolan D. C. Lewis and Bernard L. Pacella, p. 265.

alities, a combination of social, medical, and other therapies will be invoked. In cases of severe pathology the chief patient or patients or the child exposed to the pathological situation may have to be removed from the home to a controlled environment.

The guidance agency [2] tends to accept only those dissocial children whose behavior is primarily psychological or psychogenetic in origin, namely, primary behavior disorders with conduct and habit disorders and neurotic traits; normal children reacting to environmental stress; children with educational disabilities of emotional origin (not provided for in the school system) and mild psychoneurotics. It does not accept for psychotherapy, generally speaking, cases in which there are processes which might lead to deterioration— children having organic brain disease, post-encephalitis, convulsive disorders, psychoses, or severe psychoneuroses.

Psychosomatic Illness

Although most children with physical complaints are taken to a clinic or to a hospital, some do reach child guidance agencies and have to be there carefully sifted. There are few, if any, chronic illnesses which do not give rise to changes in the personality which are comparable to psychoneurotic changes. When the chronically ill are taken by caseworkers for special reasons, treatment is then carried on cooperatively with a physician. Parents often explain a child's behavior on the grounds of illness, whether real or fancied, and their explanations and projections must always be taken seriously and carefully checked. Obviously, any physical complaint has to be medically studied to see whether illness is actually present—the first essential being a careful health and developmental history. Physical illness, either in the child or in the parent, may be a disguise for emotional problems to which one or the other stubbornly clings. Al-

[2] At the Jewish Board of Guardians the policy is to accept for treatment cases which are primarily psychogenetic in origin. It does, however, take borderline cases, which include a good many psychosomatic and prepsychotic children, because the diagnosis at intake is uncertain; beyond that it takes a few cases in close cooperation with the consulting psychiatrist and other physicians for controlled experimentation. This seems legitimate in view of the fact that for some of the types medical science has at present very little to offer, and therapy may relieve, in part, the child's suffering. Routine review of diagnosis by a psychiatrist is indispensable.

though psychosomatic medicine is developing rapidly, it may be a long time before the average pediatric clinic is equipped to furnish psychotherapy to child and parent, so it may often be practical to arrange for cooperative treatment with an agency practicing psychotherapy.

It is important to detect as early as possible the child who is frequently out of school with chronic colds, or "cold habits," sinus, or asthma; the adolescent who is subject to frequent stomach upsets and other gastric disorders in school; and others with similar behavior. Since studies of allergic reactions suggest that the trail leads back to the mother, it is not surprising that children with behavior disorders whose problems also lead back to the parents, may present allergies as a part of their total picture. It is not yet established in psychosomatic medicine whether certain types of personality produce disease or whether continued psychic tension brings out disease or, as is likely, whether both interact; the social worker is particularly concerned to reduce states of chronic tension in these children whenever he finds them, and at the source. It is undoubtedly true that all disease has a psychic component, just as all behavior may be said to have physical, psychological, and social components. The next step after psychosomatic discoveries is to link psychosocial discoveries in a total consideration of the human event.

Aggression may be channelized through projectile vomiting or enuresis or other physical expressions. Obesity may be the externalized outcome of hostile aggressive demands, first directed against the mother and then toward others. The fat child who lacks friends or is the butt of jokes, who gets into mischief to gain attention or withdraws into himself, may either be picked up in the obesity clinic or be referred to a social agency because of the poor quality of his relationships. Functional illness is often the last defense against facing profound disturbance in the emotional life, and only in early stages is the disease process usually reversible. Because simpler structures are involved in a child's problem, the whole organism is more responsive to treatment. Headaches and vomiting are common in high school pupils, because school is the strongest reality for the adolescent and here pressures stir up the deeper conflicts. Although asthma is an allergy disease, it is often strikingly associated with parent-child separation. The patterns which lead to psychosomatic complaints are said to be established probably before six or seven. It is always more difficult to help children after the damage has taken place. Mothers are often resistive to admitting that a child's disturbance is psychogenetic, insisting on medical treatment. Escapist tendencies are general, and doctors are sometimes unconsciously their accomplices. Social workers should try to avoid an either/or position and encourage a physical examination, while telling the mother not to be surprised if no physical basis is found.

An organic disease or handicap in any member of the family, particularly in a child, tends to center interest on the invalid, arousing attention in a way which, though superficially solving his conflicts because of the secondary gains and satisfactions from such family concern, brings complications in its train both for the patient and for other members of the family group.

Often it is found that to focus on the physical difficulties of a child assuages the parents' own anxieties and keeps them from focusing on their own problems. The mother's overprotectiveness and concern for the child's health may be a reaction formation against deep-lying attitudes of rejection. Many persons under strong feelings of guilt may consciously or unconsciously equate illness with punishment. Children often do this. The conflicts which are wreaked on others by the child who acts out may be worked out on the self in psychosomatic, conversion, or other symptoms. The roots of the behavior disorder and of the physical disturbance alike seem to be planted in the home garden. At bottom we shall find the familiar picture of a disappointed child expressing the frustration-aggression-anxiety syndromes through all sorts of patterns. Some children seem able to make very good use of psychotherapy before the defensive structures have become rigid or the disease processes chronic, especially if the familial environment can be modified. The child guidance agency, after all, starts where the "battle for the child's soul already is raging," that is, in the home; its techniques are best designed for undoing or mitigating current damage, rather than for a therapy which reaches into the deepest layers of the personality. The unconscious of the child is more easily accessible—in fact, some of what will be later completely repressed, or what has been left after partial repression, is still going on before our eyes, if we have eyes to see. With psychomatic disorders in children the question of expert therapy directed to the environment—parental, home, and school—is also of the essence. If treatment is carried on in a social agency, medical consultation and follow-up are concurrently maintained to make flexible adjustments of the total therapy, as indicated.

A word about stutterers, since so many referred children show some speech deviation or disability, may be said here. Most speech disorders, including stuttering, are assumed to reflect disorders of the total personality, and the stuttering itself is usually regarded as a psychoneurotic symptom. Some conditions are mild, and especially at preschool ages they do clear up spontaneously, though possibly sometimes in favor of other symptoms. In most cases known to the child guidance agency stuttering is part of a syndrome found in youngsters who are deeply disturbed.

Dr. Peter Glauber [3] interprets the personality of the stutterer as resembling on the one hand the make-up of the behavior disorder with narcissistic (oral) traits, and on the other, the compulsive neurotic, and this description seems to fit most of the cases. The struggle between active domination and passive resistance acted out through a partial blocking of the speech function is in essence a struggle with the rejecting, but controlling, mother. Hostility is always embedded in this symptom. Although for the stutterer the conflict has already been internalized, parental urging and reproof, frustrations and over-attention to the symptom in school, make continuing pressure an acute irritant. In the stutterer one usually finds the rejection-overprotection syndrome, with overanxiety and pressure by both parents. Feeding difficulties are common, as are gastrointestinal and other functional symptoms, which seem to bring the stutterer close to the psychosomatic group. This symptom, a defense of the ego (considered to be a character trait, not a habit disorder), cannot be

[3] Glauber, "Speech Characteristics of Psychoneurotic Patients," *Journal of Speech Disorders*, IX (March, 1944), 18–30, and "A Social Psychiatric Therapy for the Stutterer," *The Newsletter*, American Association of Psychiatric Social Workers, XIV (1944), 30–34.

attacked directly. The conduct disorder expresses aggression outwardly; the stutterer says to himself unconsciously, "Can I or can I not express my aggression safely?" In contrast to the behavior disorder he feels inferior and vulnerable. Speech is his vehicle of aggression, not temper or quarrelsome behavior. The impulse to speak is, therefore, under pressure of anxiety, checked by the compulsive defense of stuttering. Stuttering as a defense only partially succeeds, so the child is usually disposed to get rid of the symptom for which he is criticized and which still leaves the possibility of anxiety.[4]

As with other forms of hostility and aggressiveness, the child needs great acceptance. To ask him why he stutters would be to ask him to face the objects of his resentment. Insight, therefore, is not an immediate goal. Play interviews with younger children are designed, again to quote Dr. Glauber, "to take the weight off the speech muscles." In discussions of play, school, and home occurrences, the patterns of aggression as disclosed may, perhaps, when pointed out, be accepted by the boy or the girl more easily in another frame of reference than in the symptom itself. At nursery-school age, both individual and group therapy to release the aggression and to socialize and strengthen the ego away from passive compliance or waves of resistance may prove rewarding. Warm acceptance of the jealous and controlling mother is essential, or she will be antagonized, especially if the child improves. The more she gives up the rejection-overcontrol pattern, the less the child has to struggle in a vicious circle of resistance-compliance.

The picture of a stutterer [5] with a neurotic mother whose strong masculine drives are characteristic is found in the following case of an eight-year-old boy. Male children seem particularly to arouse in such mothers rivalry and hostility.

Dave was unhappy, unable to concentrate, asthenic, fatigable, with a mild stammer which has now receded in favor of a marked reading difficulty. There were some atypical neurological features, which did not

---

[4] There are many theories about stuttering. We are here following discussion by Glauber and van Ophuijsen, which seems to fit so many cases at the Jewish Board of Guardians.

[5] See also cases cited on pp. 243–265 for clinical pictures of stutterers.

appear according to specialists to have significance. The I.Q. was high average; the Rorschach showed hostility toward the mother and sexual disturbance. The mother was cold, dominating, perfectionist, efficient, and methodical, herself neurotic; the father, a mild-mannered man, was very dependent on his wife. The boy craved attention from him and got it on a passive level. The pregnancy was accidental; the mother wanted a girl.

Admittedly the child was a disappointment. There were the to-be-expected feeding difficulties, rejection covered by attention, resulting in food fads. A heart murmur, not found consequential, gave rise to further overprotection and to keeping Dave a sissy. He not only was a sissy, but he was also thoroughly infantilized. He wore Eton jackets, Peter Pan collars, and alternately fought and ingratiated himself with the school children (dominance-compliance). His mother identified him negatively with the father, of whom she was contemptuous, and he was compared unfavorably with the older sister. She was equally aggressive toward the boy and the father and "managed" them both.

The mother asked for advice for herself and discussed the boy very little; she had an immediate resistance to treatment; her defenses were strong; she was afraid of being "psyched"—that the worker would "size her up" and that "they would get nowhere." [6]

She spoke much of herself, but coquettishly, superficially, and with a brittle façade. She prepared lists of questions to discuss (more defenses). She thought both psychiatrists and social workers too badly adjusted to help her, yet she continued to come. She wanted to leave home and to go out to work; had marked masculine drives; admitted her disappointment with her husband and her wish to manage him (this "psychological separation" from the husband is common). She struggled to control the interviews as she controlled everyone else. When the boy came for an interview he didn't stutter much, although later, when the worker (in response to an admission about his reading difficulty) interpreted that he was afraid he wouldn't say the right word and so would not read at all, he accepted this with a startled flash of insight. He had a compulsion to repeat certain phrases at the end of each sentence (stuttering is like a compulsive symptom). The worker paid no attention to this symptom, as such, but was accepting and giving both in conversation and in play.

[6] A similar picture by Dr. Glauber in the article cited is interesting.

It is important, in view of the narcissistic side of the stutterer, as with the primary behavior disorder, to give fully and easily, that is, instead of helping the child to talk or sitting passively by and so forcing him to talk, the worker gives the "words so much overvalued by the stutterer." Instead of helping to finish sentences, which is the wrong way, the worker may help by paraphrasing, clarifying, or amplifying what the child has already said.

He talked and modeled, the worker participating freely. He "looks like the pig" he is modeling. They discussed animals: polywogs, dogs, and rats. He knew "women who make rats of their children." He was "dumb," "a rag picker," "a clown." (Autocriticism was very strong.) The toy bird sang for him only the song "Please Don't Hurt Me." Sex preoccupation and play were recurrent. The play was always aggressive.

This boy fits into a classical sex picture in that he is exhibitionistic, exposing himself at school, and his guilt about masturbation, brought out in veiled terms, showed strong underlying fear of castration at the hands of the mother. At the same time he has a passive dependent relation to his father, who had carried him upstairs and down because of his "heart condition," bathed and indulged him. There is a strong craving for identification with the father.

As the aggression was steadily drained off, he became freer to talk. He thought he was bad; made his mother nervous; wanted to make mischief for her (strong hostility). He admitted fear of being hurt, overwhelmed; everyone told him what to do (the struggle between dominance and passive resistance). He became more relaxed; he began to read a little more easily; the stuttering diminished.

In this child the conflicting wishes to speak and not to speak were expressed first in a stutter and then in a reading difficulty, with almost complete inhibition of producing the required words. In other children the fighting-submissive reactions are found. Since speech tends to be overvalued, the combination of play, modeling, and conversation proved here a good medium for the release of hostility in a therapeutic relationship.

A not uncommon sequence in development seems to be difficulty with feeding, with talking, and with reading, and then stuttering—

or stuttering and then difficulty with reading. Stuttering is sometimes then dropped and sinus or headaches or other physical disturbances make the child's life miserable.

Although the epileptic child is not often treated in direct therapy by a caseworker, the combination of medical, social and psychotherapeutic measures may occasionally sustain and improve such a child, if not cure him. In the following case the child stuttered very badly also.

Jerry, a refugee, age seven, was referred by the school. The child was very difficult. Jerry never got along with other children, and the mother wouldn't allow them in the house. There was a history of feeding problems (he was bottle fed till five), convulsions, general nervousness, and stuttering. He was terribly timid, afraid of every sound, sensitive, and easily hurt. He was never permitted to go anywhere alone, was extremely infantile in all behavior. He was failing in school and thought all the teachers unjust to him.

Neurological examinations and encephalogram showed epilepsy and the "epileptic personality," e.g., strong impulsivity, peculiar reasoning and perceptions, lack of restraint, ego-centricity, selfishness, abnormal sensitiveness, and irritability.

Jerry was found to be extremely unhappy in his home, his father being disinterested, aloof, and severe, his mother domineering, masculine, rigid, and overprotective. She feared Jerry would grow up and reject her, like her other men folk. The little brother was preferred. There was marked parental disharmony.

The boy reacts to all new situations with a wish for protection, with feelings of inadequacy. His insecurity is based partly on his sickness, but has been increased by traumatic experiences, especially at the hands of his mother. His anger, hostility, and aggression mount because he is not able to accept any limitation or frustration, which he regards as a withdrawal of love; he reacts to frustration with anger instead of acceptance. His epileptic seizures and stuttering seem to have much the same value in blocking and in explosion of hostility.

It was recognized that Jerry's basic character pattern could not be changed, and at first the goal had been only to establish him under neurological treatment at a hospital.

This program was not carried out, as the mother would not use the crowded neurological clinic. The family doctor, meanwhile, had no solution except to increase medication and instructed the mother never to let Jerry out of her sight for a minute. She returned to the guidance agency, feeling in a confused way that something more might be done to help her and Jerry. Jerry, in his first contacts, had established a quick transference to the worker and wanted to continue. The consulting psychiatrist, who was himself also a neurologist, advised that the worker should attempt therapy.[7] It seemed worth while to try experimentally to help this boy control his anxiety and aggression, which were too great for him to bear. The therapeutic goal was to help him to learn how to deal with frustrations in a more mature and less self-destructive way.

Mental Illness and Psychotic Episodes

Outright psychoses, which are rather infrequent in the child population, wherever competent medical facilities exist, are not commonly seen in the social agency. If they do appear, a careful intake worker can usually spot them on history and the type of complaint made and refer them at once to the consulting psychiatrists. But prepsychotic or marginal cases are not easy to detect, especially since in children mental illness does not present a static picture. Social workers deal with many withdrawn children who may be autistic and self-loving, but not necessarily schizophrenic. In schizophrenia the boundaries of the ego, first blurred, are then narrowed as the ego retreats within itself. The psychotic cannot repress or deny, as the neurotic does; he projects instead. Psychosis is his only means of solving his conflict. His ego structure is weak and tends to deterioration. Careful diagnosis of the disease by a psychiatrist and close supervision are indicated in any combination of therapies—direct, or environmental, or both. But because child guidance is addressed to releasing the processes of growth which have been inhibited not only by disease but also by other factors, schizoid children who seem to relinquish with great difficulty the habits of early childhood are not uncommonly discovered among the cases brought to the social agency.

---

[7] The course of treatment is discussed on p. 239.

Early schizophrenia or schizophrenic episodes, which are more often found than other psychoses,[8] are difficult even for the psychiatrist to diagnose definitely, as there is much overlapping with behavior which suggests other classifications. The psychiatrist may recommend social therapy, since treatment directed to reducing strains in the environment and improving relationships may not be in vain even if the schizophrenic process itself cannot be stopped. A child depressed by the loss of a parent may look a good deal like the schizoid personality, and anxiety attacks may be not too unlike epileptic or choreic behavior. Reactive regression may sometimes be so marked as to suggest the earliest stages of a psychosis, yet the disturbance may be temporary and may clear up completely.

The schizoid personality may appear to the parents an odd but gifted child. He may personify animals or other creatures with a good deal of charm. If he asks for books in his world of fantasy, he may get approbation for being a scholar. It is only recently that the eccentric child who is noncompetitive or very shy or quiet has been recognized as a serious deviation, and he is more often given attention by school authorities than formerly. If he is brought early to the child guidance agency, there are two important interrelated avenues of treatment open—to try to socialize him environmentally, and to offer a sustaining relationship. This is really a single avenue, since the relationship is the bridge to the interests and outlets he so much needs. To coax him out of his estrangement from reality and to tempt him to accept living things is a task which requires devotion, patience, and skill. The schizophrenic child usually shows bizarre or odd behavior reactions in play, which a sensitive and well-trained worker will pick up and bring to the immediate attention of the psychiatrist. The true schizophrenic, in his regression, gives up most emotional relationship to the environment, but he is not like a child, although he behaves like a child. In his delusions and projections he uses all his life experience up to the point when he started to regress.

There is no evidence to date that the child guidance agency has had any permanent success with cases of early schizophrenia. Prob-

[8] Bradley, "Psychoses in Children," in *Modern Trends in Child Psychiatry*, pp. 135-154.

ably most cases in which there are gains lie in those borderline areas where no deteriorating process is actively operating.[9] But since the social treatment for all withdrawn and disinterested personalities is much the same, a certain number of cases have been carried experimentally, under supervision of the psychiatrist, and some improvement has been noted. Another reason for taking a few such cases is that the family may be helped supportively while the schizophrenic episode runs its inevitable course. These children are often discharged from hospital after the episode as having "no psychosis"; then a period of direct psychotherapy may prove helpful in slowing down or averting recurrence. Both before a breakdown and afterwards, a single warm relationship, whether in the family, in the agency, or in the community, may have the effect of a lifeline to reality. Such supportive relationships are reenforced by activities—occupations and interests in the outer world—just as occupational therapy is carried on in mental hospitals. Schizophrenics do not always have difficulty in relating themselves to a person, but as with all psychotics, active help must usually be given, because there is so little strength in the ego. Interpretation, except for simple explanations of medical or social programs, has to be put aside, and the personality is helped to repress and to carry on in reality.

A common family constellation seems to be an extremely controlling, narcissistic mother, and a weak, submissive father. Whether medical experts do or do not finally agree on the constitutional factors or predisposition responsible for schizophrenia, certainly the adult family members studied do show very unfortunate attitudes. Perhaps the chief argument for entering into some of these cases on a selective basis is the opportunity gained to work with the other siblings who have been exposed to such destructive attitudes. Interfamilial stresses may precipitate schizophrenic disorders.

As cases of early schizophrenia that come to a guidance agency

---

[9] As Dr. Lowrey says in *Psychiatry for Social Workers*, p. 194: "It is worth while to remember that no type of psychotherapy has yet been devised which is effective with the schizophrenic. In that way the worker will save a great deal of energy which otherwise might be wasted. In other words, she should take advantage of every bit of improvement, but not feel that it is the result of her efforts or the result of any particular type of psychotherapeutic approach." Other research is, however, more optimistic.

usually present extremely complicated clinical pictures, illustrations will not be given here.

Obsessional and Compulsive Neuroses

Even though the guidance agency avoids as far as possible accepting severe psychoneurotics, a certain number of obsessional and compulsive children remain in the case loads, largely because analysts are not available. During the oedipal period anxiety may arise from the conflict with regard to the "parents as a couple"; obsessional thoughts, either passive or impulsive, may occur between six and ten, and compulsions as a defense against the obsessional ideas.[10] The nature of the obsessional thoughts is determined by the personality trend, but it is always symbolic. As long as a threatening situation can be avoided, as by a phobia, the child may be able to manage; if not, there will be a regression, possibly with compulsive acts to bind the anxiety. A true compulsion is always a disagreeable, unavoidable experience. The things one feels one "must do" because one likes to do them are not compulsions; urges are not compulsions. Compulsive acts are devices to neutralize fear. Even though the obsessional neurotic never carries his tormenting thoughts into action, he does not know that he will not and so must build defenses against his anxiety.

Because obsessional impulses characteristically aim to harm the self or someone else they often lead to another obsession, namely, that one is "going crazy" (as distinguished from the behavior disorder's [11] "I guess I must be crazy"). A secondary gain resulting from the fear of going crazy is being sent to a hospital, where one can be at once protected against one's own impulses and punished by the incarceration. Severe obsessions always have a history of adolescent and childhood symptoms. The onset of the fully developed neurosis is a reaction to something which has touched off earlier anxieties related to the content of the obsession. Adolescents may suffer from tormenting obsessional thoughts of doing harm to themselves (including masturbation) or to their parents. Often these thoughts also are equated with the idea of going crazy.

[10] See p. 33. Obsessional trends may be seen even earlier—around three.
[11] See p. 59.

Many compulsive mothers are socially admired as good parents. They may be perfectionist about their children and their house-keeping. Both men and women are good workers. They may function very well until something disturbs their balance. About all case-work can do, with the present knowledge, is to strengthen those compulsive acts which are most constructive. Another type of obsessional mother is one who is tormented with the thought of harming her children in some way. The child guidance agency treats a good many such persons, as well as the rigid, perfectionist sort.

A thirteen-year-old boy, the older of two siblings, was referred by his mother because he was "rude," arrogant, willful, and had food fads, which had been impairing his health for many years. The maternal grandmother took care of the child.

At the age of eight months he had refused to eat and had lived on a starvation diet for several months. Then the food fads began to develop. He ate few foods and no vegetables, and for nearly two years ate only one kind of meat. He was very much underweight and underdeveloped. He showed evidence of precocity, having talked at four months and having been able to recite the alphabet at thirteen months. He was irregular in his eating and sleeping hours. From early childhood he had been argumentative with his mother. When he had to give in to her, he argued philosophically the value of doing so. He had always been a sickly child and had often had a sore throat. At the age of three he had had a tonsillectomy, which was a very traumatic experience for him. When he was three and a half years of age, the mother returned to work, and for the following six months the child cried every morning.

There was a history of petty stealing at the age of six, when he took small amounts of money from his mother and his grandmother. He was in the 4th term at high school, and in spite of his superior intelligence (I.Q. of 143) he was not doing good work. He put off doing his homework and stated that he worked best under pressure. He had fear of falling, and occasionally nausea and headache, which appeared to be conversion symptoms.

At the time his baby brother was born, twelve years after his own birth, he went on a severe hunger strike, and on one occasion he fainted in school. He was ill in bed for two weeks and explained his illness as a "nervous breakdown." He would argue with his mother about the proper care of his brother and explain, "I was spoiled, why shouldn't my brother be spoiled too?" He often felt exhausted after school examinations. He revealed a most active fantasy life. A word or idea which occurred to him led to multiple associations. He had no real friends, but used acquaintances in the promotion of his hobbies: the collection of stamps, little ships of a military nature, recipes, and statistics. He planned in detail harbors for his ships, and would figure out minutely whether the harbors were large enough to house the ships. He had a tremendous amount of scientific knowledge, read considerably in the field of psychology and philosophy, and on the subject of vitamins. He showed a marked perfectionistic drive; he amassed information regarding sports both of a statistical and historical nature.

The mother, who was frustrated both in her marriage and in her work career, had little interest except in the boy's intellectual achievements, about which she nagged him. Her comment was that she never really learned to become a woman and that if she married again she would need to learn how to be a wife. She felt quite useless as a housewife. She wanted to be a journalist, but her own mother had opposed this plan, wanting her to be a teacher. The boy, on a number of occasions, questioned whether his mother really loved him. He said his father didn't "aggravate or tear him down" as much as his mother did. His father took courses at night, and the son expressed concern about his father's health lest his work plus his studies might be too much for him. This was compensated for by making elaborate vitamin (compulsive device) prescriptions for him.[12]

An emotionally isolated personality such as this may try to use his intelligence as a bridge of contact to others, since he has no other bridge. The narcissistic drive of many parents of children with a high I.Q. is to show them off to others, thus further contributing to their isolation. This boy had a relation to reality through his stamp collecting and the collecting of model ships, so that he could connect his knowledge with actual conditions. He had, apparently, turned his sex curiosity into scientific curiosity. Although it may be hoped that relieving pressures in the environment and offering intensive therapy will be helpful, because the compulsive tendencies arose before the age of eight, the prognosis would be guarded. Referral to a psychiatrist was refused by the parents.

Compulsive persons have a tendency toward superstition. Even if

---

[12] For the treatment of a compulsive neurotic see pp. 294–296.

they laugh about superstitions, they half believe in them, and it is this attribution of magical tendencies to thoughts and actions which is perhaps most familiar to the worker with obsessional and compulsive children. The child who acts out, because he cannot bind his aggression, often looks to magic to aid him in securing his desires; the compulsive child tries to bind by magic his hostile thoughts against the parental figures, to whom he still has infantile attachments. It must be remembered that the development of a compulsive symptom cannot be stopped as long as the conflict and the stimulus are present, since the symptoms are built up to avoid anxiety. Since a compulsive neurosis means regression to an incestuous object choice (further regression leading to the giving up of this in favor of narcissism), it is clear why a transference type of therapy is not adequate to reduce the anxiety in these severe neuroses. Even though the personality structure of obsessional and compulsive persons— because they are primitive, archaic, and rigid—is not very susceptible to therapy, the presence of so many compulsive neuroses of various degrees of severity in social case loads makes experimental, carefully controlled treatment inevitable in order to find ways of redirecting these crippling tendencies and preventing great damage to others in the family, as well as the central patient.

Psychopathic Personalities and Neurotic Characters [13]

The term "psychopathic personality" is unsatisfactory. Authorities differ on definition, since it is not considered to be a clinical entity. Popularly speaking, psychopathic personality is suggested by overt delinquency and law breaking or markedly unconventional behavior, great emotional instability, and overdetermined sexual irregularity. The disturbance usually begins early in childhood and continues throughout the life of the individual. Psychopaths are typically impulsive, but do not profit from experience. The psychopath is "antisocial," but technically he is instinct ridden or propelled by his urges.

[13] See Chapter III. Dr. van Ophuijsen suggests that the terms "primary conduct" or "behavior disorder" shall always mean "a reaction to environmental influences"; "neurotic character" means a "conduct disturbance of the oedipal type"; while "psychopathic personality" should be restricted to "constitutional inferiority." Jewish Board of Guardians, "Primary Behavior Disorder in Children—Two Case Studies."

In normal growth, love and aggression become fused; in the deviations, love and aggression are split. Primary aggressions may be directed against the self, as in psychotics, or against others, as in delinquents and antisocial persons. The psychopath is usually recognizable by his pathological sexuality, pathological emotionality, or amoral behavior; sometimes he combines all three. The person with a primary behavior disorder and the psychopath are both self-loving, but the former can give up his narcissism for love if there are sufficient compensations; the psychopath will not, because his primary fixation does not permit object love.

It is always hard to distinguish the retarded, inadequate, infantile personality with superficial affect from the true psychopath—and perhaps there is no such person as a true psychopath. There are aggression, absence of (or deeply buried) guilt feeling, and narcissism both in the primary behavior disorder and the psychopath, but the psychopath has a more abnormal emotional life, sexuality, and asocial and amoral behavior. He seems to have a distorted rather than a deficient super-ego. The neurotic delinquent attacks society and is punished in return; the psychopath exploits society and may or may not be caught. Psychopaths, like alcoholics, may have very pleasing personalities, which they may use to involve others deeply in their problems. They manipulate other persons like puppets for their own ends.

In the *Unbearable Bassington,* Saki (H. H. Munro) has drawn a good likeness, in lighter vein, of a psychopath in the petulant, irresponsible, and totally inconsiderate Comus:

His mother could never overlook the fact that out of a dish of five plover's eggs he was certain to take three. The boy was one of those untamable lords of misrule that frolic and chafe themselves through nursery and preparatory and public school days with the utmost allowance of storm, dust and dislocation . . . and come somehow with a laugh through a series of catastrophes that has reduced everyone else to tears.

There is still some dispute as to the etiology of this condition and whether very early deprivation can create the psychopathic personality. The fact that so many psychopathic personalities come from families showing great social pathology makes differential diagnosis difficult. The congenital factors which are assumed to be present may be part of a family tendency, or the family environment may be enough to account for the results. Usually the diagnosis is made by excluding such classifications as primary behavior disorder, defective intelligence, structural disease of the brain, epilepsy, the neuroses, manic-depressive psychosis, and schizophrenia.[14] For the worker it is, perhaps, less necessary to understand the precise genetic formation than to understand how the primitive impulsive tendencies are perpetuated in characteristically aggressive behavior, which presents great difficulty in any uncontrolled environment. The child guidance agency may receive by direct referral, especially from the court, a considerable number of these children, either psychopathic or neurotic characters, of whom the following are fairly typical.

Sarah, fifteen, I.Q. 95, was referred by the court as defiant, disorderly, and given to stealing. The family was known to many social agencies. The father, dull and sickly, but always fond of Sarah, had died when she was thirteen. The mother, very infantile, gave most of her attention to an illegitimate child, to whom she was devoted.

The mothers of many of the psychopaths studied seemed to be weak, overindulgent, and childlike persons; the fathers were often found to be harsh, punitive, or colorless, so that protection and training were not properly given and restraints could not be internalized by the child.

Attempts at psychotherapy with Sarah failed from the start. She was also given two Big Sisters, but made no progress with either. She was unresponsive, demanding, always bragging about boys. She was sent to camp, but was returned home after one week for annoying everyone. She was then put into group therapy, where she was raucous, loud, orally aggressive; she was dropped after five months' trial because she insisted on keeping the center of the stage. She had a chip on her shoulder, used obscene language, and was comfortable only when she could stir up trouble with other children. She wanted to go to Hollywood in order to out-dress, out-star, and humiliate the other girls. She had no feeling of guilt when she

---

[14] Preu, "The Concept of Psychopathic Personality," in *Personality and the Behavior Disorders*, p. 924. See also Brown and Menninger, *The Psychodynamics of Abnormal Behavior*, and Fenichel, *The Psychoanalytic Theory of Neurosis*.

did mean things, being alternately all sweetness and then bitter and cruel. Any good behavior was ingratiating and was preliminary to trying to hurt or to dominate.

Here one sees the inability to relate oneself which makes direct therapy so difficult—a lack of will to conform—and the infantile, amoral character which offers so discouraging a prognosis. The psychopath learns little from experience.

A twelve-year-old boy from a broken, deteriorated home was referred by Children's Court for a series of petty offenses, stealing, and destructiveness. This boy complained of everything, was competitive, unreliable, and undependable. He told fantastic lies about his family. He loved to start things, get other boys into scrapes, and then skip out from under. He was often very clever about getting by. He demanded both gifts and attention, and could often be very charming and disarming before he let the giver down with flippancy and ridicule. He seemed to have little capacity to relate to his cottage parents, and other children; he could relate only intermittently to the worker. Although he showed a little improvement while at the institution, after release he immediately got into trouble again. Subsequently he was inducted into the army.

It is not known whether he managed to get along there or not, but military authority may have controlled him.

A sixteen-year-old girl wanted to run away from her socially pathological family. One brother was in a state school for feebleminded delinquents. There was marked economic and emotional deprivation—harsh and destructive attitudes in the brother and the father. At first she was diagnosed as a normal girl in an acutely destructive situation. She seemed friendly, genial, and outgoing and she had a good intelligence. It soon became evident that this pleasant manner was superficial. She was a jitterbug, an exhibitionist, lazy, insincere, quarrelsome, jealous, and provocative. She exploited her acquaintances until they were exhausted. Sent away to camp, she was impudent, noisy, familiar, flirtatious, and used much bad language. She was determined never to marry. She appeared quite comfortable in her own solutions; she was planning to be a police woman, and by not marrying she "would make all men happy."

She was hyperactive and had murderous thoughts against her family, which she enjoyed; she had little ability to plan realistically or to take any responsibility. She continued to have very confused identifications with both parents, to whom she had strong attachments. She proved to be bizarre in her talk—affected and eager to impress. She was responsive to praise, but did little to earn it. She was content to stay as she was, with no insights and no deepening roots or relationships. She continued her difficult behavior at school, at home, and with the caseworker. She was helped to secure several jobs, but kept none of them. She remained flighty, domineering, and increasingly involved as a prostitute with men in a basically hostile relationship.

Having an illegitimate child is sometimes a good way for a psychopathic girl to involve a man if she can, and it would certainly involve the family in her "disgrace." While some unmarried mothers are the victims of circumstance, others unconsciously make victims of those who cross their path. Psychopaths commonly have very brief relationships with the father of such a baby and a very poor reality sense in planning. Sometimes the mothers casually want to be rid of the baby; sometimes they plan for it as for a pretty doll who will never grow up or call for any responsibility on their part—just something to pet or through which they can take revenge on others. Psychopathic personalities readily vent their aggressions on strangers. Little girls often show their aggression with their dolls, boys on dogs and other animals. Grown up, they take it out on their children.

Psychopaths, because of their lack of super-ego, distorted and deficient guilt feelings, poor capacity for insight, and poor reality sense, are hard to treat. Therapy is especially difficult because of their lack of ability to form close human ties. All persons look alike to the psychopath—merely as hindrances to his purposes or else as objects for exploitation. If there is basic anxiety, it is so deeply repressed that for all practical purposes one cannot get at it. However, even if psychopaths are unpromising, they have various degrees of accessibility, since the degree of rigidity of personality differs, and some seem able to relate to a limited extent, although they have always a tendency to try to dictate the conditions of treatment.

A restraining institutional setting is often a great help. A child may say: "If only you will *keep* me from doing so and so." He feels more secure if there are definite rules. He needs a nonpunishing authority from without, as he has none within. Restraints on his aggressiveness are helpful, but aggressiveness against him is paid back manyfold. If the worker is strong, friendly, definite, concrete, and accepting, the psychopath will sometimes become dependent and compliant, especially if a steadying environment can be maintained. The psychopath is not easily bound in treatment, but "bounces" away. Any lasting change occurs only if inner pressures are reduced. Guilt, if it exists, is very deeply buried or distorted. Social workers have found that money can serve the same purpose with a psychopath that it serves with a child, satisfying what Anna Freud calls "stomach love," but such bribes do not settle anything. The psychopath relates only as the therapist feeds his narcissism. Giving things to a psychopath may be the only language he can understand. Because of the client's urgency to disturb other people's lives, the therapist may soon get "fed up" and terminate the interviews, instead of using a slender thread of relationship to help the psychopath face his own responsibility for his troubles. If his ego thereby becomes strong enough to develop a symptom which disturbs him, he may, though he probably will not, accept treatment. However, there have been some fairly successful cases, and when success does occur one may either congratulate oneself on one's patience or assume that the diagnosis was wrong. It is best to treat psychopaths when they are young, because once the psychopath is a parent, little can be done except to place his offspring. Although one should like children if one is to work with them at all, it is particularly important that these "bad" children shall appeal to the worker, or he can help them very little.

The neurotic character [15] (this term also being unsatisfactory), although having many features in common with the psychopath, is less primitive. In the normal person the impulses are adjusted to reality, repressed and sublimated; in the neurotic character the impulses, fixated at childhood levels, are carried out in such a way as to ensure

[15] L. G. Lowrey speaks of psychopaths and neurotic characters as "abnormal personality types which have no specific relationship to any of the psychoses or neuroses." They suffer from "blind, instinctive, irresistible impulses, with an especial propensity to destroy."—*Psychiatry for Social Workers*, p. 240.

punishment. The oedipal situation is not solved, and the person grows into adulthood with an imperfect sense of restraining reality and defective inhibitions. Whereas the neurotic solves his conflict by exhibiting symptoms, the neurotic character solves his in action. He behaves as if perpetually trying to satisfy childish needs. He can stand little tension; he reacts to frustrations with temper, or sullenness, or attack, or rebellion. The neurotic character suffers from unconscious guilt, inferiority feelings, depressions, and self-damaging activities. Even though his actions harm others, he continues to harm himself in some way, also. His neurotic needs are usually taken care of by attacks on society, which is ready to punish him. Perhaps there is no personality entirely without guilt, but in this respect the neurotic character stands midway between the psychopath and the psychoneurotic. In general, psychopaths are more aggressive and disruptive than are neurotic characters, who are poorly motivated, confused, poorly integrated, and often in need of reinforcement from "the gang" in order to commit their dissocial acts.[16] The psychological content of conflict (oedipal material) seems to be the same in the psychoneurotic and the neurotic character, but the satisfaction of instinctual desires is more important to the neurotic character than is adaptation to reality or the forming of object relationships. The extent of neurotic conflict varies as does the degree of development of the super-ego, so that few generalizations as to treatment can be given. Much more clinical study of the role of authority and discipline and of what Redl calls psychologically produced "group defenses" is indicated. Therapeutically supportive and constructively educational measures, both inside and outside the institution, seem to promise most at present, unless a high degree of anxiety should offer an avenue for deeper treatment. The essence of these distinctions in all forms of behavior disorder lies in the difference in motivation. The psychopath, like the person with primary behavior disorder, preoedipal type, does not act out because of unconscious conflict, but because of his need to exploit the environment in his own way. Whenever the behavior is a symptom of unconscious conflict the

[16] Redl, Fritz, "The Psychology of Gang Formation and the Treatment of Juvenile Delinquents," in *The Psychoanalytic Study of the Child*, p. 367.

client is likely to be more accessible than if there is a primary constellation or a constitutional defect.

Recapitulation

All organic conditions of a pathological nature react strongly to emotional disturbances and present great difficulties in diagnostic thinking. For cases of organic disease and psychosis the safest therapy lies in psychiatric hands. Social treatment aims to supply as good an environment as possible—one which will not arouse anxiety or threaten the client's slender defenses. For psychotics, supplementary direct psychotherapy, when indicated, generally tends to aid repression of the impulses by supporting the ego functions. Even though the ego is circumscribed and turned inwards, there is likely to be some healthy part to which a sustaining relationship can be addressed, thereby increasing self-confidence and self-esteem.

Social programs for crippled and handicapped children, for any of the disabling diseases of childhood, are beginning to take into account psychosocial factors and the need for direct psychotherapy, as well as medical, social, and educational therapies. For all physically and mentally ill children the closest kind of medical-social cooperation is necessary. Severe psychoneuroses do not seem amenable to transference forms of therapy, and deeper treatment is, in general, indicated (except that supportive and appropriate social therapies should be supplied if needed).

While exceedingly good results have been attained with some mental defectives, direct therapy is so costly, even when the client has good intelligence, that habit training and educational social methods usually seem more practical. Dull children, however, are often very sensitive and can be as much helped by the therapeutic approach as can any other type of child. One should not, however, expect quick results. Psychopaths and neurotic characters who "dramatize" their "primitive impulses" and develop chronically deviated and pathological social behavior offer very limited opportunities for psychotherapy today except when within a controlled environment. As with other severe disorders, a few cases are taken, chiefly for study, and then all the resources of the clinical team are used. Early diagnosis, screening, and controlled differential treatment are indispensable. Careful review by medical and psychiatric consultants is indispensable. The practical question is what program of prevention the community is willing and able to afford.

Chapter VI

DIRECT TREATMENT IN THE
THERAPEUTIC PROCESS

Psychotherapy in child guidance is a fusion of psychoanalytically oriented psychiatry and social therapies.[1] The treatment plan, or design, derives from an understanding of the clinical diagnostic process, and from a flexible evaluation of the functioning of the total personality. In the broad field of social service a great deal of direct gratification of real needs is given with the intent of subsistence and welfare, any therapeutic effects being incidental. In child guidance, however, practical and emotional gratifications subserve the main therapeutic intent, becoming tools or phases in a therapeutic process. Because psychotherapy deals with the faculties of thought and feeling and with their integration in character and behavior, learning through perception and self-awareness is important. But learning takes place only under certain conditions favorable for self-education and therefore for change. Psychotherapy, in its narrower sense, begins only after basic needs are met and when the clients have physical and mental capacity to use it. The deteriorated home, like the badly deteriorated personality, must be treated by social, medical, or institutional measures, the ultimate solution lying only in prevention.

Aims and Methods of Psychotherapy

Psychotherapy is invoked when there are distorted needs, when the deprivations or frustrations occurring in the gratification of "real" needs have created an emotional illness or character deviation, the etiological basis of which has been described in earlier chapters. Psychotherapy offers experience which can change the patterns and release energies and capacities for change and growth. Psychotherapy

---

[1] In this chapter the stress is on the two-person relationship, often called "direct treatment." See also Chapter VII.

cannot supply "real" parental relationships; it is a special technique applied *within* the living experience, but not as a substitute for it. It aims to strengthen the person's ability to deal with real life situations, helping him to meet his own basic needs, both economic and affectional. Psychotherapy is designed to affect the total functioning of the personality.[2] According to Dr. Nathan Ackerman, it means a person to person relationship, "with progressive exposure and dissolution of the pathological patterns of defense." It attempts to relieve anxiety at the roots. It involves fully the use of transference and the handling of resistance mechanisms. "Concealed fears, hates, and blunted pleasures must be exposed," and the true self be given the opportunity to exert itself. The patient must be sufficiently freed from fears to participate in satisfying new experiences. The corollary is that in child guidance satisfying and constructive opportunities for new experiences in the family and in society must be made available, and the whole process must be therapeutically conditioned.

Psychotherapy in casework is always interpersonal—in family and child guidance it always concerns itself with the family constellation, not merely as environment for the "patient." Instead, there is normally more than one "patient." Diagnosis is always dual. There must be a clinical diagnosis whenever there is a person undergoing treatment, whether child or adult, and there must be a diagnosis, or, perhaps more accurately, an evaluation, of the family constellation— how it is balanced, how it interacts, on what basis it manages to function as a family. In the child patient the problem is diffused throughout the personality, and balance among conflicting forces is not stable; in the parent the disturbance may be more or less diffused, yet it is usually localized and defined in regard to the child brought for treatment. The client must recognize that the child is a problem, or has a problem, in order to come at all, or at least to continue to come. The client may, with deeper insight, place the problem at the level of his own relationships, thus feeling or being helped to feel his self-involvement as a *parent*. The client then may come to feel, under

[2] Ackerman, "Psychotherapy and 'Giving Love,' " *Psychiatry*, VII (May, 1944), 129–138, and "What Constitutes Intensive Psychotherapy in a Child Guidance Set Up?" *American Journal of Orthopsychiatry*, XV (October, 1945), 711–720, and other papers.

treatment, his self-involvement as a *person,* with inner diffused difficulties. If so, the case worker may carry on appropriate therapy, or may refer the more deeply disturbed adults to a psychoanalyst. For the child, the line is less easy to draw, more of the unconscious usually being brought into the therapeutic process and ego building and sublimation goals being more inclusive. In direct therapy are used, in various combinations, help in: (*a*) expressing unconscious drives; (*b*) minimizing the effect of the repressive super-ego or building a super-ego (depending upon whether the problem is more one of anxiety or acting out); (*c*) adapting to the concepts of reality, both as represented by the person of the therapist and the outer world. Whenever drives are released the child must also be helped to measure himself in a real world, or confusion will result.

In many aspects of social casework the client must involve himself in the treatment process only far enough to effect a change *for* himself; in psychotherapy the self-involvement is deep enough to effect a change *in* oneself. In less intensive forms of "counseling" rational discussion may result in a client's improvement because he understands better the factors in his situation and has gained confidence in himself. For more disturbed persons such a procedure is inadequate. In any psychotherapy there must be enough potential ego strength in the client either to change or to sustain adaptive mechanisms constructively.

The Therapeutic Attitude

The central dynamic in all psychotherapy may be regarded as permissiveness—a special kind of "love" called "acceptance." Ordinarily parents give their children an acceptance far greater than will be given them in the outside world. They love and admire their children, who thrive in this culture of praise, affection, and sustaining approval —in good times and bad. Problem children have almost always been deprived of this experience, partially or completely. The child's experience with the therapist, therefore, may be his first exposure to the sort of deep acceptance that he has lacked hitherto. The therapist is not a parent or a substitute parent, yet he plays a "parental" role. He must be a good friend, yet not a friend in the ordinary social sense.

The therapist is never the real love object, though the patient, especially the child, so regards him during the period of treatment.

Life is full of all sorts of accidental relationships, which run from the most trivial to the most profound. A therapeutic relationship is different from other human relationships in that its purpose is healing. True, there may be some reciprocity in it—the therapist may benefit indirectly or incidentally, but the main characteristic is that there must be one in the experience who wishes to be helped—that is, a patient, or client, and one who wishes to help. The therapist uses himself as the chief dynamic in treatment. It is not true to say that "he offers nothing except himself," since in social work he usually does supplement direct treatment with practical services and environmental aids, as indicated, but the healing element in the main lies in the relationship which enables the client to use better the resources within himself and his environment. The therapist gives of his understanding, of his own ego strength, and even of his own super-ego. The therapist uses his whole self as consciously as possible; the patient will use his whole self, much of the time demandingly and naïvely, but probably with increasing insight. It is only after the therapist has learned to use himself wisely that he can wisely use other tools. The therapeutic attitude permits the client to learn that he has nothing to fear. Here he may talk about forbidden matters and here find the courage to make new efforts on his own behalf.

The "love" of the therapist consists of warmth, concern, therapeutic understanding, interest in helping the person to get well. This is a clinical or professional development of a natural quality. The therapist does not give love in the ordinary sense, just as he must not disapprove of or dislike what the client is, says, or does. His diagnostic sense must guide him in expressing and timing his efforts to gratify and to support the patient. Consistency, neutrality, and firmness, as well as warmth, enter into the therapeutic relationship. Giving love is in itself not enough—its assimilation by the client must be feasible.[3] The empathy which the therapist feels toward the client presumably is at a mature level of object relationship. He is able to "identify"

[3] Ackerman, "Psychotherapy and 'Giving Love,' " *Psychiatry*, VII (May, 1944), 129–138.

because he has passed through the same emotional development and is now willing consciously to enter and to share in the client's life experience. Willingness to identify with the person and to enter with him into the realm of his feelings must be distinguished from countertransference. The social worker, like any other therapist, has to be aware of the possibility of countertransference in himself, that is, irrationally liking or disliking, the client, and must guard himself against this and control his emotional reactions in the interest of the patient.

The Transference Relationship

Whereas in all social casework an accepting and tolerant attitude is essential, much, perhaps most, help, service, or treatment is carried on with relatively mature persons caught in some tangle of external events or circumstance or having some physical disability which interferes with their social functioning. Skilled use of relationship in such cases is, of course, still the medium of help—the handling of the relationship is what characteristically gives the professional quality to any social service, but the phenomena of transference may be minor or, for all practical purposes, absent. In other words, the social worker conducts many interviews in which the client uses the relationship sensibly and rationally for the purpose of changing his circumstances or possibly his ideas, rather than with the intention of changing *himself*. For the less mature and self-directing person if any real change of attitude or behavior reaction is contemplated, some use of transference must be assumed. A certain amount of the unconscious within the transference must be expressed and assimilated in new ways for change to take place. The weaker the ego the stronger the transference which must be built up for new identifications to be formed.

Depending upon the type of person, the kind of problem to be solved, the techniques and controls used, transference may or may not strongly enter in. Mature egos which deal successfully with life's problems do not use relationship in this way, because they have outgrown the need of it. Only if they are stricken with severe illness, shocked, or otherwise in a period of disorganization, do they show significant transference reactions. Those who are whole do not need a physician, only those who are sick; and those who are whole do not use a relationship in the same way as those who are less whole. Many persons with a warped character structure find it very difficult to use any object relationship whatever. But in general it can be said that unless and until there are transference phenomena a therapeutic situation is not likely to exist. Various techniques used to control the depth of transference should be distinguished from the phenomenon itself, the dynamics of which must be understood.[4]

There has been much confusion in the use of the term "transference." Parental and sibling relationships and attitudes are carried over and projected quite unconsciously upon school teachers, employers, and friends. One might say the more mature the person, the more "real" and less displaced are his relationships. Characteristic relationship patterns are composites of all the significant relationships in one's life, although the earliest are the most strongly determining. In the strictest sense, transference means the displacement of irrational and inappropriate attitudes derived elsewhere upon the therapist.[5] It is because the therapist is in a position to help him that the client tends to transfer his early or childish feelings to such a person, and to reenact emotional experiences with previously significant figures. In classical psychoanalysis the type of patient likely to seek help, the technical procedure used, and other factors give the transference neurosis a special significance. Modifications of it take place in other types of therapy. In psychotherapy motivation for change is rooted largely in the transference relationship, within which release of feeling, self-awareness, reality testing, and gradual emancipation can take place.

In child guidance the problem is by hypothesis already emotionally charged so that a transference relationship of some intensity is essential. The therapeutic situation, then, is one in which the client who more or less consciously wants help, feels a readiness to accept

---

[4] Ross and Johnson, "The Growing Science of Case Work," *Journal of Social Case Work*, XXVII (November, 1946), 273.

[5] Alexander and French, *Psychoanalytic Therapy*, p. 73: "Transference is the neurotic repetition with relation to the analyst of a stereotyped, unsuitable behavior pattern based on the patient's past."

help when he finds someone who cares enough to help him. From this point on, a state of transference exists through which everything the client says or does is affected. This applies both to the parent and to the child—although for the child, transference phenomena are different, since he is in the process of growing up and the real parents are still actively operating in his situation.[6]

In the therapeutic process here described the worker, by assuming an accepting, tolerant, friendly, and permissive attitude, induces a basic and, in the main, "positive" transference within which currents of negative, positive and mixed feelings may run, but the basic positive transference holds throughout the period of treatment. This creates an atmosphere favorable to the laying aside of defenses, and to being helped to lay aside defenses, and is the medium for learning new habits of thought and feeling. If the transference maintained is largely negative, it is likely that the client will break away.

In psychoanalysis the identity of the therapist is purposefully kept vague so that the patient can use the therapist fully according to his own inner needs, thus permitting a wide range of displacements. The problem of the sex of the worker in less intensive psychotherapy remains to be studied. While women workers may sometimes assume for the child paternal characteristics and men workers, maternal characteristics, it seems probable that the dominant transference to a woman worker remains typically that of the mother, and to a male worker, the father, transference. The fact that the client who is immature and dependent develops transference attitudes, does not mean that he may not also display "real" attitudes of liking or disliking, warranted affection or suspicion or resentment, but usually in treatment the emergence of "sensible" feelings, attuned to realistic appraisal of the worker, is part of getting well, just as sensible feelings toward the parents are part of growing up. The transference is utilized to enable the client to elaborate his feelings toward others. It is the medium through which the older person can best recall and the child act out his feelings; it is the medium for getting reliable history; the emotional climate for acts of practical service; the means of release and catharsis; the basis for insight and reeducation, and as a bridge

[6] See Chapter VIII for fuller discussion of this.

to other relationships and sublimations. Or, put another way, the relationship permits the client to reveal himself, discharge his tensions, unleash his emotions, bring fears and aggression to the surface, and through this experience to be helped to new perceptions of himself and his world of reality. In addition, transference is used for emotional support when the ego is weak, when the defensive structure should be maintained, when there are rigid personality structures, deeply fixed childish traits, severe illness—mental or physical—or old age, or very deficient intelligence. In supportive therapy the intent is less to effect change in the personality than to sustain through relationship and to reduce environmental pressures in order to stabilize the personality.[7] It is a peculiarity of the transference phenomenon that a person seems able to talk about things which he does not ordinarily talk about and to express things in play usually not so fully expressed. One wants the child to be able to talk out and act out as freely as he would have done were he actually a little child in the presence of a wise and loving parent. As treatment progresses, the center of gravity shifts to a greater and more confident use of the self by the client.

An interesting aspect of the transference phenomenon in social work should be noted. It has long been observed that persons interviewed at "intake" by one person may break off when assigned to a second worker, no matter how carefully the change was explained in advance. It is agreed that under certain transference conditions it would be better, if possible, to let the first worker continue. It is less often, however, remarked that some persons seem to pass from one worker to another surprisingly well. After the initial disappointment has been ventilated and, if the new worker accepts the client without irritation (countertransference), the client then settles down more securely than ever. It is common for him to remark that Mrs. B., who may be tall, dark, and heavy, looks exactly like his former worker, Mrs. A., who was fair, short, and slight, and he may be sustained more than ever by finding that the therapeutic attitude in which he was just beginning to have faith really exists. Under what conditions the transference is weakened, and when reinforced, deserves careful

[7] In psychotics, transference has certain modifications.

study. That the basic positive transference can spread constructively beyond the two-dimensional relationship seems probable.

Dynamics of Change

The center of the therapeutic process lies in the transference relationship, but we have yet to show more precisely in what way it is involved in change. To understand what happens in therapy one must recall what happens to the child.[8] In the little child satisfactions are magically brought about by the parents. In the gradual socialization of the child as he grows out of his narcissism, the parents, who are too powerful to fight, become the perfect figures, and the child overcomes his insecurity by trying to become like them. The child grows away from a magical sense of his environment to increased ability to manage his environment, and in contact with parental and other reality the primitive urges are gradually repressed. Imitation of the parents becomes psychological "identification" in a social and ethical, instead of a physical, sense. With the successful incorporation of super-ego, the child is emotionally more detached from the parent, since he can now be guided by his own increasingly reasonable feelings of right and wrong, as based on experience with the outer world. This identification with parental maturity in general, and specifically with the parent of the same sex, is partially achieved during the oedipal phases and repeated and finally stabilized during adolescence. In normal development, in which identification becomes possible because of the parent's sustaining love and wise prohibition, the child is integrated within himself and able to establish object relationships with others. In less normal development, capacity to relate is dependent, ambivalent or, at its poorest level, narcissistic and exploiting or infantile.

In therapy the stages of constructive identification have still to be reached by the client and are now achieved in the experience itself. The transference permits the child "to regress" to the earlier levels of development (that is, as soon as he is accepted he goes back to the level where he had satisfaction before), and so to make a fresh start on the problem of constructive identification with the therapist. It

[8] See Chapter II.

must not be thought that the child's whole personality is fixated at these earliest levels, but some of it is, or at least some of it is still vacillating in its identifications. In order to establish a positive relationship, a person, whether child or adult, must have experienced such a relationship at some time in his life so that he has a need of it. The child reproduces or repeats his emotional reactions of an earlier age—all the conflicts he has had in the past, either negative or too positive feelings which have gone beyond the permitted limits. The fact that the therapist does not make a countertransference disarms the child. The child does not achieve anything by reenacting of the patterns. Those patterns are affected by the permissive, tolerant attitude of the therapist, and so the child is forced into a new attitude, which is free from distortions, and he can draw on his own potential strengths for insight and change.

Regression should be understood, not as a falling back to, but as a reactivation of an earlier level of functioning. The most usual cause for regression is frustration. The client who comes to us already having met with excessive frustration in life experience has made a partial regression which is not acceptable within his normal environment. The basic positive transference which appears to be on the early (preoedipal) level before the conflict situations and ambivalence of the next growth period have become activated, makes it possible for the child to express primitive feelings and images. In accepting the regressive behavior and thoughts the worker is careful not to regress with the client through countertransference. Since one does not get angry, or give in, or judge him, this pattern gives the child little satisfaction, and he is stimulated to give it up and try something different. Thus, energies are freed which can be applied in new ways. The child may be wavering in his development among neurotic traits, symptoms, and character disorders, but he cannot be stopped abruptly by a magic formula. The therapist moves along with him slowly as the good parent does in real life, modifying the patterns which make for limitation on his growth. Therapy allows the neurotic child's energies to flow away from the super-ego and thus be available for sublimation. Therapy helps the child with a behavior disorder to condense and repress his aggression in the service of the newly achieved conscience. Therapy is aided by the fact that the organism has a natural tendency to move towards higher levels of integration.[9] "The therapeutic rule," according to Dr. van Ophuijsen, "is that the therapist must never interfere with the tendency to find a new departure." The child is convinced, in therapy, not that he is always bad or that he must be always good, but that he can be accepted when he is bad as well as when he is good. The courage to change comes from identification with the therapist, which brings with it enhanced self-esteem and self-valuation. The child does not feel entirely unloved and unlovable, but until now he did not believe that he had the power to change. Or perhaps we should say that the behavior disorder does not know that he wants to and the neurotic does not believe that he can. While there must be enough discomfort or tension to make the person want to be well, it is when the tension is discharged or disappears within the transference that the condition is favorable for learning through new identifications. True, the child does not want to get into trouble, or does not want the discomfort from which he suffers or the consequences of his acts, if dissocial, but all this is overshadowed by the unspoken wish to identify. This seems to be a component of our deepest drives. Thus the patient develops some of the strengths out of which socially adjustive habits and attitudes may be acquired.

Whenever less energy is needed by the ego to repress the continually upsurging impulses, the ego has more power to repress and the symptoms, if not entirely removed, are less pronounced. The person, as we say colloquially, is now able to live with himself and able, therefore, to function more successfully in reality. The correction of faulty developmental experience is made more effective if the life situation can also be modified. Although a more complete assimilation takes places in a child patient who is accessible to therapy, the essential dynamics of change are much the same in the adult. The child has less to take back or relive and farther to go.

[9] See Mowrer and Kluckhorn, "Dynamic Theory of Personality," in *Personality and the Behavior Disorders*, p. 67. See also Hartmann and Kris, "The Genetic Approach in Psycho-Analysis," in *The Yearbook of Psychoanalysis*, pp. 1–22.

Resistance

Not all objection, opposition, or stubbornness is "resistance." The normal person has a structure of essential defenses which he relies on in meeting strangers, ideas he doesn't agree with, and situations which he does not like. Technically speaking, by "resistance" is meant defenses against *treatment*—the client may not want to be treated for any number of good as well as many poor reasons, or refuse to permit a child who needs treatment to have it. Resistance therefore must be recognized and appropriately handled. Early resistance, at intake for instance, should be distinguished from resistance which arises in transference. In the early stages of treatment there may be reluctance which covers some sort of fear of the unknown, association with unpleasant similar experiences, or more basic forms of anxiety. Although there are no formulas for handling resistance, quick recognition of its appearance, friendly warm interest, explanation of the agency's procedures, the bringing out of specific fears, telling the client why he is being seen, accepting the person and encouraging him to continue his visits, offering concrete services and definite appointments, promptness and consideration all play a part in reducing the degree of such resistance in persons who are at all accessible. In addition, resistance may be commented on when the worker is sure of his ground. But defenses should not be indiscriminately attacked. Initial resistance is handled overtly only if it is really blocking the client from going on and the friendly common-sense methods of making a person feel secure and at ease do not work.

The client may show resistance in a number of ways—by refusing to give history, or by pouring out so much data that it overwhelms the worker, or by insisting after a brief period of treatment that the child is well or that things are going better so that there is nothing to talk about, or by actually refusing to come again or to let the child come again. Such resistance usually has to be handled frankly. It is sometimes wise to show very resistive parents that they are not ready to accept help. This may sometimes result in a more favorable reapplication in the future. The same thing may be done occasionally, with good results, for a child. Efforts at conscious cooperation should be accredited as well as unconscious opposition recognized. Extremely harsh and rigid parents who will neither accept treatment for themselves nor their child present, with rare exceptions, a closed door. Some anxiety or self-distrust is essential.

To stay away too long gives the child a chance to organize his defenses. To the obstinate child everything appears coercive. The therapist does not coerce, but explains to the child why he should come for treatment. The child with a primary behavior disorder doesn't want to be helped with his "problem," but he usually does want to be helped with the *consequences* of his acts. "Perhaps I'll come every two weeks." "No, I think you should come every week if I am to help you." Bargaining is as bad as appeasing in therapy. Often a child will make a blanket denial that the problem exists—"Everything is fine." Conscious deception must usually be met good humoredly, but firmly, or the child will think the therapist is stupid—that he fails to understand.

"Resistance" shows itself as an interruption of the client's expressing himself. The therapist has represented the permissive person. Suddenly the client feels that he is nonpermissive and is therefore inhibited. Resistance *automatically* develops as soon as the transference is established, when the defenses are laid aside and the therapist approaches the center of emotional conflict. The person then fears the release of his own impulses toward the therapist, as well as loss of the therapist's tolerant attitude, in which he cannot yet fully believe. He fears that the therapist will now frustrate and reject him. His impulses toward the parental image, which have undergone repression, are reactivated. (Permanent repression of the oedipal conflict in the psychoneurotic is very difficult anyway.) Early preoedipal impulses find an outlet through weak spots in his superego armor or now threaten to do so. He stops himself as though the therapist himself were prohibiting him. He no longer associates or plays or talks freely. The child may discontinue his modeling or destroy it or burst into silly talk. There is a definite disturbance of the flow between therapist and child. What has been inhibited is the expression of feeling—hostility or love or ambivalence—toward the therapist. One has to make clear to him that he is repeating an old pattern. Only if this pattern can be broken up can the energies be set free. Giving up a symptom is difficult, because it means giving up the relationship with the therapist.

Resistance should not be confused with negative transference. The client inevitably has positive, negative, and mixed feelings toward the therapist, but these in themselves are not resistance. We have said elsewhere that as long as a person does come for treatment and does talk, his relationship to the therapist is not commented upon; but if he shows hostile and erotic feelings openly, the therapist does have to comment. If the hostility persists, the therapist will lose his patient anyway, so he may, in a quiet way, verbalize the negative feeling. The worker must not confuse the very silent, inhibited child who does have a positive relationship—including the worker silently in his play, but making progress all the same—with the child who has a negative transference. Neither should this be confused with resistance. Children may play hour after hour as a means of gratification. They may have a positive feeling toward the worker; they enjoy the security of the play, but the play itself which excludes the worker from participation, is a form of resistance. Likewise, older children choose games which have a low emotional content, which, while much enjoyed by the child, may be a form of resistance. On the other hand, aggressive play in which the worker is victim and enemy, should not be confused with resistance. This may be negative transference, which tends to turn into positive as the play therapy proceeds. When play is actively or passively used as resistance, the worker may have to remind the child that he does not come to him for fun, but to be helped. Inexperienced workers sometimes, because of their own tension, bombard a quiet child with questions, when no real resistance is involved.

Release Techniques

Living out feelings in motor and verbal expression is natural for young children, and discussion of feelings in play or in the interview tends toward gradual desensitization. The inexperienced worker may permit release too quickly, thus arousing anxiety. Children may be afraid of finger painting or of any overt encouragement by the therapist of activity.[10] The worker does not often dig down to the deepest roots of the anxiety, especially in adults, but may release a great deal bit by bit. Clinical factors must be recognized, since for the person with a behavior disorder the situation may have to be molded before the anxiety reaction can be reached, and in the case of the neurotic it is necessary to move through the anxiety to the hidden aggression. Desensitization takes place slowly when the client, as he becomes free enough and strong enough in the transference to bring disturbing feelings out, moves ahead to discuss life experiences in terms of more anxiety arousing material. In situational conflicts this release of feeling may help toward spontaneous recovery. This is true of young children, especially if the environment is at the same time therapeutically modified.

That there are limits to release catharsis is well known, even though some improvement is often derived merely from talking painful things out; but a dynamic process is involved in helping the client to reveal himself constructively. The worker must be careful to arouse only as much anxiety as can be handled in the weekly interviews.[11] Caseworkers deal with anxiety, not in its symbolic expressions, such as dreams and fantasies, but in immediate reality. It can then be channelized and drained off safely within the transference. There, if not too great for the individual's capacity, defenses may be lessened and anxiety diminished. If the client has been gradually exposing feelings and patterns, the situation is pretty safe. Knowing the client is the best safeguard—what he has done with insight before, and what has been his reaction to treatment.

In phases of simple release in play the role of the therapist may be quite minimal or, at any rate, passive, but in most guidance cases in which the disturbance is pervasive, showing itself through many symptoms, simple release is not enough. In play [12] the impulses are actually discharged, so that the experience is in an even more real sense a living out of the conflict. The reduction of the intensity of conflict makes it possible to learn instead of being fixated in old frus-

[10] See illustrations on p. 94.

[11] The weekly appointment schedule need not be rigidly adhered to. More or less frequent contact may be indicated.

[12] See next chapters for discussion of play.

trations. For young children, or inhibited children who have not attained the usual levels of body mastery and skills, motor release in itself is of therapeutic importance. Nursery schools and group therapy are natural mediums for this, but the individual play interview may also be used with good effect.

To permit aggressive behavior does not imply approval, and to appease is also, in a sense, passively to condone. Neutrality and passive resistance to extreme aggression are therapeutically wiser. One must remember that the child with a behavior disorder often fears attack of some sort by the therapist and tries to ward off, provoke, and intimidate. A child who has expressed violent aggression toward the worker attempts to crawl out on the window sill. He asks whether the worker wants bad people to be hurt. The worker says with a smile that she will stop bad people, but not hurt them. The child is relieved and crawls back into the room again. Sometimes it is hard to distinguish the child's fears of his own aggression from those projected onto the environment. Every worker will have had the experience of the child who climbs onto her lap, and then suddenly strikes or bites her. Tenderness may prove too much for the unaccustomed child, and anxiety mounts; he must do something to make the worker reject him.[13] At first the child will circle around, and only as the relationship takes hold does he direct the aggression at the worker. Here countertransference, unless the worker is on his guard, is likely to throw the whole relationship out of gear. Effective catharsis must go along with integration and insight. If the child is acting out his violence elsewhere, his violent expressions with the therapist are not cathartic.

"Acting things out" brings the unconscious trends nearer to the surface, where they can be discussed, but gauging the limits which may be permitted in aggression is always difficult. Violent acting out must be checked at certain points or the child will be made confused, cynical, or anxious. Timing and "dosage" are important. Certain very impulsive, aggressive children need to be upheld and strengthened in their fight against their outbursts, or panic will result. It is a mistake to imagine that therapy offers no restraining influences, since

[13] See case of Beulah on pp. 190 *et seq.*

nothing in life corresponds to such an experience. Like the good parent, the worker must occasionally restrain, but as with the good parent occasion for restraint should not have to arise too frequently, and the authoritative restraint is never associated with retaliation or punishment, but with concern for the individual and his growth. Since the therapist wishes to impose as little as possible, there are few things in the office which must be withheld or may not be treated roughly. Once limitation is imposed, it should be discussed simply and frankly with the client in realistic terms. In one respect the child must be limited—usually by gentle physical control or verbal prohibition—he must be prevented from hurting the therapist. As the relationship grows, the aggression is usually focused on the worker. Since he is not allowed to hurt the worker, he may strike out blindly and, not receiving the retaliation he expected, he is bewildered. Here his patterns can be pointed out to him with the intention of helping him to translate them into verbal aggression. The use of substitute goals for aggressive impulses are not likely alone to be effective, unless patterns of aggression are discussed.

Reeducation, Self-awareness, and Adaptation to Reality

Just as the friendly, permissive, and accepting attitude of the worker allows the client to talk and act freely without fear or censure, so it is the accepting attitude which permits the client to turn his attention inward and learn about himself. The first aim of therapy is to give enough emotional support to let the thoughts and feelings emerge. These must be expressed before they can be commented on, and they can be helpfully pointed out only because of the phenomenon of transference. In the earlier days of child guidance, giving advice to parents was found to be of little use. This was accepted intellectually with poor therapeutic result unless the defenses had been gradually lessened so that the interpretation could be absorbed emotionally. Learning is a complicated process, especially emotional learning. If unwise parental teaching occasions the need for therapy, therapy itself involves a special sort of reeducational process leading to emotional insight.

Unless the child can be confronted with his own behavior and grasp the meaning of it, he does not break out of the vicious circle. The great unifying principle in all learning, according to Mowrer,[14] is that "all behavior is motivated and that all learning involves reward." The child can afford to learn—that is, accept education and training from the loving parents who give rewards and security. If fear of loss of love is the primary condition for the development of a conscience, hope of satisfaction is the primary condition of learning a new habit. The patient's "readiness for emotion," as Freud described it, is combined in transference into a readiness for learning about oneself, or self-awareness. Casework therapy does not aim to bring to consciousness in the adult deeply repressed tendencies, that is, infantile memories and aims, but does help the adult client recover sufficient early familial and parental memories and to connect these with his or her present handling of the child. Insight gained, therefore, sets in motion an integrative process in which the ego may have more control of the impulses. A pattern of social behavior, such as suspicion, cruelty, domination, exploitation, evasion, or jealousy, *always* emerges and is obvious to one who is trained to perceive it. When sure, because of repetition of the pattern, the therapist helps the person also to notice it. The quality of frustration or suspicion or dependency can be more or less consciously experienced by the client and defined with the help of the therapist. That this awareness may be, in part, intellectual need not disturb us, since the fact that it is gained in an emotional medium seems to make it penetrate. Conscious insight which does not necessarily cure may considerably relieve. The transference is absolutely fundamental for achieving insight, which emerges out of the clash between the client's distorted perceptions of relationship and the truer picture formed during his experience with an understanding person.

The various experiences which the client repeats over and over again will provide a single psychological constellation or trend—as for instance, feeling timid or rejected in all sorts of situations. The trouble is always something the client is *not* aware of. Story after story repeated by a mother showing how well she had managed her

---

[14] Mowrer and Kluckhorn, "Dynamic Theory of Personality," in *Personality and the Behavior Disorders*, p. 79.

boy finally brought the query from the caseworker, "But why are you so afraid to manage him?" The mother was surprised, since this was the truth. She had really been afraid of her own inadequacy since her son was a baby, but this had not been what she was consciously telling the worker. The infantile basis of her inadequacy would probably never be touched by the caseworker. The interpretation would stay on the level of helping her face her feelings of inadequacy, instead of continuing to rationalize about them. If one cannot catch the trend, the client will feel that the therapist doesn't "get him." If one catches the trend and the client also can see it, he may do something about it himself. When the client comes in vague and indefinite, it is sometimes easier to catch the trend than when he comes in organized to talk or when one tries too hard to focus. A child's random play often reveals the mood better than when he is determined to play this or that—a typical defense.

For the adult, pointing out patterns of behavior means both linking present to present and linking present to past. For children, it is largely linking present to present, for example, school and family, behavior in the office and behavior at home, except as the permitted regression in play lets the child work through earlier traumatized situations. It is usually best not to compare what he is doing in the office with what goes on at home until treatment is well established and he is beginning to make some connections himself. One rarely asks a child why he behaved as he did or says that we are going to help him find out why he stutters or has enuresis. He does not want to know why, but he may want to get over it or avoid the consequences. The comment is directed toward fears, anger, disturbance, inability to play, and so on, as the behavior emerges. Whenever there is a drop in tension through playing and acting out, the time is favorable for "adjustive" learning.

With young children the play interview is a combination of release and gratification on a level always corresponding to age and reality situations, insight taking place often on an intuitive, nonverbal level. Patterns may or may not be pointed out. Older children, for whom play may be used as a phase in treatment, are encouraged to talk as well as act out and to use words so far as possible as a means of release and communication. Each step in learning means substituting a new gratification for an old one. The incentive lies in the fact that the older habits have not proved comfortable. Every interview is a period of trial living. Tension is reduced by the repeated verbalization of old pain-inciting material. The therapist remains the lenient, participating observer, or super-ego. The child knows that here only he can do what he wants to do. This does not mean that he can smash things at home; this is made clear. The older child usually understands quite well the relationship between fantasy or play and his real attitudes. In the young child there can be unfolding and personality growth merely through acting out. For the older child almost always there must be some form of interpretation [15] but not involving the deepest level of motivation.

In the multi-patient function of child guidance, the parent can see himself projected in the child, as well as look backward toward his own childhood, so the perspective becomes significant to him. Even if the original emotional situation is not recalled, part of it is now reproduced in the child's emotional situation. Since the neurotic reacts in the same way to each environmental situation with only slight changes, the neurotic mother reacts to the child as to her own experience. If she can make the connections, it will be very important. One must never forget that though the neurosis may not be cured, relief of symptoms in the parent will go a long way toward relieving the child of conflict. The language the client uses always has special meaning. If one does not understand it, one should not be afraid to ask questions. If the interpretation "clicks," the client usually has a reaction of surprised satisfaction; if not, he will probably deny it. If the interpretation is wrong, the client's "resistance" is certainly normal, and no great harm is done, since we only object to unpleasant truths about ourselves. Still, the caseworker is well advised to be sure of his ground and of the readiness of the client to profit from the comment before interpreting anything which is emotionally charged.

In "counseling" one may actively help the client focus by discussing the situation; through the use of agency services and by clarifying

[15] Ackerman, "What Constitutes Intensive Psychotherapy in a Child Guidance Clinic?" *American Journal of Orthopsychiatry*, XV (October, 1945), 711–720.

reality issues. But in "therapy," when the conflict is internalized and one is moving with the client slowly toward self-awareness, all the clues lie within. The path is dim and overgrown. The client's present conflicts all relate to conflicts to which only he can find the way. Even though one can better guide the interview when the background and etiology are known, the treatment must still be based upon the actual material that the client produces. Whenever the client repeats, the worker should know that there is something in which he feels he has not been understood—that there is an unresolved displacement of the more basic conflict.

In the gradual incorporation of ego psychology into therapy, the worker has learned that he must appraise the total functioning of the personality, its strengths and weaknesses, through methods of interviewing which take the adaptive mechanisms into account.[16] Defenses are mechanisms which help the person to deal with reality or which may be turned by the person against inner drives. The purposes of defense and adaptation are intertwined. Defenses operate more or less successfully. Successful defenses are related to the process of sublimation, discussed elsewhere.[17] If a defense is serving the personality well in its adaptation to reality, the worker will ordinarily leave it alone just as he leaves the basic positive transference alone— that is without interpretation. If the defense is not helping the personality to function adequately, the worker tries to get the client to discuss and elaborate it until the defense breaks down of its own accord and the client is ready to relinquish it. On whatever level of action, discussion and interpretation, whenever reality factors are modified or when, through release and discussion, understanding is better, there is probably some shift in the unconscious, which results in greater adequacy in the functioning of the personality as a whole.

Interpretation is rarely at the level of infantile sexuality or of sexual aim (except as young children directly express it in play), or of translating the language of symbolism found in dreams and fantasies which come straight from the unconscious, although the therapist may often get children to elaborate their images. If he is active, it will be chiefly to notice and respond to what the client associates

---

[16] See pp. 36 *et seq.*   [17] See Chapter VII.

in reality with the dream or to the next thing he happens to say. Just as workers are taught to pay attention to what clients say first, because it is so often emotionally charged, so, after a sample of dream material or fantasy, if the worker does not distract the underground train of thought, the client is likely to produce an observation or experience which is also emotionally charged. Such a remark, therefore, can be discussed, whereas the dream material itself is not so accessible to direct interpretation. If the ego structure is sufficiently well integrated, conflicts may be formulated on a reality level, otherwise a supportive approach is more usual and the constructive defenses are reinforced. If interpretation of the defenses should be made, the conscious *social expression* or projections of the instinctual drives or the behavior would be the media, but not the unconscious impulse which aroused the anxiety and necessitated the defense. Although free association is used to some extent, "What are you thinking now?" "Please go on," most of the interviewing is eliciting specifics in the client's narration of life experience. The participation and awareness of the patient occur most often in reality discussions, wherein responsibility to work through social problems and social adjustments is encouraged. This tends to keep the client from engulfing himself and the therapist in a deep transference neurosis which on this level of therapy cannot properly be handled. Carefully spaced appointments and other controls are employed to the same end. Interpretation in the sense of "analyzing the transference" is sparingly used, and when used is couched in everyday terms such as the client himself brings out. When parents or other adults are being interviewed, the worker does not usually comment on the transference relationship unless forced by erotic behavior, overt hostility, or marked negative feelings in passive, disguised forms. In such instances he may have to handle the negative feelings or lose the client. The connection between the child's attitudes towards his own parents and his irrational projection on to the therapist will be quite obvious (for the child the therapist is nearer to a real parental figure anyway), and a comment, "You don't like me because I remind you of what your father does," etc., may be quite lightly and simply made. For the adult this sort of interpretation is less feasible, more likely to arouse hostility, and because deeper associations have not been reached, more likely to be wrong. It is true that the worker does not interpret positive transference, since the positive phases do not so often block treatment, and the child may take comment as rejection. But the line cannot be too sharply drawn, since positive and negative shift back and forth and there are all shades and degrees.

The worker, by getting the client to discuss reality situations or to elaborate attitudes toward others, keeps the transference within bounds (again this assumes that caseworkers do not treat intensively severe neuroses in adults).[18] There are, of course, exceptions to the foregoing, and it is probable that the differences between "analyzing" the transference or "interpreting," or "handling," it are in degree and depth rather than in kind. What generally results from successful casework therapy is a transference "improvement," not a transference "dissolution." The client, especially the adult client, is not likely to be "cured," but he may be far better able to function. The client who has improved will probably, on discontinuance of contact, retain a warm feeling for worker and agency, which is all to the good. If he wishes to return later for help, either for himself or some member of his family, this should not be regarded as evidence of failure. Sometimes it should warn us that the treatment given was not sufficiently radical or was otherwise wrong, but quite as often one many legitimately feel that the client's capacity to function has been conserved and strengthened by reality-adjusted periods of treatment in which the transference relationship was used only as far as the client had acute need of it.

The Supportive Relationship

Emotional support is to psychotherapy as practical assistance is to other services in social casework. Insight is not always achieved and cannot always be the aim. Support is used as a phase of treatment with many disturbed clients and as the main type of relationship with the psychotic, when the weak ego must be helped to repress the drives. It has the purpose of reinforcing self-esteem through warmth and friendliness and by these attitudes to encourage self-dependence and

[18] See Chapter XII.

efforts at reality adjustments, but does not contemplate change in the personality. There is a supportive component in most therapy, since the worker must lend some of his own strength to help the client free himself and rely on his own untried strength. In any form of therapy, along with gradual desensitization through repeated discussion of painful material, there is a corresponding movement in ego building in which each little step forward, attended by satisfaction instead of frustration, can bring more strength and greater satisfactions in widening circles.

It is a fact, however, that parents of children found in child guidance and family case loads comprise a number of very infantile personalities.[19] For such persons deep self-awareness is not feasible. Instead, the worker can usually be helpful by offering a sustaining relationship for as long as the person, here most often the mother, needs it, particularly during the period of the child's treatment. Such dependent personalities, or at least the children of such dependent parents, seem to profit from a reassuring, permissive, and protective attitude more than one might suppose. In such a transference relationship friendly counsel can be utilized, and in an indirect fashion the warmth of the therapist is conducted through the parent to the child. Interviews need not always be frequent, and the mother will continue a sort of household attachment to the agency in which she has learned to have confidence, seeking reassurance and comfort whenever she feels threatened or overwhelmed by fate. If the child is given treatment also, he may well surmount the difficulties of growing up in so feeble an environment. Alexander speaks of these cases as "interminable," [20] and if one is thinking only of the adult one might question whether the cost is justifiable, but there is good reason to believe that long or intermittent contact with the parents on a supportive level frequently has a favorable effect on the total family security, ability to function, and the growth of the children, which

---

[19] See Chapter XI.

[20] Alexander and French, *Psychoanalytic Therapy*. For such patients, for whom there is little chance of effecting a permanent change, Dr. Alexander says: "Inferiority feelings are not traced back to their origin, but are combatted with reassurance; guilt feelings are not explained but are assuaged by permissive attitudes; anxiety is relieved by the physician's assuming a protective role." p. 103.

may be regarded as justifiably preventive. For the already discouraged parents of children who come to a guidance agency, sometimes all one can give them is enough encouragement so that they will allow the child to come for treatment. They may be quite unable to use deeper relationship, and it may be sufficient for them to realize that the worker does not think them bad parents, but accepts them and appreciates their efforts for the child. By giving emotional support to the immature or weak parental ego one may strengthen those defenses which are constructive for the child. The emotionally supportive relationship may be reinforced by many forms of practical or interpersonal assistance, or it may be used to help the person discover and develop assets and talents, which is the characteristic of sublimation.[21]

The use of "authority" is closely related to that of "support." There are two ways in which this term is used—one has to do with the authority of the social order and its institutions, and the other the authoritative firmness which may be used, directly or indirectly, by the therapist, including the setting of limits already discussed. It is the task of the caseworker not to impose his own reality on the client, but to clarify with him the realities of living. But in general the caseworker disavows an authoritative personal role. He says, in effect, these are the "rules." He didn't make them, neither does he enforce them—they bind both worker and client. He will try to get the client to express his feeling about the "rules" and to discuss these feelings. He thus works within the framework of authority, lining up neither with nor against the client.

Authoritative firmness is sometimes used by the therapist when the client needs reinforcement in going through with a wise decision for himself or for his child or any other person for whom he is responsible. Very immature, infantile persons occasionally need this sort of guidance as, for instance, when it is necessary to help a childlike unmarried mother to give up her baby. Occasionally, also, the indecisive, wavering, compulsive person needs to be backed or supported to choose the more constructive of two courses of action. Such authoritative firmness should not be confused with the voluntary

[21] See p. 157.

relationship which is indispensable in therapy. If the client will not involve himself in treatment one cannot compel him to do so. If the parent is unwilling to allow the child to be treated authority will not serve the purpose. Generally speaking, whenever a child is made to come for treatment this pressure should be applied by parent, guardian, or other external means, not by the therapist. If the parent will not cooperate the case is probably lost anyway.

Differentiated Therapy in Clinical Types

In the clinical groups described earlier are differentiated the anxious child, who has been trying to batten down the hatches on his surging impulses, and the child who lets loose the waves of his aggression. There are common elements in all psychotherapy, and treatment must be flexibly adapted to shifting phases in the personality and variables in the social situation. Yet there are ways in which the therapeutic accent for psychoneurosis subtly differs from that used for behavior disorders. In the latter the therapeutic aim is for the person to achieve more self-restraint, a stronger ego and super-ego, and capacity for object relationships; for the psychoneurotic, the resolution of inner conflict and reduction of anxiety are the chief goals. The aggressive child must learn that his impulses do not and should not destroy others, that he can repress and sublimate, and that he need not continue to provoke. The neurotic child has to learn that his inner impulses may be discharged into the environment without destroying him; that his thoughts and wishes are not so terrible and need not be so cruelly and rigidly inhibited.

The child with a primary behavior disorder, because of his weak ego structure, acts out his aggression in a relationship of acceptance until he becomes able to relinquish some of his narcissism, form constructive identifications with the therapist, and so start on the road toward the establishment of inner controls and restraints. The establishment of such controls as part of the super-ego comes about, however, only if the reward is sufficient. At first the child has little to offer except suspicion and hate, for which he expects wrath and retaliation. What "guilt" he has is so deeply repressed as to be inaccessible. The delinquent (primary behavior disorder) needs, therefore, more rather than less acceptance. How often shall my brother sin against me and I forgive him—till seven times? Nay, rather till seventy times seven. All the suspicion and wariness express themselves through his use of, or rather failure to use, relationship. The client appears indifferent at first, or he may outwardly conform, quoting what people say is wrong with him, and try to be very strategic and diplomatic to the worker in order to "buy him off," as it were. In any event, he projects his image of the hostile parent upon the worker, who does not respond to his provocation, so the child must seek a new answer for himself. Acceptance does not mean denying the actuality of "badness," but accepting the child when bad as well as when good. It is the old and valid religious distinction of not approving the sin, but loving the sinner. The child is never all bad to the worker, and in time this becomes meaningful to him. The worker, something new in his experience, not because of weakness, but because of tolerance, takes a warm interest in what he is, what he likes and dislikes, his achievements, his exploits, and even his boasting. Since he wants unconsciously all the love and the admiration he did not receive as a little child, the therapist, to use Dr. van Ophuijsen's phrase, "makes himself indispensable to the patient as an instrument of his narcissism." [22] He is then bound to the therapist by his need for gratification. Gradually, in favorable cases, the interest awakens an attachment so that the therapist ceases to be merely a mirror of his ego ideal and becomes a real person (object relationship) to the child.

This carefully controlled technique with younger and not too dissocial children involves considerable gratification. In reaction to the permissive therapeutic attitude the child regresses, usually going through in play and verbally all stages of development, during which time the therapist gratifies and, when necessary, gently restrains, as the good parent does. Since the child expects not to be gratified but to be denied, he will not at first understand the friendliness. The moment a limitation is imposed or a gift denied the child with a behavior disorder becomes irritating, verbally provocative, and controlling. The worker tries to frustrate as little as possible (especially

[22] Van Ophuijsen, "Primary Conduct Disturbances," in *Modern Trends in Child Psychiatry*, p. 41.

in the early phases), and never unnecessarily. When one cannot accede to a request, the worker points out in a friendly way why, because of his age, or for some other reason, wishes cannot always be gratified. As soon as possible, aggressive patterns are discussed.

In early phases the child invokes a magical element in his struggle for power. The worker tolerates the wishes, but not the violent action. Although the child always knows in his heart of hearts whether one "approves" (therapeutic understanding) of him or not, he does not expect approval of what his family and his culture do not permit. The emotional support which he gets through tolerance and understanding serves as a protection against his own destructive trends. Self-assurance is built by attention to the child's real accomplishments and real gains. Convinced of one's good will, he may slowly come to trust one further and so finally himself. He will have many defenses against the therapeutic approach, but as he lays his defenses aside, one by one, he may be very responsive. The therapeutic intent is always to help the child resolve his aggressive conflicts "so as to release expression of need for love"—indispensable for growth.

Since the child with a primary behavior disorder has not hitherto experienced parental love and protection, he has not achieved capacity for object relationship. Persons to him are tools to be used for his gratification. For him the process of identification and object relationship is all a new development. The artificial reliving has to take place in order to make over what was done in the past. As the new relationship takes hold, the child begins to express more positive feelings. These, in turn, are followed by ambivalent reactions, attachment to the worker dominating, until finally the aggressiveness is harnessed so as to be used constructively in super-ego formation. As his ego matures and strengthens and he can internalize prohibitions, he is enabled to use his aggression for education and growth, instead of in battles and weakening fears. He can handle some of his own "badness."

While a positive giving relationship is important for emotionally deprived, frustrated, and aggressive children whose problem is learning how to live with or to relate themselves to anyone, the same approach to the child whose problem is predominantly intrapsychic may result in failure. A permissive relationship is inadequate, and it becomes necessary to gain access to the conflict which is causing the behavior. The child is already oversevere with regard to the primitive desires which his ego cannot tolerate, so that the therapeutic approach is actively guilt relieving. The therapy is to remove bit by bit the inhibitions, until the primitive impulses find expression and can then be synthesized through insight into the personality.

In the neurotic who has had some love and has, therefore, some capacity for an object relationship, a positive transference is readily established; in the child with a behavior disorder it must somehow be brought about. One should never try to stimulate transference in the psychoneurotic, who will try "to wangle" too much. He is already dependent, and has demands which are very hard to satisfy. One neither gives in nor reacts with sympathy. He must find out that his demands do not work. The neurotic in his own way attempts to dominate. He has idealized the parent image, but he is prepared to give up infantile desires if someone understands what he is going through. Sometimes the demand for love is a reaction formation and is really to be understood as a denial of hostility or a suspicious testing of the worker's good faith. Although he relates to the therapist immediately, he has equally immediate anxiety. Ambivalent feelings will soon be reexperienced in the transference. He has an unresolved parental conflict, and will use the worker right away in a struggle for its solution. When a psychoneurotic child does not seem to know where to begin or what toys to play with, one is safe in assuming that he does not know where to begin with the worker.

Both types of children are in their own way fearful and untrusting, but they express this differently. The child who acts out has no trust at all. This tends to exclude the therapist, especially in the initial stages. The anxious child also distrusts, but there is a difference in both the quality and the intensity of his distrust, which is usually mobilized later in treatment. Of course, the therapist cannot win the trust of the patient if the extent of pathology prevents the child from trusting anyone. Often all one can do at the start is to avoid threatening the child, so that he will return for treatment. One cannot expect at once to disarm the child of his fears and, indeed, the worst thing one can do is to allay them, for then both child and therapist enjoy false security, while the dangers still threaten from within. Guilt, fear of punishment, feelings of weakness and inferiority are not glossed over, but are gradually desensitized through discussion. Because vague fears and undefined anxiety are worse than any, the worker tries to find out details of suffering in concrete terms. Since the relationship is fully used by the child, the more his fears can be channelized within the transference relationship, the more sure-footed will be the approach. One must "grasp the nettle, danger," firmly.

When the neurotic regresses, as he, too, does under treatment, he at first retains his guilt. The child has been torn between allying himself with his impulses or the repressing forces within the personality. The therapist, therefore, takes the side of the impulses and tries to reduce the oppressive effects of reality and the reactions of guilt, fear, strain, and need for self-punishment. In identification with the therapist, who personifies a strong, yet tolerant, reality, inhibitions are minimized and the child feels safe to express his real needs.

The quality of gratification is also somewhat different; in behavior disorders the permissiveness involves a sort of "going along with," or moderate "giving in," until the child can bear frustration; what helps the anxious child is to be made aware of his need and his puzzling ambivalent feelings, and he is relieved when he can see the distortions in them. The chief therapeutic problem lies in the fact that the child has difficulty both in giving and in receiving love. The psychoneurotic expects from the new situation what he has lost, so he tries to recreate a good relationship. But once the aggression is turned inwards, he feels himself unlovable and bad. Here, because the hidden anxiety must be expressed, the therapist is passive. The anxious child is afraid, not so much of attack, as of love itself, because it is through love that he has been punished or hurt. It is his love feelings and his acceptance of love about which he feels guilty. Therefore, warmth and activity make such children uneasy, and a greater neutrality must be observed by the worker. The anxious child, superficially driven by his need for love, relates easily, and often is quite conscious of his need for help. But as help is given, his resistance grows, and sooner or later he will feel that the relationship is disloyal to his parents. One can never replace the lost love of the parent through therapy or continue to substitute for a real personal relationship in the life experience,[23] but the worker can help the child compensate for satisfactions around infantile urges which he now must give up. The fact that the anxious child suffers and wants to be helped is on the side of therapy, but his sense of unworthiness makes him pessimistic, and his ambivalence makes progress slow. On the whole, the neurotic child's ego can be counted on to do more for itself than can that of the child who acts out and the former can bear some reality frustrations without breaking off treatment.

Identification with the therapist in the new experience thus finally permits the behavior disorder to achieve inner controls; in the neurotic, identification with a lenient super-ego in the therapist permits him to minimize the rigid and tormenting anxiety which is a primitive method of regulating the impulses. Accepted and finally self-accepted, energies are freed for expression in ways appropriate for the age of the child and his natural capacities. Whether the infantile neurosis can be "cured" by such psychotherapy is a somewhat relative matter. It depends upon the severity of the neurosis and the skill of the therapist.

Caseworkers do not pretend to solve all the person's life problems or to work on the deepest emotional levels of the unconscious, but they make use of characteristic approaches and combinations of psychological and social techniques. The question is not *whether* direct therapy and the provision of more healthy and developing life experience may be combined—in the treatment of children they *must* be combined. The question is rather *how* to coordinate and integrate these efforts by clearing the path enough so that the child may move ahead and by direct treatment to modify his attitudes and behavior so that he can help clear the path himself.[24]

Recapitulation

In psychotherapy not only must the psychiatric concepts of health and illness, including the main clinical pictures, be thoroughly under-

[23] Ackerman, "Psychotherapy and 'Giving Love,'" *Psychiatry*, VII (May, 1944), 129–138. [24] See Chapter VII.

stood by the practitioner, but also the dynamic concept of personality —the nature of the emotional drives and conflicts within the personality. The central factors in all study and treatment, which thus interweave and become one process, culminate in the relationship which the caseworker establishes with the client. The therapeutic attitude tends to induce a transference relationship which is not only a means to understanding the problem, but also the chief dynamic factor in the treating and rebuilding process. Whatever strength is already in the personality is always built upon. Whenever there is emotional illness or distortion of the personality which is not too severe, therapy attempts *some* reorganization of unconscious functions.

The release of tension through expressive techniques may itself prove beneficial (catharsis); the release may enable the person to work more rationally in real situations, and finally the release of tension may create a situation favorable for self-awareness or insight, leading to gradual emancipation and change. In casework the therapy proceeds through play (reliving), and through discussion of life experience and day-by-day events. The client tends to repeat in one form or another, with added details or going farther into the past, situations which bother him. The trends or patterns are pointed out and discussed. The unconscious material is approached in general through its projections and displacements—in adaptive and defense mechanisms. Interpretation of symbolic material is seldom attempted, nor is the transference analyzed. Controls of the transference neurosis are maintained by enabling the client to discuss everyday situations and to elaborate his attitudes toward others, by carefully timed interviews and other devices.

Self-involvement is always essential, and usually some degree of insight is sought. In work with adults the goal is usually to remove gradually certain defenses leading to partial insight and concurrently to strengthen useful defenses. For little children, release of feeling in a supportive relationship may be self-healing if the parental attitudes can be modified and environmental conditions made more favorable for growth. For older children increased self-awareness is necessary for substantial improvement. In parent-child interaction, usually one or the other *must* gain some insight during the course of treatment, but it is not always possible for both. Supportive therapy may be used both to sustain the patient and members of the family in appropriate ways and to reinforce constructive defenses. Although psychotherapy is expressed through the two-person relationship ("direct treatment" in the interview and play interview) in child guidance it cannot be confined to this dimension. In child therapy, since the infantile strivings, stimulations, and frustrations are currently going on, the integrative process may be assisted both by the direct treatment of the child and modification of the environment. Whenever there is change in conscious adaptations, there is probably some rearrangement of unconscious functions of the personality.

Chapter VII

THE THERAPEUTICALLY
CONDITIONED ENVIRONMENT

THE ESSENCE of child guidance lies in the combination in varying proportions of direct psychotherapy (understanding unconscious conflict, transference, resistance and ego defense patterns),[1] with social therapies. The child brings his reality into the interview but the therapist also reaches out into the child's world through contacts with those most concerned with his problem.

We have seen how treatment in social casework has been revolutionized by the concept of the inner conflict (the internalized environment), and how unconscious conflict may make it impossible for a person to use social experience. Before this was understood, both with regard to the child who acts out his conflicts on the environment and the child whose internalized conflicts inhibit him from growth, the cure resorted to was a shift of environment; but this cure could only be effective when the behavior was situational and reactive, before the personality development had become arrested or fixed. When the child is not ready to live in a social environment, merely putting him into one will not help—moving the child from one natural environment to another will not ensure that the thwarted or arrested growth processes will automatically operate. When it was seen that environmental shifts were in many cases of no avail, it was recognized that the same principles which entered into the therapeutic relationship could also be applied, with certain modifications, to other aspects of the treatment process. The child is helped to change both by direct approach and by prepared and conditioned environmental situations. Just as parents and children must be seen as a constellation, so the individual and his environment are inseparable and constantly interacting.

[1] See Chapter VI.

The individual cannot be expected to do all the adjusting to unfavorable environments. The environment itself must be made more favorable. Just as we expect a modern system of social security to supplement and reinforce the national economy, so the various environments to which disturbed children are subjected must themselves be modified along with direct psychotherapy. Social work has ready access to the environment and operates a number of resources. These must be not only physically and educationally adequate, but the whole environment should contain basically sound attitudes toward the child. The parental environment is the first and primary resource, and only in a good society in which the social economy and culture permit the development of mature persons can we hope to have mature parents. But beyond this the principles of therapy must be infused through all programs for the care of disturbed children. Sometimes anxiety in the child is so great that direct psychotherapy cannot be tolerated, and other social therapies may be used as a phase of treatment. Sometimes quite a long period of planned situational building up is needed. When there is some relief and some of the anxiety is reduced or repressed, direct therapy may then be undertaken. The environment is used not in a static way, but in accordance with the needs of each child. To quote S. R. Slavson: "Psychotherapy consists of removing the patient's resistance to the world, his self-encapsulation. . . . As long as the patient isolates himself either through resistance, active aggression or withdrawal, the world cannot get at him. He remains in a state of isolation or develops or continues with antisocial attitudes." [2] Social therapy is not used in place of psychotherapy, but one reinforces the other on a dynamic basis.

The possibilities of sublimation must always be kept in mind. In psychoanalysis, since theoretically the deeply repressed is all made conscious, sublimation is left to the patient himself. In casework social opportunities are opened up as well as affects drained off, so that tensions can be discharged in constructive ways. Social workers must understand not only internalized conflict between ego and impulse, and between super-ego and impulse, but also conflicts between

[2] Slavson, "Principles and Dynamics of Group Therapy," *American Journal of Orthopsychiatry*, XIII (October, 1943), 656.

two parts of the ego—as the woman who wants to bring up her children and also have a career. That the transference is used as a bridge to "real" relationships and as the incentive toward creative activities and that resources are actually mobilized are special features of case-work therapy. Ability to use sublimation, like other change, seems to arise out of the constructive identification with the therapist. It is not a defense but, as Freud says, "a way out that does not involve repression." It is natural to social work because it is a "social" quality. Social achievement, as has been often stated, has the same economic function in the healthy person as suffering has in the neurotic. The case-worker, therefore, is always on the lookout for talents and interests which can be so utilized by the relaxed, if not wholly released, personality. Supportive measures are suitable for adults burdened by life pressures, and sublimation seems particularly helpful to children, since the child is able to learn whenever (assisted by therapeutically oriented attitudes in his instructors) he can find and master new experiences and skills. The immature ego of the child must be given educational and supportive help in adapting to the demands of life. The child's capacity to adapt is strengthened not only through direct interviewing treatment, but through other social experience therapeutically conditioned.

In child guidance, therapy is addressed to the total personality, relating itself fluidly to various levels of development and facets of behavior. Its central tool, the transference, is used both to help the person to change within himself and toward constructive abreactions in social opportunities, thus strengthening the ego directly and indirectly. Environmental, as well as personality, factors must be diagnostically determined, and the treatment integrated on this basis. Since the transference is not fully analyzed or the person "cured," it is particularly important to reduce strains whenever possible, so that the person is better able to handle things for himself.

Early in any case a plan must be established, with a tentative idea of direction and expectancy. Certain considerations guide a social agency in accepting or not accepting behavior problems: the degree of psychopathology; too much distortion of reality and deterioration, as in psychosis, or too great impulsivity, or suicidal tendency, or extremely dissocial or delinquent behavior, especially in older children; the capacity to relate oneself to the therapist and willingness to participate in the process; finally, the assets within the personality—fair intelligence, not too rigid a personality structure, some capacity for responsibility and patience, and a desire for change in the situation or in oneself or both.

Certain cases cannot easily be treated in a community agency, because the impulsive acting out is so dissocial that the child has to be treated within an institutional environment. The institutional setting may be not only necessary but also a great comfort to a child with poor inner controls. Moreover, there may be community pressures which make it hard to help a child, even one having a theoretically good prognosis, once he has been identified as a "delinquent," especially if the parents have concurred in the verdict. The fact that in the older child there is almost always some internalization of parental environment means a mixed symptomatology (for example, behavior disorder with neurotic traits or psychoneurosis with behavior disorder), calls for individualized treatment as well as a modified or controlled environment.

Whether environmental manipulation, concurrent with direct treatment, dilutes or reenforces therapy is a question often raised. Active intervention with regard to the environment (except as the parent can be involved thoroughly in treatment) is usually not too effective for the neurotic child, since the problem is internalized. It is, however, often necessary for a social worker to modify the environmental factors, especially the home factors, whether it slows up the treatment or not. For young children it is indispensable. The social worker who treats both adults and children learns that he must approach reality as impersonally and realistically as possible, having in mind continuity of treatment and reduction of unnecessary pressures. The dual question in planning treatment is always: how serious is the external situation and how troubled is the person or persons caught in it. Practical factors may have to be actively shifted, as well as a therapeutic attitude spread.

Substitute Relationships and Settings

The most important environmental influence is that of the child's own home and parents, and since in child guidance the immediate family is involved in treatment, we have devoted a special chapter to this subject.[3] What we shall consider here is the use of substitute or extended parental relationships and settings. At home the parent of the young child may be intensively treated, probably with results favorable for the child; the child may be treated intensively, and the parent only in a supportive or educational way; both child and parent may be treated on several levels and with varying degrees of intensity; or the child may be removed from the home altogether (either because of extreme social deterioration or rejection of the child by the parent or because the child needs some special treatment) and placed with foster parents. Children are helped to grow up by constructive real parental and sibling experiences, but if the natural family is lacking, substitute relationships can be effectively introduced. The widespread use of quasi-parental figures is a skilled and specialized contribution of social work. At one end of the treatment range are the natural relationships—mothers, fathers, brothers, sisters, relatives, employers, teachers, friends—and at the other end the controlled professional relationships of individual and group therapy; between these two extremes there are many intermediate relationships, such as foster parents, cottage parents, homemakers and housekeepers, "big brothers" and "big sisters," and other volunteers—acting in various friendly capacities. The important differentiation between these relationships and therapy is that all these persons offer direct gratification and active intervention in the child's daily life much like that of his own family. On the other hand, it has been increasingly evident that for a favorable outcome substitute family persons must not only like children in the ordinary way but also be able to like disturbed and deprived children in a "therapeutic" way if they are to help them. For fairly healthy children suffering from broken homes—because of the death of either parent or neglect due to inadequacy rather than rejection—the use of the substitute parent is rewarding, and the more

[3] See Chapter XI.

nearly these intermediate figures can act like real parents and friends, the better, if only they are kind and sensible persons. But the more upset the child—the more he has internalized his conflict—the more essential is it that he shall encounter only therapeutically conditioned attitudes in his new home.

So much has been written about individually "placed out" children that we shall only here emphasize one or two points about the institutional atmosphere. Extreme mental defectives or sick children—epileptics, psychotics, criminals, and others for whom the community life is difficult—need specialized hospital and institutional care. For the dissocial a flexible boarding school type of program, with vocational training in addition to academic courses, shop, arts, crafts, and so forth, is helpful if two other conditions are fulfilled. First, all the personnel, including the maintenance workers, must like children and act in helpful, accepting, and constructive ways, and the key personnel (cottage parents) should have special training for their function. In addition, direct psychotherapy should be available for children who need it.

Because children in a correctional school show a high incidence of primary behavior disorder and psychopathic personality, the handling of aggression, often very hostile aggression, is a major problem, and the principle of authoritative restraint must be clinically applied.[4] The evidence is overwhelming that a rigidly authoritative and rejecting environment merely recreates the earlier struggle with the rejecting, unloving parents, leads only to a battle of wills or submission and further breakdown of the character structure. A certain amount of restraint in a good institution, as in a good home, is normal, or the children's uncontrolled anxiety will get out of bounds.[5] Experience has, however, shown that the less arbitrarily restrictive the regime, the more often voluntary relationships can be substituted for authoritative relationships, the less frequently the child will rebel and run away. Treatment, as in a good home, must be sustained and firm, but nonpunishing; the child must be given wise support against his own

---

[4] See pp. 147–148.

[5] See *Conditioned Environment in Case Work Treatment*, a monograph on the Hawthorne–Cedar Knolls School and Lavenberg Corner House, written by staff members of the Jewish Board of Guardians.

destructive tendencies; the ego must be built up to help itself through creative and satisfying activities. No external controls are as effective as those built up from within. Children are held responsible for their acts, but the therapeutic principle requires that this responsibility is shared with them until they are strong enough to stand alone.

It is somewhat idle to ask whether a school for disturbed children should be more school than home, or the reverse. Because many children come from pathological homes their social development is at an infantile level, and the importance of giving them a satisfying parental experience remains paramount. The cottage parents, while not real parents, are the center of the child's living experience, but the search for the idealized parent is always strong. Children dream that their parents loved them or, during placement, have somehow miraculously started to love them, and they run away to see whether there is not, after all, someone at home who wants them. They do not believe it, but they have the urge to put the matter to a test, disappointing as the homecoming often proves to be. The cottage parent who understands this need will have much to offer for the reduction of tension.

It has been apparent in child placing that when the real parents continue actively in the picture, the use of substitute parental figures is very complicated for a child. Because of confused and diffuse identifications the presumption for success with children placed out over long periods seems to be almost in inverse ratio to the activity of the real parents. It seems probable that just as the institutional infant with a too impersonal set of attendants or too many nurses has difficulty in forming the necessary identifications, so do young children with two competing sets of parents. Children who have had a good emotional start naturally are less vulnerable; children who have had a bad start need direct therapeutic help in solving their parental relationships just as much when the parent is actually visiting him as when he must deal with the psychological reality of the idealized and fantasied "lost" parent. The neurotic child who has internalized his conflict will need direct as well as indirect therapy wherever he is placed, and the real parent who has any capacity for parenthood should be helped to develop it without removing the child from the home at all.

The "big brother" and "big sister," who are also part of an "extended kinship" therapy, like the foster parent do not "*do* treatment, they *are* treatment." [6] Such substitute family figures must have positive attitudes toward children, willingness to give time and, when indicated, small gifts and treats, since it is the natural giving quality of the big brother or big sister which is important in children's lives.

A "friendly visitor" may combine the advantage of a supporting relationship with creative activities, of shared sports, or trips to museums, or conversational walks, and so forth. Particularly in treating the child who has a behavior disorder, who does not believe that life can be pleasant and relationships nonretaliatory, other friendly figures—big brothers, camp counselors, and so forth—may finally convince him that the world is not all inimical. The child may first adopt socially acceptable behavior to please one adult, but later he will see that satisfaction can be gained in the same way with other persons in the environment.

Very aggressive and disturbed children often cannot be helped in this way. But for mild cases and in certain stages of treatment the constructive identification with a friendly adult may give enough emotional security to help unblock the child's capacity for growth. If the child cannot use relationships well, he will not ordinarily be able to profit by a volunteer. With the psychoneurotic who, because of his suffering and dependency, clings desperately to the therapist, the problem of any other relationship is always more complicated, and volunteers can best be used after the child has considerably improved and is strengthened within himself. During intensive treatment it is important to see that the child does not receive so many gratifications outside the relationship that he will no longer want the help. The child must have enough discomfort in his outside social relationships to be willing to continue to work on his problem with the therapist.

[6] See Avrunin, "The Volunteer in Case Work Treatment," *The Family*, XXV (June, 1944), 137–142. At the Jewish Board of Guardians the use of the volunteer has always held a central place, with increasing appreciation of its importance.

Yet the child may be genuinely starved for attention and pleasures, and gratification can be at some points more safely given by the volunteer than by the therapist. Moreover, feelings aroused toward the volunteer can be discussed by the child and the therapist in the same way that they discuss the child's feelings toward the parents. The use of a volunteer is also helpful after a long period of intensive therapy, for tapering off. One must remember that since in casework therapy the relationship is never fully analyzed, the positive feelings have to be channelized toward other persons as well as sublimated through activities.

Discussion of group therapy is not within the scope of this book. Group therapy [7] is a special adaptation of techniques within a larger frame of reference. As in play, in group therapy there is acting out through processes in which the therapist or leader becomes the object of a transference relationship. The group experience is a specially constructed situation, either for discussion or shared activities. In the group the children and the therapist are of value to one another. Through the relationships in the group and the permissive environment, where the child can act out his problems, personality malformations are corrected and his social adaptations are improved. Some children learn best in the two-person relationship, others in the group reaction. Some need both. In the group sibling reactions and displacements are made possible by the passive, quiet, and permissive parent figure, who helps but does not punish.

There is some difference of opinion as to whether the therapist should be more or less active,[8] but all agree that he should be a kind, responsive, giving, and comforting person. The therapeutic elements always lie in the differences perceived by the child between the therapist's attitudes and those of other persons. As the child struggles with the differences and reconciles them with the realities of his life, he discovers new patterns of thought. With young children or those with flexible personality structure, release of tension, reduced pressures, and creative activity can be deeply educational, socializing, and therapeu-

---

[7] See Slavson, *An Introduction to Group Therapy,* and other references in the bibliography for full discussion of this topic. See also pp. 251–252.

[8] See Slavson and others, "Principles and Dynamics of Group Therapy," *American Journal of Orthopsychiatry,* XIII (October, 1943), 578–588.

tic. One can never be sure by what experience or at what therapeutic level the blocking is removed and the child starts spontaneously to grow. In group therapy, if the child gains a feeling of security, of being accepted and worth while, he feels secure in two respects, namely, with the leader and with his siblings. If the child improves by means of individual or group therapy, or both, he is ready for release and ego building in more normal life, such as settlements, Y's, Scouts, camps, and recreation of all kinds.

School Adjustments [9]

The function of a child guidance clinic in the school itself is also a large subject which cannot be discussed here. The social worker trained in child guidance can help teachers and the school personnel to recognize the troubled child and temper educational with therapeutic attitudes. Cooperative efforts may include: interpretation of the child's capacities and attitudes, which may assist the school in regrading when the child has been unwisely retarded, overplaced or placed without reference to special needs, and interpretation of the family interrelationships and the causes of the child's behavior. Sometimes adjustment of the program or providing practical services or actually transferring the child to another school may be sufficient to relieve strain or give the necessary satisfactions, but more often the roots of the child's insecurity or anxiety or trouble-making lie in the home, only to be relieved by direct treatment and the modification of parental attitudes. The child takes his family into school. When a child enters school, if he has had unfortunate home experiences, he will find the new demands very difficult. If he is also frightened or frustrated, he will have great difficulty in adjusting. If rejected at home, he may fear that something will happen to his mother in his absence—that she will die or that in some other way he will lose her forever. In a modern school in which individualized help in adjusting to the learning situation and to the other children is emphasized, much damage may be avoided; but if the school situation reinforces the home frustrations, a vicious circle may be established. Reading, arithmetic, and speech difficulties are usually signs of neurotic in-

[9] See pp. 227–234 for cases illustrative of school adjustments.

volvement which call not only for remedial teaching but also for therapy. Headaches, dizziness, and stomach disturbances are associated with the desire to be dependent or other infantile attitudes. Because school is the most important reality for the older child, he tends to focus his conflicts there.[10]

Ideally, the school should have all the necessary educational tools, as well as a therapeutic attitude toward disturbed children. If relatively unskilled examiners give Rorschach tests the result may be fraught with danger. The best child guidance practice would, we believe, insist that interpretation of the test (given only on the recommendation of a psychiatrist) be carefully correlated with all medical, psychiatric, and social findings. The preparation of the child for this test is always important, and there is some evidence in favor of giving it unobtrusively along with other psychometric tests. Some children approach any test in a matter-of-course fashion, but for others a test causes great anxiety. The school has much to offer by way of individual and group opportunities for educational satisfactions and achievements which are so important to the child's growth. These educational and recreational satisfactions should be adapted to give the individual the appropriate emotional gratifications for strengthening his ego. Mutual cooperation and interchange between educational and therapeutic agencies are essential.

After-school hours and Saturday mornings do not allow adequate time for treatment, even though the parents of older children may be seen during school hours. Unfortunately, stigma may still be attached both by teacher and pupils to excusing a child from school for a weekly treatment appointment. Until emotional illness comes to be accepted as simply as physical illness, appointments are usually best made for after-school hours. If for a very disturbed child special arrangements are necessary, the fullest understanding and cooperation by the teacher must be sought. Children take their cues so completely from the deeper attitudes of the leader or teacher that if a skillful and well-adjusted teacher accepts the fact that the child is to have treatment as a matter of course, the children will do likewise; or if

[10] Cf. pp. 218 et seq.

they do not, their education in the principles of mental hygiene will be needed to improve the situation.

True school phobias are not fear of the school itself, but are displacements upon the school situation of unresolved parental problems. Absence from school provides the child with a secondary gain. The anxiety must be channeled where it can be handled in reality. Firm, kind, and consistent attitudes of parents and teachers are essential, but the child will need a great deal of concurrent direct therapeutic help from the worker. In dealing with school phobias it was once common to keep out of school [11] the child who was under treatment. This aggravated his neurotic anxieties and made it still harder for him to leave home and return to school. The present emphasis is to help the child work out his anxiety in the school itself. This has to be achieved through the efforts of the school personnel, parent, and social worker. Once back in school, the therapy can proceed at whatever pace is necessary. Further cooperative efforts among family, school, and social worker to build up security slowly in the child by familiarizing him with rooms in the building or leaving him alone for a short time with a friendly person, his parent having inconspicuously withdrawn, prove better for the anxious child than abrupt separations from parents, enforced stays at school, or prolonged absences.

The Use of Camps

Camps, which furnish opportunities for experience in group living, are resources available for treatment as well as simply for vacations. Camps used for disturbed children should be run according to principles of group and individual therapy. For these children, as well as for those in institutions and schools, the whole experience should be made therapeutic. If the personality can be loosened up and the ego strengthened, there is improvement all around. Since different children have different and rapidly shifting needs, all the activities program should be oriented to treatment as well as to educational and recreational principles.

[11] See Chapter IX for discussion of treatment of school children.

Camp may reactivate the child's basic fear of being sent away from home. Parents sometimes bring pressure to bear on agencies to send their children away, often with a good deal of rejection behind the request. Because we enjoy vacations ourselves, we may jump to the conclusion that the child is longing to go, when instead he may have great fear. Under these circumstances it is important in preparation to learn the child's fantasies about camp. One little boy, who had been forced by his mother into very mature attitudes, said he wanted to go to camp because he knew he was supposed to like camp. He didn't dare say that he feared it. At camp he developed obsessions, felt that he must commit "one bad deed a day," and finally became so aggressive and depressed that he had to be sent home. There must be some readiness for the camp experience on the part of parent and child, which means preparation—often a period of treatment. Social workers need to know both the child and the camp. Usually the child should have shown some ability to dress and care for himself, as well as some ability to relate to others, before he is sent away.

A child may not have developed sufficiently to be able to bear separation from his parents, or both he and they may need active support in taking such a step.[12] He may fear camp as a punishment—feel bad and abnormal—but if the separation is properly timed and integrated in his treatment he may test out his new perception of himself through constructive identification with the worker in a favorably conditioned environment. During treatment he has begun to have a different perception of himself: that he can be good and can overcome his fears. If he finds he can succeed in camp, he has received another boost toward a healthy attitude; but if he is sent to camp before he is stabilized somewhat and fails to make a proper adjustment, he may become very discouraged and feel that the agency also has failed him as well as his parents. Before going to camp a disturbed child should be aware of his own problem and know that he is going away to get a different kind of help—another opportunity to work it out. A child who is fearful needs to know that he will be given enough protection, and the very aggressive child may need to know in advance that the counselors will give him help in controlling his

12 See illustration on p. 237.

aggression so that he won't get into so much trouble. It does not help the aggressive child just to be turned loose with an opportunity to let his aggression out and so be rejected by the group. A girl whose problem was to learn how to control her aggression knew she would be rejected by other children if she didn't control it. An arrangement was made at camp by which the child agreed to go to the caseworker when she could not control her own tension and spend an afternoon under her wing instead of with the children. For the first time in her life she was able to stay in a group without being thrown out.

The actual camp equipment is less important than the quality of the personnel—director, counselors, and maintenance staff. All have to be attuned to accepting, permissive, and considerate care. There must be outlets for aggressive behavior in the children, and the usual cycle of release, support, self-limitation by the group, and ego building, through noncompetitive activities for the most part. Disturbed children need to learn to participate, and so use their energies more constructively. Motor patterns of achievement developing into skills are helpful in ego building. The strength does not come from winning and losing events and trophies or from submission to routine, but from gradually developing one's own capacity to do things and relating oneself to group activities more harmoniously. Morale, which is akin to a strong group ego formation, seems to come from good leadership, common interests, and acceptance of one another's purposes. The child needs help in forming constructive identifications and in feeling that he belongs, which is very difficult for the rejected, aggressive child. He does not come to camp with an already-established feeling of social obligation, but has selfish and personal interests and demands. As we know, the child who has a behavior problem both wants to be liked and has a deep defense against being liked. His images for identification are incipient and blurred at first, and his relationship to the camp leader is on the infantile basis of being liked. He has to grow in order to identify, and he has much resistance to this.

Both provocative and neurotically aggressive children are hard to handle at camp, and should be sent only after careful consideration. It is hard for them to accept the behavior pattern of the leader in place of their own prestige as being a problem and so the center of attention. To become like the leader is to lose face, to become a sissy.[13] These hostile children characteristically have no attention span and no activity span—no capacity to bear tension. Their strong identification with the group on a sibling basis interferes with transference to the leader. They are happy only in aggressive drives, "chasing and being chased, attacking and being attacked." If such a boy accepts the others in the group and then turns his hostility toward other gangs and groups, he does not get over his hostility. Such children, if they want love, seem to demand it only so that they will not have to change. Whenever they feel a liking for the adult coming on, they become restive and provocative. They may try to force the adult to do something which they can dislike and resist, or they may put on a front of good behavior to avoid being helped.

The camping period is so short that a technique which provides for release of aggression without other support may prove anxiety arousing. It seems clear that it is unwise to send disturbed children to an ordinary camp having routines and competitive sports which the healthy child can take in his stride or to a so-called "progressive" camp in which there is not enough support or restraint for the weak ego. When there is acute sibling rivalry or rebellion, and defiance against the parent, these patterns will show themselves at camp. Camps may be badly oriented to children's needs, for instance, the compulsively neat child may get extravagant praise for keeping his tent neat, the very thing he shouldn't do. The disturbed child not only should have had a considerable period of individual treatment before going, but there should be follow-up and individual or group therapy between summer placements. Children should go to camp for several successive summers so that they can see their own growth and achievements. "This year I can climb the tree which I couldn't climb last year." It is important that the achievements are unobtrusively accredited, just as in treatment one accredits each little de-

---

[13] For discussion of such group behavior see Redl, "The Psychology of Gang Formation and the Treatment of Juvenile Delinquents," in *Psychoanalytic Study of the Child,* p. 367.

velopment or bit of insight. Year-round treatment for disturbed children, with camp intervals used as periods of trial living away from home and the worker, is the newer concept. Children sometimes use camp as an "escape" from therapy, and sometimes this is an indication of greater health and the beginning of ability to go on by themselves. For the neurotic delinquent, long-time treatment in the therapeutically conditioned institutional school may be better than short periods at camp.

Camp should be interpreted to parents as not only a vacation but also a treatment experience, and their support should be enlisted. The child senses at once whether the parent wants to get rid of him or whether there is an element of wanting to help him in the parent's action. Preparation for all forms of separation, whether through camps or institutions or child placement, is a most important function in child guidance. Sometimes the parent expects too much from the camp experience or is unduly alarmed if on a balanced, less starchy diet the child loses weight. One has to be careful neither to respond to parental pressure to send a child to camp for long or repeated periods, which can only be regarded as punishment, nor to make a deal with the child that he can come home if he doesn't like it. The fearful child cannot be introduced into the new environment gradually, so the preparation has to be pretty well completed in advance. The fear of separation from the mother, especially with insecure children, can be handled, the fear can be reduced, and attachment to the camp leader substituted, if the parent and the camp personnel are all attuned to helping the child (who will probably regress at first in camp) to move slowly outwards into new living experiences designed to be, not frustrating or threatening, but supportive and strengthening. In certain instances when it is advisable for the caseworkers to visit a child who has been a patient, it is important to tell the children that they are coming and how many children they will have to see, so as to avoid competition and jealousy. But usually it is better to encourage the parents to make the visit or to take the gifts, attend the camp ceremonies, and so forth; it is also a good idea, when feasible, to have meetings of the parents during the winter to develop an

understanding of the purposes of the camp. This is in line with building up the parental capacity, whenever possible, to give appropriate
gratifications to the child.

Again the tendency to make the whole of the camp a therapeutic
experience is balanced by the equally wholesome tendency to make
it a real living experience. It is perhaps easier administratively to shut
parents away from camp and try to make homesick children "forget
them." The excuse is that "parents disturb the children," but the
reassurance to the child in hearing from and seeing parents should
outweigh the difficulties. Part of the orientation of a modern camp
should include a good orientation to the parents as real parents with
real responsibilities.

Recapitulation

Family and child guidance agencies are in a favorable position to
see children before the patterns of disturbance and illness are fixed,
when they may still be reversed and through treatment "outgrown."
This is more likely when direct therapy with the child is reinforced
by a supportive educational process making full use of social opportunities. The therapeutic intent is also to influence or adjust the
personal environment (parents, teacher, institutional personnel)
towards the quality of permissive acceptance which will enable the
child to use more of his energies for growth. Psychotherapy thus allies itself with or infiltrates the life experience. In fact, the distinctive
characteristic in social work and particularly in child guidance is this
tendency to work simultaneously to reduce inner strains and outer
pressures so as to achieve a therapeutic result.

In very pathological social situations a combination of emotional
support and practical social services may be all that is possible, and
also when the personality is very limited, or infantile, or rigid, or
aged, or deteriorated, or psychotic. When parental attitudes cannot
be modified, removing the child from the conditions of pressure may
result in improvement when a favorable therapeutic attitude in substitute parental figures can be induced, especially when the child
himself can receive direct treatment in his new environment. Change
of environment is not sufficient for the child who has already

internalized his problem. A child with a sense of failure in school can be helped if his program can be modified and his teachers' attitudes made more tolerant, as well as direct therapeutic efforts geared for self-awareness and self-direction.

Therapeutic education aims to achieve a better balance, channeling, and distribution of energies so that they are available for growth instead of running wild (acting out) or being absorbed in severe repressive activities (psychoneurosis). In a therapy which goes less deep into the personality than does psychoanalysis, there are certain compensations in that social outlets and life experiences are therapeutically conditioned. As Hoffer says, "The outcome is determined by constitutional disposition, strength of the component instincts, the oedipus situation, and new identifications." [14] The therapeutic identification in the transference relationship is by no means the only one, although it is very powerful. In sublimation, which is related to the mechanism of identification, the impulses are drawn off into activities which strengthen and support the ego and aid in its adaptation to reality. The combination of direct and indirect therapy makes it easier for the client to act in harmony with the normal impulses and with better balanced controls. In mastering instinctual tendencies, the immature ego needs a good deal of assistance. The closest collaboration among therapist, educator, and all those in intimate contact with the child, on a broad social range, will increasingly, we believe, become the method of dynamic programs.

[14] See Hoffer, "Psychoanalytic Education," *The Psychoanalytic Study of the Child*, pp. 293–307.

Chapter VIII

TREATMENT OF YOUNG CHILDREN

WITH THE strengthening trend in social work toward the direct treatment of children, there has been also a shift toward treating younger children. In psychiatry child therapy has been a more recent development than adult therapy. In psychoanalysis it was found that techniques discovered and developed for the adult patient had to be considerably modified for children. Melanie Klein, a pioneer in child analysis, believed that only "depth psychology" carried on by the psychoanalyst was applicable to the treatment of children. On the other hand, Anna Freud saw the possibility of considerable modification of the depth psychology approach and pointed the way toward various combinations of therapy, including educational processes. The American child guidance movement, through its unique combination of medical, psychiatric, social, and psychological knowledge and technique, developed a particularly flexible and many-sided approach to the problem of study and treatment of children. The fact that a child is growing and that his whole organism is in a fluid state gives the therapist a chance both to modify those forces which are tending to fixate the child's development and to free some part, at least, of the inner conflict through direct treatment.

The purpose of therapy for the child, as for the adult, is to alleviate guilt and anxiety, to release aggression and repressed impulses (sometimes to aid in repression), and to correct fantasies and bring the child more into touch with reality, or to encourage better assimilation of reality, or both. Since the parents are involved,[1] whether causally or not, in all problems of child behavior, they must be brought into the treatment process in some fashion. The mothers of young children and of most older children must be helped. If the

[1] See Chapter X.

parents' participation is lacking, the entire treatment process is seriously handicapped. Most mothers do not express responsibility for the child's difficulties at the outset. Usually the problem is projected. As soon as the child is in treatment, resistance in the mother tends to develop—either to the child's treatment or to any expression of her own involvement in his problem. Some mothers refuse to tolerate any discussion of their own life experiences, and the degree to which they can make connections between their reconstructed life experiences and the child's present problems greatly varies. Request for direct advice as to how they should handle the child is often a form of resistance. Asking for help for the child without assuming responsibility in any way usually means that the parent will create a conflict for the child which will sooner or later prevent his coming to the agency. A little child cannot relate himself to the worker unless his mother can also relate herself to the treatment process, and even an older child if he feels parental disapproval, may break off. Time given the parent before seeing the child may be well spent.

After They Leave the Nursery

There is no easy definition of a "young" child, but the age range discussed in this chapter is arbitrarily defined by the fact that children younger than three are not often because of behavior problems seen in the social agency having guidance functions, unless the social agency is of a child development type. In family casework mothers under treatment for other matters may incidentally discuss the behavior of the small child if he seems destructive or upsetting or "queer" to them, yet the behavior may be within normal range. This is all the more true because the three-year-old is, one might say, a "natural behavior problem" and his mother is, at one time or another, at her wits' end about his "destructiveness," hyperactivity, and messiness.

The nursery years have been years of physical maturing and of learning to make social responses, in which the mother is the central figure—"mothering," after purely constitutional and biological elements, being the essential gratification. During this period the child has been making rapid intellectual development and gaining muscular control, and he is branching out into use of his newly found motility, which puts him in touch with a larger area. To the adult this may appear like an active clash with his environment, yet the self-assertion is absolutely essential for growth. The "destructiveness" is incidental to exploratory play, since his motor development makes taking things apart much easier for him than putting them together. Ever since he has been a toddler he has been widening the range of his experience through physical adventure and experimentation, handling, pushing, taking apart, throwing and dropping, climbing and inspecting all over the apartment or house. If the mother can provide for the gratification of these needs in the home environment or in the nursery school and be helped to see the importance of these experiences for growth, there is less likelihood of distortion or fixation. The grabbing and demanding phases normal also for this age may be accompanied and succeeded by spells of negative behavior, disobedience, and obstinacy. This, too, may be part of a normal self-assertion, and the child of three who for the *first time* begins to protest in negative as well as positive self-assertion is probably not one to be alarmed about. If his mother can be brought to understand that much of his behavior is perfectly normal for his age, the whole thing will subside as the child goes on about his main business of growing to be four. If the obstinacy becomes a battle of wills, one can be almost certain that the struggle, having been started much earlier, was provoked by the mother.

The three- and four-year-olds are moving from social reflexes and responses into social relationships. They love companions of their own age. They may occasionally run off to neighbors. They are competitive with other children, boasting of their own exploits, depreciating other children. They do not want to share the mother or the nursery-school teacher, for it seems to them, as one child psychologist [2] puts it, that "sharing is like sharing an apple." If one child gets half, then there is only half left for the other, and he has no way of knowing that relationships aren't like this, too. The three-year-old finds it hard, because of imperfect physical coordination, to do two *motor* things at once, such as eating and talking, or dressing and talking.

[2] Washburn, *Children Have Their Reasons*.

The four-year-old can do this, but he is just beginning to work on an even more intricate scheme of things, which for the next year or two gets harder and harder, namely, he has to learn to get on with two parents at once. In most well-ordered households, if the father looks after the little child, he does it according to patterns laid down by the mother, and the child does not highly differentiate the two figures. The child has, so to say, no marked "sexual" preference; but soon he must solve for himself the question of self-identity as a little boy or a girl.

A three-year-old has a great deal of trouble with his body, because he has been learning to control his motor impulses and to please his parents, who want him to be clean, not dirty. Actually, he himself regards dirt, perhaps including excreta, with favor. At four he is better able in motor control to conform to what is expected of him, and he is sociably inclined. But the five-year-old [3] has to master a whole new set of impulses in the oedipal conflict. He cannot understand his tensions; he may regress and act out all the destructive and uncontrolled behavior which he is expected to have outgrown, or he may express his frustration and jealousy in erotic, verbal or nonverbal, aggression, which is even more bewildering and embarrassing to the parent. The five-year-old appears efficient. He is a great talker, saying many serious things, the meaning of which he has not grasped, but which may sound extremely advanced to the adult. He is really quite dissocial in spite of his grown-up manner on occasion, although he knows the difference between "must" and "must not." He has a sense of duty; he has begun to construct; he can do quite nicely with his hands, but because he acts like a grown-up, one can be easily led astray unless one recognizes that his ideas of reality and unreality are fluid. He says with the same poker face, "My daddy is going to take me to the zoo tomorrow and for a long, long ride on the ponies," which is entirely probable, and "My daddy can pull the moon right out of the sky and make the biggest bomb." The first statement may be exactly as untrue as the second, but you would never know it just by listening to him. Unless prepared for the shifting line between fact

---

[3] All these ages should be regarded as approximate, not literal; the emotional growth of the individual child varies as much as physical growth.

and fiction, the parent, teacher, or worker will find the unreliability confusing. The worker cannot let himself be fooled by these stories, yet he must take them seriously, for the five-year-old takes himself very seriously.

At home the child is at the peak of trying to solve the problem of social relationships in the family—to find out who is to be dominant. Like the adolescent, he is having a terrible struggle with his impulses. He likes to play with fire both literally and figuratively, but he is scared underneath of what will happen to him if he goes too far. He projects—"I am going to kill you" (before you kill me). He may translate it into action with a sudden slap, behavior which the parent fondly thought he had outgrown. The outbursts of the five-year-old are particularly startling and unexpected to parents, since he has appeared superficially to have achieved so much social "poise," precocious wisdom, and beginning skills. But the precocity is unstable and uneven, and underneath the surface all kinds of violent impulses are surging, which occasionally break through.

The five-year-old is a great diplomat, wheedler, and exploiter. He is a specialist in stirring up the troubled waters of relationship, with which he is preoccupied anyway. To mother he says, "But daddy says I can," to father, "Mother says I can." If caught, "Well, anyway, God said I could." He makes quick and volatile identifications with mother, father, and other children. He is highly imitative. If in a group he takes leadership, he is likely to relinquish it quickly because it frightens him. His occasional deviations in behavior in wetting and soiling are disturbing to his self-esteem and very disturbing to his parents. He regresses easily under frustration, although he can as easily be reassured, soothed, and encouraged to go on growing up. If little attention is paid to the lapse, and love and encouragement are given to the child, the difficulty is short-lived.

The eight-year-old finds the adult who says "My, my, how you've grown" an unmitigated bore, but the five-year-old doesn't mind it. The idea of growing up is a ready consolation when adults get too big for him. Mostly he wants to hurry up and be like daddy and mummy—in spite of the fact that he is quite ready to kill them off in a fit of rage. The wise parent listens calmly to aggressive threats and quietly limits too aggressive behavior, which may later be drained off happily in play. Even in the normal situation many parents are disconcerted by the violent reactions and attachments of the five-year-old. The little boy may become very aggressive toward his father and very much devoted to his mother. The little girl may have nothing to do with her mother and be very critical of her. It is even more puzzling, because at the same time they claim all the prerogatives of their own sex. The parent is naturally offended if he does not understand that this is a normal stage in growth, just as are the earlier selfishness, negativism, and "destructiveness." The parent of the older child may do then what the mother sometimes does with the younger child who has turned away from her—"I don't like him because he does not like me." This, of course, makes the child worse. The child, in short, can make the parental environment as sensitive to his problem as he is himself. With all the startlingly quick development and change, each year has its own achievements and problems, each function of feeding, walking, talking, speech, elimination, and exercise has its special importance. But it is the first six years or so, when the super-ego is being formed, which seem to put the greatest strain on the ego's ability to integrate.

The Task of Therapy [4]

The guidance agency rarely sees infants and toddlers, partly because adults do not always recognize exaggerations and distortions in the earliest developmental stages, and partly because neither mothers nor nursery-school teachers like to admit that they cannot handle little children. For most nursery-age children the mother's fear of social criticism will make her try to keep the situation smoothed over even when it is already badly tangled, rather than confess her failure. But it is in the upper range of the three-to-six period that the child, because of his great social mobility and the complexity of the adjustments he has to make, tends to come to the attention of the guidance agency. The three-year-old who has been normally attracted to mud

[4] Special acknowledgment is made here to the seminars on the treatment of young children given by Dr. Nathan Ackerman for the Jewish Board of Guardians' staff. See also list of papers in the bibliography.

and sand and dirtiness may by four start a reaction formation as a
defense against his disorder. If he has been over-trained up to this
point, he may rebel or develop fears about getting dirty. Young children may show marked anxiety over finger paints and clay—touching
them gingerly or avoiding them altogether. The child of three or
three and a half brought to a guidance agency may be said already
to have had "a past," a past of struggles over feeding and toilet training and other body habits. A guidance agency occasionally sees a
young child who has an exacerbation of the fears which began between two and four—of the dark, of inanimate objects, of all the
familiar objects which suddenly become eerie as the imagination
develops—but this is less common than to have children whose difficulties are more overt. Infantilized children are not likely to be
brought in until the prolongation of dependent behavior, continued
from the nursery years, has the effect of inhibiting the child from
playing with other children or causing school failure or unhappiness.
The already disturbed child is likely to be either more chronically or
more violently aggressive than the secure child, who will have many
sunny and serene intervals. Obviously, the child who has always
fought his mother over feeding and toilet training will have a difficult
time in the complicated solution of his relationship to the "parents as a
couple" problem.[5] Parents who fight back prevent the child from
a successful solution, since the child is already afraid of attack or
punishment for his wishes. The more he is afraid, the more he may
show aggression. If the disconcerted parents, on the other hand, give
in to the aggression and lose control, the child's fears may increase,
and once again a vicious circle is established. The parent who argues
with the child, but gives in, is often the same parent who insists on
dominating. A price is always exacted for the child's yielding.

The child who comes to the guidance worker has brought more
aggression, either overt or suppressed, than the average child; has
taken his parents harder and prolonged the rivalry situation with
both parent and sibling. For him the blissful state of so-called "latency" does not begin, and may never really ensue, since one turmoil
succeeds another.[6] He is still struggling with his parental solutions.

[5] See pp. 30–33.   [6] See pp. 211 *et seq.*

While the four-year-old child is beginning to dream of wolves and dogs, the really frightening dreams which crowd in at five, six, and seven, bring anxiety along with the aggressive desire to possess and not to share.

The aim of therapy is to take the child again through those periods in which gratifications have been incompletely or mistakenly given and, in the strong dependency of the transference, to offer appropriate gratifications and small doses of frustration which the child can assimilate, thus correcting the distortion, removing the fixation, and assisting the child to a normal super-ego function. Through identification with the therapist, infantile behavior can be left behind and the energies used to control the aggression, to meet the demands of the rapidly expanding personality, and to assist in the internalization of reasonable inner sanctions and restraints. The needs of the young child for protection, love, security, and encouragement to experiment are met, for the most part, in the therapeutically controlled play situation in which self-expression leads to self-direction.

Transference in a child has a different coloring from the same phenomenon in the adult relationship.[7] Since the child's ego is immature and incomplete the therapist is closer to a "real" parent in the child's mind. Transference is based on specific feelings, but the feelings of affection, fear, hatred, and evasiveness are in the child all fused together or very quickly shifting. It is hard to say whether or not the feelings are as "irrational" as in adult transference (the image of the therapist is no more accurate), but certainly there is a quality of "real" support offered by the therapist and a corresponding quality of "real" attachment and dependency natural to such an age,[8] along with the transference phenomena. For the most part, the worker plays the part

[7] See pp. 127 et seq.

[8] "Even if one part of the child's neurosis is transformed into a transference neurosis, as it happens in adult analysis, another part of the child's neurotic behavior remains grouped around the parents." Anna Freud in "Indications for Child Analysis," in The Psychoanalytic Study of the Child, p. 130.

"As a rule the child does not develop a transference neurosis. . . . The analyst may become the target of many of the child's sexual or aggressive impulses, and occasionally and within a limited scope he may play the part of one of the parents. . . . There is no need for him to repeat his reaction vicariously since he still possesses his original love objects—his parents—in reality."—Bornstein, "Clinical Notes on Child Analysis," in The Psychoanalytic Study of the Child, pp. 152–153.

of the parent of the same sex, because the child had concrete ideas and knows the adult world chiefly as "mommie" and "daddy" figures. The child easily carries over to any adult person his patterns toward his parents. Children whose fathers play with them relate quite easily to male workers, for instance. In many guidance cases one finds an "uncompromising demand," described so well by Pavenstedt and Andersen,[9] for a mother person, which can hardly be described as transference, but as dependency on a "natural" parent. The child who does not get love and understanding from the parents will seek these overtly. Nevertheless, the therapist is nearer being a real parent to young children than to older children or adults. With infantile children and those having behavior disorders the worker often nourishes and gratifies needs rather than at first approaches internalized conflicts, but as soon as the child is ready the supportive relationship may be dropped, frustrations may be imposed, and the removal of intrapsychic obstacles to growth attempted. Only experienced workers will know how far to go—when it is feasible to permit bodily contact by taking the child on one's lap, for instance [10]—and when cooking, eating, reading, or singing together may have the double value of gratification and bringing the child into a participating rhythm with the therapist.

The Meaning and Use of Play

The distinguishing technique in therapy for young children is in the use of the play situation or "interview." Play is used because the young child is best able to express himself through activity. Play offers opportunity for growth, for release of tension, for practice in new achievements, for testing and development. Through it he learns how to meet new situations, to increase his motility, to bring together fantasy and reality and distinguish the two, to build ego strength, and to dilute frightening and traumatic events by reproducing them in harmless disguises.

Anyone who wishes to work with children at all must be able to

[9] Pavenstedt and Andersen, "The Uncompromising Demand of a Three Year Old for a Real Mother," in *The Psychoanalytic Study of the Child*, pp. 211–232.
[10] See case on p. 197.

play with them. For some reason the use of play in the treatment of children has assumed a mystical and esoteric quality as "play therapy." The term is misleading. It is not the play which is therapy, it is the relationship which the child experiences. The child uses play to communicate with the therapist. The child creates his own environment, and as he manipulates his environment the therapist, through participation, guides him—the play roles themselves being often the chief means of "interpretation."

The parents of problem children, out of their own perplexities and disturbed emotions, have made one mistake or the other, that is, extreme license, or frustration, or inconsistency, so that one of the functions of play in therapy is to help to a better balance of drive expression and internalized sanctions and controls. Release on a motor level is particularly natural and helpful for young children if it takes place on the basis of a therapeutic relationship, and so can be utilized purposefully. A common misconception is that *first* one establishes a relationship, and *then* comes to understand. The truth is that it is the understanding of the child, what he says and what he does, which promotes the relationship. As soon as the child feels secure he will communicate his private thoughts in some fashion.

In treatment, play not only provides progressive release from tension but also relieves current conflicts by actually communicating fantasies. In adult analysis the patient brings up deeply repressed past material; in casework interviews discussion of painful incidents both in the present and in the past is carried on, but in play the child repeats those disturbing events which are presently active at home. He discharges his emotions and transforms frightening or unpleasant experiences into more pleasant ones. Thus he can assume a "role other than the one assigned to him by a cruel fate." [11] Play is used to reach the child on whatever level he finds himself in his regression or fixation and within the transference to help him make a fresh start toward higher levels of development. Through play the child is permitted to release anxiety and hostility; to repeat symbolically with-

[11] For a study made at the Jewish Board of Guardians see Knoepfmacher, "The Use of Play in Diagnosis and Therapy in a Child Guidance Clinic." *Smith College Studies in Social Work,* XII (March, 1942), 217–262.

out criticism forbidden bodily preoccupations; to weave stories about and relive traumatizing situations; to work through the confused identifications and erotic aggression of the oedipal period; to find strength and confidence in his own ideas and activities; to lay aside binding defenses; to externalize painful feelings of failure, inferiority, and shame; and slowly to bridge the gap between dreams and reality, learning what is and what is not "make believe." In short, through limiting and encouraging, permitting and restraining, the child is helped to consolidate and balance those diffuse strivings which a more enlightened parental attitude could have helped him to integrate in the ordinary course of familial and group associations.

As an adult is helped to remember as much as possible and to make connections between past and present and between one current conflict and another, so, too, the child, acting out repetitiously in play, is helped to make connections between what he is doing here in play and what goes on in the family. The normal child who passes rapidly through levels of development often hardly has time to assimilate educational limitations on feeding, toilet, and body habits, aggressive and destructive behavior. When there has been unwise parental handling, he may have had neither enough time to assimilate nor enough gratification to sustain the discipline of learning. Play in a treatment relationship may help him assimilate or reassimilate these "growing pains" in a less charged atmosphere and with symbolic but neutral media, such as water, clay, paint, and a "family" of dolls. Up to about five or six, play is the most natural means of communication—later play is largely used for preliminary phases with difficult children and as a means of diagnostic observation. A very disturbed older child may need this form of interview, or other problems may dictate the use of play beyond the younger age range for phases of treatment. Since the development of speech is rapid between four and six, verbalization is important to encourage along with the play as far as possible, without, however, forcing the issue.

What is it that a child is trying to say in a play situation? Repetition of one theme over and over means that in some way he has not been understood. If one does not understand, one should ask questions. How does he talk to the toys? What kind of vocabulary does he use? Is he rigid, blank, meek, aggressive? Does he smile to get approval? Is he triumphant or frightened? The total functioning of the child in the play is our concern. With the child who has a behavior problem, it is important to let the aggression come out where it can be discussed; with the anxious child, it is important to bring out the fears. But since the therapist should not arouse more anxiety than he can handle, the process is often slow. Fast or slow, the child's unconscious must be constantly in communication with the sensitized worker. If the worker is not aware of the child's unspoken messages, the play is merely play. Many inexperienced workers allow the child to play on indefinitely when nothing of therapeutic significance is emerging. If, however, the caseworker is continuously alert to the child's need for help, the play will be charged with meaning. The relationship allows the child to move from the generalized to the specific situations which bother him.

The essential element in the therapy comes from the worker's correct *perception* of the meaning of the child's play within the relationship. In other words, as the child's play projects or transfers onto the worker forbidden feelings and wishes in a permissive atmosphere, anxiety is released and progressively reduced. The response of the worker (and by this we do not necessarily mean "interpretation," but "acceptance" based on true understanding) is both educational and healing. The "therapeutic" attitude,[12] basic in all psychotherapy, is of special importance to children as the *new experience* which they can assimilate through repetition. The subtle emanations of feeling—its nuances and overtones—constantly interact both in therapy and as therapy. The child then communicates his personal life through everything he does in the office. In group therapy through play the child is put in touch with partial or "moderate" reality, and the *group reactions* become a form of "interpretation" to the participant. In individual therapy the patterns of play are usually commented on by the worker as soon as the relationship is secure enough to permit it. In building an object relationship the ability to strengthen the ego comes simultaneously. The relationship with the worker permits the play to be used this way, and as far as possible everything which af-

12 See p. 125.

fects him should be brought into the relationship. A child who had great castration anxiety finally succeeded in constructing a ship. "Will you keep this ship for me?" he said to the worker. "Of course I will." No doubt the ship meant something of masculinity to him, but the precise symbolism did not matter so much as that the child was seeking support from the worker in his struggle toward integration, and was seeking permission to grow up.

When the child says, "Can I have this gun?" it is almost never a simple request. A child may employ a baby kangaroo or a baby doll figure, but he rarely names the toy after real members of the family cast. This is particularly true when the incidents to be played out are highly traumatized. The worker in his response uses the child's play symbols, just as in the interview one talks the same language and follows the drama the child offers until he, himself, abandons it. For instance, when he names the doll "Betty"—if the worker says, "Who is Betty?" the child may block. If he asks, "What is Betty doing?" the child may show him now or later very clearly who Betty is—indeed, she may represent several persons in turn. As in *Lohengrin,* there is too much magic in a name for the little child to give his secrets away lightly.

Little children are so busy finding themselves in a world of reality that they do not appear to have, or perhaps the worker does not have access to, their fantasy life much before the age of four. Night terrors and phobias are, of course, found, however, as early as two or three. Probably each body function—sucking, defecating, drinking, masturbating—is translated into some sort of fantasy. Among the earliest and most engrossing ideas are birth fantasies, and these persist well into latency. Fears of being eaten or destroyed and threats from animals are common. The child is unconscious that he fears parental anger and punishment. Play is the safety valve, and any observer of child play is struck by the fact that the doll parents are so much more punishing and savage than the real parents ever are, and the good qualities of indulgence are of the fairy-godmother variety. In therapy, although the worker should understand most of the more common symbols—and in fact the symbols used by a child are often obvious—interpretation of fantasy is not typically given other than the participation in play which shows the child that he is understood. Although play is a substitute for free association, it is not entirely free, nor with weekly interviews is it always sequential. It is astonishing, however, how often the child carries on after six days precisely where he left off, showing that the current is really unbroken. However, meanings are not always apparent, and the worker must be on guard against premature or irrelevant inferences. Bornstein cautions us here.[13]

The multiplicity of meaning in a child's play may lead to misinterpretation, but even if, under favorable circumstances, the play permits detailed insight into the child's conflicts and the ways in which he tries to master them, we should still hesitate to interpret his symbolic play action because of the significance of play in general. Play is the first important step in the process of sublimation. Continuous interpretation of its symbolic meaning is likely to upset the process before it is well established.

Some children use repetitive patterns of play to avoid discussion as a defense or a barricade. When the saturation point is reached, the worker may have to comment on the fact that the child is afraid or upset in order to get the anxiety and hostility out into the open again. On the other hand, he may need a long period within which to work out his anxieties. Inhibition toward play is sometimes an indication of neurotic limitations; sometimes it is a form of resistance; sometimes there is physical or mental incapacity. It is not true, however, that a child who is silent is necessarily shutting out the worker. He may be extremely aware of the worker's presence and be actively including him.

One wants to make the child comfortable as soon as possible, and he is often made more so if the therapist responds to his first move but does not initiate the first move. If that is not possible, one may, perhaps, draw him gradually into the relationship by a glance or a question or by letting him do part of the worker's "play" or drawing or other unobtrusive pursuit. The therapist must become important to the child early, and usually the child's need will make him circle warily, ever a little closer, like a curious squirrel. There is no rule, of course, for getting into touch with children (and sometimes it is quite difficult) other than liking children and being genuinely sure

[13] Bornstein, "Clinical Notes on Child Analysis," in *The Psychoanalytic Study of the Child*, pp. 151–166.

of one's therapeutic role. If the worker is not sure, the child will disengage himself from "contact" with the worker in his play, and will remain obdurately outside the relationship.

An obsessional child, who would not talk and greatly feared being killed, spent his play interviews in making tiny objects which he wanted to have pasted on the worker's wall. This was the only evidence that he understood the relationship and was using the transference. For a year the worker had to instruct the janitor to leave the wall alone, and the child's anxious inspection over and over again told the worker how much he needed this help. After a long period he stopped doing this and was able to talk. Everything the worker does, once transference has been established, becomes therapeutically important. It is the inexperienced worker who does not know that there is a bond or compact between him and the playing child, a blindness which the child will take advantage of. Any discussion of shared activities by the skilled worker becomes a discussion of the child's "problem." As the child plays out his narcissistic wishes to be exclusively loved and all powerful, as he plays out over and over again his rivalries and attachments, the worker has an opportunity to help him modify these attachments. Insight, as it takes place, is fused within the personality as a reaction of the total personality of the growing child—that is, "insight" becomes part of the growth process. Whenever the child does something new, one tries to tie it up with his general behavior so that he, too, can understand the trend. Release of the instinctual behavior has to be slow, lest the child feel guilty toward the mother, who does not permit these things.

A child correctly senses that play is not for the sake of playing. Although he may try to turn it into play, using this as a defense, he will at once know when he is being understood. A worker does not promise a child everything because he would be unable to carry out such a promise. Promises build up an unreal belief in the child that he can get anything he wants by asking for it, which is not possible. It is important to distinguish legitimate requests by the child from the quality of asking which is insatiable. If one wants a child to progress one must make the next step attractive, but insatiable children often don't really want what they request and are not satisfied when they get it. They will spoil a gift from the worker or hit a worker who shows them affection. Continued gratifications may make the child feel better, but the underlying disturbances may be then inaccessible. When the friendliness and play become gratifications or ends in themselves, he has to learn that he does not come merely to play.

A child may have been told by his mother or even by the worker that he is coming to play with someone friendly to him. This is better than to have him believe that he comes to be punished. A little child cannot easily grasp the therapeutic intent of the play until he has experienced it, nor does he understand abstract ideas like happiness or unhappiness or "treatment." Sometimes even a very young child understands that he is coming for help, but ordinarily one has to help him understand. The child usually knows that "something is up," because he knows he has been "bad" or disappointing to his parents. One must give the child some clear orientation as to why he is coming. If he does not know, it adds to his confusion and mistrust. It is better to find out why he thinks he is coming than to give a theoretical explanation of the agency's function. He is told that he will be seen regularly. He may put his name on the calendar, if he is old enough, and otherwise encouraged to start "to work."

A child must be allowed to feel as much anxiety as he can tolerate, allaying his anxiety by slow experimentation, as he finds that the therapist is not dangerous. The more specifically fears are defined, the safer the relationship is felt to be by the child. Generalizations or discussions of remote problems in the child's life take the child out of the relationship and so out of treatment. Children have concrete fears and experiences. They understand the worker better when he is concrete. This does not mean that a child should be answered literally when he asks for information, because often it is better to get out the fantasy or fear behind the question. When he expresses in some form his fear that the worker will do something to him, one must recognize this or one will, perhaps, lose him. If a child is falsely encouraged, he may cover up his problem altogether, retreating into demands for gratification or other defenses. As soon as the child is able to translate his feelings into words he is encouraged to do so, but for many young children this process is slow.

Handling aggression in the play situation is always difficult. Aggression, as we have said, is a perfectly normal phase of growth, particularly during the period when the child is trying to find his place in the family circle. It is reasonable for the little child who may have been pushed and yanked around to want to take his turn at pushing other children around or to be active and aggressive in play with a compliant worker. In young children it is often hard to distinguish hyperactivity and hypermotility from aggressiveness. Since the play interview encourages the discharge of tension through acting out, a great deal of aggression flows forth. The fact that the aggression is so easily turned against the therapist is disconcerting and alarming to the young worker.[14] Adults often do not realize that they can be frightened by a young child's violence, and taken unaware they may react aggressively and appeasingly in turn. It further frightens the child, who senses the alarm at once, to know that the worker is frightened. This proves to the child that the bad impulses are very bad indeed and that perhaps magically the wish can really be effective —again because the child's sense of reality is still tenuous. It is not good therapy to placate a child for an unexpected outburst and then stir up hostility later when one feels ready for it. Nor is there virtue in letting a child indefinitely, or extremely, play out his aggression, for if unchecked it will become worse. One "tolerates" rather than "accepts" aggression. Tolerance is a systematic device for controlling aggression. One must allow aggression to be discharged, but one neither licenses nor discourages it. Sick children pay too much attention to their own fantasies of aggression. First one learns not to punish, and then not to sympathize with the wrong things. The basis of tolerance is for the whole child, who has some good in him, as well as bad.

A five-and-one-half-year-old girl, Beulah, hostile and provocative with children, was dominating, demanding, and had temper tantrums if crossed. She showed nail-biting, thumb-sucking, and feeding difficulties. There was a background of severe rejection and inconsistent handling

---

[14] See earlier discussion on giving love, p. 138.

on the part of both parents, especially the mother, who openly admitted she didn't like her and was cruel to her.

In the first interviews the child ignored the worker and talked into the dictaphone—a long story made out of nonsense about some "neighbors," but full of disconnected hostile phrases—"if you want to be a fish, go live in a dish," "if you like beef stew, go live in a stew," etc. She paid no attention to the worker other than to print her own name in the worker's appointment book. In the second interview she played with the dolls' house, talking constantly. Once she commented that the lady puppet should have a wand like the fairy godmother in Cinderella. "To do what?" She smiled teasingly—"Oh, you know"—still keeping herself aloof. She wanted to take the dolls' house home, which was refused in the usual way—that it doesn't belong to worker, but to the office.

In the next interview she complained of the toys. She demanded one of the glass animals and was given her favorite to take home (yielding to a demand). She played a little, opened all the desk drawers, found some cakes, demanded one, and ate it greedily, didn't include worker either in play or conversation.

In the fourth interview she displayed a valentine, said it was prettier than the card the worker sent her when she was sick, criticized the toys again, fussed with the dolls' house, lost interest, said she would draw a picture for the worker (letting her in a little), but didn't like the picture afterwards and drew numbers instead (retreating from contact). In the fifth interview she criticized the toys, but said the dolls' house was nicer than the house she lived in. She wanted the worker to play checkers now, exulted when winning, was very annoyed when jumped; became very angry when worker spoke to her mother when she came for her. Worker appeased—"If you will let me talk to your mother this week I will talk only to you next week." She said worker could talk only for one minute, demanded paints, and then spilled three bottles over table, chairs, and floor; was pleased at effect.

At her sixth interview she handled the toys roughly, demanded a story, climbed onto lap of worker, who hugged her warmly. She immediately climbed down and demanded ice cream. They went to the drug store; she demanded a second soda; this was refused. She asked for a doll in the showcase; this was refused; asked for a greeting card, which was given to her, and she left in high spirits. The next interview was the "pay-off." She came in scowling, hated the toys, wanted new things, turned up her nose at the finger paints, tore the dolls' house apart that she had liked so much. Worker made no effort to stop her, but commented, "Beulah is mad at me!" At this, her face became distorted with anger, "I hate you! I never wanted to come to this place!" Worker asked what kind of place it is. Worker said maybe she was scared by a strange place and feared what worker might do to her. She stamped her foot: "Your face stinks, and I hate your mouth worst of all." Worker commented: "Beulah doesn't like what comes out of my mouth." "I hate you! I hate you! I'm never coming back!" Worker, who had slipped from one mistake into another, first by giving in to demands, then by taking her on her lap and cuddling her—now tried appeasement again: "There's a swell little girl" (Beulah knows better) "and we can be friends and talk about what happened at school." Beulah considered this shrewdly, "I'm going away, and I won't come back again."

With this greatly deprived child, apparently arrested at an infantile, narcissistic level, who wants continuous gratification, the worker makes a natural mistake of trying to give love through hugging her, through verbal reassurance ("I like you"), through ice cream sodas, and so forth. A child may need, without being ready to receive, affection. Beulah's bitter cry at home was, "It's not fair." Little children have poor capacity to bear tension, and such a child as Beulah has little self-control. Accustomed to severe rejection, even cruelty, from her mother, excessive warmth only increases her tension and anxiety. She is quick with defenses against hostility, but less secure against a friendly approach. A consistently relaxed and interested attitude might have been easier for this child, who had no normal attachments. A second principle of therapy seems to have been violated by the attempts to appease the aggression. This has the effect of increasing the child's tension and anxiety within herself.

The aggressive child expects to be disappointed, and yet he is impelled to tease and to provoke. First, one lets him release his aggression, limiting only as much as is necessary, frustrating as little as possible, in order to see what is going on. The first therapeutic effect is in the catharsis, or discharge of tension, and the tolerance, patience, and lack of reprisal or punishment, unexpected because so unlike what happens to him at home and in play with other children. This has always the element of a mild "shock" therapy—the shock of forgiveness. Then, as soon as one knows what he is expressing, one begins gently to point it out and so help him to see it himself. The child rapidly apperceives the fact that here is an adult who understands his need to be aggressive, yet who does not approve of the aggressive act. When the worker does not take the behavior at face value, but recognizes the wish to hurt or dominate or love which it represents, turning it back to the real wish, the child is usually restrained and will often turn to verbalization. Permission to be aggressive has to be related to the appropriate level of development and interpreted in appropriate ways. Limitation of aggression against the person of the therapist is always necessary, both for safety's sake and because actual domination by the child is unrealistic, arouses too much anxiety, and is generally nontherapeutic in its effects. The child's violence often covers real panic.[15] One may see the emergence of fears immediately after the expression of hostility. It is better to limit excessive destructiveness for the child, since he cannot yet control his own destructiveness. Both the negative fearful child and the overtly hostile one, each in his own way, are trying to force the worker into counteraggression. Ultimately the child discovers that the danger which persists in all his other relationships is not found here.

Avoidance by play, which excludes the worker, often means anxiety or anger. On the other hand, the child's demand for the worker's participation may be in order to control or to weaken the worker's attempts to influence the problem behavior. The dictation of roles often represents a need either to dominate or to evade a particular issue. Hostility is usually easier for the worker to spot than is passive avoidance. It is hard to guess what the child is avoiding, and one has to try to get him to explain. Children may stay away either because the experience is disagreeable or because it is pleasurable, but the anxiety is not thereby resolved. If the child does not talk or play, the worker may busy himself with something else, waiting for him to be comfortable enough to speak. The worker must be relaxed and not join in the battle of wills which the child may want to provoke. In any form of therapy the patient must agree to come. In psychoanalysis he

---

[15] See pp. 55–65.

must agree to the rule of free association. In any therapy he must be willing to talk and to reveal himself. The child must be helped to come, and sometimes this calls for firmness as well as friendliness. His parents must be willing to bring him. It is not wise for the therapist to force him to come, but often quite legitimate pressure is put on the parent to see that the child does come, especially during initial periods.

Play Materials and Setting [16]

The play materials used in a guidance agency are those long tested in ordinary living as appropriate for a particular age range. The universality of the appeal rests on the universality of the motivation. The basic toys which reflect various levels of development become channels for expressing the whole personality. Sand, clay, plasticene, shells, buttons, water—all offer to the young child easy access to his unsolved educational problems. He can enjoy his messiness and satisfy his original impulses in acceptable forms. There are available, also, cannons, soldiers, guns, darts, and knives for the display of aggression; blocks and other materials for constructing and building; water and paint as outlets for toilet problems and for creative activities; the doll family for study of the body processes and, more significantly, for the social relationships; clay and crayons to express the ideation; and so forth. Older children not only use paints, but leather and tools for self-expression and "acting out."

The play things should be simple, homely, and stimulating to fantasy in the child himself; materials should be malleable enough to be manipulated in the direction of the child's desire. Any inexperienced worker, looking into a toy closet or at a toy shelf, is astonished at the poor, defaced, and worn materials which week after week hold the attention of children. True, the child may demand new toys, but this more often happens when the relationship has developed to the point

[16] At the Jewish Board of Guardians the stage is rarely set with playthings. The set play technique is perhaps more appropriate when a child has a specific phobia. The free association approach in which the child chooses his own media is preferred. Occasionally a specific device is used, such as cooking and eating together or making fires in a bucket for a therapeutic purpose.

at which the child is seeking gratification from the worker rather than gratification from the toy. Frequently, of course, children make their own toys, following out their fantasies from the start. In therapy it is not the kind of plaything, but the use which the child makes of the plaything which has significance. Diagnostically, what he chooses and how he proceeds throw a great deal of light not only on the problem but also on his affective reaction to the problem.

In general, the child is allowed to play as long as he will with one set of toys, rather than expose him to a great many, so that he may develop his own ideas and fantasies. If he moves too rapidly from one toy to another, it is less likely that a trend will develop which can be followed. Initially one may take any spot in the child's interest, either in play or in verbalization, and follow his reaction. Young workers tend to impose their own notions.

The child models a sea gull and says it is about to light on the water. Says the worker, "It's nice, isn't it, the way he just floats on the water and doesn't have to move his wings." The child agrees. Worker: "Wouldn't it be nice if you could be a bird like that when you want to run away?" "But suppose," asks the child, "there was a storm, what would happen to the bird?" Worker: "I guess he would go sit on the boat if the storm was so bad he couldn't fly." "Yes," says the child anxiously, "but what if the boat sank?" "Then I guess he could find a box to sit on, don't you?" "But what if the box sank?" "I don't think it would," says the worker cheerfully, "but then maybe he could find a stick to sit on."

"The child appeared satisfied with this," commented the worker. But, unfortunately, it is the worker who is here stubbornly optimistic and whose wishes dominate the play with false reassurance. For the most part, it is better not to choose the toys for the child, or propose play, or tell the stories. Occasionally the device of telling the child's story by attributing the events to another until the child himself takes over the role is utilized successfully. But if the child is pushed into activity chosen by the therapist, the unconscious trends cannot come to the surface where they can be effectively dealt with. What the child does first often is the clue to his preoccupation.

Illustrations Showing Use of Play

Disturbed children under treatment quickly tend to move to the situation where the difficulty lies. Sometimes this represents the binding of the emotional interest in the current situation; sometimes regression to the level where the frustration occurred. The expression of traumatized behavior does not follow any coherent pattern; it weaves back and forth among dependency of the baby, destructiveness, toilet play, and the oedipal problem. It is not easy to show a logical step-by-step procedure by which the worker gives opportunity for release, enters into the fantasy, interprets either verbally or by diagnostically informed play participation, offers gratification, or introduces diluted and gradual frustration, but we shall give in condensed form illustrations of these processes.

A little boy, five years old, very precocious, with an erratic father and a neurotic mother, had been sent to the hospital with pneumonia at the same time that his little sister was ill. When he got home his sister was dead. In his play with the worker he forever made up stories and poems about animals who had lost their families. He was very aggressive. He took a pistol and shot himself—he shot the baby doll, the pictures of baby girls. The worker was a "pistol packing momma" (she would avenge herself on him). He shot the baby kangaroo. He gave the father and other dolls a present of a new baby. "Everybody looked at the new baby and said it was cute, and so did the little boy doll." "Did the little boy think she was cute?" asked the worker. "No, he was very unhappy." He made the worker build a fire and burn the baby up—he was suddenly anxious. The worker said in the play, "Yes, I was angry but I didn't mean really to burn the baby up." He was still anxious. He played telephoning to mama. "Is there anything that worries you, little boy?" "Yes, that my mother won't forgive me," and so on.

These plays were repeated in countless variations until some of the piled up tension and anxiety over the death of the little girl, whom he had often wished away, were assuaged. Left by the death of his sister to possess his mother all by himself, she appears as a "pistol packing momma." His own fears lest he should be sent away because of his badness, and perhaps die, were also clearly elaborated with both mother and father figures. He must continue to act out these anxieties until the worker's forgiveness in play scenes can be finally incorporated as forgiveness instead of retaliation, with relaxation and self-acceptance.

An illustration of how play can be used in a shared activity to release feeling and oral inhibition and to play out a traumatized growth period is in the following:

Clara was a three-and-a-half-year-old child, brought in by her mother because she presented serious food difficulties. She was entirely uninterested in food, had no appetite, sat at the table day-dreaming, retaining food in her mouth. She vomited frequently. She was a thumb-sucker. When Clara started thumb-sucking at two, she was sent to a nursery school so that her mother could go on working. She taped the child's fingers. There was a constant battle between her and the little girl, who said, "I don't want to eat in your house."

The mother is compulsive, obsessional, and has made a ritual of feeding the children. She forces herself and her love on the children through eating. She fears death, and food is important in keeping her and the children alive, but because she is so impoverished and rigid herself, she really cannot give herself to ("feed") anyone else.

When the child was first seen, she was a tiny, fragile-looking youngster, 5 lbs. underweight. When she inspected the toy shelves, she took dolls and toy furniture. She put two dolls to bed, covered them up, and told worker they were sleeping. She was going to prepare some supper for them. Worker wondered what they had for supper. "Milk, eggs, and cereal." "Would they like that?" She did not answer, but began to feed them. Once she pretended that one of the dolls had spilled the cereal, and she said she had put too much on the spoon.

Here there is much inhibition of feeling rather than panic and tension, but release is equally needed. Therapy proceeded along the lines of continually playing out the feeding problem, permitting oral dependency, and, in this instance, offering considerable gratification. The worker wished to give a secure experience in a loving relationship. "She fed the doll, giving her cereal and eggs. The doll left some of the food, and Clara, as 'Mommie,' threw it out, then she spanked the doll." Often she showed great anxiety as she reproduced eating difficulties in her own way. Somtimes in the office the dolls would "eat" greedily the "string beans" or other "vegetables" prepared on the toy stove. As she played out repetitively these scenes in cooking and eating play, she improved very much at home.

It was very important that a relationship be formed with this child and to get her to be able to want something and take something from the worker. At the start she had taken toys and played in such a way as to isolate the worker, but later she was able to include her in the play and to accept things like a piece of candy, which she would eat. This she had never been willing to do at home. At the end of the treatment she could eat the food they had cooked together. This came after the worker had been able to bring out some expression of her hostility toward the mother, as expressed in the doll play. She seemed to make some connection in this also between the mother in the doll play and the worker. After this had been brought out, she was more relaxed, friendly, and able to accept.

In a case cited earlier [17] the worker helped a boy to derive gratification from the expression of his oral needs—offering him candy and cookies to eat during interviews. His mother and his nurse had given food with aggression—here, as a symbol of love, he could enjoy it. (There is a phase in treatment when a positive transference being established, the worker has to be on guard against being pulled over into the child's ecstasy.)

In another case, a four-and-one-half-year-old child was completely cured of food fads through interminable play with a tin can and dried peas, in which was repeated over and over again the pressure upon eating brought by the mother. Only toward the end, when the child was better, did the worker comment on the problem the child was solving, yet there was continual awareness by the child of the meaning of the play. The bond or compact of understanding was evident in almost every gesture. The symbolic play language of the worker and the child was mutually comprehensible. Concurrent treatment of the mother was, of course, carried on, but not intensively, as she responded quickly. The child needed and received a long period in

17 See p. 89.

which to release hostility and aggression toward the mother and to assimilate the new experience.

An example in which a five-year-old boy expressed problems which were handled in the play interview is the following:

Sidney had been running away from home, was reckless and aggressive, and had uncontrolled toilet habits. He said to himself in kindergarten, "I don't want to cry. I must learn to fight," indicating his insecurity in the socially demanding situation. He felt weak and expected to be attacked.

In the first phase he expressed only aggression, using guns and toy soldiers with anxiety. He almost at once began to model clay figures with intense preoccupation with sex differences between the boy and girl figures. He had all sorts of fantasies about eating people up and being eaten up in turn, and from the start began to reproduce the parental scenes, first the father, who was bad because he hit the child, and then the mother, because she did the same, but later overtly he dramatized intercourse. He moved from aggressive play to verbal aggression, using "shit" and other anal expressions. Sometimes he regressed to baby play, nursing with the dolls' milk bottle or feeding the doll. These infantile themes were succeeded by quite grown up observations, such as that the nipple of the milk bottle was made that way to "control the flow of water." [18] As he felt more secure, his verbal aggression mounted and he used all the nursery words for toilet behavior, and took great pleasure in rhythmical repetitions. His infantile drives were still active, oral and anal intermingled. He was attached to his mother and felt great hostility toward his father.

In the next phase he expressed his aggression toward the father, interspersed with birth fantasies. He became able to verbalize his feeling about his father—that he beat him; that he wanted to hit back and hurt him. "My father is angry at me, but I am more angry at him." "Is it because you cannot fight back?" He nodded. After a limitation by the worker he was angry, and this was interpreted. "Are you still angry at me?" "No, but at my father I am always angry," he said.

There was then a phase of erotic aggression directed toward the worker. He modeled her in clay, making a great point of the sexual organs. She did not permit bodily contact, but he often tried to outwit her; tried to bump into her; to handle her. He permitted himself to be diverted

---

[18] See the precocious wisdom of the five-year-old on p. 177.

into aggressive sexual drawings. The worker was relaxed, but always was quick to anticipate his moves, and did not often have to limit him directly other than to say he must not hurt her. Most of it was brought out in play. He would drop a bomb on her house, take all her clothes away and bring them to his house. "You will be naked," he said triumphantly. Then he was frightened. She smiled at him and said, "Is that how you would like to see me?" He nodded. The worker related this to wanting to see his mother. (The activity was translated into verbalization and thus handled.)

The play against the father became more intense and even more violent. There was very little disguise. Once, after he had played out a situation to his satisfaction, killing the father and sleeping with the mother, he became very anxious. "Do you like yourself?" he asked the worker. The worker said that sometimes she was not quite satisfied, and then she wanted to know what the trouble was, but on the whole she liked herself quite well. " Do you like yourself?" Doubtfully, he said, "Yes." Anxiously, "Do you like me?" "Very, very much." He said, satisfied, "Then so do I." The worker controlled his erotic attacks by interpretation of a simple sort. He tried to stick his paint brush into her eye; stopped, he tried to paint her arm. When the worker said, "'You really don't want to paint my arm, but something else," he smiled, agreed, and stopped. He was always angry after such an interpretation and turned to shooting or killing play. The worker said, "It is all right to be mad at me, but don't hurt me." "But I want to hurt you," he said. Worker said she was always careful not to hurt him, because she was fond of him, and this again helped him to control himself. After a great deal of verbal erotic aggression he suddenly said in comment on the doll family, "Could I be married to my mother?" He answered this himself, "No, I could not be married to my mother, but I could be married to another mother, couldn't I?" The worker said this was not possible, although he would be grown up some day, too, and would marry a girl and it would all be a little different.

To encounter the erotic wish always presents a delicate problem in response. Sidney had played out his wish crudely, then symbolically, but with anxiety, regression, and guilt phases replacing one another. The worker, in the long run, wants to help him change his object choice—repress and sublimate in appropriate ways. The worker has to guard against being pulled into a position of rivalry with the mother, and also against unconsciously encouraging the child in his fantasies through countertransference. She accepts the wish, reducing his guilt, but turns it in the direction of reality controls. When, as "Superman" in his play, he fantasied intercourse with the worker, it was necessary not only to encourage him to verbalize but also in some degree to interpret the transference. Intensive concurrent work with the mother resulted in changing the sleeping arrangements, for he had constantly been stimulated, and teaching her not to punish the boy. Interference in a reality situation which is actively damaging the child is often essential. In the case of the young child, cited earlier,[19] whose father was away from home and whose mother worked, all Miles's desires for his mother emerged one after another as soon as the worker succeeded in getting close to him, but improvement did not set in until arrangements could be made for the mother to stay at home. This boy immediately regressed at home to an infantile stage in order to keep his mother's love, but this was regarded as a "benign" and healthy regression. Miles needed his mother at home, and when she was helped to make the decision to stop work, progress was rapid in treatment.

A boy of six reproduced his anxiety fully in an early interview.

His mother was a full-blown hysteric, the father was very immature and indifferent to the welfare of the children. The boy had always slept in the parental bedroom; he had seen many fights between the parents and every aspect of intimate marital relationship. He now had sleeping disturbances —screamed, mumbled—he had convulsive attacks, continuing enuresis, many fears of bodily injury, excessive masturbation. He didn't want to go to school. There was some reality in this, as he was so aggressive that children did attack him. He had always dominated his mother, who was extremely inconsistent.

In his play, he involved the worker at once. They must play with airplanes, which are bombing and killing people. There was much fighting and terror. The worker was to be sent in a plane to bomb London, but he would remain—he could take it. The planes were on fire; he was terribly burned. He lost all his features; he was blind. He walked through the dark feeling for the worker. "If I find you, I will kill you," he said, and then with a beaming smile, "I shall be your husband now, OK." He shot 100 Japs and came to the worker to have medals pinned on him. Immediately

[19] See pp. 87 *et seq.*

afterward he told the worker he intended to marry her; he was a hero. He very slightly cut his finger and was very frightened about it. He went through an elaborate play with an airplane propeller, in which he brought out very clearly masturbation fantasies. His mother had beaten him when he masturbated, and he had great anxiety about this.

In an older child the oedipal situation might be repressed or disguised, but a six-year-old divulges it very clearly. The whole triangle, the aggression, the castration fears and the panic were here played immediately in war games and repetitively thereafter. A worker might hesitate to interpret, in the above case, the child's blindness and search for the worker in the dark (as for the mother), but she would show in some way that she understood his fears (although his fears, because he looks when he isn't supposed to look, etc., will sooner or later come out in other ways where they can be more easily handled). This is not to say that the transference material would not have to be handled directly if necessary by a skilled worker.

Sometimes in the four-to-six group, where one expects exaggerated aggressiveness, one finds the timid youngster who cries easily and plays with younger children. In determining what is pathological one must be careful to distinguish temporary upsets, the normal tendency to be afraid of the outside world, and the anxiety which is a response to inner aggression. A fearful child is afraid of any efforts to approach him because of the power of the adult. In treatment the worker must be always careful not to make too positive advances which seem like the counteraggression the child fears. Sufficient passivity enables the child slowly to indicate his tastes and the areas of his conflict.

The following case shows the handling of confused identifications and erotic aggression—treatment being carried on from four and a half until the child was nearly seven. Threatened by the birth of a younger sibling, disappointed at an age when the father attachment was strong and incompletely integrated, Kate has decided to be a boy. Toward the latter part of the period of treatment considerable interpretation is used.

Kate, at four and a half, was overactive, aggressive, and bossy. She constantly hit her younger sister, age two, and her parents. She used bad language and showed a great deal of sex curiosity. She had various habit disorders, such as food fads and persistent nail biting and enuresis. The developmental history was negative, except that due to the illness and pregnancies of the mother she was placed for a few weeks as a baby, and again at two.

The mother was a deprived, infantile and dependent woman, herself neurotic and self-centered. Her attitude toward Kate had always been inconsistent and weak. She gave in to the child completely for material things, but had not a great deal of warmth for any of the children. Kate was very much attached to her father, who gave her a good deal of attention.

Seen at the office, this child appeared bright and attractive, but excessively boisterous and aggressive. She showed great need for approbation and affection, though she was wary and defensive. She alternated between being very affectionate and abusive, trying to hug and kiss the worker at one moment, and at another to strike or shake her; the latter reaction occurred whenever the worker tried to limit her in the interview from hurting herself or being destructive. She found it difficult to leave her mother, but rather quickly engaged in doll play, in which she reproduced some family scenes, especially feeding and toilet training, and also excessive affection shown by the mother doll to the baby, representing her sibling rivalry situation. At the end of the hour she wanted to take all the toys home with her.

The usual phases are gone through; the small child tells her story through play. The worker, by participating in it understandingly, transmits acceptance, which enables the child to go further with reduced guilt.

During early contact Kate illustrated the grabbing stage so common at this age, wanting everything for her own. She went through all the nursery development in her play, nursing the baby, playing out all varieties of wetting herself, had an orgy of sloppiness and smearing with the clay, and then showed marked preoccupation with the problem of sex differences. She modeled phallic figures that were indeterminate mothers and fathers, wanted to investigate the worker's body, and this was handled by interpreting that she wanted to see whether she looked like the mother or someone else. She seemed to know that only little girls have babies, but she had her doubts and wavered on this point. She had moods of uncertainty as to whether or not she has a "peepee," and then accused the worker of talking in a dirty way (projection). She was clearly relieved to know that she could talk as she liked in the office. Occasionally she regressed in destructive play or painting. When the worker cleared up the mess without comment, she was frightened. "I didn't do that." "You are afraid I will be angry." "Yes." "I am not angry. If we mess it up, we just have to clean it up."

The child is much relieved to get this support for the ego against the impulses. The worker allows gratification of the sex interest through socially acceptable channels—playing out, modeling, and discussing.

From the start her play showed confusion of identification as to whether she thought herself a boy or a girl. She had apparently engaged in sex play with a neighbor's little boy, and she reproduced this repeatedly. She continued to be preoccupied with wetting and soiling problems in the doll family, and enjoyed smearing with the paints. She was aggressive and dominating. With any limitation she resorted to yelling and tantrums. She used many sex expressions and reassured herself; "Are *you* sure I can talk any way I want here?" "Yes, *I* am." Repetitive themes in doll play were various sleeping arrangements in the family (clearly related to herself and her parents), the preferred status of the baby doll, and her own wish to be a baby so that she would be loved. "Hattie, the baby doll, wants everything she sees. The big sister doll must give them to her all the time." "Doesn't the sister doll want them for herself sometimes?" asks the worker. "Yes, but Hattie is only a baby." "Even if Hattie is only a baby, she shouldn't have *everything,* should she?" Kate didn't respond to this, but became angry. Later she said, "See how nice I can be if you don't get me angry." Worker asked what made her angry. She did not reply, but became quite affectionate (denying the whole rivalry discussion).

As the relationship deepened, she became jealous of another little girl seen by the worker. The worker recognized her feeling. After singing a little song, "My mother kissed me," she began to giggle and said she would break the worker's neck, which was immediately followed by whacking the worker. She was told that she could not do that. Would I smack her back? No, I was not angry at her. She became loving again. Sometimes when playing with crayons she tried to smear the worker's blouse and had to be restrained. She demanded presents. She tried to snuggle on the worker's lap. Worker said that she wanted to be her little girl. She repeated all the bad words she knew. "Perhaps Kate says these words to get her mother angry." "Well, sometimes I do."

Over and over again a child may say to the worker without any sense of unreality, "Take me home with you." "I wish you were my mother" (or father). A child is rarely subtle in his demands, and if the worker seems kinder to him than his own mother is, why not a new one? It is similar to wishing the parent dead or away to wish for a new mother. The child cannot possibly understand the implications of either wish, but he will learn, through play, that he cannot destroy the parent. He learns that the worker sees his hostile aggression, is not afraid of it, and still likes the goodness in him. An insecure or menaced mother cannot love a child whose badness she fears, but though he destroys the worker over and over again in his play and games, he learns the steadying and clarifying distinction that he may feel as he does but may not act as he pleases, and so he comes to understand and control his impulses, without excessive guilt.

As there were neurotic tendencies involved, the worker with Kate maintained a neutral attitude, trying to turn her bids for direct expressions of affection back into the play situation.

There was much play and considerable verbalization about the neighbor boy, with marked demonstration of penis envy. The worker became more active in commenting on the expressed wish. In play and in modeling there was also some simple sex instruction based on the child's drawings. She developed indecision. She didn't know whether to make a man or a little girl in a fur coat. "Perhaps you think it is more fun to make a man?" "Yes, a man works and gets so much money," she said, evading the issue. She discussed the advantages of being a boy in detail. Following such discussion, she expressed great curiosity and interest in the worker, seeming to be able to identify with her more. In her play she often pretended overtly that she was a boy, but gradually became able to think it was more fun to be a little girl. There was interpretation that she was angry at her mother for not making her a boy, which was accepted by the child.

This child, like many little children, seemed at home with colloquial sex words and had little modesty or inhibition about using them. Body functions do not seem shameful to children this age, or if they have been taught to feel shame, the veneer of politeness is thin and the return to gutter language to test the parent may be a great source of amusement and triumph. The inexperienced worker beginning work in child guidance is at first startled and, perhaps, appalled by the amount of aggression these small personalities hold, and then by the frankness or coarseness of their language. The child will know at once whether the worker is easily shocked and will become either reticent or provocative, depending on the nature of the problem and the family picture.

There was very slow, but genuine, progress in helping Kate to identify with being a girl. She finally in her play decided that she would have a baby, and in all her play she became a little more girl-like. They acted out having a baby, and she enjoyed this very much, asking a great many questions. Every now and again she would become confused—"I am a big baby girl— No, I am a boy-girl."

As interpretation was given and the interest in babies developed, there was more expressed hostility toward her mother and affection toward her father. Toward the worker she began to develop an object relationship, though with ambivalence. There was a mixture of affection, dependency, and hostility, patterned after her attitude toward her mother. She was able to accept limitations; in her play which was less diffused, she was able to reveal her fantasies and questions in the sexual area. Rushed to the hospital for an appendectomy, she was sure she was going to have a baby and was very disappointed that she didn't get one. The hospital incident was played through and discussed a number of times with the worker.

During her mother's third pregnancy there was some regression, but she took care of this through playing baby, with a great deal of tenderness. When the worker tried to help her to bring out some negative feeling about the baby, she got very angry. Repetitive play about the hospital seemed to take care of her castration fears associated with the operation. She became gentle with all the baby dolls and gave them most loving care. Wanting to be a boy turned into wanting babies of her own.

She became jealous of the worker and her husband; was afraid she was going to have a baby. This was resolved in play in which they acted out how babies are born. She enjoyed this very much. When restrictions were imposed it brought out the child's hostility toward the mother figure and the strong competitive drive for the father. She proclaimed that she wanted to take the worker's husband away from her, and she often said that she wanted her daddy to be her husband. The worker explained that little girls often feel like this, but later on they grow up and have nice husbands of their own.

In this case the stages of emotional growth were all complicated by the fact that the child's alcove bedroom directly faced the parental bed. As soon as the worker was aware of this, she arranged for both children to be moved into another room.

Interpretation to the child that she wanted the mother's baby made her angry, but the direct interpretation helped to bring her into the next period of growth. She was able to admit her anger that her room was changed. As she began to identify with the worker and to incorporate more of her super-ego, there was a very obvious shift from the direct primitive expression to sublimated activities. She made her father a book full of drawings which she called a "love book," and turned her attention to getting on at school because she wanted her father to be proud of her. In a last fling, as it were, she wrote as a secret between her and the worker that she wished her daddy could be her husband instead of her father and that she feared her mother would find it out.

Whenever resistance was shown by breaking appointments, this was handled with her. Her occasional tendency to wet and to regress to baby habits was discussed in terms of growing up, and she was easily prepared for and sent to camp. Her desire to be a boy had changed from wanting to be a boy-girl to being willing to be entirely a girl and complete acceptance of herself. She became less bossy and managing and more maternal in all of her contacts. With the worker, she abandoned her aggression and was consistently affectionate. As she began to develop a stronger super-ego, she gave up her extremely overt sex play and sex discussion for more discussion of everyday events. She developed a desire to please people and get affection in return. Her adjustment in school was better. She seemed quite reconciled to the idea that she has something that boys haven't got, although she still had doubts. "I can grow up any time; I want to, but I don't want to." "Why not?" "Because my mother would take advantage of me. She makes me do too much now for *her* children."

At home she became very motherly to the younger children, both within and outside the family. She couldn't wait to grow up and have babies of her own. Her favorite game was playing she was having a baby.

Kate was at last able to relinquish the idea that she would like to be a man and to accept herself as a woman. The solution that she found for herself was that if you marry a man you not only have a baby but also can share in all his possessions. She became much less aggressive. On the whole she was functioning very well. She had an essentially intelligent and creative personality, and she used herself well in a group situation. As there were no settlement houses available where she could be helped to sublimate further by means of social activities, a special school was chosen for her, to which she made an excellent adjustment.

In the above case treatment was carried on in three characteristic phases, first in an accepting atmosphere in which the child could act out her extreme aggression and her marked oral and anal difficulties. The fact that her mother had given her so little help in early body habits made it difficult for her to outgrow them. As in such problems there was characteristic smearing with clay, playing with water, experimenting with "diaper dolls," and repetition of birth fantasies and sibling rivalry. Next the confusion in sexual identification was taken up, the stage being set with play material having phallic symbols—such as the Pinocchio doll, toy elephants, and a toy balloon. Phallic play and clay modeling ensued, in which the child's disappointment over not being a boy became very evident. As the transference deepened, active interpretation of this disappointment was made.

In the final phase this child played out anxieties over an operation, her sibling rivalry, and her pregnancy fantasies. In this last phase the child was well aware of what was untrue and what reality; her desires were conscious, verbalization was adequate, and the worker's interpretation about the whole business of growing up and being a woman could be direct and simple. Everyday situations were projected into the play situation and were discussed. The transference throughout was positive, with short-lived negative periods in the early phases when limitations were imposed and in the later phases when connections between the child's home and office behavior were made —interpretations always being made in the words or play symbolism used by the child. She was helped to verbalize the feelings which she clearly showed in her play. The child had good intelligence, good

insight, and was able to use the interpretations made, occasional resistance being slowly worked out. Her identification with the worker
was complete in that she was finally able to accept herself in her
feminine role.

Recapitulation

Young children who have been brought to a child guidance agency
have had painful experiences at birth, in feeding, weaning, illnesses
or operations, severe or inconsistent training, and various forms of
rejection and desertion. To his frustrations the child reacts with disturbed behavior, which, in turn, upsets his parents. Therapy has to get
beneath the aggression and guilt reactions to the fundamental picture,
which is always that of a disappointed child. The therapy consists in
slowly, through the transference relationship, reducing the child's
fears of being deserted, of being punished or hurt, or of not being
loved. Since acting out one's conflicts is the natural way for a child
to behave, it is possible to come right to the heart of the child's problem in the play situation. Living out an experience together within
the relationship is much more a part of child than of adult therapy,
although it is a part of all psychotherapy. Little children must be
gratified in order to postpone gratification or to find constructive
forms of self-gratification. The worker's understanding and acceptance of the wishes is translated through appropriate play and comment. The attitude of unfailing friendliness and concrete offers of
help give the opportunity to release tension and relive a badly assimilated or nonassimilated growth experience. Because an important
factor in assimilating the experience is time, therapy must proceed at
the child's pace, which may be slow.

Although the identifications of a child of six or seven are becoming
fixed and he may be said already to have developed a definite character structure, the child's fluid ability under therapy to assimilate new
experiences may change permanently the tenor of his life. Significant
changes do apparently take place; neurotic traits seem to be absorbed.
If the child can be helped to change his negative perceptions of himself, and some of his infantile fixations can be freed, the effect is that
of changing the character itself. The fact that the child's energies are

early enlisted to work at his problem is of therapeutic value which cannot be exaggerated. Because the parents of disturbed children are themselves neurotic, disturbed, immature or emotionally unstable, a therapeutic relationship is always attempted. In the case of young children, unless the family attitudes, particularly the mother's, are made more constructive, substantial improvement is unlikely. But even quite young children can learn to be participants in treatment, control some of their own reactions, and to some degree take responsibility for their actions. Play is used both because it is the little child's medium of communication and because it provides in a safe and natural way some of the instinctual gratification needed by the child as he learns to meet reality demands.

Chapter IX

TREATMENT OF THE OLDER CHILD

THE NURSERY years should have given the child the experience of
parental love and denial, encouragement and discipline, some mastery
of body processes, practice in locomotion, and speech. The next years
—three to about six—bring contact with other children, such as siblings, in the kindergarten or on the street, when new associations
introduce problems of rivalry, competition, and learning to share, the
whole framed within the family and the neighborhood sub-culture
in which he is growing up. Elementary mastery of skills, ability to
dress oneself, construction and motor skills of various kinds, become
incorporated within the ego. The nursery child may have become
aware of sex in terms of body differences, but he is not yet clear
whether he is a little boy or a little girl and whether he is going to
stay the way he is or acquire the characteristics of the other sex. With
the three-to-six-year-olds, exposure to adults and to other children has
begun to give the child a sense of a social self, as the earlier years have
given him a sense of the bodily self. He is aware of his appearance and
ready to measure himself against other children in status and achievement. Even though the little boy may prefer girls' games, he knows
that they are girls' games, and the little girl is aware of the difference
between boys' and girls' prerogatives.

Whatever variants of the "oedipal situation" are found in the normal child population or in other cultures, it is fair to say that the matter assumes great importance in child guidance. Although among
psychiatrists, psychologists and educators, the critical emotional periods may be differently weighted, there is general agreement that the
child's devotion to his parents, particularly the mother, in the nursery
years, culminates in a struggle which, far from being a pathological
experience, frees the child from the bonds of infantile affections. As
the child passes successfully through the "oedipal" stage, his iden-

tifications with his own sex clarify and settle down into permanent security. Intellectually, physically, and emotionally the child is ready for the complicated demands of school, of playmates, and of broader experiences and tasks. The so-called latency period, when the turbulent impulses have been repressed, should permit the child to turn his whole energies to the business of learning and growing and enlarging his horizons. After the solution of the oedipal conflict, the parents have taken a firm hold, but as ideals in the imagination. The significant repressions accompanying latency and the automatic inner controls serve the child well as he sallies out into the larger world. Popularly it is assumed that these expanding horizons replace the child's conscious preoccupation with sex differences and that he no longer has any sexual interest, but this is not entirely true. The curiosity becomes active in disguised ways and is satisfied by informational books, trips to the zoo, and movies. The boy or girl who has not been properly instructed will still want to know where babies come from, but he may take this curiosity out in a passionate interest in finding out how things are put together, in puzzles, or through the rituals of the gang. The child shows his defenses by having secrets from adults, by caves with concealed entrances, by sign languages and other mysteries, some frankly sexual in nature.

In latency the shift away from the parent, begun in the physical aspects of birth, weaning, and the physical dependencies and attachments of little children, becomes a strong swing. The ego is both expanding into social experience and differentiating itself. With the acquisition of each new idea and skill the clinging to the parent is diminishing. Hyperindependence in a young child can be as much of a deviation as extreme timidity and inertia, but in latency adventurous behavior becomes the rule when status (through skill and leadership) is sought with the group. The secure child who has been successfully solving the problem of sharing the parent has little difficulty in solving the problem of sibling rivalry and its displacement on schoolmates. But as there appear to be constitutional factors which make for greater or less aggression, greater or less sensitivity to the quality of parental protection, so it may well be that some children have greater sensitivity in the area of learning to share. Certainly the spacing between the births of children and family habits of competition may increase or decrease the difficulty. But fundamentally sibling rivalry is serious only when the child already has a parental problem. The mother who is flattered when the children race "to get to her first," who subtly or overtly prefers one child, *provokes* much as she may earlier have provoked in feeding and toilet training. For the children of such mothers the normal competition and rivalry of group association may be frightening and burdensome.

The Task of Therapy

But the children coming to a guidance agency at six, eight, or later do not present a harmonious picture of emotional and social stability. Major frustrations during nursing, toilet training, habit formation, locomotion, and the rest have distorted or seriously crippled the personality development. The "golden age for parents," when the child's restless and unpredictable strivings seem to be harnessed, does not emerge. The child who has a behavior disorder is still acting out his earlier conflicts and does not know how to postpone gratifications; the excessively anxious child is anxious because the repressions do not wholly succeed. By now the overindulged and overprotected child is unhappy as he measures himself against his comrades and finds he cannot do or is not allowed to do what the others do with such enthusiasm and mutual challenge. When beginning school the normal child has many clear patterns of independence or conformity; the disturbed child already has patterns of behavior which are a liability in the freemasonry of childhood's social gatherings.

Characteristically children present disturbances in three main areas of social development—in one or in all at once: (1) Because they have not worked through their relationship to their parents, they show confused sexual identifications; (2) because they have not worked out their relationship to their siblings they have poor relationships with other children, tend to have few friends, display excessive competition, aggressive or submissive behavior; and (3) because of deficiencies in the ego aspects of growth, they are likely to show a significant lack of achievement in one or more important skills appropriate for the age range—speech defects or educational disabilities or organic handicaps, or they may be markedly inept at games or any one of a dozen skills, which makes them feel inadequate and inferior with their peers. The child who may now be said to have his "own" problems (apart from the parents) may often need his own worker, although if he is very timid or dependent, the process of disengaging him from his mother may have to be slow.

The most obvious thing about these disturbed children is that they have not progressed into "latency" in the usual sense. The infantilized child no longer sees any sense in growing up. It is still fun to be a baby, because it is thus easier to manage people. Later, the revolt against the parents may start in extreme and peculiar ways. If not actually infantilized, yet by six many children have suffered considerable ego damage in some part of the personality. Children who have not been rejected at birth may have suffered a secondary series of traumatic experiences because of poor appearance or poor intelligence or some other failure. They may not have proved to be an ego asset to the parents, or not so much as some other child in the family. Such children lack self-esteem, develop inferiority feelings and timidity or aggression as a reaction formation. Cultural discrimination may exacerbate these inferiority feelings in the upper part of the age range and during adolescence. In the average home the presence of little brothers and sisters is useful, both in terms of learning social relationships and as natural allies against the parents. In problem children rivalry situations, because of feelings of insecurity with regard to the parents, linger on and become barriers against give-and-take relationships with schoolmates. In latency, the "inadequacy" constellation replaces, to a large extent, the "sexual" constellation as the overt area of conflict.[1]

But at this stage the disturbed child who should normally be turning away from body interests may be still partially fixated. Masturbation, which should have receded from attention, may be secret or defiantly overt, although in either case the child will not want to talk about it. Most of all, if the parental situation has not been comfortably worked through the child is still struggling with his primitive

[1] See Chapter X, p. 247.

impulses and is still confused in his identifications. Just as unsolved problems of early habit training characteristically tend to recur with the preschool child whenever he is frustrated or frightened, so unsolved problems of sexual identification persist in disturbed children to a surprising degree well into latency and puberty. The whole situation is intensified by the inadequate role frequently played by the father. What the rejecting mother does to the little child the unwise, harsh, weak, or indifferent father contributes to the failures of the phallic period. Society is far readier to intervene and provide mother substitutes than to provide father substitutes. Whether or not the fatherless boy (beyond the nursing period) is worse off than the fatherless girl is not precisely known,[2] but in child guidance one observes that the boy who has had little or no opportunity to form wholesome identifications with his father continues to have great difficulty.

In latency the child with infantile neurosis will show a rigid stiffening of defenses. He may do very well at schoolwork, but feel a failure in all his relationships, or one symptom may succeed another. The child who has a primary behavior disorder, who represses very little, is uncomfortable in a different way. Because chronologically he is growing up, the average person expects him to repress his impulses, but actually he is not able to do so. The anxious child always suffers from self-limitation. Because of the expectations of home and school, both types of children have a great sense of failure. The parents of children who act out are especially worried because the child is maturing physically and his emotions are obviously not under control. They see such children as "wild," and indeed they are wide open and very vulnerable. The parents' fear and distrust exaggerate the child's own fears and self-distrust as he enters the high-pressure period of puberty. The anxious, self-limiting child may less excite parental concern until failure in some special area belatedly touches off alarm.

As we have said, while normally there is a swinging back and forth until each step in growth has been adequately mastered, in disturbed children these levels have not been firmly established and the child

---

[2] See English and Pearson, *Emotional Problems of Living*, p. 90 *et sqq.* See also Chapter XI on the Treatment of the Family.

is still uncertain, or else a portion of his personality is already fixed at a lower level. The task of therapy, therefore, is to free and integrate at the growth level appropriate for the child's present development. Social workers engaged in therapy discover very soon that direct play or interview treatment with the objective of insight for children in latency is very difficult. As Melanie Klein points out:

"Children in the latency period present special difficulties of their own [in analysis]. Unlike the small child whose lively imagination and acute anxiety enable us to gain an easier insight into the unconscious and make contact there, they have a very limited imaginative life in accordance with the strong tendency to repression which is characteristic of their age. . . . Their ego is still undeveloped and they neither understand they are ill nor want to be cured. Added to this is the general attitude of distrust and reserve so typical of this period of life." [3]

Even though disturbed children may be accessible as a much younger child would be, in latency there would be withdrawal from intimate communication were it not for the phenomenon of transference. The worker uses the transference relationship to help the child discuss his everyday problems of school and leisure time adjustment and to move from discussion into constructive activities. Treatment which is aimed at strengthening the ego rather than removing defenses seems most to go along with the natural flow of development. The ego is strengthened and integrated, particularly in the younger flexible personality, through the living experience as well as through the integration which comes through direct psychotherapy. A great deal of treatment during this period is properly to try to reinforce constructive defenses through social casework and groupwork. This is not to say that limited goals in insight are not attainable, but it is important by social and educational means to help the child to greater security and self-esteem through achievement and warm supportive attitudes in his natural environment, as well as through the therapeutic relationship itself. It is also fair to assume that a child under active treatment *uses* the living experiences in an emotionally charged way that is beneficial. "Insight" is a component of the total treatment situation.

[3] Klein, Melanie, *The Psychoanalysis of Children*, p. 94.

In transference not only does the person recall and produce more but also it would seem that there is a heightened sensitivity for other relationships.

In normal latency the child does not want to have to think about his primitive desires, and he resists very strongly any attempt to stir them up. Whereas the little child has few and quite transparent defenses, of which simple denial is a common expression, in latency the child has built up defenses of one kind or another against dangers from the environment, from within himself, and from affects which are associated with these defensive structures. Young children frankly express erotic material. In adolescence erotic material again comes to the surface, and one may find extremely frank verbalization of feeling about the parents (although the sexual aim is usually disguised). But in latency the defenses are strong; it is unusual for the youngster to speak easily of his feelings toward his parents, nor do these feelings come through clearly in games. Often the child has to be understood from a whole chain of evidence—from history, verbalization, and the aims of the games played. Therapy, which aims in part to help the child lay aside his defenses, is therefore at this time going against the grain. Insight not only may not be successful, but may easily prove harmful. Tension is decreased through opening new outlets and discussing associated problems quite as much as through uncovering "forbidden" topics.

When the child has been taken into treatment during the oedipal period or earlier, with marked release of tension and improvement, the worker should not be disturbed if in latency the repressing forces start and the child turns away, or seems suddenly to give very little material. This may well be the signal to taper off in favor of educational, recreational, and group resources alone. Technique suitable for the earlier period may have to be radically changed, and in many instances discontinued. A "rest period" during latency has often proved useful. If there is reactivation of the neurosis at puberty, the child may come back and may again be receptive to interviewing treatment.

If the treatment has progressed far *before* the stiffening of the defenses takes place, the problem must be evaluated somewhat differently from that in which one encounters the defensive structure at the outset of treatment. In the former instance one should be on the lookout for periods of *true* quiescence (being on guard if the child is of the compulsive neurotic type or ill), which often represent signs of growth and strength and tells us that the child is ready for sublimation. It takes skill to infer the direction that ego-building and sublimation may take—aptitude and other psychological tests proving valuable. If the right type of sublimation is found in connection with treatment, the new satisfactions will diminish the strength of the conflict. In effect, faced by social reinforcements, one of the inner combatants gives up the struggle, and the child is freed to invest his energies elsewhere. Casework therapy, like progressive education, uses the situation itself as a stimulus for the modification of behavior. But this alone, especially for the more neurotic children, would be of little avail were it not for the experience the child has in the transference relationship.

School engulfs older children and adolescents and becomes almost their entire world.[4] In school, children are accepted for their personality and for their achievement—both are important. The child's formal acquisition of skills has brought certain pressures upon him, particularly in the ego area. He is more aware of his appearance and whether other people like him or not, and the things which he fails to master may induce a great sense of inadequacy and failure. This is a period, too, of "learning the rules" of work and play. The school child's trouble seems to center in several clusters of difficulty: fears about failure in work or in play; difficulties with the teacher (a tie-up with the unsolved parental figure at home); difficulties with schoolmates. Seven-year-old children who have a very strong consciousness of standards bring quickly into the play interview many of these fears of inadequacy.

Cases of educational disability and handicap are treated by the school through specialized devices, and certainly less diffused personality disturbances can be greatly helped by remedial teaching and the adjustment of the program. Because disturbed children suffer from a sense of inadequacy and lack of basic skills, it is important that

[4] See Chapter VII.

the ego be strengthened, whenever indicated, through such efforts. The child cannot cope with his program unless he has concrete help. Tutoring may or may not be sufficient help in itself, but it can become an excellent medium for therapy, because the retardation is usually an inhibition of the learning process as a whole. Whether or not the therapist should, if competent to do so, engage in the remedial teaching, since all learning is a discipline, is a moot point, but it is obvious that remedial teaching which is therapeutically oriented will be more beneficial to the child. When the inhibition in learning is part of the unconscious conflict, as in neurosis, remedial teaching will not in itself be likely to be effective, since the underlying neurotic disturbance may not be reached.

Dull children, because of lack of progress in school, suffer painful assaults to the ego—"dull children" meaning those with limited intelligence rather than those who are functioning on a poor level because of emotional blocking. The parents of such a child are usually disappointed in him, and the rejection and teasing experienced tend to make the child withdraw into asocial behavior or lonely pursuits. In therapy, therefore, he particularly needs both acceptance by the worker and gratifications in his environment. Individual treatment has to proceed at a slow pace, and pointing out trends must also be on a simple level. For essential ego building cooperation by the school must be enlisted and the program must be adapted to give the child a sense of achievement. Frequently such children project all blame for personality difficulties onto their stupidity, using this as a defense against insight. Limited insight is, with patience and skill, however, possible to achieve. After only six months of treatment one eleven-year-old boy with an I.Q. of 84 was adjusting well at school and pitching his expectations for himself at a higher level. The family also was brought to more acceptance. School, camp, and group therapy were all used to bring this boy to the point of greater self-acceptance and self-confidence. Since poor intelligence cuts off certain areas ordinarily useful for sublimation, one has to be particularly careful to find channels accessible to the dull child. The rewards, when these channels are found, repay the effort. Treatment is especially significant when viewed in terms of prevention of delinquency.

Modifications in the Use of Play [5]

With older children, as with younger, the play interview is used to help the child to release inhibitions and disapproved impulses; to relive traumatic experiences; to build up self-confidence by sharing activities in a friendly atmosphere; to encourage and limit so as to help the child find his own way to self-control and constructive balance. Play, for a little child, is the chief means of communication; but for the older child it is introductory or a means toward verbalization unless the child is much retarded or atypical. Family relationships are the whole world of the little child, who reproduces family scenes with the dolls. The older child's play has a larger orbit, and his games, while still motivated by the family constellation, show more complicated forms of expression and more indirect and elaborate schemes of relationship. Whereas the individualistic creations of the younger child show not only the direction of his feeling but also the components of his real situation—the older child is more guarded, more structuralized, and more symbolic in his use of games, building airplanes, and the like. Young children play out what the mother wants them to do in toilet matters, eating, or sleeping arrangements or else show clearly what they are resisting in the home discipline. Older children are not always so easy to follow, and the whole matter may be obscured by the fact of regression. Play by young children may or may not be on a lower age level; play by older children is usually a form of "regression" to an earlier developmental level permitted by the accepting attitude.

Whether or not we make a distinction between a child who is "playing" and one who is "acting out" is immaterial. Children play, they act out, they talk, they shift from one medium to another. Sometimes the child is quite conscious that he is pretending; sometimes there is very little pretense or a very thin layer of pretense. There is an age differential in the level of acting out to which the worker responds in appropriate ways. The little child, when angry, will urinate openly on the floor; a little later he will play out his aggression with the dolls; the older child will be still less direct and more

[5] See this topic in preceding chapter.

symbolic. The little child says quite simply, "I made wet"; the older child, whose defenses are aroused, maintains that it was an accident, or plays out enuresis interminably with the dolls; the still older child has great difficulty in admitting enuresis at all, or masturbation. The problem for the therapist is different when he sees a five-year-old acting like a two-year-old, and a much older child acting like a two-year-old. This may be a temporary regression, or it may be serious symptomatic behavior. In fact whenever a child of eight or nine with normal intelligence plays at all consistently like a very young child, one has to consider the possibility that the child is sick—possibly incipient schizophrenia.[6] Most children moving into new situations suffer temporary attacks of regression, from which they spontaneously recover. In the treatment relationship children do the same thing, that is, they may again retreat beyond a threshold over which they have once stepped. If a child is transferred to a new worker, there is almost always regression. Increased security within himself and with the therapist permits him to move on at his own pace. However, at the appropriate time pointing out the patterns will help the child to make a new start. One must distinguish the relatively chronic regression or fixation of disturbed children from the regression occurring in treatment because of the permissiveness of the therapeutic attitude.

An older girl, chronologically aged nine, who was somewhat dull and emotionally retarded, baffled an inexperienced worker by violent swings of behavior. This girl had been lazy, disobedient, aggressive, demanding, with marked rivalry with an older sister. The child had suffered from very severe toilet training; the mother was compulsively neat, clean, and driving. In the first phase of treatment one worker had both mother and child, and the child was extremely reticent, inhibited, occupying herself mostly with trying to keep the worker's shelf neat and tidy. She used finger paints with great caution.

The worker followed along in her careful and rigid play without fully recognizing the underlying anxiety. When the case was divided, as it perhaps should have been earlier, the second worker was extremely permissive, not sensing the volcano smoldering in this dull, neat girl. Sud-

[6] See Chapter V.

denly Nina seized on the finger paints and proceeded to go on what can only be described as "a binge" or "a bender." She made a terrible mess; she splashed paint everywhere—on the table, floor, walls, and her dress; she gloated; she said the mess "was beautiful"; she admired it extravagantly; she wanted the worker to admire it. Then, overcome with anxiety, she rushed away to get her former worker and the mother to view the spectacle. When the mother, far from admiring, was horrified, she quickly retreated to her defensive patterns, insisting on playing checkers in a very grown-up way for several weeks.

The worker, aware of the need for infantile satisfactions, should, however, have allowed a more gradual and, therefore, less anxiety-arousing expression. Here the initial sedate and housewifely behavior probably put the worker off guard and left her quite unprepared for the violent regression. For a young child a therapeutic attitude towards released impulses in itself may give sufficient opportunity for growth. For an older child, some verbalization of the conflict situation is usually necessary—"At home perhaps you can't splash things about, but it is all right here with me in the playroom." The child must repeat and project on the therapist his patterns in order to be helped. The worker (unless in purely diagnostic situations) is not an onlooker, but whereas with the young child sharing is complete and gratifications direct, with the older child more discussion must be utilized to help him incorporate the new emotional experience. Given a good home, ordinary associations with children, and good luck, even bad experiences can be met with self-healing or spontaneous recovery. But the parents of problem children are so disturbed that the children are continually stimulated toward neurosis or conduct disorders by what goes on at home. Very disturbed children may be seen, if indicated, through quite long play periods, or two or three times a week, to assure abreaction, always remembering that such abreaction is an extension of transference phenomena. For children not too disturbed group therapy seems often to offer an excellent method for abreaction. Not only in groups is play felt by the patient less as a regression, but the presence of other children supplies the deficiency for the child who in the ordinary day's rough and tumble does not have friends to tell things to or on whom to work out tensions, fears, and aggression. Neurotic children usually need individual treatment, involving interpretation as well as the therapy of abreaction.

Sibling rivalry is entirely normal for the little child, but under favorable conditions the older child who has established the fact of parental affection does not need to be so competitive. The disturbed child's interest in what another child does in the office may be still on the primitive basis of competition rather than of jealousy. Generally speaking, if the problem is sibling rivalry, in a behavior disorder the worker meets it by some form of reassurance that this time, or these materials, or this interest, is the child's and his alone (at least until he is secure enough to discuss his pattern); if the problem is oedipal jealousy, verbal recognition is usually indicated, but always in homely terms which are familiar.

"Interpretation" of play behavior is modified for older children. One may interpret the impulses of the small child directly: "You are mad," "You want to hurt me." That is, one points out the impulses (and if necessary to control the erotic aggression even the sexual aim), but one cannot interpret the symbolism of playing with fire or crashing in an airplane to a nine-year-old boy in the same way. For the older child interpretation is in the ego area, where the social patterns are now strongly forming. The child says, "I don't like the teacher," and one may discuss how his pattern of annoying the teacher is the same as his behavior at home and, perhaps, here at the office. It is the outer expressions of which the child is conscious, with which one works. He verbalizes his inferiority in achievement terms—"I don't know how to play ball," "The fellows beat me up"— and one interprets his feelings of inadequacy in the same way. To a little child one may say, "You are afraid of this or that," or when the doll is decapitated, "There goes that horrid baby," to which the child will assent with glee, particularly if the worker's cheerful tone does not arouse anxiety. Although interpretation may be direct, it is so only when one really understands. Inexperienced workers are likely to say (with reference to the dolls), "This is your father (or mother)," or, "Is this your baby sister?" which may not represent the true state of affairs and may make the child feel that one is a very stupid person. Guesswork with the older child is even less useful.

Illustrations of the Therapeutic Process

In the following cases of children between the ages of six and eleven, because of the disturbed latency, the usual developmental stages have not been firmly established, so that many phases of treatment seem to overlap with those appropriate for younger children, discussed in the preceding chapter. Therapy includes expressive play techniques, discussion of everyday occurrences, interpretation of behavior trends and concurrent or tapering off activities to promote socialization. Efforts aimed toward sublimation usually come after a period of abreaction, toward the end of treatment, when the child is stronger. Concurrent efforts to reduce or remove pathological features in the environment are made.

At the lower end of the age range under discussion is a six-and-a-half-year-old boy who was behaving at a much younger level. The therapy included release of aggression, coupled with careful limitations, with permitted periods of regression used by the child to experience forbidden activities through the symbolism of play.

Matthew was referred because when just starting school he was quarrelsome, could not get along, was stubborn, spiteful, hyperactive. While there was nothing marked about the developmental history, he seemed to have been extremely restless from birth, possibly on a constitutional basis. There was a problem in nursing and excessive masturbation at about three.

The outstanding familial factor was that the father deserted during the mother's pregnancy, so that Matthew had no contact with him at any time. The mother was inconsistent, neurotic, helpless in her relationship with the child, alternately punitive and seductive. She made what were equivalent to castration threats over the boy's masturbation, and this remained a tension between them.

Diagnostically Matthew was regarded as having a primary behavior disorder, preoedipal type, with so little repression of aggression as to be the background for a character defect.

Matthew was a stocky, handsome child, verbal, outgoing, provocative, teasing, aggressive. He started at once to complain about his mother's constant punishment of him and described how he fought with her. He was flighty, distractable, used bad language, wanted to try all the toys. He was very unruly, made a nuisance of himself, told how he outsmarted everybody. When the worker imposed any restriction he was angry and complained that the worker did not like him. This was discussed with him, but he shrugged off the explanation. He spattered paint, first all over the office, and then over the worker. The worker interpreted how he equated any restraints with the worker's not liking him. He used all the bad words he knew—"shit," "ass," etc., to provoke a reproof. He bragged, he boasted, he bullied. He denied that there was any difference between boys and girls—they both had a "pecky." (His lack of a father seemed to have left him with a real confusion about men and women.) He spilled a great deal of water. He painted and he smeared—with much anal suggestion—and he was demanding and infantile. He regressed to the destructive and whining level of a two- or three-year-old. He knocked his blocks about wildly. He said he was unable to pick them up. He wanted worker to tie his shoelaces. During one period the worker had to give him things to eat to meet his need for dependent satisfaction.

The child behaves at an inappropriate age level, and the worker permits extreme regression during several interviews, before pointing out the pattern, how on the one hand he wants to be a very little boy, but actually he wants to be a big boy too, which Matthew at first rejects and then comes to accept. The grabbing, demanding, wild "destructiveness" is excessive in both quality and quantity. He becomes a helpless baby. He can do nothing for himself; the worker has to give him everything. He is very competitive. When he shows the defects in a toy another child has made, the worker sees this correctly, not as jealousy in the oedipal sense, but rather the infantile quality of inability to share, and so comments on his right to have his own place and his fear that the worker will not care for him.

He threatened to break the door down and screeched. When the worker restrained him from assaults, he complained that he was being hit. This was commented on. He retaliated by saying that he would draw a picture for the office girl, but not for the worker. The worker gave him permission good naturedly. He offered a great deal of fantasy about fish and how mother fish make babies, but this, too, is on a preoedipal level of birth fantasies (complicated by the absence of the father).

He is a narcissistic little boy with intense fears of being hit and attacked, his aggression towards his mother and the worker having more the tone of childish hostility than of erotic aggression, although flashes of oedipal conflict are seen when he is about seven.

After six months of treatment his behavior calmed down somewhat, his play was less random, with more periods of constructive activity. He easily reverted, however, to competitive games. In contrast to his rough language, he used fewer vulgarisms, and if he did, he said "Excuse me." He began to show some signs of growing attachment; was occasionally considerate, although the worker was careful to let negative feelings always be expressed. Some of the hostility had been redirected into play. From spilling water he took to watering the worker's plants.

When they played store together, he occasionally had phases of cheating. He outbargained, overcharged, and otherwise victimized the worker, who pointed out his need to dominate. In his play he still had spells of wildness, which, as the worker repeatedly explained, arose from fear of being hurt. He occasionally showed marked anxiety after an outburst and was very fearful that he would not be allowed to continue. He began to accept limitation without so much rage and fear and was able to use more play channels for his aggression.

Although games of this period are about Hitler and extremely complicated "triangle" dramas and sexual dances with the dolls, he continues to appear oblivious to the significance either of the aggression or the relationships displayed. But when he makes a great din in miniature battles, because he wants "so much noise that everyone will be deaf," and the worker asks what it is that he doesn't want him to hear, Matthew smiles. He stops the battle and immediately recounts an everyday occurrence of a teacher's "strictness" which is bothering him. The (male) worker, as father, is willing to permit and discuss the sexual dramas. The worker says in effect, "I know you are afraid that if I hear (understand) I will not approve, but will punish you. You are ashamed of these sexual drives, but it is not forbidden to wish when one is young, and I understand these feelings." The child, who has appeared oblivious, does not respond in words, but he smiles; guilt is relieved, and he is able to move along one pace on the path of healthy repression. Because of the worker's "forgiveness," he is now able to express the guilt problem in terms of a strict schoolteacher—an appropriate field in which to discuss the latency child's conflicts. Through repeated abreaction and phrases of realistic discussion of school problems, but with a minimum of interpretation, Matthew moves slowly toward more mature and independent activities. With any frustration, he easily falls back into suspicion of the worker.

At eight he was able actually to build an airplane, which he did not destroy, but took carefully home and was simultaneously affectionate. (The worker was now a person, not a tool for his pleasures.)

He had made so much improvement during this period that he was placed in group therapy [7] with three other boys, under an experienced worker. He showed at first much of the same behavior as in individual treatment, was obstreperous and demanding. There was a bigger boy whom he couldn't dominate and he resented this. He was angry because the worker did not take his part. Group therapy was a new experience for him and he was able to discuss with his worker in detail what happened when he couldn't have his own way, or could not retaliate. It was a surprise to him that he could discuss these things instead of fighting them out or running away. He became conscious of other persons in the group —that refreshments must be shared, instead of being exclusively for him. When he learned this he no longer needed to eat his lunch in the worker's office when he came for his interviews.

He became less afraid of his destructive impulses and could finally accept and even give love. The therapist continued as super-ego until the boy acquired sufficient inner strength.

Remedial reading had been arranged, and Matthew was now functioning well at school, where his good intelligence was an asset. The boy was sent to camp and later placed in a boarding school to help him work out the male identification which had been started with the worker.

The following case shows treatment related phase by phase to each developmental problem of a six-year-old girl, culminating in the achievement of a reasonably normal "latency" period.

Margaret was referred to the child guidance agency when she was six, because she was slow at school, had a tendency to vomit, was self-protective and fearful of criticism. Her first-grade teacher was hostile and

[7] See discussion of group therapy in Chapters VII and X.

often frightened her. She had many fears—of fires, of being killed, of being left alone. She was diagnosed as having behavior disorder with habit and conduct disorders with neurotic traits.

The home situation was unfavorable—the mother tense, rigid, and cold. She was harsh to the older girl, now fifteen, and had never wanted either her or the patient. The marital relationship was unsatisfying and unhappy. This mother was concurrently treated to show her on a conscious level how she might express her feelings in an atmosphere of acceptance and understanding, instead of the scorn and rejection which she feared because she believed that she was abnormal (homosexual trends).

In the first phase of treatment Margaret was destructive and infantile. She entered into overt toilet play with a barrage of sex words; was destructive with toys and messy with clay. She played out fire scenes, showing one area of her neurotic fears. Her play was restless, discontinuous— jumping from one thing to another. The next cluster of fears came out about school. Over and over again she played the cranky teacher and the frightened child. A great deal of hostility was released, the worker being identified as the nasty teacher. After a while the worker took the role of an understanding teacher, which the child resisted, but finally got a great deal of assurance from the fact that she, the pupil, could be so bad and still have the teacher, in the play, like her. After letting her act out her dislike of the school, the worker reverted to the role of being the accepting person, and tied up her expressions of hostility with her relationship to the teacher.

Her drawings were of the Cinderella type, with much self-criticism. Sometimes, her anxiety overwhelming her, she could neither play nor verbalize, but wrote notes, largely to the effect, "Do you like me?" "Yes, I do," with endless variants. She was anxious that if she were not neat and clean in every way the worker would reject her. Her perception of the difference between the therapeutic attitude and that of others was immediate: "I asked Margaret if she thought I did not like her if she got dirty. She immediately retorted 'You are not my mother, you are my "philosoph." Of course you are different.'" As she became more secure and the transference deepened the worker was able to impose some limitations on her destructiveness, such as not scribbling on the walls. She was angry, but was able to accept them. She then overtly began much more to bring in the problem of sexual curiosity and preoccupation with body differences, interspersed with "the mean teacher" play. The school situation was so traumatized that she had great need to repeat it. She wrote many notes stating that she loved the worker because she loved her, which were continuously demands for reassurance.

Because of the neurotic elements, it was felt that the destructiveness and aggression could be limited, and dolls and other material which were substituted were readily utilized. The child still wavered between neurotic formations and conduct disorders.

Margaret wanted the worker to take her to her (the worker's) home. "I would love to be your little girl." The worker met this by telling her she was her "girl" when she came to the office. Her confusion about sex differences was worked through in clay modeling, and this, in turn, precipitated discussion of the fact that she actually was engaging in sex play with an older boy. The fears multiplied—of the dark, of fires, of illness, of being bad. The doll play became ferocious. The mother doll was killed repeatedly, and the girl doll was severely punished. Whenever Margaret tried to substitute the worker for the doll figure, she was limited, and this made her very angry. The worker always recognized her anger with appropriate comment.

During all this period she continued with phases of toilet play, school play, and all the other areas of her fears, and she seemed to get relief from her fear of dirt in finger painting. As the real situation with the boy seemed important to precipitate, playing with balloons (phallic symbol) was deliberately introduced, as she seemed more able to fantasy with these than with the dolls. This led her to associate being chased by a man and attacked and finally to discussion of her sex relationship with the big boy, about which she seemed to feel no guilt.

Meanwhile, the Rorschach showed phobic material, compulsive behavior, active fantasy life, and very strong castration fears. Her intelligence was found to be of high average capacity, apparently blocked by anxiety. She had good common sense and contact with reality. Her personality was not too rigid, and the neurotic disturbance did not seem too fixed.

During the first phases of treatment the main purpose was to release pent-up hostility, which, because she became at once so wild, demanding, and destructive, had to be restrained. During the first few months of treatment the vomiting disappeared. As she became secure, she accepted limitation on her aggression and began to reveal her sexual preoccupation—sex behavior which could not be permitted (carrying on active sex relations with a fourteen-year-old high school boy). Institutionalization was considered, but dismissed, and because actual controls were impracticable, it was decided to use the transference more fully for interpretation. The sexual activity was a continuation of an infantile pattern, with complete absence of super-ego formation. Margaret was functioning on the level of a three- or four-year-old child; all she feared was punishment. One sees here the precocious activities of a possible sex delinquent. She was preoccupied with the marital relationship between her mother and her father. She began a theme openly which was to be recurrent—that she wanted to marry her father, but could not because he had a wife. The next step was to consolidate a primary identification between Margaret and the worker, with the aim of tying up her gratifications with the value of the love object.

The worker encouraged her to a very full revelation of all her behavior and feelings about this boy. Recognizing that the worker was not criticizing her, she was able to speak frankly. She reported sex pleasure, fun, and small presents from the boy in question. As treatment progressed, it was clear that there was no connection in the child's mind between love and sex. She had no reason in her experience with her parents to connect sexuality with love, but sex activity only with someone one does not like. She had a small boy friend toward whom she felt real affection, and he was introduced into the discussions. After some weeks of this, Margaret stopped her sex activities. She said, "Well, I haven't done it for four weeks now." "You haven't?" "No, because what do I get out of it? I get presents, but that's all." She insisted that the worker had told her that it was not good for her, which was not so. The worker commented that that must have made her angry. This was all reproduced in play, but actually the connection with the older boy stopped.

In the next phase there was a sharp change in the relationship—the child began to see the worker as an object for affection. She expressed a great deal of curiosity about her husband and her marital relations. Sent to camp (a stormy period) she renewed after her return from camp the discussion about the worker's husband as if there had been no interruption. Her affectionate relationship, however, was in terms of primary identification, not yet full object relationship (the development of the super-ego being always dependent on the creation of a conflict between the feelings of love and hostility for the loved person). So far there was no hostility expressed toward the worker, but only infantile curiosity. Precipitating a conflict situation was arranged, the father to be brought into the office.[8] This was dramatically successful in arousing conflict, although she had never shown any feeling about the coming of either her mother or her sister (each had a separate worker). It was arranged that Margaret and her father should come together. She did not like this at all and tried to block it. She began extremely hostile and jealous play in which she poisoned the worker and took her husband away. In the next interview her first remark was, "Let's continue what we were doing last week, you know, my taking your '*father*' away." She again played scenes in which she took the worker's husband-father (she used the words interchangeably) away with great hostility. As more and more hostility was expressed, the worker had to be on guard against countertransference, since the child had become very unpleasant. When the hostility got out of bounds, the worker occasionally would say, "You know why you are so angry at me," and this in itself seemed enough control. After the father-incident hostility reached a peak. She drew up lists of names of good and bad children, the worker's name heading the bad list. In the school play the worker was demoted, hit, slapped, and sometimes killed. She became demanding, critical, calling the worker a liar and other names. In an interesting interview she discussed the father's visit and then averred, "That wasn't my father—I fooled you. It was your husband." This was followed, in turn, by her becoming tremendously concerned that the worker was going to have a baby.

Margaret's earlier confusion and desire to have a penis have now changed to a wish to have a child. The worker discusses her jealousy with her in the next interviews. It is interesting that throughout the treatment the child's preoccupation was so intense that she always began precisely where she left off. The underground association between weekly interviews and outside experience and interviews is strong. The aggression is gradually being turned into an inner struggle, the primary identification with the worker becoming the basis of the super-ego formation.

She remained insistent that the worker should have a baby, but more in reality and less in jealousy terms. She stopped the school play and talked

[8] See Chapter XI.

realistically about school problems. Most of the wildness had gone, both in the office and at home, and she was getting along much better at school. She showed that she was ready to leave. She wrote down the address of the agency—"In case I leave this place and will forget." In her dress she was modest instead of exhibitionistic. Discussions with the child moved to an educational, reasonable level about what went on outside the office. She continued to do things to get approval and praise, dancing classes were arranged for her, which she greatly enjoyed. The Rorschach showed great gains in self-control and self-reliance. She was again sent to camp, where she made a good adjustment. The identification with the worker was complete; she wanted to act like her and be like her, and she copied her handwriting, her hair arrangement, and her dress. She became affectionate toward the worker, and from this point the case moved rapidly to conclusion.

The worker carried this child over a period of nearly three years through a very disturbed latency, helping her to achieve a super-ego, make normal identifications with her own sex, and develop moral judgments. At first hostility was aroused, then ambivalent feelings were resolved in favor of a positive giving relationship. At conclusion there seemed to be no evidence of fears, and behavior at school and in outside activities was normal.

In the case of a seven-year-old girl,[9] absorbed in day dreams, bright, but not getting on well at school either in class or with other children, one sees an interesting transition from free acting out and verbalization of conflict, to the strong repressions of latency.

The history showed a neurotically depressed mother, an easygoing non-assertive father, and in the child, feeding difficulty, nail-biting, masturbation, sibling rivalry, vomiting, temper tantrums, and fears. The diagnosis was primary behavior disorder with neurotic traits. The father was devoted to Bessie. Until about five, when a baby brother was born, the child slept in the parental bedroom, and the relationship between father and daughter was always close.

Though predominantly infantile, she was in many stages of development all at once. She was hostile to, rather than identified with, her

[9] Knoepfmacher, "The Use of Play in Diagnosis and Therapy in Psychiatric Case Work," *Smith College Studies in Social Work*, XII (March, 1942), 217–262.

mother. She was preoccupied with oral and anal material; had confused sexual fantasies of all kinds about masturbation, sexual attack by "bogey men," etc. Cooking and eating with the worker relieved the feeding problem in about six weeks, with finger painting and clay modeling, and many allusions to smells by the child. The worker accepted her interest and pleasure in these things and would comment occasionally. "Sh, don't talk about it—it's not nice," said the child. "Yes," said the worker, "when you grow up you feel it is not nice, but when you are small you like to smell it and have other people smell it." "How do you know all these things? Do you still remember them?" "Partly I still remember how I felt when I was a child, and partly other children tell me how they feel, so that I know." There is extensive verbalization both with and without play scenes about sex differences, and the parental intercourse which she has witnessed. Expression was always uninhibited. During the later part of the first year there was less fantasy and more realistic reporting of intimate sexual curiosity about the parents, and sex play with the little brother. During the second year, in the first six months interviews were less frequent. She became preoccupied with Bible stories and used them to help incorporate new moral judgments. The worker helped to clarify what was forbidden now, but would be permitted when she was grown. She identified fully with the worker, became interested in having babies, and then began to taper off. The worker kept stressing how she was growing up, and she was able to leave off the feeding difficulties and the sex play. She became sociable and successful at school and got along well at camp.

During this period she stopped revealing material which hitherto had been so freely expressed, telling the worker to "shut up" if there was any allusion to it. Before leaving she regressed a little, and she failed in arithmetic. This was handled now on the social instead of the interview level by giving her a tutor who had good therapeutic understanding. Bessie showed remarkable insight as to what had happened. With regard to a plant she was watering, she spoke of all the stages a twisted plant propped up with a stick had gone through to grow—"That is just like me—I was small; I needed a lot of care. You were my stick, but now I don't need a stick. I can walk alone." She talked into the ediphone—"I have been coming here for a long time, and now I can manage alone. I will come to visit if I feel like it, *not to talk, but to play and have a good time* (the old free expression now completely renounced in latency). She also found a neighborhood club which she enjoyed.

While still having a tendency to be oversensitive about any criticism from her father, it was felt that she was doing very well, and if further upset occurred at adolescence it was probable that her mother and she would again seek and use help.

An example of "school phobia" is the following:

Billy, a ten-and-a-half-year-old boy, had ceased attending school because of acute anxiety and vomiting. He had gone through the third grade with many absences, but was unable to continue. A change to a strict teacher aroused all his fears, as he believed he would be forcibly kept at school and not allowed to go home. Actually the failure to go to school was a symptom of his unresolved oedipal conflict.[10] He was diagnosed as having acute anxiety hysteria, superimposed on an infantile character disorder. Later a kind young teacher who tried to gratify him only made matters worse and aroused anxiety and guilt reactions. The mother had always infantilized the child, but whenever he was bad, had threatened to send him away from home. This threat was reinforced by the fact that an older step-brother had run away because he was bad. The father was a steadier and more mature person, who had inconsistently disciplined the child, but was willing to cooperate in treatment from the start, bringing the child for interviews and moderating his discipline.

During his early attendance at school Billy had many crying spells, and when the anxiety reached its peak, unfortunately the school had acquiesced in his neurotic pattern by letting Billy stay at home, which gave him the double gratification of staying with the mother and of tormenting her. When he did not have to go to school, he got along well in other areas, which is quite common in early stages of a phobia (so long as the ostensible situation can be avoided, the person is comfortable).

The first phases of treatment consisted in play which symbolically expressed hostility toward both parents. He felt himself bad and feared that his mother would desert him altogether because of his badness. The nature of these feelings was not known to him. At first he was very protective about school; he "liked it and his teachers," only he was afraid. Although his parents had been cautioned to avoid threatening him, they had already done this too often. He played many fearful games, in which he was kidnapped and his father would not ransom him.

A more realistic and less protective method of handling Billy was sug-

10 See discussion in Chapter VII.

gested to the teacher, and the authority of the school was invoked to make him attend school.[11] When the worker attempted to get at the basic anxiety and help the boy express some of the infantile feelings and desires, Billy's reactions to his own admissions were belligerent and provocative. The worker did succeed in helping Billy to see and admit that he was using the school to get even with his mother, but that at the same time he was punishing himself.

The early sources of pleasure had been incompletely repressed, and it was these pleasures that the child unconsciously feels are bad, although he has projected the difficulty onto the school. The child's super-ego has become as threatening and as strict as that of his parents. Billy continues to long for magical aid from the outside to meet his feeling of inner helplessness. As an overprotected child he has inadequate strength to meet reality frustrations, and the habit of avoidance has set in.

At the beginning the worker makes the mistake of not insisting that the boy go to school, by which she seems to accept the boy's projections and excuses that the danger lies in the school instead of in the conflict about the parents. If there had been less concentration on symptoms, or if the case had been picked up earlier, when the child was first sent by his mother to kindergarten (where he had had an outburst of aggression and anxiety), the real phobia could have been better attacked. Billy clings to his mother because of his fear that she will send him away and that his father will not "ransom" him. The severe super-ego makes him disguise his feelings in complicated symbolic ways, which are not readily accessible to this level of therapy. The fact that this boy is now in pre-puberty, when the drive to repress is particularly strong, is an additional consideration in not attempting to touch the strong erotic motivation. Although at closing Billy was showing a generally good social adjustment, which was a real gain, it may be assumed that there will be trouble ahead.

A case [12] which illustrates how an exceedingly fearful school child

[11] E. Klein, "The Reluctance to Go to School," *Psychoanalytic Study of the Child*, pp. 263–279.

[12] This case is reported from a different angle in Juliana Knoepfmacher, "Child Guidance Work Based on Psychoanalytic Concepts," *The Nervous Child*, V (April, 1946), 178–198.

can gradually throw off his fears and be slowly desensitized is the following:

This eleven-year-old boy, Albert, undersized and undernourished, was referred because he had a great many fears—of being hurt, of failing in school, of loud noises, of strangers, of death, and of losing his parents. The situational anxiety was aroused as a result of the persecution of Jews by the Nazis in Germany and was superimposed on a basic neurosis clearly shown in the history. The boy was rejected from birth because of his peculiar physical appearance, neglected by parents, and brought up by maids and governesses. Both parents were markedly neurotic—the father unrealistic, living in the glories of the past and completely tied to his own mother, who was in the household. The child's mother, with an old history of frustrations and intense but unconscious hostility toward her own mother, was in conflict with her mother-in-law.

On examination, both neurological and psychiatric, physical defects were ruled out. The diagnosis was psychoneurosis, anxiety hysteria, with some conversion symptoms. The psychological test showed a great deal of anxiety and concern, fatiguability, and an I.Q. of 87, minimal rating. The Rorschach suggested average intelligence, with some language handicap, intense color shock, and various hysterical traits showed up clearly. The boy was brought in by the mother with the hope that he would be sent to camp, both to "force his growth" and "to get rid of him" (but she didn't really want to).

Seen by the worker, he looked like a seven-year-old child with the face of a little old man. He clowned a great deal (this usually conceals a great fear of being laughed at—the clowning controls the laughter in favor of the subject and elicits some approbation). He immediately acted out in play violent scenes in which people were hurt. He talked about South America, where he wished to return (he had been thrown much with his mother there, and they had gone out very little). He brought out at once his fear that his tonsils would be taken out. After this play and these admissions he refused to come back. When his mother brought him, the worker explained seriously to him that he should come in spite of his resistance so that he can be helped with his fears. He said he wanted to forget his fears, and the worker reminded him of them. He did not see how talking could help him. The worker said that if he would share his fears with someone they could fight them together, while now he is alone. He remained suspicious about what would happen to him. He consented to come only if half of the hour could be devoted to studying, because he never could "finish his home work" and was afraid of failing and being obliged to lag behind his class. The worker permitted this at the start, recognizing the anxiety.

But he did not keep his bargain and insisted on doing his home work without intermission. When the worker pointed out that he was doing these things in order not to reveal his fears, he was angry and told the worker to "shut up."

After the United States entered the World War he became the picture of misery. He seemed to shrink in size and be utterly withdrawn. He could hardly utter a sound. The worker succeeded, bit by bit, in helping him to play school. One repetitious singsong was: "Fears, North America, South America, morning, afternoon, night, Africa, Pacific, Atlantic, fears." There was no escape for this little boy; no oceans to keep him safe. However, the repetitive play of school seemed to help him. He succeeded in coming alone to the office. He began to talk about his fears directly, but he often insisted on reading instead of talking. When the worker commented, he was angry: "Leave me alone." He punched the stuffed animals. The worker said, "This is how you want to treat me. You are angry because I make you come here and talk about your fears." "Do other children have the same sort of fears?" "Yes. They come here, and we help them with the fears." "Well, I'm glad I'm small, because if I am, there is not much that can happen to me." He wanted to run away after this admission. He continued to set up defenses by way of reading and studying in the office. The worker made the comment that he did not come here to do his home work, he came for something else. He insisted he was wasting his time. The worker agreed. Yes, he was wasting his time, and why must he do so? He complained of school. (The worker pulled this into the relationship) "what can a teacher know about me?" The worker says, "You mean, 'What can a social worker know to help you?' " He admitted this. He was terrified about going to the dentist. The worker managed to help him discuss it. Castration fears were very close to the surface. He agreed to go, but got sick. The worker patiently went through the whole cycle. They played shipwreck, South America, school, the dentist. He got great relief out of this. He loved to both tell and to act out his fantasies. He finally was able to go to the dentist. It did not hurt him much, and he was greatly relieved. All this took about a year.

There was a struggle again in getting him to camp. "It is too difficult. I cannot adjust to it." The worker accredited his strengths, reminded him how well he had done in camp the preceding year, which was true—his skill in games and the drama. The worker pointed out ways in which he would be able to excel in life. He got a great deal of release from painting in violent colors—pitch black or red. He associated these with being sick and well, respectively. Before his tonsillectomy—"I want to be brave, but you make me scared." The worker says, "I don't make you scared, I only acknowledge with you that you are scared." He broke one appointment before he was able to go through with it. On the way to the doctor's office he muttered aloud, "I am scared, I am scared, I am so terribly scared." He continued to utilize play, both inside and outside the office, to act out his fears. It was all violent and dramatic, and seemed to relieve his intense preoccupation. The dominant theme was always being hurt. On his third camping trip he unexpectedly asked for a Scout knife for a gift, and this was an improvement in the light of his constant fears of being hurt and cut. When he came home from camp, complaining of rough treatment by the other children, fears of being hurt, and that the food was making him lose weight, his family regressed with him and insisted that he should not go back. The worker made a home visit and talked it out. She remained firm. She did not want Albert to stay at home. The family expressed all sorts of anxiety about him—his fatigue and his loss of weight. The worker stood her ground and winked at Albert. He laughed and said he would go back to camp. The worker was careful to draw the mother in to support the discussion.

Whether or not it is advisable in the course of sustained treatment for the therapist actively to intervene in the home setting is, of course, controversial.[13] Opposition to a mother has to be carefully managed, but here it seemed justified and well timed. The boy was much relieved to have this active ego help at a critical juncture. There were too many secondary gains for him at home, which he was making the most of, much as children do who refuse to go to school. This was a turning point. At camp, which was a progressive and understanding one, he did extremely well, and after he returned home he entered the Boy Scouts and began to taper off. He gained in height and weight, and while not tall, was physically normal. He was able to enter high school comfortably. It need not be assumed that the therapy helps

[13] The problem is sometimes less complicated in a two-worker situation; here there was only one. Active interference should be distinguished from knowing and making use of knowledge of the child reality which is always assumed to be important.

such a boy to *grow*, but release of the crippling fears enables him to eat better, sleep better, use camp, have the necessary medical attention, and all the rest. Whether a more intimate psychosomatic connection is present is not known. In this case there was a protracted contact, much ego support, and many ego-building outlets. The boy also created through drama and intellectual interests his own avenues of sublimation. Psychotherapy with family and child, direct interviewing, and social therapies were all closely integrated throughout.

If the child is handicapped organically, the battle may assume heroic proportions. In the case of the seven-year-old epileptic boy, reported earlier,[14] the stakes were high from start to finish. Though play was used incidentally, this boy was well able to articulate his difficulties and was encouraged to do so. The early phases of treatment had been largely permissive and supportive, letting Jerry's hostile feelings be expressed to the worker. He showed all the same mechanisms to the worker as toward the mother—threatening to run away, accusing the worker of not loving him, becoming very hostile whenever he was limited. He was abnormally selfish, sensitive, and timid.

All through the first phase nothing was done to thwart him, and he was allowed to bring out his hostility in any form, with complete acceptance. In the second phase, especially after he had epileptic attacks, the worker discussed what had happened to him and what the medical treatment would be. He was well prepared for all examinations. However, he resented the worker's participation in the medical program he disliked so much, so she said lightly, "Here comes Mrs. Buttonmaker and does the same thing as his mother, sends him to a doctor and makes him take pills." He was a little mollified as he agreed that he was angry.

In the early doll play he expressed his fears: "Jerry talked in a soft voice to the baby, saying, 'I know how you feel. Shall I tell you I have selected the most wonderful sunny hospital for you, the best and kindest nurses? But I know you are afraid they will cut it off. But don't be afraid, they won't.'"

Fears of being hurt assail this frail little boy, including castration fears. This child, like most children, personalizes an injury or a sickness, tending to blame the parent. The earliest fears of being hurt

---

[14] See pp. 107–108 for diagnostic picture.

and of loss of love are all caught up in the totality of a handicapped person. As he gained full security with the worker and could verbalize his feelings, she tried to bring his problems more completely into the transference with the aim of insight and better organization of his strengths.

"My mother doesn't love me because she won't let me play." This was discussed with him. Later in the interview he asked if he might leave earlier. "Do you want to find out if I, too, must control and not give?" He nods. "Then you are asking for the wrong thing. You should ask for more time from me so I can help to cure you quicker." (This direct suggestion is used so that the child may later use this as autosuggestion.) When he was not able to go to camp, he said defiantly, "OK, I can take it." "Perhaps that is not so easy as you pretend." He became very angry at this. "You are always making things difficult for me—no, that is not true. I make things difficult for myself." Kept waiting, he said, "I do not like to wait. You know it is not good for my health to wait. You are wasting my time." The worker acknowledged that he was angry when made to wait— "but sometimes you yourself do not use the time, because you will not talk about what bothers you." (She tries to involve him more earnestly in efforts to be well.)

Cautiously the worker tries to bring out the aggression in order that he may understand the mechanisms of the disturbance.

He had great anxiety about his first trip to the office alone. The worker, too, was anxious, fearing that he might have an attack. He read her thoughts. "Don't worry—I will be all right." It was a great struggle, but after that he came alone. "When will I be rid of my sickness?" he lamented. He recapitulated all his fears—that he believed the worst of everyone and that he was getting angry still when things didn't come his way—and then added, "But you make me able to overcome my difficulties." "I am glad, but that is not yet the real cure for you." "Yes, yes, I know, I must learn not to be fearful at all." The worker said with a smile, "Well, only if it is something really frightening—like a lion." "But you are the lion," said the little boy. From this he went into elaborate fantasies— that his father was a lion and would tear him to pieces, but his mother must save him. (This is one of the few times in the transference when the worker apparently becomes the father figure. For the most part the mother transference holds.)

In all his play, especially in competitive games, which he insisted on, it made him very angry when he lost. Even when the worker helped him to win. "I am getting so terribly angry," he would say, "I want to kill everybody." "Is this how you feel when you get angry?" "Sure, that's why I am afraid." "We all feel that way when we are angry, and still we do not kill." He was able to let the worker win one game. "I am glad, though, that I have won more often than you, because otherwise I would have to be very angry with you." When he complained of his mother, as he did constantly, he said, "I have an enemy in the house." The worker accepted this, but sometimes tried to show him that his mother did have affection for him, which was true. He always found this hard to believe.

With a boy as sick as this, it was necessary to give him this kind of reassurance very often. He still had moods of great suspicion and anger at the worker.

By now he called her "Mama," and she occasionally called him "Sonny," the symbolism of which he well understood as a "play" relationship. He wanted the worker to come often to school and explain to the teacher how he should be handled. "How should you be handled?" "With great love," he replied.

Careful environmental work was done to explain Jerry's problem to the school and to the camp where he was sent. Another worker, meanwhile, was consistently working with the mother, trying to have her accept him more, at the same time giving him more independence.

Jerry came to the office with his mother. He immediately announced that things were going very badly with him. The doctor had prescribed three pills. Also, he didn't want to come anymore. "I always get into trouble when I have to come here. My mother is angry at me because she has to bring me here, so she hits me; then I get angry at her, and it's not good for me to get angry. It's all on account of *you*." Also he didn't want to go to camp. The worker said that it was difficult—they hadn't been able to talk it over because she hadn't seen him in such a long time, and that if he didn't want to go to camp, he didn't have to go; she told him he should have his examination for camp so that if he changed his mind he wouldn't have lost his place. He softened a little and asked about the camp. Was it the same as last year? No, it was a different camp and there would be no Robert (a bully). Jerry said that he had been afraid, but if she could promise there would be no Robert, he was ready to go.

By her own example and by discussion she tried to help him face and bear frustration a little better. He was usually made very angry by this. He accused her of not helping him, but of making him more nervous. She pointed out that his trend was to expect the worst from everybody. He admitted it. The worker always talked to him, he said, as if he were strong, but he was really weak. Worker said he was stronger than he thought and pointed out that he got much stronger in camp. (Which was true; the camp had done an excellent job in building up his ego and helping him to progressive achievements.) About this time he told about his epilepsy, which had started when "my father screamed at my mother, when I was three" (apparently between his second and third years, a characteristic age for beginning epilepsy). He was very resistive to taking his pills. He wanted "to take the worker instead." "I said I was in him just as much as the pills. The pills he swallows of me he can think about as often as he wants to. Both I and the pills are going to help him." Once when he complained about his mother the worker pointed out that although he said he hated his mother, he was developing into a somewhat similar personality. He said he was fighting this trend in himself, "but I have to be like *somebody*, and I can't be like my father." [15]

He gave a long lecture about the United States. When he finished his lecture, he suddenly embraced the worker and said, "I would like to marry you." Worker asked him whether he remembered what he had talked about the last time. "You mean about my wanting to marry my mother?" (He had not explicitly talked about that), "but I don't want to marry her, I want to marry you." "This is still the same wish, because I am in many ways like your mother—I am married, and I am much too old for you. I wish you to find a nice girl who would love you as much as I and your mother together."

In discussing his camp experiences afterward he spoke with admiration of the counsellor, but then retracted—"The counsellor has to be nice to all the boys." "I think you mean me, too. You think because I am a professional person I do not have an interest in you." "Yes! When I first came here I used to say I wanted to live with you. If you would only live with me I could be good, but you never took me home with you." "Yes, I knew you were hurt, but I knew you didn't altogether want to leave your real home." "Maybe, but I want my parents to be very sad and lonely and

[15] The importance of the identification mechanism discussed in Chapter VII.

call me back." This gave an opportunity for the worker to discuss with him that his wish to leave home meant that the family must change, but not he. He resisted this, but showed that he partly understood, because he explained the difference between an "attack," which comes suddenly and is stronger than he, and a "spell," which comes when he knows he might get an attack, but he catches it in time. This was discussed with him as meaning that when the anger reactions were too strong he could not control the on-rush. When the worker paused, he finished himself—"and then the 'attack' is on myself, because I am afraid to 'attack' others."

During the later period there had been a shift in treatment in the direction of insight. Earlier the worker had, perhaps, been too much of a "real friend" to this boy, doing too much for him, buying him birthday presents, all of which he was frankly enjoying, and therefore he was not working hard enough to be cured. His attacks had ceased, except for one short spell during a frustrating experience, but his stuttering became worse. Previously, when the worker had tried to discuss this he had insisted that it was not the business of the worker, but of his speech teacher in school, who had told him that he could "control the stuttering by speaking slowly and rhythmically." Thus he was able to shut the worker out. At this point in the treatment, however, he was willing to have the stuttering brought in and discussed, which illustrates how problems are, bit by bit, brought fully into the immediate therapeutic relationship.

After this he seemed eager to reach the point where he could do more for himself and not need any pills at all. When the interview time had to be changed, he was angry. "You are just like my mother, you want to keep me forever with you—no, I guess only until I am cured." The worker recognized with him that he had improved and could go on by himself in many ways.

This case shows clearly how the dynamics of the conflict, expressed through whatever behavior, are the same: his ambivalent feelings toward his mother; his excessive demands for love and attention from his rejecting parents; his inability to accept frustration without explosive aggression (partially inhibited in the stuttering symptom); his dependency and insecurity about growing up. The case also illustrates one of the "danger situations," namely, the prolongation of the helplessness of infancy, to which Freud called attention. Jerry could not deal with the stimuli and pressures from the environment or the psychological tension, because of his weak ego structure. The therapy, repeated with infinite patience, was with steady support, to give him practice in meeting frustration until he could feel that he need not respond to frustration with anger. The damming up of tension inside him had made him want complete freedom to behave as he chose, which was, of course, impossible. He must consent to the idea that he came to the worker to be cured and that he must work on his problem himself before improvement could take place. The third Rorschach showed gain, and a recent Rorschach confirmed the gains shown in all his social relationships. The consulting psychiatrist, who was also a neurologist, believed that since Jerry had made such striking improvement under therapy he would be able at some point to go without medicine and give up the attacks altogether. Follow-up on this case confirmed this judgment. Obviously, such gratifying results in ill children must be regarded with caution.

An interesting observation made by several caseworkers is that a child who may have used treatment in a very matter-of-fact social way, with strong defenses, sometimes shows in a flash of fantasy or play how real has been the insight. Sometimes when the patient is tapering off, an intimate emotionally charged situation may be produced—as if to say, "now at last I am able to bring out the traumatic situation which has been bothering me."

A ten-year-old boy, somewhat emotionally retarded, had lived through a very traumatic situation at the time of his father's death from cancer, when he was about eight. He had been carried in both individual and group treatment, and the play was almost wholly calculated to let him bring out his aggression, with very little insight emphasis. Some of the treatment was social therapy. He had been given a "big brother," to whom he was greatly attached, as he had still some confusions about male identification. He had progressed well in the group and in individual therapy and had made two successively good camp adjustments. He was getting along well at school and, with the worker's consent, felt that he should discontinue treatment.

In the last interview he suddenly took out a doll set and reproduced very faithfully a sick man lying in bed with a little boy kneeling beside him. He commented in response to a question, "This little boy is nursing his father." There was a discussion of the feelings the little boy doll had about nursing his father, and how the father had died, but there seemed to be very little anxiety. He played out the association as a sort of last confession, and then he was able to leave.

The educational process, ideally, should integrate knowledge and growth toward socialization. When fears overwhelm the school child, he makes an active alliance with the therapist against worries and getting into trouble. Both support and environmental changes may be needed to reinforce the ego from within and from without. School programs for disturbed children cannot be adjusted without understanding the real dynamics of the conflict. Although limited goals in insight are often attainable, it is important through social and educational means to help the child to greater security and self-esteem through achievement in his natural environment, as well as from the therapeutic relationship which itself predisposes to a successful use of these other avenues. In latency, perhaps even more than in other periods, interviews are focused to a discussion of everyday behavior, and the child's reactions to these everyday problems brought in. Moreover, direct interviewing therapy is used concurrently with, and recedes in favor of, educational procedures and opportunities for sublimation.

Recapitulation

All disturbed children tend to expect danger or fear being hurt by the adult world. For the little child expressive techniques are much used, and since he projects his expectations upon any mother figure, an experience of gratification, kindness, and acceptance, especially if parental attitudes can be modified, may be healing. For the older child, in whom the repressing forces are well under way and the swing from the parents is vigorous, technique must be considerably shifted, allowing always for the fact that disturbed children do not go into latency in the usual way and so may have to be treated at times like younger children. Parental fantasies are now displaced on more remote figures, such as that of the teacher. Experiences in social reality of many new types crowd in, and new defenses, both useful and harmful, are built up and harden. In treatment, defenses and disguises built around these remote images and intricate reactions cannot be directly approached, nor may the damage be so directly undone. Play has become more complicated and its defensive structures more ingenious than with the younger child, and verbalization must be encouraged, because it is appropriate to the child's level of development.

Deep interpretation, which is a tool so rarely used in casework therapy, is perhaps least appropriate in latency. It is the worker's understanding of the emotionally charged responses rather than the occasional comment, which flashes the signal to the child and relieves his tension. "Interpretation" is most frequently expressed in the effort to help a child verbalize the everyday conflicts with which he is struggling. Getting these feelings articulated, mutually recognized, and accepted convey essential meanings.

Because social reality is imminent and fears of inadequacy are overwhelming, integration through life experience is emphasized. The therapist's concern lest any approach to the social milieu may dilute the transference relationship, while an important technical consideration, does not appear altogether justified. If the worker has steadily brought the child's reality into the transference relationship and is surefooted in timing moves and handling reactions, the transference need not, we believe, be adversely affected by appropriate social therapies. The fact of transference helps the child to integrate inner and outer. The transference in a supportive relationship is also used as a bridge to social outlets, to support the ego, to help the child manage his defenses constructively, and to open up avenues for abreaction and sublimation. The underground connection between one experience and another becomes electrically one circuit, and even with weekly contacts the emotional experience and the everyday discussion are doubly charged. Thus the child is finally enabled [16] to deal with his problems in his own way, with all the self-understanding of which he is capable and all the social reinforcements which may be necessary.

[16] In all our discussion it must be remembered that seriously disturbed children should be treated by the psychiatrist or analyst. See Chapter V.

Chapter X

TREATMENT OF ADOLESCENTS

Social workers have always treated large numbers of adolescents, because it is in the very nature of adolescents to be "wayward"—to come into conflict with the culture. Moreover, the proverbial "high spirits" and strong restless energies of youth, physiologically so essential, predispose to a situational "delinquency" while the adolescent is struggling to achieve a new social balance. This passes when the ego strengthens enough to handle the impulses and stability is gained.

The Period of Storm and Stress

So much has been written on puberty and adolescence that it seems unnecessary to do more than review the elements which especially influence the therapeutic approach. In this discussion we follow the usual age definition—that the period of puberty, characterized by body changes, is in the western hemisphere from about twelve to fifteen years, running into the adolescent or "teen age" period, approximately till twenty-one. The difficulties of the latter part of the range are contributed to by the economic and cultural factors which prolong dependency.

In many grade and high school children feelings of insecurity and the longing for, as well as the rejection of, dependency, are recurrent. Dr. Franz Alexander emphasizes this in a recent article.[1]

In our present days, another nuclear emotional conflict stands out [in addition to the oedipal conflict]. It centers around emotional insecurity, a conflict between competitive ambition and stress upon individual accomplishment, and a deep longing for dependence and security.

Whether there is or is not an "additional" nuclear conflict rests with

[1] Alexander, Franz, "Present Trends in Psychiatry and the Future Outlook," in *Modern Attitudes in Psychiatry*, p. 61. See p. 214.

psychiatric research to determine, but for the adolescent period the outstanding problem found is certainly the feeling of inadequacy. In addition to the skills that the grade school child must achieve in order to have self-regard and the approval of his social world, the adolescent must acquire skills which make him feel strong in himself and attractive to the opposite sex. The older self is an acculturated self, and the adolescent must prepare for a career which will bring him credit and recognition. The preference towards this or that career is unconsciously motivated (unconscious ego); the channels are created or blocked by the particular culture in which he lives, the specific direction and steps are consciously chosen by the youth and influenced by his immediate associates and advisers. Adolescence is a no man's land; the adolescent himself is an "in-between-ager." In each child's development there is always instability, the move forward and the back swing, as each physical and emotional stage is being slowly mastered. These swings become even more violent, the moves forward and the regression more frequent, and the cultural pressures greater during the adolescent period.

Within the range of adolescence there are two roughly distinguishable stages comparable to the oedipal and the latency periods. In the earlier stage the preoccupation is with strongly erotic, though disguised, feelings toward the parents. What the five-year-old aggressively acts out, the younger adolescent—as soon as he feels secure—*talks* out: all his complaints against and attachments for one or the other parent. The adolescent tries to formulate a word picture which will gain him acceptance. Later the preoccupation is with problems of heterosexual achievement and the success and failure theme. But whereas the grade school child sees his problems, because of strong repressions, in terms of success and failure, adequacy and inadequacy, the adolescents' sense of success and failure, dominance and submission, is always closely associated with the sense of adequacy as a man or a woman. Even those who think that the oedipal conflict has been overstressed in evaluating the younger child's development tend to agree that the onset of puberty precipitates the parental triangle in all its emotional intensity. Social identifications normally achieved through the parent-child relationship from infancy to six or seven must have taken place to confirm the preponderant choice in favor of one's own sex. Just as children who come to guidance agencies between four and seven show more than ordinarily confused sexual identifications, so ten years later this same problem, if not successfully treated or outgrown, recurs as a major theme of adolescence. The little child's problem is predominantly maturation; the adolescent's physiological adjustment is translated into socio-cultural terms. The nursery-age child is interested in body differences; the five-year-old, in finding his place as boy or girl; the adolescent, in his sex role in the larger world—what Dr. Hyman Spotnitz refers to as "the reproductive constellation."

Parents are better prepared for the physical changes of adolescence than for the mood swings—the bursts of affection and repulsion, of tenderness and indifference—of their unpredictable offspring.[2] Not usually able to accept the full impact of the ambivalent, erotic behavior, directed in disguised ways toward themselves, they are thrown into a panic, and their distrust of their own as well as their children's impulses adds new burdens to the struggling youth. The adolescent feels psychologically rebuffed and let down by his parents, much as the younger child in the oedipal phase feels rebuffed when overt erotic aggression is not permitted. The child's feeling about parental prohibitions of a physical kind are now expressed in other terms, such as, "My father won't let me stay out"; "My mother won't let me dress like other girls." The little child feels that he is not loved; the adolescent feels that he is not understood, which is essentially the same thing.

The Task of Therapy

Clinical diagnosis is especially important, because at adolescence one must be prepared for shifting as well as mixed clinical pictures. It is hard to distinguish, particularly in the volatility of adolescence, the children who have taken the fork of the road which leads them

[2] As Lippman points out, extreme reactions are more likely to occur in individuals who were disturbed before adolescence. Behavior problems which often seem of great intensity may be only acute emotional outbursts which clear up. Lippman, "Treatment of Juvenile Delinquents," in *Proceedings of the National Conference of Social Work*, 1945, pp. 314–323.

to act out their oedipal problem on society [3]—in stealing, unmarried motherhood, or promiscuity—from those who have taken the fork of the road leading to symptom formation. The adolescent reaching a guidance agency who has been described as having a conduct disorder usually shows some neurotic traits, and the neurotic is there because of asocial behavior or social failure. History, rather than current behavior alone, must supply the diagnostic conviction. When marked conduct disturbances or marked personality changes have their onset just before or during puberty, the possibility of schizophrenia must be kept in mind.

Bisexuality is constitutionally present throughout life, and a homosexual phase during early adolescence is part of normal development, but full-blown homosexuality (constitutional factors not being present) arises from inability to solve the love and hate relationships of the oedipal period. The normal identifications become mixed or fixated, and the child is hampered in moving forward into heterosexual relationships.[4] A young person in whom homosexual impulses are strong may become panicky or form symptoms for which he seeks help. It is important to distinguish what is normal in quality and quantity for the adolescent period. Strong transferences of either a loverlike or a homosexual nature are to be expected and may be transitory. Severe cases of adolescent homosexuality should presumably be treated by psychoanalysis, but cures are no more common than with any other serious type of neurotic or delinquent personality. The drive of the adolescent for independence and freedom from family ties, coupled with his insecurity, will sometimes make the young person, on his own initiative, seek advice from adults outside the family, but he will be more likely to do so if of the psychoneurotic rather than the conduct type of personality disorder. Because at the outset of puberty the impulses tend to overwhelm the ego—the balance of power being upset by the physiological changes—it has long been known that supportive relationships and social outlets for tension—sports and recreation, shop work and arts—are important.

[3] See van Ophuijsen, "Primary Conduct Disturbances; Their Diagnosis and Treatment," in *Modern Trends in Child Psychiatry*, pp. 35–42.

[4] See p. 227.

Social workers are cautious about embarking on intensive therapy because of the instability of this period. Psychoanalysts themselves have been conservative about suggesting analyses for adolescents, because anxiety and panic states are so easily aroused and the weak ego may not be able to bear the demands of insight. The question is not whether to offer psychological help to disturbed boys and girls, but in what areas and on what levels.

In meeting the difficult problems of transition from childhood to adulthood, both individual and group therapy have much to offer. In fact, the established success of social groupwork as a natural medium for the adolescent suggests one of the main considerations of psychotherapy at this period—that the caseworker, as well as the groupworker, should consciously use social instruments as part of the therapy. As Slavson, Buxbaum,[5] and others have pointed out, since the family cannot satisfy sex needs, the group is a transitional device which makes it easier for the young person to move into heterosexual relationships. Group support and restraint are helpful to the egoistic, turbulent individual. Group therapy is most effective when the conflict is reactive; when expressed in the ego area (feelings of inadequacy, inferiority, excessive dominance, shyness), and when there is chronic fear of failure (as expressed in avoidance of competition or of physical encounter).

Young persons who lack normal sibling experience find group therapy profitable. Group therapy tempers the sharp winds of association and competition with small doses of achievement in an accepting, permissive atmosphere, which allows the person to integrate and assimilate as he goes along. Experiments in group sex education for adolescents have probably raised as many questions as they have answered. "Interview group therapy" is provocative of new and significant techniques.[6] Interview groups for adolescents seem to have the effect of stimulating remarkably frank and intimate discussion of parental relationships and sex, and inhibited youngsters

[5] Buxbaum, "Transference and Group Formation in Children and Adolescents," in *Psychoanalytic Study of the Child*, pp. 351–366.

[6] See Gabriel, "An Experience in Group Treatment," *American Journal of Orthopsychiatry*, IX (January, 1939), 146–169, and Slavson, "Group Psychotherapy with Children," in *Modern Trends in Child Psychiatry*, ed. by Nolan D. C. Lewis.

who are protective under individual therapy may be able to use the less highly charged atmosphere of group therapy and find relief in knowing that their disturbing feelings are common. However, the very frankness of the discussion may precipitate violent reactions—anxiety being easily touched off in the adolescent—which have to be watched for and perhaps picked up in concurrent individual treatment. With fairly severe psychoneurotics the risk is great, and individual therapy appears more appropriate, certainly until the adolescent has worked out a good deal of stability for himself with the therapist. The sex of the group therapist presents a technical problem of no small importance, and much more experimentation in this field would seem to be indicated before definitive conclusions can be reached about many of the above problems.

Because the adolescent is between two worlds, but reaching out toward new experiences, he tends to identify with someone not like himself. Because he feels inadequate, he often chooses strong figures—movie stars and other leaders. Characteristically self-centered, vacillating between dependency needs and drives for independence, his need for self-assertion makes him want to act out, and his preoccupation with his own conflicts turns him toward himself. Because of his narcissism the first approach may often be like that taken with a child having a primary behavior disorder. The adolescent first relates to the therapist on the basis of liking to be liked. Thinking so much about himself, he often enjoys talking about himself, his conflicts, and his problems, as he does not do so freely at eight and nine. In general, if the youth can identify the therapist with his ideals, there is a strong transference. The adolescent must be given clear ideals and images for identification, and constructive defenses must be reinforced.[7] As these boys and girls move from their parental images to object relations with the worker, they derive great support from the mature life experiences of the loved person—his or her marriage, children, career, and so forth. Cases repeatedly show this borrowing and the incorporation of ego strength. Moreover, as the adolescent works toward reality in transference, he can accept the imperfection of the therapist

---

[7] Zachary, "A New Tool in Psychotherapy with Adolescents," in *Modern Trends in Child Psychiatry*, pp. 79–88.

more easily than that of his parents, and so come to rely on and to test his own strength more fully.

The question of using the transference to interpret the parental relationship is always difficult. Again one must distinguish object love—the attachment, hostility, or ambivalent feelings towards the parent—from sexual aim, shown in infantile modes of pleasure finding and satisfactions which persist in the unconscious. Casework therapy does not attempt to uncover in any detail such early thoughts, actions, and fantasies or to confront the person with his feelings about them. Outside of analytic experience most people do not have these memories. With little children, sexual things are frankly expressed and so must be handled equally frankly; with children under the strong repressions of latency, interpretation of sexual material is usually inappropriate and unacceptable, and the child's troubles are discussed in everyday situations; in puberty and early adolescence, sexual aim is again near consciousness, and disguised wishes are freely verbalized. Such wishes are now presented to the worker as dreams, fantasies, and extravagant talk about the parents. Insight, to some degree, has to be given in order to help the adolescent free himself. In general, however, the parental relationships to which the young person is now reacting with such intensity are discussed with regard to his rebellion, hostility, deep and puzzling attachments, resentments and jealousies, but not the incest content. The boy, for instance, can be helped to see that he likes to have his father away from home so that he can have his mother to himself, but he is not faced with implications of this preference. When this formulation is not enough the worker may occasionally be forced briefly into a more drastic position for interpretation of the sexually charged material, especially if this is directed in the transference unavoidably toward the therapist. But only very experienced workers are able to do so. Rather, we would say, if the adolescent must be helped at all consistently on this deeper level, he should be referred to a psychoanalyst.

The social worker uses the transference in a supportive way to help the adolescent bring out his conflicts, to discuss them, and to help him channelize them in socially acceptable ways. In later adolescence, which is more like latency, the repressions settle in again, and the adolescent can and will discuss his sexual feelings (including sexual aims), but now in less anxiety-provoking ways with regard to boy and girl relationships. As in any stage of emotional growth, this is not achieved at once, but the adolescent may swing back to intense outbursts about the parent. In the case of Peggy, illustrated later in this chapter, the girl returned again and again to the parental theme, although moving jerkily forward into heterosexual relations appropriate to the age. One girl, whose mother accused her of inducing her father's death through her behavior toward him, "which brought on pneumonia," felt so guilty that she was completely inhibited, had a delusion that she was ugly, and that no one could love her (that her badness was written in her face). She made a strong transference to a woman worker and was able to discuss her violent hostility toward her father for "letting her down." The meaning of this "letting down" was never fully brought out into the open, yet the metaphors used were transparent—her father always had understood her; he was a "partner"; they were "a team"—her mother was always "offside." When her father left town on a job, her mother had "kicked him out of bed," and so forth. She got as far as facing the fact that she had wanted her parents to get a divorce, and from there on the treatment went in the direction of helping her choose a career for herself. The worker was able to help her so much with her general feelings of inadequacy, the roots of which are so clear here, that finally she could accept her beauty, and she became a model.

Men workers are much needed for adolescent boys, although for certain boys an older maternal person can be very helpful. For cultural reasons even, if there were no technical objections, many parents do not like to have their daughters interviewed in therapy by men workers. Because of the straining at parental bonds, therapy is conducted usually on a two-worker basis, the parents either having their own worker or not being intensively treated. It is important to obtain parental consent whenever an adolescent, especially in the younger age range, applies for help on his own initiative. The timing of the decision as to when and how to bring the parent in is delicate, and it is a great temptation to overlook or greatly delay getting in touch with the parents when the adolescent is strongly upset and hostile toward them. It is dangerous to go far in the treatment of minors without parental consent, especially as the severity of the disturbance is often difficult to evaluate. Gentle firmness on this point is usually acceded to by the young person.

Although the problem of the adolescent unmarried mother should be within the range of guidance, it is infrequently so recognized. Community resources for such girls are restricted, for the most part, to institutional maternity care and placement or adoption of the baby.[8] The girl herself in many instances gets too little or unskilled attention. There is no one type of unmarried mother, but it is quite clear that many of these girls fall within the classification of behavior disorder, oedipal group, with some admixture of neurotic traits. Some are psychoneurotic; a few psychotic. Limited intelligence and poor reality sense are commonly found. There are also many narcissistic infantile (preoedipal) types found in the case load.

Since adolescence is a period when the impulsive life is strong and the ego not too secure, it is to be expected that any disturbance of the ordinary controls of society, increased tensions, dislocations of living routines, and the rest, predispose young people to a high incidence of acting out. The less normal the times, as during wars, the more the number of "normal" girls who fall into this situation. The general observation that one is safe in making is that a large proportion of these adolescent girls have never successfully solved their parental relationship. In fact, one can remark in this group how many immature girls seem to act out their own aggression and anxiety through the very process of having children.[9] Study of the adolescent unmarried mother shows every version of unresolved oedipal conflict, often accompanied by a secondary conflict of extreme feelings of inferiority and inadequacy carried forward from the earliest years and increased at this period.

Since the adolescent is predisposed to fantasy, many pregnant girls have an active fantasy life, both about the lover, often idealized, and about the baby. Some deny the experience altogether, do not believe in their own pregnancy or that the baby can be real, until the arrival of the baby punctures the defenses and leaves the ego unprotected.

[8] See pp. 118 *et seq.*   [9] See Chapter XI.

Many of those who cling to the baby as someone to take care of are the most infantile, deprived, and have the least reality sense. They cannot think of the good of the baby, but are concerned only with their own need for a comforting relationship. There is, of course, a normal narcissistic preoccupation during pregnancy which diminishes after the birth of the baby. But in the infantile personality the need for a love object all one's own, accentuated by chronic affectional deprivation, makes the baby an extension of the self in a narcissistic relationship in which growth is hampered. Many girls find it hard to admit any responsibility for the conception of the baby, and the family attitude, which may also regard them as "victims," reinforces the immature tendencies. One difficulty in the whole guidance process is that the girl does not usually seek help in early pregnancy, and because of the practice of early adoption for the baby's sake there is little time for emotional growth in the mother. Because bodily preoccupation is normal and conscious needs, medical and material, must be immediately met, a warm, maternal relationship is called for. Since adequate treatment of the topic of the young unmarried mother is not feasible here, illustrations will not be given.

Illustrations of the Treatment of Adolescents

It is not easy to give examples of the treatment of adolescents. In the cases studied at the Jewish Board of Guardians the writer found, a might be expected, a great range of problems, many psychological and social variables, differentiated treatment, and a good deal of experimentation by the staff. In general, one can say that the transference relationship was used to help the young person release and sort out his feelings, discuss his life problems, strengthen constructive defenses, and open outlets to express aggressive and sex drives in healthy ways.

A fifteen-and-a-half-year-old girl, Peggy, was referred by the mother because she could not manage her. Peggy was doing well at school and had a good many friends, but was difficult at home—demanding, critical, stubborn, and competitive with her older brother. The diagnosis was psychoneurosis with behavior disorders. The mother was a fairly stable person, however, she had had three abortions and had not wanted this girl. The father had at first been extremely indulgent and affectionate to the little girl, but at adolescence he began to take a very active role in disciplining her, including beatings. The developmental history was essentially negative except for many fears—of the dark, of insects, of animals, of getting deaf, and of being a cripple. At the time of intake she was subject to intense rage reactions against her parents.

As we may expect, her first preoccupations are with the immediate parental triangle. In this case the girl still has confused identifications because of the rejection by the mother and the close but ambivalent relation to the father. She has not been able to identify with her mother. Expressing ideas as to feminine-masculine components in the conflict leads her into discussion of the oedipal situation.

Peggy was always a tomboy, had no boy friends, provoked her father so that she would get a beating, loved to get even, both with him and with her mother. She had slept in the same room with her brother until she was fourteen. He was a very effeminate boy, and she had an unresolved but ambivalent tie with him. She had a great many masturbation equivalents—nail-biting, skin scratching, and other habits. She overtly verbalized that she could not stand her mother, wanted to murder her, and had fantasies about this with obsessional coloring.

This sort of violent expression is not uncommon with unhappy adolescents, reminding us again of the overt aggression of the younger child going through the oedipal period. In a little child, who has no idea of the abstract concept of death, his wishes may be a direct expression of anger and frustration. In the adolescent such expression is, of course, more serious. Hostility is carried over from the time when the parents stood in the way of direct gratification, and the obsession is a disguise for the repressed wish. It is important to remember that as adults we can repress only what is already associated with repressed material; we control other material. In the case of Peggy, one must ask whether this is real aggression or obsessional thinking. Real aggression is not torture; often it is not uncomfortable, but satisfying. An obsession, always uncomfortable, is a defense against more torturing thoughts. In real aggression Peggy would want to get rid of the annoying mother; if obsessional, she would be tormented by the thought that she wanted to get rid of her mother.

Peggy was glad her mother was mean to her, because if she were nice she would have to be nice to her, and she would not want to. She did not want to feel guilty about her mother. She would choke her mother with a towel and go to a show—nobody would ever know. Her mother has never protected her and does not protect her against her father's beatings. Last year she did not go away to the beach with her mother to have a good time, but stayed at home and kept house for her father and her brother, who did not appreciate it. Her mother should not have let her do this—put her in this position. (She states the oedipal situation here very clearly.) She had always been jealous of her brother. He was the one to get the mother's love. That is why, she supposes, that she got so angry with him that she could not control herself.

In this triangle, with the brother sometimes taking the father's place, she can hate the brother more easily than the father. In her ambivalence she gives the positive to the father and the negative to the brother. The mother constantly eggs the father on to punish the girl, without being aware of her own motives. In this tense, unresolved oedipal situation the girl can see no solution for herself except to leave home. She has a real case against her parents, but what she does not know is that she wants to hang on to the situation. In her daydreams she invents a kind mother, and this is her picture of the foster mother if she should go into a boarding home. The fear of "going crazy" is basically fear of loss of control of her obsessional murderous thoughts.

As the worker helped her to bring out her hostility, bit by bit, it disturbed the balance that this girl had made for herself of getting satisfaction and comfort by being punished, hitting back, and being punished again. When this pattern was broken down to some extent through treatment, she wanted to break away from both home and agency. (She doesn't want to change herself any more because she partially recognizes that the change goes too deep.) Her pattern had been seduction, punishment, retaliation, and as soon as the transference was well established, she began to provoke the worker; showed marked hostility; said the worker was just like her mother. She wanted the worker to be unkind, otherwise she could not stand it. She expressed great jealousy of the worker's interest in her brother, whom, in fact, the worker had not seen.

There is a sado-masochistic quality in the relations between the father and the girl, which she shows clearly in dreams and daydreams. Actually, she wants to be treated with violence by her father.

The social worker did not attempt to go all the way back into the unconscious basis, but used the transference to discuss the girl's overt preferences and antagonisms. The sexual aim was not discussed, and there was no attempt to bring this into the girl's consciousness. Sometimes, when the worker encountered too much resistance, she said in effect: "You are treating me thus and so as you do your mother," but the fantasy behind the transference was not made conscious. It is unnecessary to show the many ways in which she revealed her attachment to her father. Whereas a little child would have brought this out in doll play, we see the theme clearly in the emotionally charged interest of father and daughter in animals and in their quarreling over whether he would give her a canary or a goldfish (baby equivalents). In discussion she admitted that she wanted to get her father angry, then he would want to hit her; her mother would be afraid that he would injure her, and at the last minute she would be forced to take Peggy's part against her father.

This case follows, so far, a common movement—the confused identifications, with the complication here of inverted identification with the father rather than with the mother. The child has been hampered in moving forward into heterosexual relationships, the unresolved oedipal struggle activating at adolescence, in this instance, latent homosexual impulses. Therapy must be aimed toward increasing capacity to love others through a combination of insight and support.

Peggy turned away from boy friends and formed strong attachments with girls. As the primary conflict was partially worked through in discussion, the themes of the later stages of adolescence became more accented. The discussion centered around her feelings about girl friends and boy friends. The boys she at first disparaged in favor of a violent attachment to a girl friend. The acute discussions about the parents receded, and her attention centered on her appearance—she was rather fat—her attempts to gain the interest of boys, and her retreat from them. Inferiority feelings were for the first time met and faced, although actually the girl was intelligent, pleasant to work with, and had a successful social time with boys. (With older children and adolescents these inferiority feelings are second only to the unresolved oedipal situation as troublemakers.) In this period Peggy was having a violent adolescent crush on a high school girl.

This, as a passing phase, is nothing to be alarmed about, but since the confused identifications are already a problem, Peggy is panicky. If the homosexuality becomes a persistent and preferred mode of life, it is a type of character disorder which does not easily yield to psychotherapy. The conflicts then are lived out with gratifications which serve as a defense against treatment. Much homosexuality in adolescents normally is sublimated, but homosexual parents, or parents who themselves have confused identifications, are likely to produce deeply disturbed children. Fortunately, in this case treatment was instituted at a time when the feminine impulses could be reinforced.[10]

She told how she competed with boys; how she used to envy them, but now she was changing and felt differently. "It is not so hard being a girl as it was before." She felt helpless, because boys were stronger than she, so now she had turned feminine. "I feel I can control the boys in other ways. I can get Dick to do anything I want by saying please and rolling my eyes. I don't feel helpless any more." She discussed with the worker wanting to get married and having a home of her own. This was a great improvement on running away from home. She loved children. She would like to be a mother, but was afraid to, lest she be like her own mother, who had made such a mess of things. When she failed an English test in school, she was in a panic, and this was used in discussing her fear of failure, her feelings of inferiority, and her wanting to be grown up and not grown up. She spoke about the happy time when she was seven or eight, when "we lived in the country and there were no worries, school was easy, and boys—you didn't have to be afraid of them, as boys and girls that age *are treated alike*. It's a lovely age." (This is a good description of the latency attitudes.) "Now I am frightened; school is not easy. Maybe I am not intelligent enough for college." (She has a high I.Q.) "I want to be a housewife, anyway." She boasted of her domestic accomplishments—cooking and sewing, although she has to sew the opposite way from her mother.

The repressed wishes were now taking the form of acceptable outlets. Her father admired her cooking and gave her praise for it. She got recognition for a womanly function and enjoyed it. She discovered that one of

<hr />

[10] It is interesting to compare this case of straightening out confused identifications, under psychotherapy, with the six-year-old discussed on p. 227.

her boy cousins was very nice. The boys and girls went out together in a group and had secrets. The worker commented that it was natural to have something secret between them, and she said this was exactly so, and it was very satisfactory. Her ability to form heterosexual attachments moved rapidly. She saw the connection between one of her beaux and her father. "Every little thing he says or does reminds me of my father, but I have found a way. I whine and pout and so I get my way." She saw that this was the way she had waged contests with her father and wondered if it was the best way to get along with a boy. She dropped the girl friend. She felt "melting and tender" toward her best boy friend. Of another child who wanted to run away from home she said: "He can do one of several things. He can fight; he can brood and put it inside of himself; he can run away; or he can wait until he is grown up and forget and forgive." This was said with deep feeling and with obvious insight that she was talking about herself. It became increasingly clear to her, and she was able to verbalize that in order to get love one has to give it; that she must give consideration to other people.

Toward the end of the treatment she recalled terrible childhood dreams reproducing the oedipal situation. The worker made no comment, but there was considerable relaxation after this, and they returned to discussions of everyday events, school, and the boys. Shortly after this she said she wanted to stop coming. She was grown up. She was manicuring her nails, following a reducing diet so as to be "perfect for my beau when he returns from the Navy."

Some fears of sex and of her own masculine preferences persisted. She slid back and forth between homosexual and heterosexual aims, just as the little child wavers in his levels of motor or speech or toilet achievement. She had given up her father as a sexual partner, but she held on to him for a long time in identification. Sometimes she came to the office nicely dressed, sometimes disheveled and in slacks. She was able to accept the worker's marriage and to express adult envy of her. Some aspects of transference had to be actively handled, e.g., she resented worker's illness; it reminded her how she resented her mother's illnesses; she thought that mothers "should never be ill." The worker here recognized her disappointment in her, and the resistance and the fear that she would be rejected.

In the transference the worker is at first perfect like the forgotten idealized parents, then tries to help the girl accept the worker's shortcomings, "Yes, I failed to understand you"—"We both must try to improve, must we not?"—and finally to look for ideals outside the parental relationship.

There are several interesting phases of this case which are of general application, such as Peggy's desire to leave home—either after an emotionally heightened tussle with the brother, which aroused incest fantasies, or whenever maternal conflict became too acute. In such instances discussion has to help the adolescent face the reason why the home situation cannot be changed; why the person might change himself enough to handle it; or, if placement is contemplated, what is the youngster's idealization of the foster home? One may ask what she wants or expects in a foster home? Peggy, in describing her ideal mother, would say: "If I did something nice, she would praise me; but I believe if I did anything good and she praised me, I'd just die." Peggy's feeling that she cannot trust her mother is basically a guilt feeling that she does not deserve her mother's praise because of her feeling for the father. The feeling that she does not deserve praise—without going to the ultimate root—can be commented on sometimes more easily with respect to dreams about the wonderful foster mother she longs for than when directly projected onto the worker in the transference. Both in individual and "interview group therapy" many girls are helped to progress from curiosity and vague fears about sex relations to a healthy interest in child bearing and rearing. A girl, whose conflicts at home had pushed her into a wage home without the worker's handling her fantasy about it beforehand, found that she could not stand it because the foster parents "hugged and kissed each other too much." Sometimes youngsters run away to punish their parents—retaliate in a hostile childish fashion—hoping that their parents will follow them: sometimes it is clearly an oedipal version. Frequently real choices and real courses of action must be faced in social work, since the client asks practical help in doing this or that. The therapeutic element is deepened whenever the worker elicits the fantasy around the choices and knows the motivation, but motivation need not always be interpreted for the person to apperceive something of the emotional significance as he elaborates the ideas.

Erotic material at adolescence is always more difficult to handle than in the little child. In Peggy's case, when the girl reported her sacrifice of herself as a drudge at home for her father and brother while her mother was off on vacation, there were so many layers of defense that the worker let the issue pass for a more favorable opportunity; in another case, when a girl expressed herself as being perfectly happy whenever her mother went away, the worker's well-timed light comment—"I guess you are happy when you have your dad all to yourself" brought a flash of insight, without arousing too much anxiety.

To a high degree the adolescent turns outside the family group to ideals which include not only hero and saint but also superman and villain. Sometimes delinquency is far more acceptable than the unconscious wishes. With all young clients the therapist may exercise or suggest restrictions which the child cannot yet fully exercise for himself, and so protect him against his own impulses. If the personality continues to carry a load of aggression well on into adolescence, it seems to be like having a too-prolonged high blood pressure, when actual bodily changes take place. If aggression becomes habitual, there is no known way of remaking the character in which the changes have occurred. Prevention in early childhood seems the only hopeful approach.

In the treatment of the older neurotic character one often sees a person wholly given up to his impulses, who strives to make the worker his conscience. Resistance to being brought into treatment is characteristic, and the worker has to be more active, more outgoing, and more emotionally ready to handle initial and, perhaps, prolonged, resistance. Delinquents have neither the desire nor the strength to ask for help. They deny, disguise, and conceal, or if they admit their difficulties, it may be a trick to disarm the worker so as to elude him. Authoritative [11] firmness is often necessary—if possible resting on a structural rather than a personal basis. Sometimes one can win the delinquent's confidence by doing something for him that he wants, like arranging a more satisfactory school program or averting some of the consequences of his misbehavior. It is unfortunately true that

[11] See p. 147 for authority.

the techniques involved in the clinical concepts of permissiveness, acceptance, and release are more fully worked out than those involved in authority and restraint. That these should be equally clinical is not now a matter of argument. The problem is one for intensive study and experiment.

Since puberty places great strain upon a weak ego organization, it is important that energies blocked by educational disabilities should be unblocked before the disorganization of the adolescent period sets in. Adolescents, who have great fear of failure, whether dull or bright, often have dread of failure in school, where the fantasy of a punishing parent may be reactivated. The parents' overvaluation of school success heightens the conflict for many children and adolescents. The importance of school adjustment in latency is again emphasized.

A sixteen-year-old boy, Alfred, who had anxiety hysteria, was referred because of school failure, unhappiness, and depression.

At first Alfred had attributed his difficulties (fears of riding in the subway, of being killed, of failing in school) to the death of a neighbor, which had greatly shocked him at the age of eleven. This was associated in his mind with his father and fears of his own death by heart disease. He had begun a babyish sort of stammer at this time, which persisted and made him afraid to recite in school. His conflict was increased by the separation of his parents, throwing the boy and his infantile mother, who herself had had several breakdowns, together.

After some preliminary contacts with the school and with the family, the boy was assigned to a man worker, to whom he made an immediate transference. He placed his problem quite directly as that of preoccupation with himself. From the start he had a good deal of insight. He felt his worry kept him from doing well at school and at music, which was the thing he cared for most. He elaborated these anxieties. Early in the transference he described his relationship with his father, who made him feel low, inferior, and lacking in confidence because of his constant criticism. On the one hand he wanted his father to love him, and on the other he feared being a sissy.

With this boy, as with other neurotics, the conscious attitude that he cannot do certain things covers an unconscious attitude that he will not—or doesn't want to do them. The neurotic picture originates in identification with the mother (he fears and wishes to be helpless like her) and hatred and impotence toward the father. The boy's over-determined piano playing is a conversion of his drives, which, unlike a true sublimation, does him no good. He feels pressure in the head and panic whenever he plays. He lives in a conflict between a will to achieve and a desire to fail, which is analogous to the confused parental images he retains. The repressed aggression and sexual wishes have led to the appearance of symptoms.

This is a good illustration of the way in which older children and adolescents often present their problem, namely, in the ego area—inadequacy, feelings of inferiority and weakness. Throughout the case the worker handled Alfred, not on the level of sado-masochism (he enjoyed being treated violently by his father), not as having an inverted, unresolved oedipal situation, although the boy showed passive homosexual trends, but discussion was focused on his feelings of dependency, weakness, and failure. The worker was fully aware of the deeper roots, and from time to time the boy showed flashes of insight, but the nuclear anxiety was not the main theme at any time.

After five or six interviews the boy recovered many early memories—of fears, night terrors, and panic—all associated with his parents. (In transference unconscious material comes up. When not in transference events are *remembered*. This is less therapeutic.) The worker was passive about these revelations, but began to bring out and comment upon the boy's patterns of submissiveness and evasion. The parents' reconciliation gave opportunity for discussing Alfred's current feelings about them; his admissions of inability to take responsibility at school, to stand up or to face things were handled largely in running interpretation dealing with his attitudes toward responsibility. Sometimes it was taken up directly in terms of the relationship—failure to keep appointments, etc. He described things that he and his mother did together to make his father jealous. He admitted only hate of his father, although he brought out quite clearly that as a child it was not so much concern over his hate toward his father as his fear lest his father might harm him. After such a revelation he would become protective. He had a good deal of insight into his stuttering.

After much release of feeling he complained of discomfort in his ears, feared the worker didn't understand him, begged him to have confidence in him. He was afraid worker would turn against him as his father had done.

A doubting, negative phase, so common in anxious persons, ensued. He had a strong desire to break contact because of having revealed so much and a wish to get well quickly without working further on the problem. The anxious person has to work hard to get well, and doubts about recovery should be frankly admitted by the therapist.

At first the worker did not react to the repetitious narrative and did not question the boy. Because the worker did not do this, or handle the boy's doubt of his ability, the boy broke appointments and then came in with a psychology book about his "problem," as if to say, "Since you do not help me, I must help myself." The worker participated in his reading interest, did not thrust the implied criticism aside. "Tell me about the book." The boy presented his problem through an intellectual discussion and felt better. He expressed an ambivalent desire to be helped.

Generally, when a person repeats his story in great detail it is because in some way he feels he has not been understood, as is true also in the repetitive play of children. The worker might have brought this out: "Why do you tell me this again? What is it you want me to understand?" The client, regarding such questions as a display of interest in him, will rarely resent them. The boy, in complaining that the worker doesn't understand him, was projecting onto the worker his negative feelings about his father. He expected that the worker would turn against him.

He knew stammering came from a feeling of helplessness and that he used his helplessness to get attention and pity from his father (who criticized the stuttering and tried in every way to help him overcome it). He enjoyed being the weak, handicapped person. He made the connection for himself: The worker, unlike his father, does not condemn him if he stammers. If relaxed, he does not stammer. Why, then, does he not relax, he asks himself? Maybe he does not want to relax. Perhaps if he relaxes and doesn't stammer, the worker will think him improved and give him up; so he does not want to give up the stammer. The worker pointed out the ways in which he used his helplessness to gain sympathy in school. He saw this with real insight. He admitted that he used his stuttering to evade responsibility so that he would not have to recite. He moved nearer to his problem. Why must he stammer with the school principal, who is good to him anyway? Why with his father? Does the worker think that by always being as helpless as the mother he may retain the father's interest? Does he think so? Well, he doesn't know—he just wonders.

As he continued in interview after interview to talk about his father, we are aware how central in the boy's problem was this relationship—its role in changing him from a "wild brat," as he called himself, to a submissive, neurotic child. When the father disciplined and belittled him, the aggression was first overtly expressed, then displaced on the image of the father. The father image, which was then incorporated as part of the severe super-ego, made him turn his aggression against himself. He could no longer fight back, but accepted the position of being weak because of his identification with his mother. This position he both liked and resented because of his confused identifications (here passive homosexuality).

The boy is not aware of his deeper conflict, but only of the difficulty caused by his symptoms. The worker comments lightly on his repeated clashes with school and other forms of authority. An extremely talented pianist, his fears of failure paralyze him. When the boy brings up a memory of an old conflict, this is linked with his present behavior in school or elsewhere. But the worker does not interpret the basic neurosis; he *formulates the trend* (conflict with the father's authority), but not the unconscious meaning of the trend in terms of the inverted sexual aim, nor does he interpret the transference, in which the boy is submissive to him as to his own father. Rather, after helping the boy to make connections between the old remembered incidents of frustration and angry feelings in childhood and his present sense of frustration and inadequacy in all his activities, the worker uses the positive transference relationship, first to point out the repetitive pattern and then to help the boy into educational and other interests (sublimation). The ventilation of the conflict as expressed in ego functions seemed sufficient to help Alfred to go on with his music and studies. He became more aggressive with his father, using his rivalry constructively by asserting his musical prestige, in which the father could take pride.

This boy gained insight about his passivity and submissiveness and how he was using these as defenses against his extreme hostility toward his father. He recognized his tendency toward self-effacement as a means of warding off hostility and gaining acceptance. He saw some of the secondary gains of the speech difficulties and was able to relate this to his general pattern of wanting sympathy and to be dependent. There was definite indication, with only this much insight, of growth and improved function. Toward the end he not only had mobilized enough energy to be graduated, but he showed considerable betterment in speech and ability to plan about jobs. Analysis would have operated at a deeper level.

As is well known, the delinquent adolescent does not easily use individual psychotherapy, nor is he easy to handle in group psychotherapy. The problem is complicated by community attitudes towards the juvenile delinquent which bring pressure on worker, family, agency, and patient alike. If the total environment counteracts whatever is done, there is little alternative but to remove the patient. Intramural therapy, to provide both acceptance and boundaries or restraints, is therefore indicated. Sports, shop work, vocational interests can all be offered to help the youth lessen tension, achieve skill, and enhance self-valuation and self-respect. The socially pathological temptations and stimuli of home, or neighborhood, or both, are thus eliminated or at least reduced. The specifics in institutional treatment for this group include nonpunitive authority—the other constants being a therapeutic attitude and outlets adapted to relieve adolescent pressures and strengthen personality achievement.

Demands made upon delinquent youngsters have to be slight and not too frequent at first, since they are so resistive to treatment and enter into transference on such negative and primitive levels. Institutional activities may be so graduated as to provoke less rebellion or anxiety. Whenever repressions are loosened up, it is easier to get at the central constellation of difficulty. The realistic framework of institutional life touches off reactions which may suddenly bring the repressed feelings to the surface and create insecurity and sometimes panic. The fact that the young person is physically accessible may make efforts at individual and group therapy (which would never attract at long distance and over weekly intervals) more feasible.

This fourteen-year-old girl, Isabel, was referred by the Children's Court as being disobedient beyond her mother's control, incorrigible, and having temper tantrums. The mother wished her sent away from home. The girl was seen as emotionally deprived, thoroughly rejected, and somewhat dull. Her behavior seemed to be retaliatory. The diagnosis given by the psychiatrist was multiple neurotic character traits on a background of general inadequacy (neurotic character).[12] Both parents had been married previously—the mother divorced, the father never divorced from his first wife. There has been great marital tension, arguments and quarreling, and periodic separations. (Except for the consistent rejection, the history was essentially negative.)

Isabel had been placed during her first three years three times. She was actually away from home until she was six and one half. In the foster home she was a good natured, happy child, demanding much affection and very dependent. Returned to her parents, she was never accepted by her mother, who called her names and punished her severely, always favoring the younger sibling. The father, who also rejected the child, favored the oldest boy, so that Isabel felt "just like a boarder in the house." She had few satisfactions in school, because she was graded beyond her abilities. Because of dissatisfactions at home and in school she truanted early and frequently. Her I.Q. was 87, in the upper end of the dull range, although she might have done better except for her strong feelings of inadequacy. She should have been, but was not, placed in an industrial high school.

She appeared discouraged, unhappy, stubborn, and sullen, having periods of being ingratiating and dependent. At the time of opening the case she had begun to steal in a petty way from a neighbor for whom she did errands. She was punished by her parents, but also punished herself by not eating. It would appear that the aim of the stealing was, in part at least, to pay her family back for their strict standards. She was sent away to camp for a brief respite, but did not do well there. After a school failure, she refused to go back there, where she had already felt so frustrated. She expressed her feelings definitely when preparing for the court hearing. She said she would tell the judge: "I do these things because they don't love me. My parents treat me like a stranger in the house, not like the other children. I have to get even with the family." She didn't think she was a bad girl, but her family did, she said. Because of the hostility at home,

[12] See discussion of neurotic character in Chapter VI.

the stealing, and the truancy, commitment for institutional treatment
was approved. She herself seemed to welcome the decision.

In the early phases of this case there had been some question of a
possible diagnosis of psychopathic personality, but it seems clear that
the behavior could be accounted for by the extremely depriving background and that the girl herself was reacting with guilt and self-
punishment,[13] which emerged clearly in the next phase of treatment.

When Isabel was first admitted to the institution, she found it difficult
to get along with the other girls; she was so eager to be accepted. She
continued her strong feelings of hurt and defiant retaliation because her
parents did not write to her, send her clothes, or otherwise show interest.
She was demanding of the caseworker for clothing and privileges, and
wanted a "big sister" who would be a "friend" to her. The worker was
careful to clarify the areas in which she did not have jurisdiction, which
were rules of the institution, and maintained, within these limitations,
a warm, therapeutic relationship. Isabel attached herself almost with violence to the worker, especially whenever she had a strong impulse to run
away. She often said she was a bad girl. The worker's role was to let her
bring out these feelings fully. Unfortunately another social worker had
to take charge of the case. Isabel said: "You are the third social worker I
have seen. It doesn't help to see social workers." The worker accepted that
it was hard to have changes and gave her a great deal of warmth. She
responded to this with tears and a strong, dependent attachment was made
to the new worker.

After a period of sullen dejection she began to speak of her feelings
about her mother, who had never loved her, pleading in the next breath
that her mother really must love her and excusing her because she was
sick. It was arranged that Isabel could take a small job outside the school
grounds (looking after a two-year-old boy), since she had little satisfaction
in the regular school program. This gave her a real lift. She related
warmly to the cottage mother. After she became secure with the new
worker, she brought out her feelings freely about sex, her own masturbation, and sex behavior of other children in the school. She got comfort
from such discussions. A "big sister" was found for her so that on week
ends and birthdays she could have little celebrations, since she got so little
happiness from her trips home. The worker gave her ego support about

[13] Showing the neurotic ("oedipal type") formation in the primary behavior
disorder.

her appearance, her diet, her clothes, her hair, and accredited all her efforts to be neatly dressed and attractive. She copied the worker's dress closely. She verbalized the feeling that she always felt badly because her mother had put her in a home. She didn't want her. She used to do bad things to make her mother angry, and was never sorry for them. She always wanted to get back at her. She knew she was just like a stubborn little baby, always wanting her own way. Maybe if she had acted differently her mother would have acted differently. "Maybe my mother isn't so bad. Maybe I just think these things about her" (expecting the worker to deny this), "she couldn't *really* be this way." The worker continued to encourage expression and release, with no interpretation. Suddenly Isabel admitted an obsessional thought: "It is hard for me to fall asleep. I just lie there thinking." "What about?" "Such crazy things." "What crazy things?" "Well, sometimes of what's going on at home; what my mother is doing; what my brother is doing. Gee, one of them has had a serious accident. I see them run over by a trolley car, badly hurt, sometimes they're even killed. I get so upset. I quickly turn around and knock on wood. God forbid that it should happen." After this she was depressed and anxious.

Here is the beginning of an obsessional syndrome, with the commonly associated idea that she must be going crazy to have such thoughts.[14]

She tried to reassure herself: "I certainly want my mother to be well and happy." She had nightmares along the same lines and got relief from telling about them. She became very anxious lest this accident might be what she wanted to have happen. Lots of things she was angry at her mother about, but she never wanted that. Worker explained that anger expresses itself in funny ways—in thoughts and dreams. This was an angry dream, but she need not take it literally as an omen. She was much relieved.

Shortly after this she became freer with the boys and girls in their socials and was able to enjoy herself more. She spoke, with some help from the worker, of her relations with the cottage parents, and discharged some of her feelings.

During the caseworker's vacation the girl ran away from the institution, but she had a miserable time at home; there was an open break with her mother. This proved quite salutary. She was able to express at the same

14 See discussion on pp. 111 and 258.

time negative feelings for the worker. She needed somebody "to be stricter" with her, "to punish" her. She expressed the idea that she was "easily led" and needed someone to hold her back. She just wanted to do anything. When these feelings (unresolved oedipal feelings) came, she felt she must run away or do something bad.

The mother transference to the worker—the good mother this girl has never had—was very strong throughout this period, but she was ambivalent too. She wanted to do things on her own, and she wanted to have the worker decide things for her. This was recognized with her. She said, "I never had such confidence in my mother as I have in you."

After the break with her mother there was a period of depression. As the worker continued to accept the aggressive, hostile feelings often expressed in the interviews, she was able to work out a healthier type of mother ideal—not the "perfect mother" of her dreams. More and more she was able to assert herself as an individual and make plans for her parole. It was arranged that she would live at a girls' club and have a factory job. She had applied herself well to all her jobs on the campus. Finally she began to taper off. Her mother was begging her to come back and live with her, probably for the wages, and she was able to say that basically her mother had not changed and that she would not go. While she was guilty about her resolve to live away from home and "let her mother down," she was able to go through with it. She had matured enough, however, to offer to help her mother financially instead. Shortly after this she became engaged to a steady, reliable man, introduced him to the worker, and was able to express the feeling that she and the worker had worked through a great deal together. For awhile she kept up contact with her former cottage mother. She finally outgrew this, but considered her a life-long friend.

In this case the institution was used as a living, but restraining, situation in which Isabel experienced acceptance, encouragement, security, and opportunity. In the therapeutic relation with the case-worker she increasingly was able to air and so sort out her feelings about her relationship with her mother and finally to accept her mother's rejection of her as real. At the same time, she was helped to develop certain abilities which she had, in efforts which were given backing and accrediting. For a long period Isabel's dependent striv-ings had to be satisfied both by the worker and by the cottage mother. Finally she became aware of her ambivalent feelings toward people she liked, and through this to understand her feelings toward her mother, the impossibility of change in the home, and the importance of planning for herself in a constructive way. It was interesting that after admitting obsessional thoughts she had to run home to reassure herself that her wishes had not killed her mother. As she was able to discuss this experience later with the worker, she worked it through repeatedly and was apparently freed. The basic masochistic structure of wanting to be handled strictly and wanting to be punished was not changed, although she was far more able to plan satisfying and rewarding experiences for herself. At the end of the period, given the rather inadequate personality and dull intelligence, the level of in-dependent achievement exceeded expectation.

Recapitulation

In the disturbed child the problems of puberty and adolescence are exacerbated. The girl who has been confused about her sexual iden-tifications, who may have built up satisfying defenses in being a tom-boy, is now forced by the realities of body change to face the break-down of these defenses. The child who has not been helped to internalize restraints is now driven headlong by his urges. The child who was anxious before is doubly constrained to find inhibitory mechanisms to bind his impulses. The normal reaching out toward independence and freedom from the parents may be feeble or else expressed in violent revolt. In either case earlier unresolved over-attachment may be suspected. Psychotherapy for adolescents not only encounters those general psychological resistances but also reckons with the fact that opportunities for growth have been denied and capacities impaired. Measures to increase intellectual and work skills and so enhance self-esteem and prestige are therefore important.

The transference relationship is fully used by any adolescent who is accessible to psychotherapy. As in other therapy, the depth of the transference neurosis is carefully controlled by various devices already discussed. As has been well said, "the aim is the maximum of production with a minimum of intensity." [15] The young person is helped to grow into independence through strong identifications with a worker who reinforces constructive defenses and offers an ideal, while sanctioning the adolescent's efforts to be himself. These identifications are the more important because the question of confusions and inadequacy feelings about one's role in life are so much a part of the problem. "Interpretation" is more a matter of the therapist's grasp of the problem than of any special sort of verbalization to the client. Emancipation, plus a workable interpretation of the drives through ego building achievements and sublimation, are the goals. Despite all the difficulties encountered in the treatment of adolescents, in some ways the therapeutic aim is the clearest. Through being understood, he comes better to understand himself and to be "on his own." Understanding is not only expressed *through* the transference relationship itself but also is actively used to help the young person into experiences and opportunities which will give him skill and strength to take his leave of the worker, as of the parents.

[15] Ross, Helen and Adelaide M. Johnson, "The Growing Science of Casework," *Journal of Social Case Work*, XXVII (November, 1946), 273–278.

Chapter XI

TREATMENT OF THE FAMILY

In carrying forward through the three preceding chapters description and discussion of the therapeutic process, the device of relating the treatment to a consideration of the developmental level (age range) has been used. Understanding *both* the stages in growth *and* the clinical diagnostic picture is essential for any worker who is attempting to adapt therapy to the real needs of the child. Yet even this is not enough. Just as the dynamics of the family group must be fully grasped to arrive at accurate diagnosis, so the same dynamics must be fully utilized in treatment. Recognition of the interpersonal aspects of social casework has long been expressed by the phrase "the family as the unit of work." Through many changes in philosophy, through shifts in emphasis and technique, this concept has remained unchanged. In economic assistance it was early seen that the provision of income carried with it certain implications for family relationships as well as for survival. The fact of a reasonably assured income through the social security program permits more objective investigation of those psychological factors which hold family life together either on a wholesome or a neurotic basis or tend to promote family integration or disruption. This is doubly important from the angle of child conservation. But it is of little avail to reduce infant mortality, or even to assure the economic survival of the individual, if he is not to grow up emotionally and spiritually strong, confident, wise, and kind.

The Dynamics of Family Life

Any social worker must have a specialized understanding of the complexity of the living situation. The case loads of many types of agency show a high incidence of acute situational problems arising from illness and temporary dislocations, brief family separations due to external causes, relatively uncomplicated income, and management problems. The skill of the social worker consists quite as much in knowing how to deal with simple things simply as how and when to go deeper when necessary. But in child guidance many of the mothers are disturbed, frustrated, nervous, anxious, and tense; some have masculine drives; some very little love or respect for the husband. Emotional readiness for parental partnership is limited. There is often marked parental friction, and often disagreement not only as to the care and upbringing of the children but also in other matters.

Mature parents, by not invoking magical powers of infallibility, omniscience, and omnipotence, gradually, in an atmosphere of love and common sense (which is another way of saying "reasonableness") free the child to outgrow them. In the deviant family, the overwhelming forces of love and hate and power perpetuate a sort of magic bondage long after childhood, or else the parent is violently and cynically "debunked" by the protesting child, who sees through the magical parent because there has been so little of the real parent there for him. Thus there is a cycle of mutual rejection. Thousands of women who dislike domestic duties and are irritable with their children may appear to be rejecting mothers, but actually are not so and rarely come to guidance agencies. Just as it is normal to like and dislike one's parents, so it is normal for parents to have negative and positive feelings toward their offspring. Probably there are no mothers, certainly very few, with no feeling of love for the child. Most mothers feel guilty when they have moments of natural hostility toward their children, but the mother who really rejects her children continuously feels resentful and so continues to punish them or herself.

It may or may not prove to be a valid assumption that in giving birth to a child women are likely to recreate in their children any unsolved part of the oedipal situation. If a person may act out her conflicts by creating new beings rather than by forming symptoms, then the child, when actually upon the scene, may certainly become the field in which the parent presents her own narcissistic wishes, aggression, and anxiety. The public has tended to be more alarmed by divorce statistics than by the picture of the precariously balanced, rejecting, or neurotically tied family, which is the classical setting for the behavior problem and anxiety-ridden child. Although many neurotic individuals function well in life situations—even on the level of brilliant social contribution, severe neurotics and neurotic characters perhaps function least well as parents, especially when the "repetitive core" of their neurosis gets in the way of, or actually is worked out through and upon, the children. Parents who are not a real couple at all, in the sense of adult mating, produce some of the worst types of child pathology. Just as in the individual, there may be internalized conflict which keeps the person from complete self-realization, so the marriage of immature or partially matured persons, while offering "adjustment" for the partners themselves, presents many difficulties to the children caught up in the warped structure. It is these families which neither succeed nor fail and do not break up which become the clients of clinics, particularly of social agencies.

All children at times must interfere with the life and pleasures of grown-up persons, but normally mature parents take this in their stride. In any census of a guidance case load one will find the rigid, stern father, and the oversolicitous mother, whose solicitude conceals much hostility toward the child, the weak father and infantile mother, or the ineffectual father married to a woman who dominates the whole family with severe discipline or equally controlling anxiety. The nature of rejection, however, is much more complicated than it has perhaps been customarily regarded. When education abandoned the traditional view that parental love is an unchanging and universal quality, there was a tendency to swing to the other extreme and regard overt expressions of hostility, as well as overindulgence, as evidences of complete rejection, in direct or compensatory forms. In the guidance agency one becomes aware that one is dealing with very mixed types, much ambivalence, and all degrees of parental capacity.

Serious rejection usually stems from the original experience now carried over to a second generation. It is not this child the mother rejects, but this child has touched off her feeling of being unloved by her own parents; her own immaturity and emotional instability. The child intuitively senses these deeper currents and seems to enjoy having his parents upset about him. Certainly, with an uncanny accuracy, children reproduce what the parents fear the most. Sometimes the rejected child makes good use of his uncomfortable experience by developing constructive defenses of independence or creative interests or good school work, but like the woman who struggles too hard to be a good mother, these overcompensations are at a great cost to the personality as a whole.[1] Clinically, as stated earlier, there seems to be reason to assume that primary behavior disorders in children are reactions to gross and early parental neglect, or total rejection by one or both parents. Anxiety, combined with behavior disorders, perhaps, is more usually indicative of disturbed parental relationships caused by interacting neurotic needs in the married couple. The more severe the parental pathology, including adult psychopathic personality, the more likelihood there will be of correspondingly severe disturbances in children.

There are many punishing fathers in a child guidance case load and many recessive, ineffective ones, but since men usually are at work during the day, the pressure upon the child is not so continuous.

One may ask why it is that one child in a family seems to suffer so much more than others. Why does the mother pick out one child for special rejection rather than another? It is seldom that all children in a family are equally disturbed, unless one is dealing with a psychopathic or much deteriorated group. One can only assume that one child touches off the same problem that the parent himself has. The parent does not recognize the link with his own life experience, or, if he does, he fails to understand its meaning. He will say: "This child is just like me," but this may not be so, rather the child reminds him of an older "me" or of persons close to that older "me." This child may be just like his own sibling, or this child may remind him of his parents, or, even more deeply, this child may be an extension of his hidden impulses. Sometimes all the children touch off emotional problems of the parents, but more usually it is one child who especially elicits old responses, or perhaps this one is more "allergic" to the family aggression or anxiety or both.

The problem may be transmitted from parent to child through the

[1] Burgum, "Constructive Values Associated with Rejection," *American Journal of Orthopsychiatry*, X (April, 1940), 312–326.

stream-of-unconscious motivation. The mother may be so fearful of the old in herself that she restricts the child. The parent is likely to be less conscious of his attraction toward than of his feelings of repulsion against his son or daughter. A little girl's overattachment to her father, who may have unconsciously seduced her, may provoke the mother into a natural jealousy and normal irritation. Even overt cruelty may not always be a sign of rejection. Witness the case of a somewhat promiscuous but kindly woman who has given a great deal of affection to her daughter until she began to show signs of uncontrolled behavior. Anxious that the girl should not be the same kind of offender that she is, she attempts to restrain her through extreme punishment. Only when the mother's chain of behavior can be broken, through a relationship to a worker who restores her own self-respect, can she relax a little with regard to the child.

A couple came in bringing the problem of their fourteen-year-old daughter. The man was handsome and vigorous, the woman shabby, old, and tired looking. The man complained volubly about his daughter, "who is a charming, brilliant, gifted girl, now behaving wildly with the boys. Everything she does is wrong. She paints like a Jezebel." The father is terribly worried and tries to restrain her; she calls him names, and he punishes her severely. He cannot tell the worker how bad she is now and how upset and disappointed he is. The worker noticed that every time the father protested that the girl didn't love him, he got emotionally upset. When he told how when he went into hotels and the older men "made passes" at her, he almost had apoplexy. The worker asked a few questions. There was a boy, who had died; the mother had never got over this. This girl was adopted, and from babyhood she had been brought up by the father. He bathed, dressed, caressed, and showered attention on the little girl. His wife was neurotic and preoccupied by grief.

The worker here has taken him away from his accusations and hostile discussion of the girl's present behavior and gets the real story—his great attachment to the little daughter. Does the man see the incest motif? No, probably not. Does the worker try to make him see it? No, certainly not.

The worker said mildly and sympathetically that it was hard for him to let his little daughter grow up and have men friends. He denied it, but in a later interview he grudgingly admitted it, but said, "Isn't it natural not to want her to run wild?" The worker agreed. He brought his wife to the interview saying, "Of course I do not want to have any secrets from my wife when I pour my heart out."

But he not only has secrets from his wife, but from his own conscious thoughts. The worker discusses the "object love"—it is hard for us to let our children go to other people for love instead of to ourselves, but she does not bring out fully with either father or child what went into this intimate father-daughter relationship. In such a case under treatment the father may come to put two and two together enough to recognize that he was jealous of other men's attention and so change his behavior on a social level from so much punishment and restriction of the girl, and this would be one step into the unconscious, but the self-understanding may not have to go deeper than that, nor does the worker usually try to resolve the basic repressed feelings involved—certainly not for the man and not for the girl in the middle of the instability of adolescence. With the girl, the worker might go beneath the intense expression of revolt against and dislike of the father's behavior to some admission of her fondness for him, but for the most part the interview would be kept to the more conscious aspects of the relationship.

Cases are often found in which the parents incite the child to an aggression which they themselves have inhibited. A boy is urged to stand up for his rights or to fight the other children; a girl to speak up, or to act in this or that aggressive way. A mother's compulsion to act as a "good" mother may cover deeply hostile impulses. On the other hand, there may be periods of affection or, at least, pleasant relations mixed in with what seems to be an otherwise unbroken pattern. The reason that a child never seems quite able to accept the fact that his mother doesn't love him is because sometimes she does. In some complaints it is quite clear that the mothers feel that the fathers are more accepting of the child than they are. Often this feeling is expressed with real resentment, because of residual traces of rivalry and jealousy. In a secure home with favorable attitudes, little children tend to work out normal attitudes of sibling rivalry long before adolescence, but the immature parent—insecure, unloved, and overcompetitive as a child—married without working through his or her problem, may now be in fierce competition again. The emotions appear to be fixed at a childish level—"this child of mine is very dependent or bad and annoying, and I have to bear all the hurt."

In any child guidance case load a proportion of cases will be found in which the family attitudes are so destructive that the goal of treatment must be to help the parents relinquish the child to placement, but for the most part placement is not the objective in a guidance case load. The parents, whether hindrance or asset, continue to keep the primary responsibility for the bringing up of the children, and the social agency has no choice but to treat parents in some fashion. The question becomes not whether therapy can cure these psychoneurotic and seriously disturbed adults, since with present knowledge and equipment it certainly cannot, but to what extent it can ameliorate home conditions, affect parental attitudes toward the children, and so improve the social functioning of the family. Extremely harsh and rigid parents who will accept treatment neither for themselves nor for their child present, with rare exceptions, a closed door. From time to time parents have been put on the defensive by the attitude prevailing in "enlightened" circles that there were "no problem children, only problem parents." Today's emphasis, which again stresses parental responsibilities, also points to a wider and more constructive use by parents of what the community is offering in the way of family and child guidance—with real acceptance of the parents themselves.

The Task of Therapy

In child and family guidance one sees children whose parents somehow manage to struggle along or who seem, superficially at least, to want to struggle along, so that attempts must be made to help them within the home setting. We may, perhaps, take it for granted that in most parents coming to a guidance agency of their own volition there is some wish to keep the child, although this may be a wish to keep him unchanged, and there may be no readiness in the parent himself to change. Perhaps in about half the applications received mothers indicate at the outset some awareness that they are playing a role in the child's difficulty. In other cases, as soon as this is recognized the mother may be thrown in to a panic and withdraw because of guilt, unless very carefully handled.

At the beginning of the child guidance movement it was observed that for any modification of the child's behavior the parents must be treated, but as one caseworker has commented, "at one time it was thought to be a simple matter like pouring water—so long as the parent pours water, the child will be wet; if we can stop her pouring water, then the child will be dry!" At first the attempt to make a parent stop "pouring water" was on the level of intellectual advising. But bit by bit it was discovered that treatment carried out solely on an educational level, directed toward specific ways of handling the child, was not often successful. As a therapeutic orientation was gained, history taking became a vehicle not only for information leading to diagnosis but also for bringing out the parents' feelings toward the child, and in the acceptance of these feelings a transference relationship was established which, in turn, could be used for further release of feeling and possible insight. Treatment of the parental situation, then, has become not merely one angle for treating the child, but an integral part of the therapeutic process. Theoretically, both parents should be brought into the treatment relationship, but in the American culture, since the mother, especially when there are young children, is most involved, it is usually she who is most actively engaged in the process. In the family guidance of the future, more effort must be made to bring fathers actively into treatment. Siblings come into focus both as individual patients and as an environment for the chief patient. Moreover, any well-conducted agency will be in contact with other agencies which are concurrently, or have been previously, engaged in treating other members of the family. The larger relationship world of the older child and adolescent have already been discussed.

The objective is to help parents see the connection between their problem and the child's, and if improvement within themselves is not possible, perhaps to help them act out their conflicts in other ways. In all family difficulties the question of who provokes whom is basic: with disturbed children, the parents must usually first have been the ones to provoke. Having a disappointing child, they correctly sense the child's disappointment in them. The worker, by helping them to elaborate their attitudes, can ascertain how they feel about their role as parents and give them enough security in their parenthood so that they are willing to make changes. The caseworker must evaluate whether the parent is "centrally or peripherally involved" in the problem. How much is the parent's destructiveness directed toward the child, and how much is it a displacement from some other person —the husband, for instance? Can the parent be made aware profitably of the real object of the hostility and control it either by conscious effort or through sublimation? If the disturbance, as is likely, is intrapsychic, how much is really connected with the child's present problem, or is the child only incidentally the target?

Not only is the mother the parent who is culturally most concerned in bringing up children, but psychologically there are traces of the original biological unity in the mother-child relationship.[2] With the young child, generally speaking, the child's problem is the same as that of the mother. As the child grows, he slowly resolves the tie, although by hypothesis the disturbed child is less likely to have resolved it. The question, then, is not whether the mother should be treated, but to what degree and on what level must she involve herself and come to understand her self-involvement. Age, health, intelligence, rigidity, or elasticity of character structure, capacity to use insight, all must be considered in the parent as in the child. Because the problems themselves stem from distortions in the parent's own life experiences and outlook, now displaced upon the child, the total emotional climate becomes the milieu of the therapy. One must consider both the overt interaction of parent and child, and the deeper layers of emotional disturbance which play into this interaction. Here, as in all therapy, one must begin with the surface expressions, those which are visible, conscious, and actively stirring the parent to action, whether or not deeper treatment is ever to take place with the parent as "patient." It may be that all one can obtain from a parent is active or passive cooperation in allowing the child to come for treatment, but this is a minimal condition.

[2] See Silberphennig, "Mother Types Encountered in Child Guidance Clinics," *American Journal of Orthopsychiatry*, XI (July, 1941), 475–484.

The essence of the therapeutic aim is to approach the parents, not as obstacles to the child's progress which must be smoothed away, but to enlist them in the search to remove obstacles in the child's path. The pain of self-revelation can be borne only slowly and as one becomes secure in the relationship. As in all therapy, a conscious educational process directed toward helping the parent to give the child more freedom or wiser restraint can be effective only if there is some degree of transference. There must be emotional change in the parent before there can be change of attitude or behavior. The therapeutic permissive attitude in the worker toward disappointments, anger, hostility, anxiety, and guilt feelings must be present from the outset. There must be genuine and complete acceptance. The first objective, and often the major one, is to make and keep the insecure and guilty parent secure with the therapist. An emotionally supportive relationship is usually necessary, particularly for infantile, narcissistic personalities who need to be allowed to become dependent for a time, or intermittently. But if there are insatiable dependency needs of an infantile type in the grown person, workers will try to meet these through realistic solutions.

Caseworkers, like other therapists, have not always been sufficiently sensitive to the parents' own satisfactions or to their expectations about their children. If the father has been projecting an idealized father image on the son, he is upset when the boy falls short. When the boy becomes defensive and aggressive, this seems to justify his reproaches. Or mothers who want to give their daughters all they did not have in their own lives, to bind them thus with eternal gratitude, are resentful if a girl tries to free herself. Many parents who come to a child guidance agency are already deeply self-critical. Almost anything the worker says may be felt as an additional criticism which they are unable to bear. Just as the child patient has to know that we do not think him all bad, so does the adult need to have his strengths as parent accredited. The neurotic parent with repressed hostility is quick to suspect hostility and criticism in the worker, and both acceptance and neutrality have to be carefully balanced. In effect the worker says to the parent, maybe if I could help you be clearer about your feelings, you could help the child yourself. But the caseworker is not able to treat successfully in the specific area of the parents' handling of the child unless he understands the parents' character structure and ideals for themselves. The parent intuitively recognizes whether he is understood or whether he is regarded merely as environment for the child.

The question "What is the matter with me, or with my child?" covers so much anxiety that the slow road of self-interpretation is the only safe one. If the mother can be less sick only by keeping the child sick, one has to help her not only to accept changes in the child but also to find new gratifications for herself. While everyone knows that adolescents need help about their parents, it is not so often realized that the parents of adolescents can be made very insecure by their behavior and also need help. Parents come to accept that it is not terrible to have some negative attitudes toward and some preferences for one or another child. Attitudes of self-blame which the mothers present at intake do not necessarily represent a good prognosis. When they say they are doing something wrong, this self-accusation is often a reflection of what someone else has said, and one must not let oneself fall in with this pattern. It may be only a plea for reassurance and comfort, not real expression of insight. The blame is often combined with excuses: "I am to blame, but I am so nervous I cannot help it." There may or may not be much guilt behind the expression. It is important always to see how she feels about her role as mother. Can she accept her failure, or does she blame her husband, her relatives, or the school? Was she ever separated from the child, and what happened then? Was she ever separated from her own parents? The parent may be merely giving lip service to the cultural ideal of the "good" mother. There is, however, always therapy in the fact that the parent has been able to recognize the difficulty and bring the child for help. This strength is built on until she can admit her own need.

Sometimes one cannot treat the mother at all, or at best incidentally; sometimes she sees herself only as the means to enable the child to receive treatment. She may bring him in or allow him to come in; she may give information about him; she may pay for his treatment if financially able; she, in short, may give cooperative assistance. The responsibility of keeping a young child in treatment remains the parent's, not the worker's; older children must be allowed by the parents to come. The worker does not have and should not assume the right to compel a child to come for treatment. Sometimes the mother is completely inaccessible, and the most one can hope for is that she will not interfere too greatly with the child's use of the agency. If she really does not want the child to change, little good can come of treatment. Sometimes she is too infantile to do anything for herself or make effective efforts to change. Any mother is less likely to block treatment if she receives adequate support and encouragement for herself. Sometimes she is ready and willing to involve herself to the extent of discussing the child and her attitudes and behavior toward the child, but easily becomes panicky or withdraws if the interviews encroach on the deeper levels of her feeling. Sometimes she comes to see the connection between her own problems and those of the child and is ready for the fullest kind of participation.

In most referrals, "complaints" against the child are produced early. Later, if the worker maintains a therapeutic attitude, hostile and aggressive feelings toward the child are uncovered. Since most parents want the child to behave better, they are willing that he should be helped to a truer understanding of *himself*, but they fear the child's ability to make a truer evaluation of them. They are afraid of the child's "telling on them," just as the child fears what the parent may be telling. The painful aspect of all therapy is that we must "tell on" ourselves. Sometimes the parents' reluctance to face the child's emancipation is handled through discussion of the use of the agency, where the feelings of wanting or not wanting help for the child are often projected. Sometimes the resistances are handled through material that the parents bring up either about the child or about themselves and their own sense of adequacy is encouraged. There is no one way of moving in. A progressive emphasis has been, when indicated, to ask parents whether they were *willing* to have the child treated— thus trying to get more active response and participation from the outset—conscious commitment instead of vague acquiescence.

It is usually necessary to bring out the dependency needs and frustration-aggression feelings, as well as the anxiety. In determining the love-aggression balance in the parental demands, one must remember that repressed aggression may only show up as overanxiety.

The more hostility is repressed, the more anxiety will be shown. In general, neurotic parents are likely to be exacting of help for the child and sometimes for themselves, although one must always be ready for the recoil from treatment of overdominating mothers when the "mother-child monopoly," [3] as Dr. Levy calls it, is seriously endangered. Therapy with such mothers (along with the release of hostile feelings toward the child) must be firmly held to the purpose of treatment and the importance of parental self-involvement. If the neurotically demanding or infantilizing mother is unable to engage herself in the process, a supportive relationship will accomplish nothing. "Delinquent" parents (neurotic characters) tend to reject all forms of help. Psychopaths have the knack of entangling the worker as well as community forces in their domestic difficulties before they drift casually out of treatment. Childlike, narcissistic personalities, themselves the product of infantilizing experiences, whether of overindulgence or overdomination, or neglect in the nursery years, must be allowed gratification and dependency along with practical assistance, and educational processes. Sharing the mother's burdens in various ways may have the effect of helping her to free the child to have more friends, to be driven less hard in his studies, or whatever.

Parents who cannot accept their part in the child's problem often argue that the problem is due to disease or intellectual limitation. The mother, for instance, may solve her own fears in a projected anxiety about the child's health. His being sick keeps her from having to face her basic anxieties, just as having a problem child in any guise keeps her from facing her own marital and inner problems. If the mother has symptoms of her own, the worker can gently direct her attention to these and so begin to get her complaints related to herself. Obviously, much support has to be given whenever she is being helped to face her fears. When a parent insists on being furnished with a specific I.Q. instead of an interpretation of range, capacities, and interests, one can usually infer, as with the demand for a medical examination when there is little symptomatology, that aggression and rejection are involved. It is probably better to try to treat the mother's anxiety, suspicion, and resentment than to be bullied into ac-

[3] Levy, *Maternal Overprotection*, pp. 203 *et sqq.*

quiescence. If the parent uses the worker's "passive resistance" to such demands as an excuse to break off treatment, she will do so anyway. Since parents do and do not want treatment, one has to discover in what sense they do and do not. Parents must know they do not come just to bring the child, but must themselves enter into a relationship to help him. Often there is great initial resistance. The mothers who urge interpretation of the child's behavior in many cases must be gradually directed back to self-interpretation.

One cannot disarm hostility all at once, but the worker remains steadily nonthreatening so as to encourage the parent to allow the child to come and to go on coming herself. Particularly when the mother is ventilating hostility toward the child, the worker must be warmly supportive and able to accredit whatever there is of the positive and maternal. Young workers fail over and over again because the very hostility which they have tried to elicit turns them against the parent. Sympathetic identification with the parent must be sincere as well as consistent, or the parent will be overwhelmed by what she is revealing. It has become increasingly clear why the older technique of gathering material *about* the child from the mother on an intellectual level was so disturbing, and there is no easy answer, since it is important at intake to gain enough history to make some sort of decision about the case. On the other hand, recognition that the parent needs acceptance as a person, not merely objective advice, has affected all technique. One must understand not only the child's problems but also something of the parent's own life frustrations, must make not only a clinical but also a character diagnosis, and the level of therapy must be adjusted to the kind of character. Obsessional persons are afraid that something terrible will happen to their children, they do not know quite what. Often they function very well as parents until a situation comes up which hits directly at the core of their conflicts; the compulsively good care of the children then breaks down, and they get panicky. Getting rid of anxiety is never a smooth curve, and the workers are careful not to unravel more than they are able to rebuild. For this reason, treatment may be used to reinforce the parent's constructive defenses for himself as a person and as a parent, rather than toward uncovering deeper layers of motivation.

Although therapy is first aimed at a release of feeling in an atmosphere of acceptance, the rejecting mother may be too self-protective to admit to resentments. As soon as a mother sees that the problems lie in her own feelings and behavior, she may withdraw the child. When the mother, however, is accepting of the child's treatment and his behavior is mild, often she need be seen less frequently in treatment. One might say that the minimum for therapy would be readiness to let the child take help; in still more favorable situations parents should have a readiness to take and use help for themselves, and for a therapeutic result they should become able to see the interconnection between the child's problem and their own behavior and needs and how, in turn, their needs are related to their own early life frustrations, hostilities, and anxieties.

Mothers who have failed to bring their children up successfully, especially if the child must be placed, feel humiliated. Perhaps the mother cannot separate from the child because of her guilt over her original rejection—just as the child cannot easily separate because of his anxiety lest he lose his mother. By supporting whatever is positive in the mother's wish to keep a child, one sometimes can help her to let him go. When the mother can neither accept the child nor separate from him, the worker, recognizing in a friendly way the rationalizations, may help her gradually to permit him to attach himself to the worker or to another "mother person." This is not likely to work out unless the mother is also helped to channels of interest and gratification outside of the home, because she is neither willing nor ready to face the real problems in herself. Support and sublimation must, therefore, go hand-in-hand for most mothers of this type.

As in all therapy, the transference relationship is the medium of release, of self-awareness, of new efforts. The degree of transference must be controlled, and this is usually done by keeping close to the reality of the child's problem. There is a technical dilemma here, because, on the one hand, not much progress will be made unless the adult "client" uses the transference to talk of herself and to "relive" enough of her emotional experience to make connections between her inner life and that expressed in her handling of the child. On the other hand, going too far in that direction may involve the worker in an unmanageable transference neurosis. The psychoneurotic mother is likely, turning quickly from discussion of the child's problem and probably of her husband, often with no stimulus from the worker, to go like a homing pigeon straight to her own traumatized parental and sibling experiences.

In favorable cases connections made by the parent and pointed up by the caseworker lead to sufficient self-awareness, change of feeling tone, and assumption of responsibility for her part of the difficulty to help the mother modify her handling of the child. In more severe neurosis, when nothing less than a deep transference will suffice to reach and meet the client's need, psychoanalysis must be considered. This is not to say that certain caseworkers particularly well equipped for therapy [4] may not go deeper than others, but in the main the child guidance configuration is one in which the central conflict, already focused in the parent-child relationship, is held to that perspective. In certain instances, when the parent in treatment, either father or mother, out of violent rivalry or jealous dependency must push the child aside in favor of his own needs and demands, it will be necessary to clear up early the question—"For whose sake then do you come for treatment?" Control is especially important, since the parent cannot be allowed to become so dependent that he will be unable to function in reality as the parent of the very child whom he is bringing for treatment. As soon as transference establishes itself and he feels the stirring of his own irrational impulses toward the therapist, resistance will develop, with fear of criticism and loss of love. A sustained attitude of acceptance and consideration for the person in his role of parent tends to check the rise of excessive negative and erotic feelings toward the therapist, which sooner or later would be sure to interfere with the child's progress. Experience at the Jewish Board of Guardians parallels that of the authors of *Psychoanalytic Therapy*,[5] namely, that in helping the patient to make social adjustments it is not always desirable for the therapist to be the sole repository of the patient's emotions. It is not regarded as clinically unsound if the therapist becomes "the object of one part of the patient's displace-

[4] See Chapter XI.
[5] Alexander and French, *Psychoanalytic Therapy*, pp. 46 *et seq.*

ment, and an individual in his daily life" (particularly in the parent-child relationship) "the object of another." Transference can spread constructively as well as be diluted.[6]

If the overprotective or overdominating mother is asked to give up her child as love object and so meet head on her own primary problem in the marriage relationship, the result may be overwhelming, unless a supportive relationship is maintained. The very infantile mother who does not assume full responsibility for the child because she has a pattern of behavior which depends on the direction of others requires inexhaustible patience. So long as the worker permits dependence, the mother can, perhaps, manage the child quite adequately. The worker remains the understanding "counsellor" to whom she can apply for relief from strains, tensions, and a sense of inadequacy. In many instances control of overdependency is kept by not seeing the mother too frequently, but letting her seek assistance whenever the "going gets tough." With a normally mature couple there is some "rearrangement of affection and love" after children are born. Infantile persons must be helped to some such rearrangement or redirection of affection. Immature, dependent women may get enough reassurance through the transference to assume more responsibility. But generally treatment must be sustained long enough so that the child, also concurrently in treatment for himself, has developed enough to go on in school and use other constructive influences more or less "under his own steam." In such cases it is particularly important to enlist active participation by the father.

Resistance to treatment is shown in many ways. The mother may protest that the child is much better, as a way of making it unnecessary for him to come in any longer. She may actually resent signs of improved adjustment in the child. There are, of course, very practical reasons why it is hard for a mother not only to bring a child in, but to come herself for another appointment. Obviously, the mother must really suffer and want to help to be willing to go through with it. Skilled workers who know how to accept, reassure, generalize the difficulty, and help with reality problems can do much to relieve fears and resentments and thus deflect them from the child. The acceptance

[6] See p. 130.

received my be translated by the mother into a greater display of affection toward the child or, even more important, in giving him more freedom to grow up.

Illustrations of Treatment of Parents

It is not easy to demonstrate the wide range of approaches to the parent-child configuration [7] since treatment runs all the way from supportive help, both practical and psychological, to intensive treatment of the parent as "patient." Because mothers are more commonly participants than fathers, most of the examples are of the former. In all cases the children were concurrently in treatment. Two illustrations of treatment at the supportive level follow.

In a severe reality situation, practical assistance was given and environmental opportunities opened so that the mother could move out into a life of her own.

A nine-year-old boy, with an older brother, fourteen, was referred as restless, overactive, having a vicious temper and intense sibling rivalry. The diagnosis was behavior disorder, conduct type. The child had been raised in a disturbed, broken home, the father coming home only one day a week, with arguments and quarreling. His wages were supplemented by public assistance. The boy, I.Q. 107, was doing barely passing work in school, reacting in an understandable way to the reality situation. There was little distortion in the character structure, although he was constantly attacking his mother.

The mother, a foreigner, made a strong, immediate transference to the worker. The case was not divided, and most of the early work was focused on the boy. Very little headway was made, however, until the worker, recognizing the mother's needs, actively used the transference to help her develop outside interests, supporting her right to have her own life apart from the children. She was encouraged to have fun and carry out her own ideas for constructive activities. She was able to be more relaxed in regard to the children and to engage in war work. The worker also gave her material things, which seemed to mean a great deal to her as a token of interest. Actually, she had strong and good feeling for both her sons, and the friendly support proved genuinely helpful to her. As the mother with increased relaxation and some self-awareness became less critical, the boy

[7] At the Jewish Board of Guardians.

developed a good relationship to her, improved in school, joined the Scouts, and did well generally.

Comparable treatment of a father, in social terms, in a case in which the mother was out of the home, is the following.

Betty, an eight-year-old girl, was referred for shoplifting. She was a sweet, appealing youngster, shy, obedient and submissive.

The problem seemed to be, in the main, a reactive behavior disorder due to the mother's prolonged illness, hospitalization, and, finally, death, although the stealing suggested a neurotic basis.

The father was always a hard worker, with long hours, but his wife's illness had drained away his savings. He was eager to cooperate with any plans which would relieve pressures on the older daughter, who was the homemaker, and to help Betty have a more normal life.

Since attempts to arrange for a visiting housekeeper were unsuccessful, a warm, maternal "big sister" was arranged for her, who made herself responsible for bringing the child to the office for treatment, and also for her recreation, shopping, and other normal activities. Direct treatment for the child was brief, and improvement was rapid. The father's good understanding of the problem was translated into his approach to Betty, whom he had overlooked in favor of his housekeeper daughter.

Transference may be used by the parent to move to a deeper level and to make connections repeatedly between her own family experience and the present handling of the child.

The mother of a boy of nine, anxious and failing in school, was intensively treated, through discussing current conflicts with her own parents, her present handling of the child, and these interactions.

The mother, strict, rigid and jealous, who identified her son with an insane brother, showed insight from the start. She was living with her parents and at first was unable to move out. When the worker interpreted, in response to her complaints, that she had piled up a great deal of feeling about her own mother, she was able to accept it. Worker kept close to what she was expressing. "You seem to have lived up to a standard of behavior expected." "You think it's a crime to think of yourself first." "You have reason for your resentment and feel a constant urge to help your boy specifically." Transference was strong and positive throughout. Since the worker had confidence in her as a person, she was able to hold her head up. After this she saw that there was a connection between the boy's actions and her attitudes toward them. She admitted she had always wanted someone to lean on. Her current situation was tied up piece by piece by the worker with her earlier feelings about parents and brother, and she was able to accept all of it.

Worker did not interpret the transference relationship, but consistently related present and past, encouraging the expression of hostility toward the parents. The mother was able to say that she could see a repetition of what happened between herself and her brother. But "the work of years cannot be eased in a few months." She accomplished much, and felt she had come a long way. She now saw her mother in a new light without feeling badly about it. Worker gave her frequent praise for her pieces of insight. She was able to admit that she got a great deal of pleasure out of the children, and now understood what she had done to her son.

The boy improved markedly during the mother's treatment, and after about two years she was sufficiently adjusted to carry on alone and apparently successfully.

A case in which mother, father, and child were all treated, is the following.

A nine-year-old, an only child, was referred by the school clinic, where the parents had taken him for evaluation of his mental ability. He scored an I.Q. of 127, was found to be emotionally disturbed: anxious, fearful, and withdrawn. He was shy in school, but quarrelsome and sullen at home when he couldn't get what he wanted. Moody and easily irritated, sensitive and self-conscious, he showed these qualities mainly in his relationship to his mother. Yet he would not permit her to fondle him or to kiss him. Philip and his mother were closely attached to each other. He did not like to have his mother go out lest something happen to her. He would not go to camp, since he could not bear separation from her. Yet he was as withdrawn with her and confided as little in her as to others. Since he was very shy, he always wanted her to take responsibilities for him.

The mother was a submissive person who yielded half-heartedly to her husband's domination. Philip was exposed to inconsistent handling, strict discipline on the part of the father, and oversolicitude on the part of the mother. A tense, overanxious woman, she handled the boy rigidly and overprotectively. She verbalized many fears, such as that something would happen to the boy if he traveled alone on a subway and that he should not play in the street for fear he might learn bad habits from the children. Death fears are characteristic.

Mrs. D. gave in to his wishes in order to avoid any excitement. She would stay near him until he fell asleep, always accompany him whenever he had to take the train or do any other kind of traveling. Her impulse to protect him was tied up with constant fear that something might happen to him. Thus, her fear fitted into his needs, but blocked him in his emotional development.

In early interviews Mrs. D. pressed for advice. Why is Philip so resistive? Should she force him to have his hair combed? Why is it of such importance to her? She doesn't know. Worker recognized that it must be disappointing not to get definite answers about problems like this. There are painful things in her past life, she says, that she doesn't want to discuss. She thinks these may have some effect on the child. The worker offers to help her discuss them. She reveals that her parents were orthodox, but from an early age she hated religion. When she was a little child she had a "hunchback" and her mother told her she had prayed it away. She does not believe this. She was very fearful of talking about herself. She would rather write it down. It was evident that she submitted to the husband's wishes and lacked the strength for anything that he did not want. She cried continuously. She has "always struggled so hard." Her early "experiences are like wounds that have healed up"; she is "afraid to open them again." The worker clarified with her that on the one hand she was eager to get help with Philip, but on the other was not ready to get help for herself. She wanted a reading list on psychiatry, but was able to understand that she could not solve her problems on an intellectual basis.

It was apparent from the outset that Philip's close attachment to his mother had been caused mainly by her own insecurity and need for dependency. In the beginning she had to overcome her resistance to treatment, her suspicions toward the worker, and her obsessional doubts that she ever could be helped with her problem. Coming for treatment aroused great anxiety, especially in the areas where she had put up strong defenses, such as inability to talk about her past and her health. She was afraid that her various pains might become worse if she were faced with her own difficulties. In the transference Mrs. D. was able to reveal some of her most threatening thoughts. Treatment was focused mainly on showing her her own strength, which had been buried because of her lack of self-confidence. Even such a very neurotic woman was found to have considerable potentiality for improved functioning.

In response to various discussions, she was able to let Philip spend the night with friends and come home by himself. She continued to be full of guilt and insecurity about her handling. Was she right about this? Was she right about that? This insecurity was reflected in Philip, who saw no point in obeying her. She blamed herself; she should have had more self-control. The worker tried to help her to see that she was not all good or all bad. She broke contact and went off on a vacation. She wrote the worker a twenty-page letter full of guilt and doubt. She came in at once on her return, as tense as before. She had hoped that she would be better, less nervous, but she had the same "choking sensations" in her throat. She had hoped that by writing she would be relieved. Worker reminded her that she had been warned that writing everything out would not necessarily cure her. It was not a matter of giving information which could produce the change; they would have to work together to understand the difficulty. She agreed.

Mrs. D. began to express jealousy concerning the relation between her husband and her son. She felt left out. He was a very authoritative man, managing all the household money and expenses. She secretly saved money and contributed to her own family. In a very hesitating way she began to tell of daydreaming, feeling that this was allied with "mental illness," of which she was afraid. Usually she projected her resistance about coming to treatment on physical discomforts. Worker, preparing her for disappointment, arranged for a medical examination, which was negative. Psychoanalytic treatment was not feasible.

She brought out resentment about being the drudge in her family. She admitted she did not enjoy helping her sister, but saw that it was good for her not to repress all her feelings. In her daydreams she was always the main figure, getting the attention she had been denied all her life. At first she was very protective of her mother-in-law, and then expressed criticism. Her fears came out more and more; her resentment at being deprived in childhood and marriage of love and attention. As she brought out resentment against her husband and family, she saw her own part in the conflict. She became reasonable about limitations for Philip, insisting on a few things and letting the rest go. She was able to express annoyance at the worker and resentment that she was no better. She had many mood swings, but less depression. She admitted that she had made real progress in handling Philip, was not so insecure and undecided, and was also less nervous. She still had great need of worker's approval whenever she did something wise for the boy. Worker gave her reassurance on a reality basis. She talked of her fear of emotional dependency and related this to her fear of being dependent on the worker. She connected her ambivalent feelings of love and hate with her own childhood, seeing, with some interpretation by the worker, that she had felt this way toward her son, and had not always loved him, as she imagined. She saw that her anger against religion was because her parents had seemed to give all their love to God and none to her.

She was often late, but rarely broke an appointment. Her resistance to coming was discussed, and after that she brought out more of her painful childhood. She dreamed that she had attacked Philip with a spoon, which became a knife, and was able to understand the aggressive impulses as they came out. Later she was able to admit that she once had an impulse to throw her niece out of the window. The worker discussed the universality of aggressive impulses and how they were both controlled and expressed, and she became less anxious. She was able to assert herself in a much more natural way with Philip, which surprised him very much, but he liked it.

This mother has taken out all her childhood experiences on Philip. Unconsciously she has rejected him and compensates by being overprotective. This has kept her in a state of tension. When she gets acceptance of her own suffering, she can let out her aggression. While before she had been proud of herself for being such a controlled person, one who would never show her anger and was ready to submit to her husband's wishes, she now understood that it would be better for her and her family if she asserted herself and was firm and decided in her opinions. In the later stage of her development, as she kept making connections between her past life and her present behavior, she began to see improvement in herself. She found that her former ideal of herself had changed entirely. Philip was doing well at school and making friends.

The father came, too, for help—a rigid, compulsive person. He had imposed high standards on his son, forcing him to do what he wanted. At first he was taken into treatment, but later transferred to another agency, as it seemed best not to have this closely knit family together all at once. Consultation was frequent, and the whole family interrelationships were much bettered.

A six-year-old boy was referred by the school as uncontrollable. Diagnostically he was regarded as having a primary behavior disorder with conduct and habit difficulties. His mother, a professional person, was anxious and controlling, having had many gastrointestinal difficulties and three "nervous breakdowns." She was frigid, and the father weak and uncertain in his handling of the family life and the children. Jake was the second child after a stillbirth, which had very much frightened the mother. After his birth she had her second "nervous breakdown" and a partial paralysis. Jake, breast fed only three weeks, had had convulsions from two-and-a-half months to two years, feeding difficulties from birth, vomiting, thumbsucking, severe and early toilet training, and recurrent soiling and enuresis at three. The mother said she had broken five baby carriages rocking him in the effort to put him to sleep. His first words were, "I don't want it." After a tonsillectomy at three, he was in a coma. He was persuaded to go to the hospital "to have his picture taken," and, according to the mother, he had never trusted her since.

In treatment the boy made clear what was going on (although the course of it must be omitted): "I want to hit my mother, but I can't hit my mother, so I want to hit you instead." Once he said to the worker that perhaps what he had to say to a woman of thirty-five or forty would sound silly, but he could trust her because she was pretty and brave and he could depend upon her.

In this case a great deal of the work had to be done with the mother, whose difficulties were obviously deep-seated.

Given her own worker, Mrs. Young related quickly and positively. She was responsible about appointments. Her first expressed concerns were about Jake's health; she was anxious and overprotective. She started at once projecting everything on health and school, so that the worker soon had to be direct: "How did Jake react to being given love?" She was perplexed. She hadn't tried. "Why?" She couldn't. She was able to see that her inability to show affection was bad for him, and was also able to give incidents. Worker did not feel her intellectual approach was altogether a barrier, but used it as an interest, to which she responded, and from there usually she was able to relate it to herself. Jake's behavior at school was always part of a situation where she had been ill or upset, and this was pointed out. (Health and psychological tests were negative.) She was always intelligent, frank, and open. Her resistance to treatment, however, showed that as soon as Jake was better, she felt there was no need of his going on, and she continued to discuss his problem on a physical and intellectual basis—his school difficulties, grades, etc. Each time he came in, she would have a new idea of what to do. Because of her inconsistency, worker took up with her whether she was going on or not on a regular basis. She bluntly pointed out that the agency was not interested in getting Jake good grades, and that her pressure on him was destructive. After that she came very regularly for a time. Behind her rigid aggressive exterior she showed herself to be an extremely anxious person—pessimistic, never relaxed, and never happy.

As she got into her own problem and the meaning of her relations with her husband, she became panicky and developed gynecological disorders which had no physical base. She was able to discuss this a little, recovered, and came back to a good level. She could presently go anywhere and eat anything and not be ill. Her criticism of the boy began at once and continued for months. She did not want him to have a woman worker because of her jealousy and possessiveness. She told how Jake would tell her she was the most wonderful mother in the world, but that she was unable to respond; that she had no feeling of warmth for him, and that this worried her very much. She blamed him for his school failures, identifying with the teacher against him. Sometimes she reported that he was good, and at other times "absolutely impossible." After about three months she discussed the possibility of psychoanalysis for herself, but though the worker supported her in this, she was not able to make up her mind to go ahead with it. She was able quite early to discuss her frigidity. She gave her own history freely, her self-blame for her mother's death, her feeling of being unwanted, her resentment against her step-mother, and could see how she was repeating some of these patterns with Jake. She had a great many defenses about her handling of Jake and about her relationship to men, which had all been of an exploiting, castrating type. Though she exploited men, she feared and appeased women. She connected her feeling that she had to pay all men back with her feeling about her father. The worker accredited efforts that she made to clarify her feelings in this way. She knew that her anxiety was rooted in early experiences and was able to admit that her fatigue and tensions were taken out on Jake. The marital situation improved superficially, and she was able to be warmer both toward her husband and toward the boy. She gave Jake more freedom and allowed him to go away to camp. Her resistance to discussing her relationship to the boy almost completely dropped away, and she was encouraged to work outside the home, which she enjoyed.

In this case it would seem that the treatment of the mother is the deciding factor, even though she was never able to go much beyond the area of understanding the connection between her emotional problem and that of her son. In her recognition of this and her conscious attempts to change, the boy felt accepted. He responded to this because of his own treatment, the purpose of which he clearly understood. He made very good connections for himself, his feelings toward his mother, his desire for gifts, his fear of not being loved, and he developed a less demanding and more tolerant attitude toward his mother.

The interaction of the ventilation of feeling between mother and son was particularly strong, and it seemed that self-awareness and modification of attitudes were immediately reflected from one to the other. Since Mrs. Young had a strong attachment to her own mother, intensified by her death and the father's immediate remarriage (leaving the daughter with strong masculine drives to handle alone), the question was whether she could take deeper therapy. This might have endangered a neurotically balanced marriage without putting anything in its place. At various periods during treatment, as the transference deepened, she would discuss separation and try to force the worker to aid her. The worker, who was skilled and cautious, steadily controlled the homosexual transference in favor of reality adjustments, helping Mrs. Young at last to a genuine sublimation in her career, which left the marriage intact. She tapered off on a positive note, understanding that for deeper help she would have to overcome her resistance to psychoanalysis. She was grateful for her own and for the boy's improvement, and he, after approximately a year and one half of regular treatment, is now getting on splendidly.

Less successful cases include such types as the following. The mother's poor ego structure and infantile development made it difficult for her to use a relationship.

A five-and-a-half-year-old girl, disobedient and unmanageable at home, was at nursery school very good. The father was selfish and easygoing; the mother, much attached to her own family. Soon after the child's birth she had had nervous chills and so could not feed the baby. There was not much evidence of "rejection," but the mother's attitudes were infantile. She found that caring for a child was too much for her. She herself had been spoiled and indulged in her own childhood. The mother revealed her helplessness in the first interviews: "Anita won't let me"; "Anita has no respect for me." She was constantly appeasing her. Her intention in coming to the agency was only to have the child sent away to camp. It was hard for her to use the interviews. She was afraid of the caseworker's criticism; afraid of having bothered her and of not having done the right thing. When there was improvement after camp, she said this was all due to the caseworker, covering up her jealousy and hostility, and ending contact.

A seriously rejecting mother with obsessional ideas could permit treatment neither for herself nor for the child.

A six-and-a-half-year-old boy had fears, eating problems, and generally disturbed behavior. The father had consented to placement, but the mother could not go through with this. She usually brought the child in, but could not leave him. She often stood peering through the key-hole, or went in and out. Neither boy nor mother would accept separate workers, and it was difficult to arrange separate appointments. The mother felt hopeless—sometimes she "wanted to kill the boy." He drove her "crazy." She said she was desperate for help, but revealed great resistance and ambivalence. She projected the failure on her husband and the worker. She said the boy began to torture her even before birth (illness during pregnancy). Everything she said expressed a desire to mold him. Any comment by the caseworker as to the boy's need of less control was taken as a proof that she must be wrong. She felt that she got no help. She could not see what the talks were for. The caseworker could not help—only crying could help her.

With a compulsive mother who cannot make up her mind whether to place her child or not, the outlook is difficult. One cannot expect, outside of radical therapy, to cure the severe compulsive neurotic, and all one can hope to do is to strengthen those compulsive acts which are most constructive for the children. In such cases one may need help from the father. Often the mother may have bothered him so much about what plan to make for the children that he has said she can do whatever she wants. Then she is quite helpless to act. The compulsive mother always places on the caseworker the whole conflict which has been operating within herself; she externalizes the indecision and tries to make the therapist act for her. She argues, just as she has argued within herself, and thus is able to blame the therapist for any decision.

A seven-and-a-half-year-old girl was referred by the mother. She couldn't make friends with children; she was nervous, a poor eater, enuretic, and a nail-biter.

From the very start the mother took no responsibility for Alice. Her attitude was: "I have brought my child in to you; you must do something about it." When the caseworker tried to involve the mother in discussions about Alice, she met almost complete resistance. As she admitted a little of her hostility toward the girl, she became more hostile toward the caseworker. Most of the time she discussed her own family. Once she said: "You are not supposed to help *me,* are you?" She expected only magical solutions. The caseworker was positive and accepting, but it was hard for Mrs. M. to express her anger. She showed to the worker what she did to the daughter—controlled her anger with gritted teeth.

About all the caseworker was able to do was to enable this repressed and bitter woman to express some of her anger and rivalry before she withdrew.

In the case of a four-year-old boy with a feeding problem so severe as to suggest incipient neurosis, the mother was treated chiefly in order to get her to allow the child to be treated.

The mother, diagnosed as having a severe mixed neurosis, had displaced her anxiety and guilt over the death of her own mother, an event for which she felt responsible, onto the boy. She at once directed hostility and anxiety toward the worker, although on the surface she strove in every way to placate and please because of her tremendous guilt. She herself was an unwanted overprotected child—a pattern which she reproduced in Johnnie. Her feelings of inferiority, guilt, and need for punishment were carried over into her marriage. She forced her mother to support her (perpetual dependency), wanted to leave her husband, yet made it impossible by getting pregnant with Johnnie.

She related to the worker with passionate, clinging attachment, as to a mother. The worker, by complete acceptance of her hostile feelings and acts, enabled her to express her cravings for love and understanding. Identified with her father in a negative way, a great deal of hostility and aggression was tied into eating. Sometimes she wished to overpower her husband (father) and men in general, and in these moods would treat Johnnie with the destructive cruelty with which her father had treated her. Then she would overprotect and overfeed the boy. Hostile aggressiveness grew toward worker, especially whenever she went back to living with her mother. As it was impossible to get her to accept treatment by a psychiatrist, the worker, to whom she had made a strong initial transference, was forced to continue, even though the severity of the symptoms made this case marginal for therapy. It was necessary for this woman to have her own worker.

If a child, going through eating play with the worker, finds that he is not stuffed, or reproved, or punished for not eating and then at home tries to follow this pattern, only to encounter the destructive attitudes again, the unformed personality may not prove strong enough to handle the new conflict set up. Often a direct educational approach to the parent has to be made to change ways of feeding, or else the child's discovery, so important therapeutically, that the worker is different from the mother, may be too hard to bear.

A deep dependency was permitted, with considerable overt friendly gratifications, and when her tensions became unbearable she was seen twice a week. She "would have died were it not for a chance to talk." Like a little girl, she promised to be good—to control her temper, and not to provoke Johnnie. She became possessive of the worker, expressing her love, but was not able for a long time to express her hostility. The worker used the transference to help her let the boy go away to camp, and subsequently to encourage her to do part-time work, thus taking the pressure off the home somewhat. She became more relaxed, able to discuss her treatment of Johnnie, and got conscious insight as to her need to punish him, but she couldn't go into her own motivations. She insisted she always loved her mother, couldn't remember anything about her own childhood. She had to get even with life, but refused to admit that she could ever have been hurt. Her mother was "an angel," like the worker. She described behavior identical with her present treatment of Johnnie, but did not see that it was the same. It was nearly a year before she could admit anything bad about her mother, and then she overwhelmed the worker with a burst of anger. When the worker accepted her love-hate feelings, she was able to admit slight positive feelings toward her father.

The mother could use the transference for support in use of nursery school and other necessary separations and to do work she enjoyed. But her own needs were so great that she became competitive and jealous, interfering with the treatment of the boy, despite which, on a conscious level, she was able to control her need to hurt, and the boy was able to function better, especially when not at home.

A case in which the mother was centrally so involved in the boy's problem, through seduction, that treatment was largely blocked, is the following.

Oscar, fourteen years of age, was referred for failing in school, lack of concentration, insecurity, inability to sit still, temper tantrums, being a poor mixer, and having no friends. In the past he used to soil himself and was severely punished for this. From birth, one leg was shorter than the other. He was not nursed, because of lack of milk, and screamed continuously as a baby. He was placed at twelve weeks for a short period, because his mother felt too weak to care for him, and again at five-and-one-half years he was hospitalized for two months with an undiagnosed condition, possibly polio, followed by a long period in a convalescent home. His illness may have played into his later behavior difficulties.

The mother was an old-looking woman, resentful at having been referred, denying that Oscar had a problem. Only after she talked fully of her own unhappiness and sickness was she able to discuss the boy. She was preoccupied with herself. Her mother was ill, and she took care of the younger and newborn siblings. When two of the siblings died, the father felt she was responsible for their death, became religious, and turned away from this girl, who had been assuming so much responsibility for the children's upbringing. She then began to hate and fight her father and to assert her will. She resented the fact that her father permitted her less education, and finally, though often beaten for it, she forced her father to give her the same education as her brothers. She wanted to go to college, but married, instead, an uneducated man, who "fooled" her because he was kind. She always had difficulties in the sexual area. She completely dominated both husband and sons, as she did her own siblings.

Her guilt over her relationship to her son came out early. With a different mother, he would have been a good boy—it is all her fault, but she does not want it any other way. In the first interview she denied that Oscar had a problem; he is just like other boys. She expected blame for his bad behavior, and her defense was her own misfortune and unhappiness. She, although able to do so, didn't want to pay a fee. Why do we have to take so much interest in the parents? In succeeding interviews she protested that she was a good mother; she repeated all her struggles, her illnesses, her drives to force her children to be educated and to excel as substitutes for her own frustrations. She insisted that Oscar resented coming to the agency. (This was not the case.) She did not know how to account for his difficulties—perhaps she had "given in to him too much." She could not allow him all the privileges he wanted. He was always demanding of her affection. He often said, "I'll pay you a nickel for your smile." His coming is a waste of time. Things cannot be different. She can manage him by praising him. She can get him to do anything she wants by kissing him. When she wants him to do anything, she gets into bed with him, kisses and coaxes him, and he accedes. When she found at last that he seemed to like coming to the worker, she could not stand it. When he cut his lip, she did not take him to a doctor—*she had her own remedies*. When he was younger, she took him into the "Y," where she was able to *watch* what they did and imitate them. The worker asked if she had any feeling about his seeing another woman for help (as, of course, she did). She denied this vehemently. He was beautiful only as a baby, now he is like her husband. He is still a child; she should find it possible to change him.

Here we see the need to control, to keep him as a baby, to use her own remedies, her guilt over her neglect and his illnesses, her overt seduction of him to win him to her purposes. The boy wants very much to be helped, but his mother is always making it hard. Throughout the treatment of the boy, the mother must interfere and, if possible, stop him from coming, from separating from her, from growing up. She thinks treatment is useless—"a waste of time." The worker understands that this is because she cannot permit another woman to succeed with her son where she has failed, but does not interpret this motivation, as she cannot accept it.

Deep therapy addressed to all the deep nuances of this woman's love, hate, and guilt could, perhaps, have helped to resolve her attachment to her son and her competition with other women. Here the discussion should concern itself with the question about why the mother would or would not permit Oscar to come for treatment, using the transference to help such a woman accept a mother person, without competition and guilt. This latter could, perhaps, be done without interpreting the meaning of her attachment and its own roots in the unresolved relationship to her own father, her frustrations and need to dominate all the persons in her original and present family groups, but any worker would need a very full understanding of the basic problem to treat successfully so distorted a relationship.

In an older child improvement may be possible without much change in the parent, if the nature of the involvement can be so handled that the child is allowed to come for treatment. This again emphasized the importance of the worker's being mature enough to identify with the parent as well as the child, not usurping parental authority nor replacing parental affections and never actually being in competition with the parent, for whom the child has unresolved ambivalent feelings. Oscar, who came regularly for treatment, improved.

In the next case there was a long period with the mother before the worker was able to touch the immediately painful material of her identifications with her daughter or discuss the child at all—still less the links between them.

Patsy was an eleven-year-old girl brought in by her mother because she was disobedient, defiant, teasing, critical, and demanding. She had many fears—of the dark, of germs, of illness—and was very conscious of her own body. She was compulsively clean, excessively truthful, extremely modest, feared that her mother would hurt her, letting only her father touch her—in short, a neurotic child with conduct disorders. The mother was ill before and after the birth of the child, who was not nursed; feeding difficulties and thumb-sucking ensued, toilet training was early and very severe. There were many colds and minor childhood illnesses. When the child was two-and-a-half the mother returned to work and the child was put into a nursery school, where she immediately became a behavior problem. She constantly pleaded with her mother to stay at home; only by falling ill, which she often did, could she force her mother to stay home and care for her. The mother never gave in to the child's fear of the dark, but insisted that she fall asleep by herself without lights. Patsy slept in the parental bedroom till she was seven. The father was mild and indulgent; Patsy treated him with disrespect. At four, when she had pneumonia, she had a nurse to whom she became quickly attached, but was soon sent back to nursery school, where she failed physically and behaved wildly.

The case was divided, perhaps prematurely, for early appointments were not kept. Patsy would telephone for appointments, and the mother's voice could always be heard prompting her what to say. When an appointment was finally arranged, largely through the persistence of the child, the mother made one at the same time.

At the start the mother was uncertain about coming; didn't know whom she was "supposed to see"; wasn't sure if she wanted help. She wanted a doctor, but how could she go to work and pay for a doctor, since she had a little boy at home? She was worried all the time; she couldn't afford a private psychiatrist; could go only a few times, but this wouldn't help her. She was suffering, but was ambivalent about taking help for herself and still more so for the child. Resistance was met frankly.

In all the early interviews she hardly mentioned the child, swinging directly to her own problems and her feeling of hopelessness about being helped. She was hysterical when she found that she would have a different worker. She didn't know whether Patsy needed help; maybe she was herself so upset that she felt Patsy needed help—still she was a brat. The worker assured her that Patsy wouldn't have been accepted unless she had needed help, and recognized that it was natural to sometimes feel that she needed help and sometimes that she didn't. She was fearful and tense. There was something wrong with her that she had never been able to adjust to life. She "wanted children, to have something close to her," but she must be queer, because she also wanted to work in an office. She saw her life as one of complete frustration.

This thirty-three-year-old woman, born of a second marriage, her mother having died when she was five, her father a little later, had been left with half sisters who didn't care for her. They taunted her, saying she was ugly and "a brat" (as she, in turn, always refers to Patsy). Married at nineteen to escape her unhappiness, she is deeply disappointed in her marriage, disgusted with sex relations, fears further pregnancies, and wants more intellectual outlets. She is now a frustrated, rejecting, and rigid person, with periods of depression and much anxiety. The child appears to have much the same sort of neurosis as the mother, but here one cannot get to the child because of the barrier of the mother's insecurity.

The first phase of the treatment was focused on the mother's reluctance to have Patsy treated. Admitting early, with guilt, that she had helped to make Patsy the way she was, she wanted to come if Patsy did, because Patsy wasn't able to come alone. Assured that both could come, she had headaches and broke appointments. Whenever she came, she talked about the outward circumstances of her life, protesting that there was nothing the matter with Patsy. Patsy could come only if she came with her mother. The worker held gently to the plan of separate appointments. The mother didn't like this, since it threatened the whole constellation of her dominance as parent. She broke appointments; she came late; she remembered that her sister had warned her that she should never tell anyone anything. Her resistances were taken up by the worker in a relaxed way. She was always disappointed in people. Perhaps she expected disappointment here too? This was denied.

The mother was tired of the whole family; she would like to run away. Even her little boy pounds on her beautiful mahogany secretary, but perhaps people will feel she is mean and cruel. Of course she wanted Patsy to say everything if she should come, but she would say that her mother is impossible. But Patsy wouldn't come—how can we get her to come? She was sure Patsy wasn't unhappy. The worker was slow, steady, patient; accepted her feelings as natural; didn't push her. The mother then shifted. *She* thought Patsy needed help, but Patsy said no, she could talk to her mother instead. She added fearfully that if Patsy should come in and talk, we would "understand her," but if she should only talk to her mother, it would be "just talking." The worker asked how she felt about her talking to another person. She denied any fears, but went back in a circular way to say that if she herself felt better she could be the one to help Patsy. This was followed by long complaints. She liked to talk here, because it was so "impersonal." She admitted doubt and worries about herself. She connected her own dissatisfaction in marital relations and fear of another pregnancy with her mother's pregnancies—five children in nine years, "which led to her death." She discussed her own handling of Patsy and contrasted it guiltily with the sweetness of her own mother—"When children are little, they worry whether the parents love them—when they are bigger, *parents* worry whether the children love them."

She recalled details in her childhood and recounted them fully. Later she admitted that her doubts were about being helped; she had always denied this before. People were so critical. She used to lose herself in a novel, but now she could see through it and didn't enjoy it. This was discussed in terms of her feeling of being seen through and being criticized. Worker accredited her efforts in making herself come in and talk. She would like to study psychology (identification with worker) when she felt better. She often had to be reassured that she was making progress, but the worker told her that she herself would know when she felt better and could complain about not being helped.

There were repetitive periods of recollection, especially of her mother's forced pregnancies—those children who caused her death—Patsy would be the death of her. After several such interviews, she stated that she had a relationship to the worker that she has been wanting all her life. She discussed friendship, being ignored, getting angry, taking sides, losing friends, being hurt. Worker lightly brought it into the relationship. The mother admitted her fear of being hurt, turned down, ignored, criticized by worker. After this admission of the relationship there was real change, and she seemed to want Patsy to come at last.

Mrs. R. wanted to know if a morning appointment could be arranged for Patsy so that she could come with her. The worker told Mrs. R. that she would arrange an appointment as conveniently as possible for each of them. In the next interviews she plunged into her early love affairs and sexual relations, with great guilt, but relief from tension.

Patsy was now coming regularly. She tried to explain what she talked about at the office, and the mother was now able to say, "Go ahead and tell everything you want to." In a later interview the mother felt free at last to talk about herself interchangeably with Patsy. Patsy is so much like her. Patsy might meet some fresh boys. Mrs. R. was worried lest the fourteen- or fifteen-year-old boys might attack Patsy. Patsy is naïve. . . . Mrs. R. has told her about menstruation, but nothing else about sex, and she knew that one time recently Patsy went with an adult and another child to the park and she wanted to go rowing. She didn't know you had to hire a rowboat. A navy officer invited her to row with him, and Patsy went along. She couldn't let Patsy out after dark and be worrying about her being attacked by someone. That's why she was afraid to let Patsy go anywhere alone, and Patsy had never been anywhere alone. Mrs. R. is always afraid of talking to strange men or any people she doesn't know. She remembers that she was taught not to talk to anyone. She had once met a man who asked her to do an errand for him, and she had refused. She had been taught, however, to be polite, and so she just had stood there and talked with him. He had moved her along into a hallway and put his hand on her thigh. She was very much disgusted and ran away from him. She was glad that she was wearing her long underwear so that he really didn't touch her skin. She has never had any man touch her skin. Her brother and her father never touched her—that's the way she was brought up—very strictly. They never dressed in front of each other. They always had separate rooms. Of course, she hadn't wanted Patsy to be like that. She undressed in front of Patsy and Johnny. Patsy didn't like it. She couldn't understand why Patsy was the way she used to be, when she had tried to bring Patsy up to be different. Patsy would be going to Girl Scout Camp. It was going to be very hard for her then, because Mrs. R. would be left alone at night. She was afraid to stay at home alone at night. Johnny was no company for her, and Patsy was. She was afraid that some man will come in and attack her. She had heard of a neighbor to whom this had happened. She wished she hadn't heard about it. She would like to go away for the two weeks that Patsy would be gone. She knew that Patsy would be all right; it was a good camp, and it would be good for Patsy to go, but if she could find a place to go herself, she would like it.

The worker discussed at length these sexual fears, now recalled, now projected on Patsy, and accredited Mrs. R.'s growth in being able to let the girl go to camp—a step which was, in effect, to let Patsy grow up and move away from her. To make an oversharp distinction between focusing in the area of parent-child relationship and of treatment of the parent for herself is artificial and arbitrary. Whether such a mother discusses her own problems in relation to sex or Patsy's attitudes toward sex will have the same treatment value for her and, no doubt, the same effect upon her attitude toward the child.

Divided Cases and Separation

The question of separate workers for parent and child rests on considerations as to the age of the child, the degree of parental involvement, timing, and other factors. Ideally one should work with a parent before, during, and after taking on the child as patient. To divide the case, one worker taking the child and another the mother, does not mean that the mother will accept treatment. Allocating the case from intake to two workers, unless the mother has been prepared for this, may easily arouse hostility and greater anxiety than she has anyway.

The mother must usually bring the small child to the office, and there she may be seen with or without the child. In cases where there is extreme control or dominance, the mother's willingness, when it occurs, to be interviewed separately may be an indication of her willingness to change. On the other hand, the worker may, during the initial phases at least, want to observe mother and child together in the same room, since one can then see how the little child is responding to what the mother wants him to do. Later, when other environmental influences have played fully on the child, it is not so easy to see the mother's wishes in the child's reaction. Moreover, the shared interview is a good opportunity for the mother to learn through observation, as she does in the nursery school, how a child may be handled quietly and permissively. This participating demonstration has more emotional value than telling her something about the child. In cases carried as a unit, the parent is often less fully treated for himself or in himself, but more in terms of, or as background for, the child. There are exceptions to this when, as in some of the cases illustrated, the immediacy of the interaction makes treatment of either one essentially the same thing.

One must always give a sincere reason for discussing things separately. But since it will not do to convey either subtly or bluntly that the parent has been instrumental in creating the problem, preparation involves a more constructive approach. As Dr. Allen and others suggest,[8] one should not focus on what is wrong, but on "what can be made right." Usually the worker begins with the parent's projection of the difficulty upon the child, giving the mother the same acceptance, exposing her to the same warm and permissive attitude as that toward the child, and then tries to clarify with her the necessity of participating in the solution of the problem. If the preparation is

[8] See papers in *Modern Trends in Child Psychiatry*.

successful, there is usually some point in which the mother asks implicitly, or explicitly, for help for herself, which may be the signal for giving her a separate worker. Or other opportunities may present themselves in the course of discussion. Consciously, she may not want treatment for herself, so she will not readily accept another worker. Occasionally she wants all the treatment and pushes the child aside. She may want the worker to take the whole problem over and cure the child without involving her in the process; or she may fear to leave the child because of guilt. Only by concentrating on her feelings about the child can one move to her handling of the child and to her feelings arising from her own life experience. If at the start she fears judgment as a parent, later, in transference, she will fear loss of love and rejection if she is given another worker. Aware of this possibility, it is still true that time spent in preparing the mother for a separate worker, when division seems indicated, is rarely wasted.

The child, too, may find it hard to leave the mother for his own appointment, since his central problem is usually that of growing up and being separated from his mother. All little children fear this separation, and since the interaction is so close, it is sometimes wiser to continue treatment with the same worker even after the child has been able to accept a separate appointment. The child cannot be prematurely forced into the separate identity (always a special problem for the disturbed child) which he must gradually assume. If fear of separation persists in the older child, it would indicate an abnormal need which would have to be actively worked out. Separation in child guidance is a small edition of what happens in placement. Both parents and child should be helped to participate as fully as possible in the process of separation if lasting benefit is to be expected. Attitudes of marked detachment may preclude any deep relationship being set up—the underlying fear being impossible to break through. Especially with conduct disorders for which the parents feel responsible, therapy carried on either at home or away from home may be equally threatened. Studies made at the Jewish Board of Guardians suggest that since so many rejecting parents react with extreme guilt to placement, if a dissocial or predelinquent child is to be removed, court commitment may be preferable to voluntary relinquishment. Parents, driven by guilt after placement, often seek the release of the child, going through the motions of asking for discharge, only to show great relief when blocked by the impersonal authority of the court.

Indications for division of a case are strengthened whenever there is a condition of overt hostility and aggression between parent and child. Some children, because of insecurity about their parents' attitudes toward them, may not be able to form a relationship with the worker who sees the parent. The strongly ambivalent attitudes of the adolescent toward all parental figures usually make it desirable for him to have his own worker. A practical consideration also is that a very punishing or rejecting mother may arouse countertransference in the worker, who sees the child suffering. Unless the worker is mature, self-aware, and constantly on guard, this is likely to influence treatment negatively for the mother by breaking the inner current of permissiveness and acceptance, even though controlled on the surface. After division of the case, treatment must always be closely co-ordinated, since sooner or later resistance to taking help will develop and be reflected in the child's behavior or in actually blocking the child from continuing in treatment. The mother, too, is better able to handle changes, whether for better or worse, if she is prepared for these changes before they occur. The overprotective and infantilizing mother needs to dominate through her dependency, even though the dependency itself is resisted. The mood seems to be: "love me all the way or I must hate you." Such a mother may move ahead better when discussion is directed away from the child to her own problems, and she may need the additional security of her own worker.

One does occasionally find children who make tremendous strides in their adjustment, irrespective of any *outward* sign of change in the mother, although this must usually follow a long treatment process. The drive to keep the child at home may be strong enough to make the mother control herself and behave better, even when there is no change in basic attitudes. Treatment of the child in and for himself may result in improvement if he is merely an incidental victim of the parents' aggression, neglect, or unhappiness. Since in the young child the problem is likely to be the same as that of the mother, treatment of the parent (the child being seen only occasionally) may suffice. For the young child to get better, the mother (except for very childlike personalities who make a sort of over-all intuitive response to acceptance) must achieve some degree of self-understanding. If the mother, at the outset of treatment, sees any connection between the child's problem and her own part in it, the battle is half won; if later she makes connections between the present and her own emotional experiences, improvement in the child is likely to follow. But if a particular child is an extension of the mother's neurosis, then improvement apparently can take place only if the mother's feelings are ventilated and reintegrated through intensive therapy and if the child can be psychologically detached and fortified within himself.

Recapitulation

In any form of child guidance the family dynamics must be not only understood but also utilized in treatment with differing degrees of intensity and with one worker or two, as needed. In serious disturbances residual desires and unsolved emotional problems in the adults have provoked, and are still provoking, extreme reactions in the children. The family situation in which the behavior is being manifested is the central social fact to be accepted. All insight therapy involves some kind of reliving, recreating experience. In psychoanalysis the reliving comes through the recall or return of the repressed. In child guidance, since the parents are currently acting out and unconsciously, through their own children, reliving former emotional experiences, the past is active in the immediate present in a special way.

Therapy is dependent to a large extent on what the parent is able and willing to do to meet the child's needs. The position of the parent must be considered not only diagnostically but also as the chief element in reconstruction of the family balance. Many parents expect punishment for themselves, and they use the agency to justify what they are doing, or to punish the children; in almost all cases, initially, they see coming to the agency as an admission of failure. In many, there are elements of rejection, but these may not be dominant; a sense of failure and hopelessness is, perhaps, greater. In some cases the parents essentially refuse treatment for themselves, even when they are willing to let the children continue. In practically all success-ful cases there is honest questioning at some time by the parents of their own role, followed by active enlistment and self-involvement in the treatment process.

Transference is used to help the parent verbalize feelings of ag-gression and anxiety and to make connections between early emo-tional experiences and the relationship with the child which lead to self-understanding. Because of the depth and sensitivity of the parent-child involvement, there appears to be a preponderance of supportive treatment of the parent, controlled in favor of reality adjustments. Especially for the more childlike parent, warm acceptance and sup-port, and direct educational methods whenever necessary, prove con-ducive toward releasing her inarticulate or misdirected affection for the child and freeing him to grow up. The initial focus is always the parent-child relationship—later, treatment may go to various levels of self-awareness always related, however, to the guidance objective. That the mother in discussing the child's problem is discussing in disguised form or symbolically her own emotional difficulties of the past seems to carry special therapeutic significance. Experienced and skilled workers are undoubtedly able to help neurotic mothers to a considerable degree of insight, with resultant relaxation of pressure on the child. This is not, however, if the neurosis is severe, a satis-factory substitute for psychoanalysis. If the parents derive secondary gains from the fact that their children are not getting well, as soon as treatment begins to show results it is likely to be abandoned.

Helping a disturbed child to grow up is usually resisted by both child and parent. Psychological separation should not mean, however, growing *apart,* but a new integration of the self in respect to the family constellation appropriate for the age of the child and the cul-tural factors. Ideally, to strengthen the whole family is the aim in a modern concept of treatment. The interaction between parent and child continues to be the central focus of treatment, and it is this psychological involvement and balance, awareness of which is, per-haps, the deepest factor in the success of a therapeutic approach in child guidance. How fathers may be brought fully into the process remains a paramount consideration.

Chapter XII

PREPARATION FOR PSYCHOTHERAPY
IN SOCIAL WORK

CHILD GUIDANCE is a complicated function, because in its very nature it must draw on what psychological, medical and the social sciences, offer. All the social sciences are developing rapidly, and all the fundamental assumptions are being constantly retested. Social work, although allied to other disciplines, has a distinctive function and role. Its special problems arise from patterns of social living; its special skills are directed toward preserving the balance between inner and outer forces. Its traditional concern with outer reality has no meaning unless the social worker understands the nature of personality and how a client is motivated to use reality. All social casework has within it elements of "therapy," because of the psychological use of relationship, but in any casework in which attempts to counsel in problems of human behavior are made, as in family and child guidance, the therapeutic elements are pervasive.

The practice of social work lies midway between the disciplines of healing and of education. The relationship among the professions always shifts whenever new knowledge is being assimilated. What is learned in science tends to be adapted in many forms. It is inherent in the nature of knowledge to spread. Study of *disease* will always be ultimately the domain of medicine, although shared with scientists of many specialties; study and treatment of the *person* must be shared, since the person is a social and cultural, as well as a biological, organism. Psychosomatic discoveries indicate that prolonged emotional strains lead to chronic tensions with disturbances of physiological functions, and these, in turn, are related to disturbed human interaction. As medicine has progressed from study of the disease to study of the person, the line between medicine and psychiatry has tended to disappear; in child guidance (therapy), the line between psychoanalytic and social work practice becomes, in a qualitative way and in certain areas, indistinguishable. There are many opinions as to how psychoanalytically oriented therapy can best be differentiated from psychoanalysis. Making no pretense of answering this larger question, in the foregoing chapters we have tried to describe and illustrate how psychoanalytic principles have actually been adapted in a particular agency carrying out child guidance functions. It must be emphasized, however, that experimentation, correction, and change are going on at the Jewish Board of Guardians, as elsewhere.

Any attempt to help the child achieve insight is almost always accompanied by attempts to reduce environmental pressures. In child guidance usually the pressures and strains derive from other personalities, though not infrequently programs of living, and physical and economic factors must also be shifted for a therapeutic result.

The demand for psychotherapy is steadily increasing. It is believed by competent authorities that the great majority of children now placed in foster homes would be benefited by concurrent direct treatment, but facilities are almost nonexistent. A conditioned environment for placed-out children, either foster care or institutional, in many cases has not proved sufficient. There is urgent need for more and better therapists not only in "clinics" but also in institutions, family and children's agencies, and elsewhere. Vulnerable children must be detected earlier, and a broader program of mental hygiene instituted. Even if one can assume that mentally ill—psychotic, neurologically disturbed persons, and severe psychoneurotics—will always be treated by psychiatrists, there are an enormous number of clients—less severe neurotics, behavior and character disorders—who do not see themselves as ill in any sense, but whose awareness of difficulty comes because of a breakdown in social functioning. The social worker encounters disturbances, frustrations, and traumata arising in family life and must deal with these deviations. Many persons do not have access to specialists in psychiatry and would not seek this sort of help. Social workers continually treat persons who, projecting their problems onto social factors or on other persons, do not initially seek help for themselves, because they do not recognize their self-involvement. That more social workers should be trained in therapy is inevitable: that appropriate adaptations of psychoanalytic principles of therapy will be made is also, we believe, inevitable.

Often as the person is helped to use a social service he comes to recognize his self-involvement and to press for another sort of treatment. Whether one chooses to regard this treatment as merely a component in social casework or as "therapy" or as "psychotherapy" is, perhaps, less important than to recognize the demand for the thing itself. Some who would not insist that psychotherapy must be carried on by a psychiatrist would, nevertheless, prefer to have all persons in whom psychological needs for help have become conscious referred to a clinic where a "psychiatric caseworker," if not the psychiatrist himself, will be available. With deference to such a conviction, the writer is unable to find this a realistic solution for the day-by-day needs within family and children's work, nor would such a course, even if feasible, contribute most to a dynamic practice within the profession of social work itself.

Considering the difficult tasks which social workers throughout the country are asked to do on behalf of children, the necessity of training them better for their task can hardly be disputed. The social worker who wishes to specialize in psychotherapy should, we believe, first have professional education in an accredited school of social work. He should understand social security, public welfare, cultural subject matter, human behavior, the essentials of community planning, labor problems, social legislation, and related subjects, as well as the fundamentals of medical and psychiatric programs, on all of which the basic social service programs must rest. Even if there were no other reason for obtaining such thorough grounding, if he is to take any part in positive human welfare the social worker must understand the larger social problems. Therapy at its best cannot take the place of broad preventive measures. The social worker must interest himself in standards of living and a better social order if he is to fulfil his obligations.

The question as to who should do psychotherapy can perhaps best be answered by examination of the disciplines involved in any responsible version of it. The essential point is always whether a discipline is adequate for what is attempted. Even if psychiatrists could be found, a combination of psychotherapy and social therapy is called for in a considerable number of family and child guidance cases, rather than classical psychoanalysis or a medically oriented psychiatry. Either far more psychiatrists must be trained to do social therapy, or more social workers must have training for psychotherapy, or both.[1] It is just as fallacious to try to divide the person from his environment, to assign the role of treating one to the medical expert and the other to the social work expert, as to try to divide body and mind. The question is, in part, answered by the "team" approach already established in child guidance and rapidly developing in many areas of professional practice. It is also, in part, answered by the social worker's competence, which should derive from the increasing adequacy of his professional education. There is some ground for thinking that professional social work has incorporated into its educational foundations many concepts which make it peculiarly useful as a background for psychotherapy. Granting a common denominator and the integrated practicing unit, some, nevertheless, insist that the role of the therapist must be sharply delimited from that of the social worker. In this book emphasis has been put on the purpose and characteristics of the therapy itself. Variations, depending on the structure and policies of the agency, the qualifications, philosophy, interest, and skill of the professions concerned, are to be expected in a developing field.

All social workers should have the basic training which enables them to recognize personality needs and to help the individual to take advantage, when appropriate, of specialized therapeutic services. Some caseworkers will be associated with agencies whose functions are addressed to these special needs and will be able to participate fully in the therapeutic process. But this does not impose upon social workers, in general, a function and a practice based upon these specializations. A social worker whose primary task is to help individuals who do have the strength to use "counseling" on a conscious level must know the structure of personality whether or not he is to use this knowledge intensively. In his casework he will have learned the significance of relationship in connection with social services and therefore to make use of himself as a "helping" person. The well-

[1] See Foreword.

developed and carefully controlled field practice characteristic of
social work education not only gives the student a beginning skill
in relationship which can be later built upon, but also serves to screen
for those special aptitudes which techniques of psychotherapy require.
It is our belief that specialization in psychotherapy should not take
place within the range of the two-year period in which one is working
for a master's degree, nor would advanced clinical study ideally be
undertaken before a substantial amount of practice in social work.
There is an ever increasing body of knowledge and skill to be learned
in terms of the primary purposes of social work. Since, however,
understanding personality is prerequisite for the disciplines of casework and group work, practitioners with certain interests and aptitudes will choose to deepen their skills in this field.

For specialization in psychotherapy the student must understand
the irrational and primitive emotional forces in society, the prevalence
of aggression, hostility, prejudice, discrimination, and distortion of
values, so that he can ally himself with those forces of education,
religion, and social action which would make for a wiser and more
tolerant society. These social insights he must take with him if his
therapy is not to be isolated from human progress. The student must
thoroughly grasp the clinical approach to illness through studies in
psychopathology. Many social workers today do not really know the
difference between health and illness, or how to estimate the normal
range in a child's development, or how to evaluate the capacity for
self-help in a person who is damaged in some part of his personality.

Since the essence of psychotherapy lies in the use of the transference
relationship and understanding the unconscious, the student must
have advanced instruction in these disciplines. This means that in
addition to his general field work, special assignments and seminars
must be taken under skilled teaching therapists. The student must
understand the motivation and dynamics of the transference; appropriate ways of controlling it; how to help the client resolve it in
favor of more mature object choice. He must be able to use it in supportive therapy and to open avenues for sublimation. He must understand and be able to handle resistance, and recognize and work with
the unconscious as it manifests itself through the defensive structures

and in projected forms. He must understand the nature of the fantasy life of the individual even though, in the main, he does not use the media of dreams and symbols or the more distinctive techniques of the psychoanalyst in helping the client to gain insight.

Training for psychotherapy in social work does not have the objective of training the worker to be a lay analyst, but to use the principles of psychoanalytical psychiatry in a social context. If the student wishes to be a lay analyst, there is no escape from seeking full training and official licensing in whatever way is prescribed for such practice. If the student plans to practice psychotherapy as a social worker, then he will seek full social work training, plus whatever additional training is standardized for this specialization. Not all competent caseworkers will have interest in or aptitude for psychotherapy, so that careful screening and vocational guidance are essential.

There is no substitute for liking children and having a natural skill with them. Without a warm and giving attitude social workers should not select any field of social casework, still less child and family guidance. Not every therapist can use the same approach, and some workers will always be able, because of natural gifts, to go further and deeper than others. The social worker must be a nonrigid person, sensitive to the ideas, attitudes, and unconscious feelings of others. There is never any substitute for a well-adjusted personality, and it is fortunate if the potential therapist has achieved this in one way or another. There is no reasonable doubt that a social worker will be better prepared to do therapy if he has also been analyzed. He must have a trained self-awareness—if gained without analysis this may be adequate—but the self-awareness must be considerable. He must be emotionally willing to learn about himself and others. Whether analysis is, or is not, possible, the next equipment would derive from a substantial training period in which he may carry on a number of cases under the close supervision of an analyst and subsequently with consultation.

Finally, the conscious use of the social work supervisory process over a considerable period of time is the best guarantee of the development of skill and the decrease of risk. The practice of psychotherapy is safeguarded and enriched by agency standards and controls. Supervision as a teaching method has been developed in social work to an unusual degree. There is no substitute for the practical "clinical" teaching of the supervisor. It has been adequately demonstrated that consultation even by the best of psychiatrists is of little value unless the level of social work supervisory competence is high. It seems provincial to argue that the use of professional consultants (here psychoanalysts) demeans the dignity of a social work practitioner. On the contrary, it is to the credit of social work that it so fully seeks consultation services in this and other areas. More knowledge and skill is required to work in the field of human relations than can be achieved within the ordinary education span of each profession. The reasonable alternative to piling one professional discipline on top of another is the concept of the working team. In the present development of psychotherapy by social workers, review of cases by a good psychiatrist is, we believe, indispensable, but each practitioner must understand quite fully all the tools that must be used, and much of the technical approach will be in common. A common language is indispensable; the concepts must mean the same things for any useful cooperation.

The programs of child guidance, if well staffed and having controlled case loads, are costly, but not so costly as delinquency or severe personality disturbance in adult life. Since every profession is itself in a state of flux, continuous mutual consultation, experimentation, and research are needed for a living and progressive development in the science of human relations and to establish the most effective community groupings and patterns for service. New forms of graduate education will, no doubt, emerge, designed to synthesize and integrate all disciplines which are basic in the practice of psychotherapy.

Bibliography

Ackerman, Nathan W., "Constructive and Destructive Tendencies in Children," *American Journal of Orthopsychiatry*, VII (July, 1937), 301–319.

—— "Dynamic Patterns in Group Psychotherapy," *Psychiatry*, VII (November, 1944), 341–348.

—— "Psychotherapy and 'Giving Love,'" *Psychiatry*, VII (May, 1944), 129–138.

—— "Technique of Therapy; a Case Study." Contribution to a Symposium on Treatment Presented at the 1940 Meeting of the American Orthopsychiatric Association, *American Journal of Orthopsychiatry*, X (October, 1940), 665–680.

—— "What Constitutes Intensive Psychotherapy in a Child Guidance Clinic?" *American Journal of Orthopsychiatry*, XV (October, 1945), 711–720.

Aichhorn, August, Wayward Youth. New York, 1935.

Alexander, Franz, "Development of the Ego-Psychology," in *Psychoanalysis Today*, edited by Sandor Lorand (New York, 1944), pp. 143–150.

—— "Present Trends in Psychiatry and the Future Outlook," in *Modern Attitudes in Psychiatry*, New York, 1946, pp. 61–89.

Alexander, Franz, and Thomas Morton French, Psychoanalytic Therapy. New York, 1946.

Alexander, Franz, and William Healy, Roots of Crime. New York, 1935.

Alexander, Franz, and Hugo Staub, The Criminal, the Judge, and the Public. New York, 1931.

Allen, Frederick H., Psychotherapy with Children. New York, 1942.

Alt, Herschel, and Joseph Stein, "After 50 Years; an Agency Looks Ahead," *The Jewish Social Service Quarterly*, XXI (December, 1944), 99–108.

Amster, Fannie, "Collective Psychotherapy of Mothers of Emotionally Disturbed Children," *American Journal of Orthopsychiatry*, XIV (January, 1944), 44–52.

Avrunin, William, "The Volunteer in Case Work Treatment," *The Family*, XXV (June, 1944), 137–142.

Axelrode, J., "Some Indications of Supportive Therapy," *American Journal of Orthopsychiatry*, X (April, 1940), 264–271.

Bernard, Viola W., "Psychodynamics of Unmarried Motherhood in Early Adolescence," *The Nervous Child*, IV (October, 1944), 26–45.

Bornstein, Berta, "Clinical Notes on Child Analysis," in *The Psychoanalytic Study of the Child* (New York, 1945), pp. 151–166.

Bradley, Charles, "Psychoses in Children," in *Modern Trends in Child Psychiatry* (New York, 1945), pp. 135–154.

Brown, Junius F., and Karl A. Menninger, The Psychodynamics of Abnormal Behavior. New York, 1940.

Buhler, Charlotte, From Birth to Maturity. London, 1935.

Burgum, Mildred, "Constructive Values Associated with Rejection," *American Journal of Orthopsychiatry*, X (April, 1940), 312–326.

Buxbaum, Edith, "Transference and Group Formation in Children and Adolescents," in *Psychoanalytic Study of the Child* (New York, 1945), pp. 351–366.

English, O. S., and G. H. J. Pearson, Emotional Problems of Living. New York, 1945.

Fenichel, Otto, Psychoanalytic Theory of Neurosis. New York, 1945.

French, Lois Meredith, Psychiatric Social Work. New York, 1940.

Freud, Anna, The Ego and the Mechanisms of Defense. London, 1937.

—— "Indications for Child Analysis," in *The Psychoanalytic Study of the Child* (New York, 1945), pp. 127–150.

Freud, Sigmund, Basic Writings of Sigmund Freud, ed. by Dr. A. A. Brill. New York, 1938.

—— General Introduction to Psychoanalysis, ed. by Dr. J. Riviera. New York, 1938–1943.

—— Collected Papers. London, 1924.

Gabriel, Betty, "An Experiment in Group Treatment," *American Journal of Orthopsychiatry*, IX (January, 1939), 146–169.

Gesell, A. L., and F. L. Ilg, Infant and Child in the Culture of Today. New York, 1943.

Glauber, I. Peter, "A Social Psychiatric Therapy for the Stutterer," *The Newsletter*, American Association of Psychiatric Social Workers, XIV (Autumn, 1944), 30–34.

—— "Speech Characteristics of Psychoneurotic Patients," *Journal of Speech Disorders*, IX (March, 1944), 18–30.

Glover, E., "Pathological Character Formation," in *Psychoanalysis Today* (New York, 1944), pp. 218–226.

Greenacre, Phyllis, "The Biological Economy of Birth," in *The Psychoanalytic Study of the Child* (New York, 1945), pp. 31–52.

Hamilton, Gordon, Theory and Practice of Social Case Work. New York, 1940.

Healy, William, and Augusta Bronner, New Light on Delinquency, and Its Treatment. New Haven, 1936.

Hoffer, William, "Psychoanalytic Education," in *The Psychoanalytic Study of the Child* (New York, 1945), pp. 293–307.

Jewish Board of Guardians, The Case Worker in Psychotherapy. New York, 1946.

—— Conditioned Environment in Case Work Treatment. New York, 1944.

—— Primary Behavior Disorder in Children . . . Two Case Studies by staff members of the Jewish Board of Guardians. New York, Family Welfare Association of America, 1945.

Klein, E., "The Reluctance to Go to School," in *The Psychoanalytic Study of the Child* (New York, 1945), pp. 263–279.

Klein, Melanie, The Psychoanalysis of Children. New York, 1932.

Knoepfmacher, Juliana, "The Use of Play in Diagnosis and Therapy in a Child Guidance Clinic," *Smith College Studies in Social Work*, XII (March, 1942), 217–262.

—— "Child Guidance Work Based on Psychoanalytic Concepts," *The Nervous Child*, V (April, 1946), 178–198.

Kolodney, Etta, "Treatment of Mothers in Groups as a Supplement to Child Psychotherapy," *Mental Hygiene*, XXVIII (July, 1944), 437–443.

Lee, Porter R., and M. E. Kenworthy, Mental Hygiene and Social Work. New York, 1929.

Levy, David M., "Attitude Therapy," *The American Journal of Orthopsychiatry*, VII (January, 1937), 103–113.

—— Maternal Overprotection. New York, 1943.

—— "Release Therapy," *The American Journal of Orthopsychiatry*, IX (October, 1939), 713–736.

Lewis, Nolan D. C., Outlines for Psychiatric Examinations. Albany, New York State Department of Mental Hygiene, 1943.

Lippman, Hyman S., "Treatment of Juvenile Delinquents," *Proceedings of the National Conference of Social Work* (New York, 1945), pp. 314–323.

Lowrey, Lawson G., "Psychiatry for Children," *The American Journal of Psychiatry*, CI (November, 1944), 375–388.

Lowrey, Lawson G., Psychiatry for Social Workers. New York, 1946.

Mahler, Margaret S., "Child Analysis," in *Modern Trends in Child Psychiatry*, ed. by Nolan D. C. Lewis and Bernard L. Pacella, New York, 1945, pp. 265–290.

—— "Ego Psychology Applied to Behavior Problems," *Modern Trends in Child Psychiatry*, ed. by Nolan D. C. Lewis and Bernard L. Pacella, November, 1945, pp. 43–56.

Mowrer, O. H., and Clyde Kluckhorn, "Dynamic Theory of Personality," in *Personality and the Behavior Disorders*, ed. by J. McV. Hunt, New York, 1944.

Murphy, Lois B., "Childhood Experience in Relation to Personality Development," *Personality and the Behavior Disorders*, ed. by J. McV. Hunt, 1944, II, 652–690.

Neumann, Frederika, "The Use of Psychiatric Consultation by a Case Work Agency," *The Family*, XXVI (October, 1945), 216–220.

Pavenstedt, Eleanor, and Irene Andersen, "The Uncompromising Demand of a Three Year Old for a Real Mother," in *The Psychoanalytic Study of the Child* (New York, 1945), pp. 211–232.

Pray, Kenneth L. M., "The Place of Social Case Work in the Treatment of Delinquency," *The Social Service Review*, XIX (June, 1945), 235–248.

Preu, Paul William, "The Concept of Psychopathic Personality," in *Personality and the Behavior Disorders* (ed. by J. McV. Hunt, New York, 1944), II, 922–937.

Redl, Fritz, "The Psychology of Gang Formation and the Treatment of Juvenile Delinquents," in *The Psychoanalytic Study of the Child* (New York, 1945), pp. 367–377.

Robinson, Virginia, "Psychoanalytic Contributions to Social Case Work Treatment," *Proceedings of the National Conference of Social Work* (Chicago, 1931), pp. 329–346.

—— A Changing Psychology in Social Case Work. Chapel Hill, 1930.

Rogers, Carl R., *Counseling and Psychotherapy*. New York, 1942.

Ross, Helen, and Adelaide M. Johnson, "The Growing Science of Case Work," *Journal of Social Case Work*, XXVII (November, 1946), 273–278.

Siegel, Miriam G., "The Rorschach Test as an Aid in Selecting Clients for Group Therapy and Evaluating Progress," *Mental Hygiene*, XXVIII (July, 1944), 444–449.

Silberphennig, Judith, "Mother Types Encountered in Child Guidance

Clinics," *American Journal of Orthopsychiatry*, XI (July, 1941), 475–484.

Slavson, S. R., An Introduction to Group Therapy. New York, 1943.

—— "Group Psychotherapy with Children," in *Modern Trends in Child Psychiatry* (ed. by Nolan D. C. Lewis, New York, 1945), pp. 291–305.

—— "Principles and Dynamics of Group Therapy," *American Journal of Orthopsychiatry*, XIII (October, 1943), 650–659.

—— "Some Elements in Activity Group Therapy," *American Journal of Orthopsychiatry*, XIV (October, 1944), 578–588.

Slawson, John, "Social Work Basis for Prevention and Treatment of Delinquency and Crime; Individual Factors," *Proceedings of the National Conference of Social Work* (Chicago, 1936), pp. 590–599.

Stevenson, George S., and Geddes Smith, Child Guidance Clinics: a Quarter Century of Development. New York, 1934.

Taft, Jessie, "The Relation of Function to Process in Social Case Work," *Journal of Social Work Process*, Pennsylvania School of Social Work, Philadelphia, I (1937), and subsequent volumes of this journal.

Towle, Charlotte, and others. "Psychoanalytic Orientation in Family Case Work," *American Journal of Orthopsychiatry*, XIII (January, 1943), 1–33. Round Table, 1942.

—— "Social Case Work in Modern Society," *Social Service Review*, XX (June, 1946), 165–180.

Van Ophuijsen, J. H. W., "New Fields for Psychiatric Case Work," in *The Case Worker in Psychotherapy* (Jewish Board of Guardians pamphlet, December, 1945), pp. 10–15.

—— "Primary Conduct Disturbances; Their Diagnosis and Treatment," in *Modern Trends in Child Psychiatry* (New York, 1945), pp. 35–42.

—— "Therapeutic Criteria in Social Agencies," *American Journal of Orthopsychiatry*, IX (April, 1939), 410–420.

Washburn, Ruth Wendell, Children Have Their Reasons. New York, 1942.

Wills, W. David, The Hawkspur Experiment. London, 1941.

Witmer, Helen L., Psychiatric Clinics for Children. New York, 1940.

—— Social Work. New York, 1942.

Zachary, Caroline B., "A New Tool in Psychotherapy with Adolescents," in *Modern Trends in Child Psychiatry* (New York, 1945), pp. 79–88.

Index